DATE DUE

NOV 5 1992			

DEMCO 38-297

FROM COLONIA
TO COMMUNITY

Recent Titles in Contributions in Ethnic Studies
Series Editor: Leonard W. Doob

Nations Remembered: An Oral History of the Five Civilized Tribes, 1865–1907
Theda Perdue

Operation Wetback: The Mass Deportation of Mexican Undocumented Workers in 1954
Juan Ramon Garcia

The Navajo Nation
Peter Iverson

An Unacknowledged Harmony: Philo-Semitism and the Survival of European Jewry
Alan Edelstein

America's Ethnic Politics
Joseph S. Roucek and Bernard Eisenberg, editors

Minorities and the Military: A Cross-National Study in World Perspective
Warren L. Young

The Emergence of Ethnicity: Cultural Groups and Social Conflicts in Israel
Eliezer Ben-Rafael

Minority Aging: Sociological and Social Psychological Issues
Ron C. Manuel, editor

FROM COLONIA
TO COMMUNITY

The History of Puerto Ricans
in New York City, 1917–1948

VIRGINIA E. SÁNCHEZ KORROL

Contributions in Ethnic Studies, Number 9

Greenwood Press
Westport, Connecticut • London, England

Library of Congress Cataloging in Publication Data

Sánchez Korrol, Virginia.
    From colonia to community.

    (Contributions in ethnic studies, ISSN 0196-7088 ;
no. 9)
    Bibliography: p.
    Includes index.
    1. Puerto Ricans—New York (N.Y.)—History.   2. New
York (N.Y.)—History.   I. Title.   II. Series.
F128.9.P85S26   1983   974.7'1004687295   82-18691
ISBN 0-313-23458-2 (lib. bdg.)

Library of Congress Catalog Card Number: 82-18691
ISBN: 0-313-23458-2
ISSN: 0196-7088

First published in 1983

Greenwood Press
A division of Congressional Information Service, Inc.
88 Post Road West
Westport, Connecticut 06881

Printed in the United States of America

10 9 8 7 6 5 4 3 2 1

Copyright Acknowledgments

  Every reasonable effort has been made to trace the owners of copyright materials
used in this book, but in some instances this has proven impossible. The publishers
will be glad to receive information leading to more complete acknowledgments in
subsequent prints of this book, and in the meantime extend their apologies for any
omissions.

In Memory of
Antonio Sánchez Feliciano
My Father — My Friend
For Chuck
and for Pam and Lauren,
our future

Contents

Plates

Tables

Maps

Figures

Preface

The idea for this study began many years ago when my own children were very young and I attempted to describe for them life as I remembered it in the Puerto Rican community in New York City. Discovering materials on the early settlement to be practically nonexistent, I was unable to reconcile the available writings on Puerto Ricans with my own memories of a *colonia* soundly structured by strict family values, a concern for cultural heritage, and an identifiable organizational network, so I embarked on a search which led to the study of Latin American history and the writing of this book.

I owe those individuals and institutions which participated in that search a sizable debt of gratitude. Special thanks are due to Professor Steve J. Stein, Department of History at the State University at Stony Brook, for constant support and intellectual stimulation through periods of frustration and elation. Others at Stony Brook who read the manuscript and deserve my deepest appreciation were Professors Robert M. Levine, Joel Rosenthal, and Ernesto Chinchilla Aguilar. José Oscar Alers, director of the Puerto Rican Migration Research Consortium, offered astute comments and criticism from both an academic point of view and as a second generation Puerto Rican who lived the experience. These individuals encouraged and supported my endeavor.

My own support network was a woman's group which extended real help and ego building when I needed it the most. Recognizing the special problems of women, wives, and mothers in academe, the group formed five years before the completion of this work primarily to give one another important aid and motivation. The group included Grania Marcus, Judy Wishnia, Marjorie Levine, and especially Susan L. Pickman, who was always there for me.

The Center for Puerto Rican Studies, City University of New York, provided invaluable and consistent support. Throughout my years of research, the Center's director, Frank Bonilla, librarian Nelida Perez, and researchers Ricardo Campos, Carlos Sanabria, and Hector Colón unhesitatingly welcomed me into their collective investigative circles. Similarly, my colleagues in the Department of Puerto Rican Studies at Brooklyn College shared a personal and professional interest in this study. María E. Sánchez and Hector Carrasquillo, in particular, provided guidance and inspiration.

The interest, enthusiasm, and suggestions of many others are gratefully acknowledged. Clara E. Rodríguez of Fordham University and Rosa Estades of Hunter College offered me the wisdom of their own experiences and led me to the Puerto Rican *pioneros*. Kal Wagenheim provided access to library files at the Migration Division of the Office of the Commonwealth of Puerto Rico. The library staffs of the Long Island Historical Society, Brooklyn College, and Columbia University were gracious and attentive. The Ford Foundation provided a grant which enabled me to interview migrants in Puerto Rico and New York City.

Without the help of those who agreed to be interviewed, it would have been impossible to go beyond the written work into the heart of the *colonia*. To all the migrants who offered warm hospitality and gave so much of themselves, I owe sincerest appreciation. Special accolades are due in particular to two who showed me the way back—my parents, Antonio Sánchez Feliciano and Elisa Santiago Baeza.

Personal acknowledgments are also due to Aura and Frank Garfunkel for reading the manuscript and making additional suggestions, to Richard and Vivian Cahn for real support, time, and encouragement, and to Margarita Logan and Patricia Chafe for typing and revising many times over.

Finally, to my husband Chuck and our daughters, Pamela and Lauren, who patiently traveled along with me, listening to tapes and interviews, reading revisions, and sustaining me throughout, when they would have preferred to do their own thing, I offer my love, devotion, and heartfelt thanks.

FROM COLONIA
TO COMMUNITY

Introduction

In the early decades of this century, a significant number of Puerto Ricans from the countryside and urban centers of the island began to migrate to the northern metropolises of the United States. Although small groups of political exiles had emigrated throughout the last third of the nineteenth century, it was not until after the North American occupation of the island in 1898 that critical social, political, and economic transformations in Puerto Rico triggered an increase in the numbers of people leaving for continental shores. Through the creation of infant enclaves on the mainland, Puerto Rican migrants set about establishing communities which reflected in many ways those they left behind. As early as 1910, over one thousand Puerto Ricans resided in the United States. American citizenship granted via the Jones Act of 1917 stimulated the freedom of movement between the island and the United States. By 1920, forty-five states reported the presence of Puerto Rican-born individuals, with all forty-eight doing so in succeeding censuses. In short, the decades before the onset of World War II witnessed a progressive increase in the numbers of Puerto Ricans living in the United States, a migration slowed only by the Depression, which would peak in the decades of the fifties and sixties.

In New York City and the surrounding metropolitan areas, the Puerto Rican presence became most noticeable just after the Second World War. About that time, the first systematic surveys

depicting the plight of the Puerto Ricans in the city began to appear
in print. In 1947, for example, a pictorial essay in *Life* magazine
chronicled the migration to the United States as the first airborne
diaspora in history. Such news stories coincided with investigative
reports of various social service agencies highlighting the health,
housing, and employment problems of the city's newest migrants.
Within a decade, monographs like the Columbia University Study,
the Welfare Study, and the New York City Board of Education surveys focused attention on Puerto Ricans in an effort to inform the
dominant non-Hispanic society about this group.[1]

While literature on Puerto Ricans during the fifties centered on
the economic, social, or racial assimilation or adjustment problems
of the post-World War II migration, relatively few studies emphasized the community structure of the Puerto Rican New York settlements throughout the decades before the war. Social scientists
like Daniel P. Moynihan and Nathan Glazer blatantly denied the
existence of an early Puerto Rican community and failed to per-
ceive the relationship between early support systems or coping institutions and the later migration.[2] Indeed, these particular authors
based their ideas on the notion that the process of community
building never existed on the island proper and therefore could not
be translated to the New York settlements. Thus the experience and
resettlement patterns of the larger migration at mid-century were
frequently viewed and analyzed in a vacuum without reference to
earlier community development or to the forces which motivated
the original displacement. The experiences of the pioneer migrants
in New York settlements who laid the groundwork for the "great
migration" of the later decades had clearly been overlooked.

This study proposes to fill the gap. It explores the development
of the Puerto Rican settlements, or *colonias,* in New York City during the first four decades of the century and demonstrates the existence of an identifiable migrant community during that period.
Originating soon after the turn of the century, pioneer *colonias*
charged with the responsibility of translating the Puerto Rican way
of life to unfamiliar territory generated a visual and intrinsic presence which would greatly influence future settlement patterns
between the island and the mainland. It was to those *colonias,*
vividly Puerto Rican with their *bodegas* (grocery stores), Hispanic

boarding houses, or restaurants, formal and informal support networks and organizations, that migrants came.

Focusing on the community's organizational networks, structured and unstructured coping institutions, settlement patterns and migrants' occupations, the study revises heretofore accepted interpretations of the Puerto Rican experience away from the island and builds on pioneer works, such as those of Joseph P. Fitzpatrick, Lawrence R. Chenault, and C. Wright Mills. Moreover, I intend to expand on current scholarship, particularly the research of the Center for Puerto Rican Studies, CEREP (Centro del estudio de la realidad Puertorriqueña), and the Puerto Rican Migration Research Consortium.[3]

Several issues integral to the migratory process will be dissected. How and why, for instance, did Puerto Ricans come to New York City during the first decades of the present century? What kinds of communities did they establish and what institutions or practices emerged to meet migrant needs? How did the settlements in different New York boroughs relate to one another, to issues concerning Puerto Ricans on the island, and to the dominant non-Hispanic or host society? Above all, who were the early migrants and how did they carve a definable community in the city?

Research for this book was divided into two phases. The first consisted of an investigation of United States government documents and publications, census materials, archival collections, newspapers, periodicals, and journals to determine the size and scope of the early *colonia*. Most of this research was executed while I served as a member of the History Task Force of the Center for Puerto Rican Studies, Graduate Center of the City University of New York. In conjunction with this group, an official but untabulated census, The New York State Manuscript Census of 1925, was coded and computed for 7,322 Spanish-surnamed individuals living in Manhattan's Sixteenth, Seventeenth, Eighteenth, and Nineteenth Assembly Districts. Yielding variables including the sex, age, race, and occupation, length of residence in New York City, country of origin, place in and composition of Hispanic households, the census formed the basis for an analysis of the mid-1920s Spanish-speaking community.

Moreover, while participating with the History Task Force, I was

introduced to an autobiographical manuscript detailing Puerto
Rican life in the United States, especially in New York City, dating
from the final decades of the nineteenth century up to and including the 1950s. This material, *Memorias de Bernardo Vega,* edited
by the Puerto Rican writer César Andreu Iglesias, was subsequently
published by Ediciones Huracan.[4] The most comprehensive study
on the subject to date, *Memorias* provided the leads to many
Puerto Rican associations in operation throughout the early
decades, newspapers and journals in existence, community issues,
and leadership. Once the information became confirmed and cor-
roborated, an investigation of the organizational charters on file in
the New York City County Clerk's Office, Supreme Court Building
became possible. Archival collections such as the Vito Marcantonio
Papers and the Arturo Schomberg collection in the New York Public Library also yielded valuable insights on this theme.

   While archival materials, census information, and publications
provided important perspectives for an historical reconstruction of
the pre-World War II settlements, oral interviews and popular culture also added major dimensions. The second research phase centered on tracking down appropriate oral history collections and in-
terviewing migrants who had lived through the migration experience within the first four decades of the century. The Columbia
University Oral History Project and the Brentwood Multilingual
Assessment Program on Long Island housed limited collections on
Puerto Rican settlers. The first concentrated on individuals recognized for their contributions in building the Hispanic community in
general. These were mostly community leaders, writers, or both.
The interview with folklorist Pura Belpré is representative in both
of these areas. The second also focused on better-known persons
such as Elizabeth Guanill, commissioner of Human Rights for Suf-
folk County, and others active in establishing the Hispanic Long
Island community. The Long Island Historical Society, however,
offered a fine, extensive, and varied collection of interviews with
pioneering, working-class migrants in the Brooklyn *colonia.* This
set focused on early settlement patterns, community and organizational structure, leadership, and the relationship between the Manhattan and Brooklyn settlements. Numbering close to seventy taped
interviews, half of which have been transcribed, Puerto Rican life-

styles, attitudes, work experience, family structure, and migration processes have all been recorded.

Furthermore, from June 1977 until June 1978, a grant from the Ford Foundation, "Movements of People in the Caribbean," enabled research on return migrants currently living in Puerto Rico. During this period a series of interviews was conducted with retired, working-class individuals cognizant of the New York experience between the two world wars. Their references regarding the formation of the early settlements proved essential to the overall theme, since secondary sources have been so limited in this area. Close to twenty hours of transcribed tapes and an additional twenty-five conversations were gathered with migrants in Puerto Rico and in New York City, augmenting the interviews in other collections. Moreover, as women comprised a significant percentage of the interviews collected, a description of their specific role in the development of the pioneer *colonias* became possible for the first time.

Finally, the second research phase concluded with an investigation of popular culture, particularly the music and songs which so often expressed feelings, attitudes, and concerns of the migrant population rarely found in the literature. Themes of popular songs not only set forth strains of nostalgia for the migrants' absent homeland, but also expressed nascent feelings of incompatability with the alien New York environment.

The book has been organized in the following manner. Chapter 2 describes the background of the migration to New York City, analyzing the factors which encouraged Puerto Ricans to leave the island as well as those which drew the migrants to the city and other parts of the United States. Indicating the migration occurred in response to complex and extensive continental considerations, many of these economically based, the chapter explains how and why Puerto Ricans became concentrated in the metropolitan area throughout the decades before the Second World War.

Chapter 3 explores the concept of community as described in the literature on Puerto Ricans in the mainland. It evolves to demonstrate the existence of an active, energetic, and structured Puerto Rican community which coalesced around various characteristics. These included Puerto Rican settlement patterns, increases in the

size of the *colonia* as well as in commercial and professional establishments, use of Spanish as the language of communication, and
common interests and attitudes expressed in popular culture.

Chapter 4 concentrates on the role of Puerto Rican women in the
structure of the early community. Comprising almost half of the
migrant population throughout the period of this study, women
persisted in maintaining traditional sex and family roles in spite of
their steady integration into the mainland work force. Faced with a
disintegrating and sometimes hostile environment, women devised
practices and customs designed to maintain an intact family structure while shouldering their share of familial responsibilities.
Often, women added supplementary or, in some cases, primary
incomes to the households. Practices such as taking in boarders and
child care expanded to strengthen communal bonds at a time when
the *colonia* was most vulnerable. Thus the practices which emerge
to meet migrant needs in this aspect of settlement are considered
informal coping institutions.

Chapter 5 investigates the formal (incorporated) social, cultural,
civic, and economic organizational structure and the leadership
which these groups engendered. Neighborhood clubs, brother-
hoods, federations, and professional and educational groups played
pivotal roles in defining and reinforcing the *colonia hispana*. Here
we trace the development of three organizational models over several decades, outlining the group's relationship to the community,
to Puerto Rico, and to the dominant non-Hispanic host society.
While the organizational objectives of many such groups appeared
in their certificates of incorporation, these often failed to convey
the full scope of a group's actual functions and operation. By describing the activities and concerns of several representative
groups, the chapter attempts to fill this void.

Chapter 6 examines the functions of political organization and
participation among Puerto Rican migrants. During the early
decades political participation among this group was far more pro-
lific than previously assumed. Political units numbered among the
earliest associations within the *colonia* and these concerned themselves with the social or political issues affecting the community,
relations between the early settlements and with the wider non-
Hispanic society, and with Latin American issues in general. Above
all, these were the groups which sought to serve the migrant *colonia*

as power brokers both within the Spanish-speaking settlements and with the non-Hispanic population.

Chapter 7 serves as summary. Without doubt the study of immigration, migration, and its aftermath forms an integral part of the histories of the Americas. As a Latin migration, the Puerto Rican experience and its efforts to build pioneer settlements should serve as a basis for comparisons with other Latin population movements or with Puerto Rican communities outside of New York City. Inasmuch as changes within federal immigration regulations continue to encourage and stimulate population movements from Latin countries to northern urban centers, an understanding of the Hispanic reality remains critical. New York City, in particular, continues to receive a substantial amount of legal and undocumented immigration. The problems faced by recent arrivals, whether social, in the job market, or in the community, closely parallel the Puerto Rican experience. It behooves us, therefore, to learn as much as possible about their migratory processes and resettlement patterns in order to understand other Latins in the United States.

Notes

1. Among the surveys published between 1947 and 1957 were the following: C. Wright Mills, Clarence Senior, and Rose Goldsen, *The Puerto Rican Journey: New York's Newest Migrant* (New York: Harper & Bros., 1950), based on the findings of the Columbia University Applied Social Research team on the Puerto Rican community in New York City, 1948; New York City Board of Education, Bureau of Educational Program Research and Statistics, *Teaching Children of Puerto Rican Background in New York City Schools* (1953): J. Cayce Morrison, director, *The Puerto Rican Study,* 1953–1957 (New York City Board of Education, 1957); The Welfare Council of New York City, *Puerto Ricans in New York City* (1948); Welfare and Health Council of New York City, *Population of Puerto Rican Birth and Parentage* (1950); Welfare and Health Council of New York City, Brooklyn Council for Social Planning, "Report on Survey of Brooklyn Agencies Rendering Services to Puerto Ricans" (June 1953).

2. Adalberto López, "Some of the Literature on Puerto Rico and Puerto Ricans in English," in Adalberto López and James Petras, eds., *Puerto Rico and the Puerto Ricans: Studies in History and Society* (New York: Schenkman Publishing, 1974), pp. 471–480; Nathan Glazer and Daniel Patrick Moynihan, *Beyond the Melting Pot* (Cambridge, Mass.: MIT Press, 1963); History Task Force, Centro de Estudios Puertorriquenos,

Labor Migration Under Capitalism: The Puerto Rican Experience (New York: Monthly Review Press, 1979), pp. 144–45; U.S. Commission on Civil Rights, *Puerto Ricans in the Continental United States: An Uncertain Future* (October 1976).

3. Lawrence R. Chenault, *The Puerto Rican Migrant in New York City* (New York: Columbia University, 1938; reissue, Russell and Russell, 1970); Joseph P. Fitzpatrick, *Puerto Rican Americans: The Meaning of Migration to the Mainland* (Englewood Cliffs, N.J.: Prentice-Hall, 1971); History Task Force, *Labor Migration.*

4. César Andreu Iglesias, ed., *Memorias de Bernardo Vega* (Rio Piedras, Puerto Rico: Ediciones Huracan, 1977).

Background of the Puerto Rican Migration to New York City

The pre-World War II Puerto Rican settlements in New York City continued various social and economic processes originating in Puerto Rico during the nineteenth century. As time passed—and particularly toward the end of the nineteenth century—changes in the island's economic structure increasingly led to both internal and external emigration to the mainland. Instigated by a poorly integrated labor force, Puerto Rican men, women, and children left their homes. Prior to the Spanish-American War, three migratory patterns existed from the island to the United States. Each had direct or indirect bearing on the emigration and settlement patterns of the twentieth century. Early Puerto Rican settlers came as merchants and students, as adventurers and revolutionaries, and as field and factory workers. The first migration based on commercial factors served as a rehearsal for the next two, which were more politically and economically motivated.

In the beginning, migration was influenced by a commercially oriented pattern which emerged from growing trade relations between Puerto Rican and Anglo-American colonists. Originating in the mid-eighteenth century, commerce between the two initially meant smuggling and clandestine barter, conducted despite Spanish mercantilist policies. This flourishing trade, based on the exchange of Puerto Rican sugar and molasses for basic food staples which Spain failed to provide, enriched the purses of New York, New

England, and Pennsylvania merchants. Early contacts intensified when the Spanish Crown sanctioned the entrance of ships flying the stars and stripes into Latin colonial ports during war times.[1] Commercial movements were inevitably accompanied by the transfer of people as well as commodities.

By 1830, trade between Cuba, Puerto Rico, and the Middle Atlantic states, along with resultant population shifts, reached large enough proportions to warrant the establishment of a Spanish Benevolent Society in New York City (Sociedad Benéfica Cubana y Puertorriqueña), composed of merchants from the islands. These merchants promoted trade exchanges between the islands and the mainland, a connection virtually unsevered throughout the century in spite of subsequent political or economic fluctuations.[2] More important, the formation of the Spanish Benevolent Society indicated positive expectations regarding the degree of commercial interaction between Puerto Rico and the United States that was to follow throughout the nineteenth century.

During the last third of the period, Puerto Rican molasses and sugar production depended on North American markets to such an extent that the volume of purchases made by the United States far exceeded the volume purchased by the mother country, Spain. A study by Angel Quintero Rivera revealed that 68.6 percent of the island's sugar was exported to the United States while only 0.8 percent was sent to Spain in 1870. A decade later, 57.0 percent was exported to northern metropolises, but only 2.0 percent was sent to Spain; and finally in 1897, the year before the Spanish-American War, 60.6 percent of Puerto Rican sugar exports went to the United States, compared with 35.4 percent exported to Spain.[3] Furthermore, the expansion of commercial activity between these points becomes more significant when we consider that almost all of the island's molasses exports were destined for the United States. In return, the United States, along with several European industrial countries, provided Puerto Rican *haciendas* with the machinery necessary for planting and harvesting the island's major crops: coffee, sugar, and tobacco.[4] These commercial interactions involving primarily the island's merchant and creole *hacendado* class opened the way and influenced to a great extent the selection of the United States as one entrepot for the immigration of the sons and daughters of this class. Some would come as students and others as political exiles.

It was this latter group which characterized the second migratory pattern from Puerto Rico during the island's struggle for independence. Attempts to shed Spanish rule had appeared since the beginning of the nineteenth century, reaching a climax in 1868 with the unsuccessful revolutionary attempt known as *El Grito de Lares*. Immediately after this aborted lunge for independence coupled with the failure to establish a Puerto Rican republic, and throughout the last decades of the century, many activists involved in the island's separatist or independence movement were forced to emigrate from Puerto Rico. Arriving in the United States, they rapidly organized into political units. From New York sanctuaries they dedicated themselves to a series of activities furthering the cause of independence; uniting other Puerto Rican exiles; and promoting propaganda campaigns and writing political manifestos directed toward the indoctrination of their compatriots in Puerto Rico. Joining forces with Cuban exiles and other Latin Americans also struggling in their countries' internal revolutions, they published newspapers such as *Patria, La Revolución,* and *El Porvenir* in support of Spanish Caribbean liberation.

By 1895 Puerto Rican political exiles in New York formed a branch of the Cuban Revolutionary Party's governing body and motivated the establishment of various socially and politically oriented associations all dedicated to the theme of Antillean independence.[5] These constituted the first Puerto Rican organizations to operate in New York City. They appealed not only to the political founding exiles instrumental in their creation, but to the trickle of skilled and unskilled Puerto Rican workers who began to make their homes in the city during the first decades of the twentieth century. Among this latter group some individuals had come as contracted agricultural or factory workers; others as skilled artisans; and still others had followed a pattern of migration originating within the island's internal population movements from rural to urban sectors, which culminated in emigration. While we have no way of knowing the exact numbers of migrants who came via this route, we can nevertheless trace the events in Puerto Rico which set these emigrations into motion. Predominantly composed of working class individuals and rooted in social and economic changes, this migratory wave was the largest of the pre-Spanish-American-War period. Most "common laborers" emigrated in reaction to transformations in land-usage and landholding patterns, a situation which would accelerate under United States domination.[6]

If the last third of the nineteenth century, characterized by the growth of commercial cultivation, marked the transition from an *hacienda* to a plantation system in the island, it was also a period when the increased production of coffee necessitated changes in land usage and in the structure of the work force.[7] By 1870 the creation of the island's first sugar refineries motivated an increase in commercial sugar cultivation, but this situation proved contradictory since it placed Puerto Rican sugar in competition with the Peninsula's. Spain sporadically encouraged the island's cultivation. Without a firm technological or financial foundation, and as long as Puerto Rican sugar competed with the metropolis, *hacendados* dependent on Spanish markets were inhibited in increasing their production. Moreover, an increase in the island's sugar growth meant agricultural expansion based on favorable tariff structures, available credit, technological improvements, secure markets, and a larger labor force, none of which existed for Puerto Rican sugar *hacendados* at that time. Thus, within a decade the combination of an uneven growth pattern and the general economic crisis of 1878–79 placed the Puerto Rican sugar industry in jeopardy.

During the same period, Puerto Rican coffee cultivation for European export surpassed sugar production, with various repercussions. Among these were the concentration of land devoted to coffee, the expropriation of small farms, the consolidation of large *haciendas,* and the stimulation of external and internal migrations. Since coffee production required less land and fewer workers than did sugar cultivation, the transformation from the predominance of one crop over the other necessitated changes especially in the structure of the labor force.[8] By 1873, the abolition of slavery and of laws restricting the geographical mobility of free workers in the island encouraged freedom of movement between Puerto Rican agricultural sectors. Some cane workers, for example, would migrate to the mountain coffee regions during the sugar crop's "dead season," returning to coastal areas in time for the new harvest. But the decline in the sugar industry released numerous workers who now migrated to the coffee sectors but could not be incorporated into that crop's smaller production on a steady basis.[9] Former slaves previously employed in skilled jobs or crafts in the *ingenios* also migrated to the island's urban centers. In time, the labor force of these towns provided the basis for the creation and development of large-scale cigar factories based on wage labor.

By the last decades of the century, an internal migratory wave emerged from the coastal sugar regions to the interior and western sectors of the island, which were the traditional coffee-producing regions. Equally important, internal population movements within Puerto Rico would in time give way to external emigration to other parts of the Hemisphere. Many former landowners reduced to day-worker status, along with growing numbers of landless peasants, regarded emigration as contract laborers as the solution to their unemployment problems. These early migrations were seemingly composed of workers from the sugar cane growing region and adjacent areas. That these migrations were well structured and carefully manipulated is suggested by the fact that ships expressly chartered for this purpose by neighboring Caribbean *hacendados* regularly picked up contingents of laborers in the island's southern ports.[10] Responding basically to the nonintegration of a growing work force into the island's existing relations of production, potential migrants also reacted to high taxes imposed on foodstuffs, a prevailing coin shortage, and a marked decrease in subsistence farming. All of these factors, including emigration from the island, would accelerate under North American auspices. The direct colonial relationship between the United States and Puerto Rico would further aggravate the changing social and economic processes already in operation at the close of the epoch, culminating in even larger movements of people (see Map 1).

Thus we can conclude that the migratory waves in operation before the onset of the twentieth century linked the island to the mainland in bonds which would solidify after 1898. The migration patterns in effect before the Spanish-American War brought various Puerto Rican groups into contact with New York and other industrial centers. Many of them remained in the places of their original destinations, establishing footholds in several cities. As if reenacting predestined scenarios, turn-of-the-century migrants continued to form infant enclaves, the basis for the more extensive

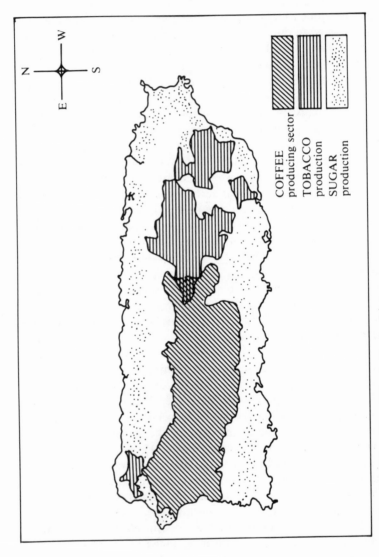

MAP 1 Traditional Land Use in Puerto Rico

COFFEE
producing sector

TOBACCO
production

SUGAR
production

migration that would follow. This was the case, for example, with the early New York settlements, shaped predominantly by tobacco workers, and with the San Francisco community composed of agricultural workers enroute to or from Hawaii.[11]

Emigration from Puerto Rico—The Early Decades of the Twentieth Century

After the Spanish-American War and particularly during the early decades into the century, Puerto Rican working class emigration increased while the migration of political exiles was eliminated by the changes in the new colonial situation which relegated the island to the status of a United States possession. To facilitate the influx of United States capital and the establishment of North American corporations after 1898, the island's educational, monetary, legal, and economic systems also underwent modifications. American currency superimposed and undervalued Puerto Rican currency based on the Spanish peso; roads, bridges, and schools were built; new curriculums intended for rapidly Americanizing the island's work force were instituted. Moreover, improvements in health and sanitation radically reduced mortality rates aiding in the process in augmenting the population at a time when changes in production methods, land usage, and land ownership could no longer incorporate them into the work force.[12]

If the patterns of emigration before 1900 emerged in response to social, political, or economic transformations under Spanish colonialism, what were the underlying causes of emigration in the twentieth century? Stated in other words, what were the factors which "pushed" Puerto Ricans to migrate after the United States occupation? At least two major theories propose to answer this question. The first, postulated by researchers like Lawrence R. Chenault and Oscar Handlin, maintained the island was plagued by an excess population, partly resulting from health and medical improvements made under United States policies, whose basic needs could not be met by the island's limited resources. The second theory, set forth in in-depth analyses of migration conducted by research centers such as the Center for Puerto Rican Studies and CEREP (Centro de estudios de la realidad puertorriquena), maintained that population movements from Puerto Rico throughout the Western Hemisphere and especially to the United States occurred in two patterns and for very different reasons: the structural movement of contracted factory and agricultural workers (such as the workers contingents recruited by neighboring Caribbean *hacendados* before 1898), and the nonstructured migration of noncontracted, working-class Puerto Ricans. Both situations responded to an acceleration of the island's nineteenth-century economic transformation, which intensified after the Spanish-American War and resulted in the creation of a marginal population. At the same time, changes in production and land ownership created a surplus working class prepared to migrate wherever it was most needed within the North American capitalist orbit. We will explore both theories in the order in which they were introduced.

The causes for emigration had been traced to overpopulation and the inefficient use of agricultural resources as early as 1901. One newspaper article of the time stated:

> The excess population [of Puerto Rico] is another obstacle to industrial development. There are only two ways to overcome it. One is emigration and the other is the establishment of agricultural stations where laborers can be taught how to grow the food needed for their own subsistence. . . . Emigration is a temporary but valuable measure. The existing population is too dense taking into account the country's ability to provide for its people. This is the case even though the island's resources can significantly support one million inhabitants and afford them comfort at least as it is understood in the tropics.[13]

The premise that Puerto Rico's economic problem was rooted in overpopulation convinced United States government officials charged with the island's responsibility to repeatedly recommend emigration as a temporary measure. In 1917 for example, a memorandum addressed to the United States Secretary of War, entitled "Excess Population in Porto Rico," recommended bringing between fifty thousand and one hundred thousand individuals to labor on farms as agricultural workers. If that was not possible, then similar work requiring manual labor might be arranged.[14] Along with the same communication, a confidential note addressed to the island's Governor Yager proposed: "Would it be possible to secure fairly good Porto Rican laborers to be brought to the United States for work requiring manual labor. How many men could be secured without interfering with Porto Rican industries and would you anticipate great difficulty, transportation being arranged from this end."[15]

By mid-1930s, the overpopulation theory continued to be proposed as the underlying cause of outmigration. In his study on the Puerto Rican migrant in New York City, Chenault said:

> During a period of about thirty-six years from the time of the census of 1899, or from about one year after the American occupation to December 1, 1935, the population of Puerto Rico increased more than eighty percent. For the approximate period of thirty years prior to 1930, the increase per decade was approximately eighteen percent. In the period from the census of 1930 to the census of 1935, however, a period of five and two-thirds years, there was an increase in number of over eleven and one-half percent.[16]

And almost thirty years later, yet another study reported:

> Puerto Rico's central problem since its annexation to the United States has been over-population. A birth rate that was always high and a lower mortality rate that has been declining steadily since 1930 have combined to more than double the population of the island in a half-century.[17]

However, the countertheory to the overpopulation premise, according to the History Task Force of the Center for Puerto Rican Studies, contended that while the island's population did in fact nearly double between 1899 and 1940, the yearly rate of increase rose only slightly. During that time, migration was hardly instrumental in keeping numbers down. Until the 1940s, death rates on the island declined slowly, and it was not until the forties that the island experienced an impressive escalation in population coinciding with the expansion of health and sanitary services into rural areas.[18] Therefore, the propensity for Puerto Ricans to remain on or leave Puerto Rico was not solely influenced by excess population coupled with limited resources, but rather by the effects of structural economic changes on the island's working class.

From 1898 to 1940, for example, the formation and decline of a capitalist plantation system in Puerto Rico conditioned the growth, employment, and emigration of Puerto Rican workers. The major branches of production—cane cultivation, sugar manufacturing, tobacco, and needlework—experienced a varying degree of relative overpopulation, precipitating both internal migration and external emigration.[19] In addition, since 1900 high unemployment predominated among men in general, but the phenomenon increased dramatically after the 1920s. During the same period, women became incorporated into the work force, particularly in manufacturing and the needle trades, and constituted a majority of undersalaried tobacco workers by the 1920s. These conditions impacting upon the island's labor force directly coincided with changes in land usage and production.

Within the first decades of the North American occupation, sugar emerged once again as the island's single most important crop. By the twenties, the concentration of arable land under the domination of four absentee-owned North American corporations and the transition from an *hacienda* to a plantation type economy was well established. In 1899, for instance, 26.2 percent of the acres under cultivation with the three major crops were devoted to sugar cane, while 71.6 percent and 2.2 percent produced coffee and tobacco, respectively. By 1929, however, sugar cultivation covered 49.3 percent, while coffee was grown in 39.7 percent and tobacco in 11.0 percent of the acres under cultivation (see Table 1). Moreover, from 1899 to 1929 there was a 230 percent increase in the amount of land under cultivation, which dramatized the enormous growth in sugar production over a thirty-year period. Astutely linking production and migration, one researcher proposed that the latter was stimulated both legally and indirectly through the passage of laws such as the Foraker Act (1900), the Second Organic Act (1917), and the Federal Statute of Relations with Puerto Rico Act (1944). Tacitly supporting the nonenforcement of the Sherman Anti-Trust Act in the island, these laws boosted the spread of sugar monopolies and indirectly encouraged thousands of small farmers to leave their farms.[20]

TABLE 1
Acreage under Cultivation with Puerto Rico's Major Crops

	1899		1929		1939	
Sugar	72,000	(26.2%)	237,758	(49.3%)	229,750	(52.3%)
Coffee	197,000	(71.6%)	191,712	(39.7%)	181,106	(41.2%)
Tobacco	6,000	(2.2%)	52,947	(11.0%)	28,584	(6.5%)
Total acreage under cultivation for major crops	275,000	(100.0%)	482,417	(100.0%)	439,440	(100.0%)

Between 1889 and 1929 the total acreage devoted to sugar production increased 230 percent, going from 72,000 acres to 237,758 acres. Tobacco acreage also increased dramatically by 780 percent but coffee remained essentially unchanged. In all, the overall increase in land under cultivation with the Island's three major crops increased by 75.4 percent for the same period.

Source: Puerto Rico Census by Agriculture, 1940.

The complete transformation from coffee *hacienda* to sugar plantation was viewed from another dimension by Angel Quintero Rivera. In 1895, before the United States' occupation of the island, the sugar industry yielded $4.4 million in exports. Two decades after the war, it had produced $74 million, representing 6 percent of the total value of exports. Conversely, whereas the United States imported close to 85 percent of the sugar it consumed before the acquisition of Puerto Rico and the other sugar islands (Hawaii, Cuba, and the Philippines), only 0.4 percent was imported by 1932. Moreover, the effects these changes in production had on Puerto Rico's internal migration and the labor force in general paralleled the changes produced by the ascendency of coffee and the decline of sugar in the last decades of the nineteenth century. But now the migration shifts were from a declining coffee sector, with its vestiges of pre-capitalist relations including non-wage employment, to a mechanized, technologically advanced plantation system designed to generate high profits. Professors Campos and Bonilla referred to this phase when they stated: "Although it maintained a high rate of profit the cultivation and processing of sugar cane was incapable of generating sufficient employment. The result was chronic unemployment that found its social expression in intensive strike activity and in the emigration of thousands of Puerto Rican workers."[21]

Agrarian workers who in the past customarily moved from one agricultural sector to the next depending on employment opportunities, now found their options limited because the concentration on a mechanized capital-intensive sugar industry displaced more workers than it incorporated into the system. During the crop's "dead season," workers who were unable to make ends meet continued to leave the island.

Contrary to the expansion of sugar cane cultivation, coffee production, whose principal markets were in Europe, and to a lesser extent the cultivation of tobacco, also underwent severe crisis after the North American occupation. New taxes, credit limitations, and the undervaluation of the Puerto Rican currency forced many former coffee *hacendados,* small independent farmers, and peasants to give up their land holdings or see them repossessed or sold on the auction block. The situation for the workers in those regions became more acute due to the rapid decline in the acreage dedicated to subsistence farming. By the 1920s, for example, the average acreage reserved for staples in the sugar cane farms fell to less than 0.076 percent per average family unit. The peasant population of the central areas, former coffee workers, and remaining small farmers unable to survive hard times began to move to sugar-connected municipalities in search of jobs.[22]

Between 1899 and 1940 the traditional coffee-producing central western mountain region extending from Moravis to Mayaguez (see Map 2) experienced a relative depopulation, but the northeastern non-coffee-producing mountain region increased in population. Cane-growing municipalities on the coast also grew along with the urban San Juan-Rio Piedras region, emerging in time as the main urban concentrations in Puerto Rico. The decade from 1930 to 1940 alone found fifty-four of the seventy-seven municipalities decreased in population. Thirty-three lost 10 percent or more of their 1930 population and six lost 20 percent or more.[23]

Furthermore, with the exception of San Juan, all of the islands' municipalities had five unemployed laborers for each available unskilled position. The job shortage partly motivated the movement of 71,000 individuals from the island between 1909 and 1940. In the opinion of one researcher, these internal migratory interludes were merely stepping stones toward eventual external emigration. Professor Maldonado-Denis believes:

> The social result of this process of progressive deterioration of Puerto Rico's agriculture has been the mass exodus of the peasant population to the cities (of Puerto Rico) and to the North American ghettos. . . . Many of the displaced *campesinos* that flocked to the urban areas did so as an intermediate step towards migration to the mainland.[24]

The traditional patterns of family life and land ties were also callously eroded by all of these transformations. Each individual displacement altered extended family values, creating among its members a propensity to move in adverse situations rather than to stay. Thus the connections between internal population movements and the subsequent emigrations to the mainland become clear. Puerto Rican workers became conditioned to traverse the island in search of better job opportunities. In time, internal movements also ended

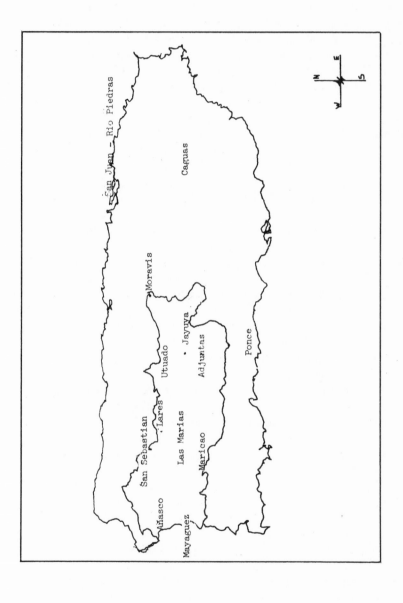

MAP 2 The Coffee Region in Puerto Rico

in frustration since the conditions motivating migration continued to be in operation throughout the island. Of equal importance, the colonial relationship between Puerto Rico and the United States discouraged the formation of native industry or internal markets which might have provided an anchor for urban workers.

The penetration of United States capital into the Puerto Rican economy since 1898 virtually destroyed the traditional pattern of individual land ownership and consolidated the dominance of large continental corporations. Almost all of the major foreign corporations, 103 out of 107, in operation on the island by 1922 were American owned. Large-scale American investments stimulated the supremacy of a one crop economy based on sugar production. Within a decade after the United States occupation, four American corporations produced 50 percent of all of the sugar cultivated in Puerto Rico. Put into other words, Puerto Rico's economy depended upon an agrarian system in which 2 percent of the island's sugar farms controlled 65 percent of all land devoted to that crop.

Moreover, the development of substantial trading outside of United States markets was virtually impossible. By the mid-twenties the United States accounted for over 95 percent of the island's exports and approximately 90 percent of its imports. Inclusion within the continental Coastwise Shipping Act meant the United States enjoyed a monopoly over Puerto Rican commercial activities. American capital investments were not limited to agrarian enterprises. Corporations performed a major role in the tobacco and fruit industries, were the major investors in public utilities, and, along with Canadian interests, owned a significant share of all Puerto Rican bank resources by 1929.[25]

By 1920 sugar cane and tobacco processing, which constituted Puerto Rico's main industries along with a growing cottage-based needlecrafts industry, increased production without an increase in the work force. From 1910 to 1934, sugar production increased from 347,000 tons to 1,114,000, but the total employment in that sector remained almost the same. The sugar workers numbered 87,643 and increased to 92,398 during that period. While 25.3 percent of the agrarian labor force were needed to produce 100 tons of sugar in 1910, only 8.3 percent were employed in this area in 1934. And tobacco production experienced a 12 percent increase in production, but suffered a 26 percent reduction in employment between 1910 and 1920.[26]

At the same time, artisans and independent craftsmen such as shoemakers or carpenters underwent a similar process of transformation in the urban centers. Threatened by an increase in the surplus work force and confronted with competition from United States manufactured goods, skilled craftsmen, unable to make ends meet, flocked to work in tobacco factories. This was then the only industrial sector which enjoyed some degree of prosperity. The numbers of cigar makers increased by 197 percent from 1899 to 1910 and the acreage under tobacco cultivation also increased during this period. In 1910, 74.6 percent of all cigar makers were working in factories of over one hundred employees; a decade later in 1920, 82 percent were employed in factories of over five hundred workers. By 1920, North American interests controlled almost all of the processing and marketing facets of this industry, and while only 4.4 percent of the island's total production was exported at the turn of the century, 19.3 percent was exported two decades later.[27] By the mid-1920s, cigar makers suffered a setback motivated by mechanization in the industry, the growth in the popularity of cigarette smoking and the decade of the Great Depression.

By the mid-twenties the effects of the Depression were deeply felt in Puerto Rico. This critical time signaled a period of contraction in the agricultural sector directly related to a decline in the trade-exchange terms, with serious effect on Puerto Rican incomes. But while the income reduction in the sugar industry was 32 percent from 1929 to 1939, tobacco incomes had already decreased by 51.9 percent in the period 1920–1930. By 1939, the tobacco industry in Puerto Rico was virtually nonexistent.

Second, the period fostered greater dependency on the United States for basic commodities at a time when the population had increased by 21.1 percent but employment had only increased by 1.7 percent, causing one commentator to point out:

> In an index where the prices between 1910 and 1914 are defined as 100, the price of Puerto Rican exports in 1937 was 92.5 and the price of Puerto Rican imports 126. . . . In order to maintain the same level of imports in terms of gross product without

inflicting a negative turn in the balance of trade, the Puerto Rican economy had to increase its gross export production to 36.2 percent.[28]

By 1939, the situation of both the rural and urban worker had changed minimally. Wage laborers received from sixty to eighty cents a day. From 1930 to 1940, the per capita incomes of Puerto Ricans declined from $126 to $120.

The situation in general led to an increase in structural unemployment, as well as an increase in the growth of a marginal work force reduced to working part-time or in miscellaneous employ (*chiripeo*). Many families were forced to depend precariously on poorly paid female work such as home-based needlecrafts. This was a disastrous turn of events because women's labor had always been considered supplementary and therefore viewed as less valuable than men's. Home sewing, as a case in point, was well known for its miserable salaries and inadequate work conditions. In addition, women generally occupied the lowest paying jobs in all of the industries where they were employed.[29]

To make matters worse, women were often employed in declining sectors. Domestic service which had employed 78.4 percent of all females in the labor force in 1899 declined to 27.7 percent in 1930 and decreased drastically after 1940. The tobacco industry, where women came to represent 53 percent of all workers as strippers and classifiers of tobacco leaves, also diminished about the same time. Between 1930 and 1935, including the period of the Depression, unemployment continued to increase and emigration continued to present an attractive alternative.

Clearly, the movements of people from Puerto Rico to the United States responded basically to economic conditions on the island which in turn created a marginal population outside of the stable work force. The search for economic opportunity once again became the motivating factor propelling numbers of Puerto Ricans to migrate, first to the island's urban centers and then across the ocean. The internal migrant in Puerto Rican cities often became part of a pool of unskilled labor working for low wages, and family earnings were frequently supplemented by women's work. Chronic unemployment seasonally rose to alarming levels. The pressure of

a labor surplus created a group geared for emigration among some
Puerto Ricans—those with resources, ambition, and a lack of
opportunity within the island's existing structure. Although
migration incorporates a wide range of causes and consequences
both for the sending and the receiving societies, there are two components which are outstanding: those factors, already discussed,
which encouraged the migrant to leave his or her homeland; and
those factors which attracted the migrant to new destinations.

THE PULL FACTORS

Job opportunities, congressional legislation, and favorable transportation routes combined to influence personal motives for emigration. For Puerto Ricans, the attraction of New York City was
largely economic. Job opportunities, above all, loom as the single
most important factor encouraging potential migration. While
some scholars caution against divorcing the "push" from the
"pull" forces inherent in the migratory experience, others insist
one factor outweighs the other. Several researchers, among them
C. Wright Mills and Harvey S. Perloff, for example, viewed the
"economic pull" forces as the stronger variable in analyzing the
Puerto Rican case. Demonstrating the relationship between the
migrants' personal employment goals and migration as well as the
correlation between the Business Activity Index in New York City
and the levels of migratory participation, Mills concluded that close
to 90 percent of the migrants came in response to employment possibilities.[30]

As a mobile labor force within the North American economic
system, migration certainly fluctuated according to business cycles
and the requirements of the labor market. While in the first decade
of this century only 554 or 37 percent of all Puerto Ricans in the
United States were domiciled in New York City, by 1920 an estimated 7,364 or 62 percent lived there. Within ten years this figure
rose to 44,908, or 81 percent, according to some counts, and in
1940 it increased to 61,462, or 85 percent, but these figures were
disputed by Hispanic groups as undercounts.[31] By 1920, forty-five
states reported the presence of Puerto Rican born persons and all
forty-eight did so in succeeding censuses. Thus the twenties appear
as the turning point for increased immigration. Significantly, while

it was a period of declining employment on the island, it represented a time of increased opportunity on the mainland.

During the First World War a shortage of semiskilled and unskilled labor in the United States activated the "pull" forces of
migration from the island to New York City. Followed by a
demand for labor during the prosperous period, 1922–1929, Puerto
Rican migrants were faced with the opportunity to work in factory
positions formerly held by newly arrived European immigrants. A
potentially growing labor force, Puerto Ricans became entrenched
in garment manufacturing and light factory work, hotel and restaurant business, cigar making, domestic service, and laundries within
a short time.[32] Based on the 1925 census tabulations for four Harlem Assembly Districts heavily populated by Hispanics, almost all
of the Puerto Ricans worked in light industries with smaller contingents represented in the commercial and service sectors and a fraction in public service employment (see Table 2). Almost a decade
later Chenault observed:

> One is apt to find a Puerto Rican in some form of building
> service, acting as a waiter, working in a laundry or employed
> in a factory. Even in the prosperous years before the Depres-
> sion employment was one of the major problems if not the
> major one, of the Puerto Rican in New York. Because of the
> great demand for labor, however, in the early years before the
> Depression, the majority of the workers from the island found
> it comparatively easy to secure work of some sort. The two
> largest employers of Puerto Rican labor in New York City
> were a large biscuit company and a pencil factory.[33]

Two factors were especially important for the growth of Puerto
Rican employment throughout this decade. The first, the passage
of the Second Organic Act or the Jones Act of 1917, created a double impact on migration: it conferred American citizenship on
Puerto Ricans changing among other characteristics their status
from immigrant to migrant and sanctioning population moves
between the island and the mainland as if they were merely reloca-
tions across state lines; and it required obligatory military service in
the armed forces of the United States. The latter provided a seg-

TABLE 2

Occupations of Hispanics in 1925 Based on the Enumerations Reported in the Census of 1925, Assembly Districts 16, 17, 18, 19 in Harlem

PRIVATE SECTOR	A.D. 16		A.D. 17		A.D. 18		A.D. 19	
Owners & supervisors	9	1.5	66	1.8	35	1.8	44	4.3
Workers in production	164	27.0	1188	31.7	558	28.8	279	27.4
Workers in commerce	14	2.3	358	9.6	104	5.4	110	10.8
Workers in services	80	13.2	233	6.2	156	8.0	79	7.7
PUBLIC SECTOR								
Supervisors	—	—	2	.1	—	—	—	—
Workers in production	—	—	—	—	1	.1	—	—
Workers in commerce	—	—	3	.1	1	.1	—	—
Workers in services	2	.3	60	1.6	16	.8	18	1.8
EXCLUDED FROM WORK FORCE								
Housewives	145	23.8	781	20.9	415	21.4	194	19.0
Children & students	187	30.8	903	24.1	576	29.7	253	24.8
Retired, not employed	4	0.7	40	1.1	48	2.5	32	3.1
N.A.	3	.5	108	2.9	28	1.4	11	1.1
TOTAL	608	100.1	3742	100.1	1938	100.0	1020	100.0

Source: New York State Manuscript Census, 1925, Assembly Districts 16, 17, 18 and 19.

ment of the Puerto Rican male population, those who served in the military, an opportunity to familiarize themselves with life, customs, and opportunity in North America. The Jones Act, therefore, significantly encouraged migration. Between 1909 and 1916, for example, the largest group of Puerto Ricans to leave the island for the United States consisted of 7,394 individuals. But in 1917, the year of the citizenship act, 10,812 Puerto Ricans left in almost all cases, en route to North America.[34]

The second factor favoring immigration was the passage of the Johnson Act of 1921. Radically curtailing European immigration, this act contributed to the expansion of job opportunities during the post-World War I period. The laws indirectly resulted in job vacancies for unskilled workers, fostering a series of positions destined to be filled by the available black and Puerto Rican work force. Signed into law by President Harding, the Johnson Act limited the number of aliens to 3 percent of the number of foreign-born of that nationality already residing in the United States based on the census of 1910. The revised Johnson Act of 1924 curtailed immigration even more by admitting only 2 percent of each foreign-born group resident in the United States in 1890. A third act in 1929 fixed the total annual quota at 150,000. With minor exceptions such as the favoring of displaced persons from Europe and alloting minimum quotas to Asian and African countries, these immigration laws remained in effect until 1964.

The correlation between population movements from Puerto Rico and the requirements of the labor market in the United States, and in particular New York City which continued to draw a significant share of the migration, was demonstrated once again during the Depression period. Formal and informal avenues of communication between Puerto Ricans in New York City and relatives on the island (referred to as the "family intelligence network"), kept potential migrants abreast of the insecurities of the Northern job market.

From 1931 to 1940 there was a decrease in the annual average net migration traced directly to employment decline. In his study on migration, Clarence Senior, one-time director of the Social Science Research Center of the University of Puerto Rico, demonstrated that there were fourteen years of high unemployment in the United States in which the net return flow to the island has been greater than the out-migration. These included the years 1921 to 1922 and 1931 to 1934, periods in which job opportunities decreased in the mainland. Demographer Vázquez Calzada addressed this very issue when he remarked, "Between 1930 and 1934 there was a return migration of almost ten thousand people, which is equivalent to 20 percent of the Puerto Rican population in the United States at that time."[35]

Those Puerto Ricans who remained in New York, fortunate enough to be gainfully employed remained concentrated in the unskilled, semiskilled, blue-collar areas working at jobs basically similar to those held by immigrant groups during the past decade. But whereas during the twenties migrants were filling positions previously slated for newly arrived European immigrants, the decade of the Depression found Puerto Ricans competing with unemployed individuals for jobs as dishwashers, countermen, laundry workers, or in maintenance. Resulting from the unusually high unemployment affecting all sectors of the labor force, workers scrambled for any available job. Workers of other ethnic groups, more experienced with the English language and United States customs, who had progressed up the occupational ladder into skilled positions now found themselves unemployed and desperately competing for menial jobs.

That Puerto Ricans continued to hold blue-collar jobs is further demonstrated by the types of jobs available during the thirties. Because of the drastic effects of the Depression in the Puerto Rican New York residential areas, the island's Department of Labor established an office in the heart of the Latin community on 116th Street in an attempt to place the unemployed migrants in jobs. Agency records for the period of its operation, 1930 to 1936, indicate the majority employed were hired in blue-collar positions (see Table 3). Of 1,977 individuals placed by the branch office, 23.4 percent were hired as laborers and in construction; 16.2 percent were placed in laundries; another 12 percent in factories; and 6.4 percent in the hotel business. The rest were employed in restaurants, garages, and in miscellaneous jobs.

Similar employment patterns continued during the forties when once again migration responded to the demands of the United States labor market. During the years of the Second World War,

TABLE 3

Jobs Secured by Puerto Ricans through the New York Based Department of Labor of the Office of Puerto Rico, 1930–1936

OCCUPATION	NUMBER OF INDIVIDUALS PLACED
Laborers and construction	402
Laundry	321
Factories	238
Porters	157
Hotels	126
White collar (clerks, sales, etc.)	121
Janitors, handymen, watchmen	110
Carpenters, painters, plumbers	109
Tailors, garment workers	75
Restaurants (waiters, countermen, etc.)	74
Garages, auto mechanics, electrical workers	67
Cigarmakers and cigarettes	53
Clerks, groceries and shipping	32
Farmworkers	11
Shoemakers	8
Miscellaneous	73
TOTAL	1,977

Source: Chenault, The Puerto Rican Migrant in New York City (New York, Colombia University Press, 1938; re-issued, Russell & Russell, 1970), pp. 74–76.

migration was limited along with all movements to and from Puerto Rico. However, immediately following the war, migration increased again in proportion to the availability of work. In the early years of the forties the North American economy went from bust to boom. Whereas unemployment in American cities exceeded the official rates in Puerto Rico in the early months of 1940, by mid-1943 the United States had achieved full employment. As had been the case in past epochs when cheap immigrant labor provided the means of expanding cities and establishing manufacturing centers, the early years of the 1940s saw a return to labor recruitment in the United States. Minorities and women were actively sought for factory and farm work. Unskilled labor was solicited from rural to urban areas as well as from bordering countries. The impoverished Americans of the Depression era were now at work.[36] Some scholars argue the labor shortages of the Second World War precipitated the motivating forces behind the large-scale Puerto Rican migrations of the period just before and after the war while others maintain that close to 400,000 foreign contract workers entered the country in response to the requirements of the labor market between 1942 and the end of the war, very few of whom were Puerto Rican. Still others propose that although World War II drew nearly eight million workers into the labor force, it was rather the demobilization of that work force and the departure of workers after the war which created a void on the labor market to which Puerto Rican workers responded. Certainly the opportunities for employment were more numerous and varied in a booming economy than could be found in Puerto Rico during the same period. The joint issues of jobs and wages continued to be ever present and decisive.

But the migration also responded to a more basic reality. This was the colonial relationship between Puerto Rico and the United States. While each influenced population movements from the island, some researchers contended the employment conditions in the United States were of less significance in generating migration than were the critical ties between the island and the mainland. Clara E. Rodríguez, for example, focused on the often neglected colonial situation in her study exploring migration motivations. She proposed:

> Of what significance to migration would these changes in employment and national income be if the colonial ties were not present? Would an increase in national income in the United States provoke migration from Puerto Rico but for the colonial ties? Would those factors that have generally been seen as facilitating the Puerto Rican migration . . . have existed but for the colonial relationship? Why weren't cheap

and easy airfares established to nearby cheap labor pools of French Canadians, Cubans or Appalachians? Would military service and the radio have been similarly perceived by Puerto Ricans but for the colonial tie? But for the colonial relationship, would the "pull forces" have been perceived, responded to, or perhaps even generated? Put bluntly, would Mayor Wagner of New York have gone to Puerto Rico to tell Puerto Ricans about the jobs available in New York?[37]

In many cases migrants were indeed directly recruited from Puerto Rico and encouraged to make the journey through offers of paid transportation and other subsidies. By 1948 the Migration Division of Puerto Rico's Department of Labor in New York City established programs to educate potential migrants about conditions in the city. Between 1947 and 1949 a yearly average of 32,000 individuals constituted the net migration from Puerto Rico, many responding to attractive offers from representatives of New York factories in search of workers for the garment and needle-trade industries. Throughout this period the United States Employment Service cooperated with the island's Department of Labor to discover where work shortages were developing and how Puerto Rican workers could best make a contribution. Vázques Calzada, representative of a group of researchers who have emphasized the connection between government policies and migration states:

> Migration has been considered by some social scientists, as well as by the majority of our government leaders, as the best solution to the demographic problem of the Island. Although publicly it was indicated that the government of Puerto Rico was not fostering migration, its actions showed just the opposite. In the population projections prepared by the Planning Board (in Puerto Rico), one of the first variables always included was massive migration.[38]

While Puerto Rican planners intended to alleviate demographic problems, New York businessmen sought to increase their productivity. So closely did the migration of the fifties remain locked into the city's business cycles that a former director of the Migration

Division of the Commonwealth of Puerto Rico's Department of
Labor, observed, "The size of the Puerto Rican migration varies
closely with job opportunities in the U.S.; i.e., when job opportunities increase, migration increases; when job opportunities
decline, migration declines." The Harvard Study of the New York
Metropolitan Region during the same period further underscored
the critical role of the Puerto Rican worker particularly in industrial sectors which might have otherwise been endangered:

> The rate of Puerto Rican migration to New York is one of the
> factors that determines how long and how successfully the
> New York metropolitan region will retain industries which are
> under competitive pressure from other areas. To the extent
> that some of these industries have hung on in the area, they
> have depended on recently arrived Puerto Rican workers who
> have entered the job market of the New York area at the rate
> of about 13,000 each year.[39]

Although Puerto Ricans continued to be concentrated in blue-
collar, low skills, low-paying sectors, especially in light industries,
restaurants, and hotels for men and in the garment industry for
women (see Figure 1), migration was nevertheless almost universal-
ly viewed as financially beneficial.

Wages and war-related occupational mobility were key factors in
attracting the migrant to the mainland, according to economists
Rita M. Maldonado and Lois S. Grey. Professor Maldonado indicated the two essential reasons for migration were (1) if the average
wage in the United States was higher relative to that in Puerto Rico
and (2) if the job market in the United States was relatively better
than that in Puerto Rico.[40] Moreover, Professor Grey concluded
migration to the mainland entailed a risk of downward mobility for
the highly skilled, but offered the prospect of upward movement
for those with lesser skills or work experience. Throughout the fifties migrants with white-collar experience tended to become
employed below their skills level in New York, but most migrants,
generally from rural areas and experienced in farm labor found
mainland jobs in factories thereby moving up the occupational ladder. Indeed, a comparison of average weekly wages in Puerto Rico

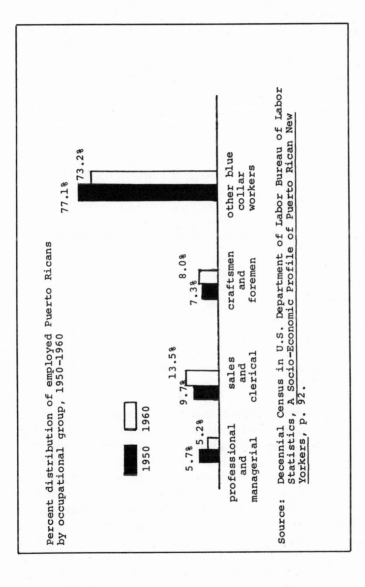

Percent distribution of employed Puerto Ricans by occupational group, 1950-1960

73.2%
77.1%

other blue collar workers

8.0%
7.3%

craftsmen and foremen

13.5%
9.7%

sales and clerical

5.7% 5.2%

professional and managerial

1950 1960

Source: Decennial Census in U.S. Department of Labor Bureau of Labor Statistics, A Socio-Economic Profile of Puerto Rican New Yorkers, p. 92.

Figure 1. The Occupational Distribution of Puerto Ricans in New York City

over a period of three decades with wages received in New York
City demonstrated the migrants were paid higher wages in their
first New York jobs than they had received in their last job on the
island (see Table 4).[41]
Thus, the correlation between the demands of the labor market
through the twenties, thirties, and forties as well as the relative
material progress that the move represented—the "pull" factors—and the high unemployment rates in Puerto Rico—the
"push" factors—is clear.

TABLE 4
Comparison of Average Weekly Wages in Puerto Rico with Average
Weekly Wages in New York City

PERIOD	LAST JOB IN PUERTO RICO	FIRST JOB IN NYC
1920s	$13.00	$19.04
1930s	$12.00	$22.62
1940s	$14.00	$31.43
Post–WW II	$14.60	$28.05

Source: Clarence Senior and Donald O. Watkins, "Toward a Balance Sheet of
Puerto Rican Migration," United States-Puerto Rico Status Commission
Report, 1966, Washington, D.C, p. 749.

But migration is a complex phenomenon involving the breakup
of family units, the determination to succeed in an alien environment, and the ability to create a better existence frequently under
hostile conditions. In spite of the underlying causes indeterminately
resulting in migrant moves, push-pull factors, and recruitment tac-
tics, in the final analysis, each individual migrant made the decision
to leave the island for his or her own constellation of reasons.
While the underlying causes for the great majority were economic
in nature, migrants commonly responded to other motivations as
well. Some migrants were the initiators of the decision to leave
while others became the followers. The true story of who these people were and their reasons and methods for coming to New York

City may be told in both statistical terms and in the personal tales of those who migrated.

INDIVIDUAL MOTIVATIONS BEHIND MIGRATION

Who were the Puerto Rican migrants? Characteristics held in common between migrants of the island's internal movements and migrants in New York during the mid-twenties reveal similarities while an additional profile of city migrants during the mid-fifties offers yet another perspective in determining a more accurate portrayal of these individuals. Based on persons tabulated for the 1925 census, migrants were: in their most productive years; slightly more males than females; more of urban than rural origins; more white than black; and because of the internal migrations within the island during the early decades, more likely to fall into skilled or semi-skilled labor groups within a Puerto Rican context. Skilled tobacco workers, for example, were well represented among the earliest Puerto Rican groups in the city, circa 1915 to 1920. The fact that 55.6 percent of the females and 64.2 percent of the males fell into the fifteen through thirty-five-years-old age bracket further defines the migrant as the "cream" of the island population.[42]

An analysis of the migrant characteristics of those who traversed the island during the decade of the thirties concludes these persons were above average in comparison with those who did not move. Professional and semiprofessional individuals were found in the migrant stream far out of proportion to their percentage of the population. While service personnel were also represented to a far higher degree among the migrants, the opposite was true of farm laborers and farmers.[43]

By 1948 migrants in New York closely resembled those who had previously participated in internal movements. These continued to be in their most productive years (between fifteen to forty-four years of age); more educated than the island average (8 years for both males and females as opposed to 6.1 for remaining males and 5.6 for remaining females); more urban than rural (82 percent of the migrants came from the island's three largest cities).[44] Throughout the fifties, migrant characteristics continued to mirror those of earlier periods with one exception. Males and females tended to move to the mainland in much the same numbers as they had done before with males predominating slightly; agewise, 70 percent of those who left the island were between the ages of fifteen and thirty-five; migrants had on the average a higher level of education than those who remained in Puerto Rico; but the later migrations appeared to be of more rural than urban origins.[45]

One migrant who was typical of the skilled tobacco workers of the first two decades was Bernardo Vega. He left Puerto Rico at a time when the cigar industry was overloaded with skilled workers. In his memoirs, Vega unwittingly revealed his personal motives for coming to New York while at the same time offering insights into the expectations of the migrant group as a whole. The following passage recounts conversations with fellow passengers aboard the steamship *Coamo* in August 1916:

> The days passed quietly. Towards the dawn of the first day, the passengers began to act as if they were all family members. We did not hesitate to discover one another's histories. The overriding theme of our conversations, however, was what we expected to find in New York City. With our first earnings we would send for our nearest relative. Later on at the end of several years we would return to the homeland with our savings. We all, more or less, set our sights on the farm we would buy or the business we would establish in our respective hometowns. . . . All of us carried our individual castles in the air.[46]

Another migrant, Homero Rosado, hoped to fulfill his goals of completing his education while working in the city. A native of Ponce, the decision to emigrate was motivated by family hardships. Leaving the island at the age of seventeen, Don Homero arrived in Brooklyn in 1930:

> I lived with my parents, brothers and sisters. We were two sons and three daughters. My parents were poor but they struggled to meet their economic responsibilities towards us. As we completed high school, our father decided the young women would continue their studies in the university but the young men would have to go to work because our father could not continue to support all five of us. For this reason I decided to leave for the United States because I wanted to

continue my education but was unable to do so in Puerto Rico. When I reached seventeen years of age I went to San Juan, borrowed twenty-five dollars for the fare and disembarked on one of the steam ships which sailed weekly, named *Jacinto*.[47]

Similarly, Antonio Rivera Hernández left Puerto Rico during the twenties in search of opportunity and a better future. Coming to New York completely on his own, Rivera Hernández was seventeen when he left the island. His decision to emigrate came after completing one year of college. Neither was he unemployed nor was he representative of the working class. What he was was an ambitious young man who, as so many like him, did not see a future for himself in Puerto Rico. In a personal interview he described the situation at the time of his departure:

Unfortunately at home we were many and I dreamt only of studying law and my father, well, we had no money . . . a poor family. We were many. We lived in an enormous house but we were many and very close in age. Well, my mother and father decided I should study education and prepare myself for the career of a rural teacher. This was an area I could not accept. I studied one year but failed to matriculate for the second. . . . To keep me from a life of decadence, my father gave me the passage to New York City. They made all the arrangements, supervision on board ship, contacts in New York City, never anticipating my shipboard chaperones would succumb to seasickness leaving me very much on my own.[48]

While most migrants failed to realize their ambitions, compromising in many cases for poor working conditions but living wages, Don Antonio proved to be an exception. He availed himself of the educational opportunities in New York City, perfected his command of English and spent over thirty years actively participating in the activities of the Puerto Rican community. Don Antonio became a dental technician, an examiner for the United States Postal Service, and was one of the first Puerto Rican insurance agents employed by the John Hancock Life Insurance Company. He also published and edited several journals catering specifically to the interests of the Puerto Rican community.

One individual whose experiences were more typical for the migrant community was Antonio Sánchez Feliciano. The youngest son of a landowning, sugar-growing family of nine children, Don Antonio saw a limited future for himself in a declining agricultural economy. His older brothers, Carmelo and Emilio, were the first to leave making the trip from the western part of the island to the capital by train, then boarding a steamship to New York City. Another brother, Fernando, had already left as a seasonal agricultural worker to harvest the crops along the mainland's eastern seaboard. Surviving the influenza epidemic of 1918, which left scores of his compatriots buried in Savannah, Georgia, Fernando settled in New York, establishing a beachhead, so to speak, for the other migrants in the family. When Don Antonio decided to migrate, he was following an example set by his brothers before him. Before his sixteenth birthday he had already attempted to stow away three times. He arrived in New York at the age of seventeen in 1926, aboard the steamship *Coamo*. With limited work experience, his brothers had already secured a factory job for him as an unskilled laborer.[49]

Yet another stowaway described an experience which was rather unique among the migrants. This individual left the island at the age of eight or nine years arriving in New York completely on his own in 1919:

> I left home because I used to go around with other bigger fellows than myself and we used to run away; in those days when a child ran away from one town to another one, some people from the police department, they brought us home, no matter how far we were in the island, they brought us home. But this time I ran away to the capital of Puerto Rico which they call San Juan. Over there a fellow, a small fellow like myself, we got into a ship. I came to this country. When we arrived here they apprehended us because we were kids. We didn't know how to run away or anything. So they took us to a ship, I think that was in 25th Street in Manhattan, and they keep us there. And from there we also ran away. We ran away until this day.[50]

One individual whose experiences were reminiscent of the internal and external migratory patterns of the early decades was Mary Geraldino. During her childhood in Puerto Rico, she lived in

Yauco on the eastern part of the island, in Ponce on the south and in Santurce in the northeast. Before settling in New York, she lived in Cuba for eight years. Dona Mary was a "follower," for it was her father who, determined to provide a better life, decided to move the family to Cuba around 1924. When she made the decision to migrate to New York, Dona Mary was almost twenty years of age. She arrived in the city in 1936, directly from San Juan, Puerto Rico, having moved back to the island several years before. Her greatest motivation for migrating was the lure of good paying jobs and a sister who had already made her home in New York.

Another woman who followed relatives on the migration trail described her experiences in the following manner: "My sister and her husband came to visit the island and they talked me into going to live with them in New York."[51] And still another individual responded:

> We were eleven, six females and five males. My father always provided for us selling fruits and vegetables at the *Puente de Balboa.* But we were poor and as the oldest female I was like a second mother. The burden of caring for the younger children was always on me. In 1930, I was invited to go to New York to live with my cousin. I went and I stayed. I was seventeen years old at the time.[52]

During the late thirties and early forties, conditions in Puerto Rico were described by most migrants as deplorable. Typical of the migrants who referred to economic difficulties was Don Rafael de León. At thirty-six years of age, a married man and father of four children, Don Rafael worked sporadically, loading and unloading fruit aboard ships. Twelve hours of work brought three dollars a day. Food was scarce at that time. If rice could be bought, it cost one dollar for 1½ pounds. Multitudes lined up to purchase five cents' worth of milk every day. Work could sometimes be gotten at the United States military base at *Isla Grande,* but there thousands of workers worked eight hours a day for one dollar. These salaries could barely support one individual let alone a family of six. Borrowing fifty dollars for his ship fare and an additional thirty-six dollars for emergencies, Don Rafael set out for New York City on April 25th, 1945, arriving ten days later.[53]

Another migrant with similar problems, Dona Margarita Her-

nández, emphasized the reasons for her exodus rested on lack of
both employment and opportunity:

> Well at that time, no, in '46, look in '46, I tell you things were
> so bad here that my husband was fired from the factory and
> upon his dismissal did not know what to do or where to turn
> to. He could not find where to make a living! The needle-
> trades industry had hit rock bottom—my husband was a
> mechanic in the needle-trades business and at the same time,
> he was the "foreman" over three hundred or four hundred
> women. . . . We were evicted from our home because we
> owed so much money. Our rent was only eleven dollars a
> week and we owed more than one hundred dollars. One day,
> a woman whom he had worked for, asked if he would be in-
> terested in going to work in New York. As you can imagine,
> we accepted, since we didn't have a chance to make a living
> here.[54]

The thirties and forties stimulated many migrants to leave,
although the return migration during the Depression period was
greater than the net out-migration. Individual migrants continued
to base their reasons for leaving on lack of opportunity: "I came to
New York because the food situation was very bad in Puerto Rico
and there was no work. One of my sisters who lived in San Juan,
the capital, went to New York. She sent for my brother first. Later
I came with my father."[55] "There is nothing in Puerto Rico. My
father and two brothers are here. I don't like it here but I hate it
there. Here at least I can live."[56]

It was not unusual for New York City to attract the bulk of the
Puerto Rican migration. The shipping lines connecting the island
and the mainland had their terminus in New York City. The settlements in New York were also older, more established, and as previously discussed, formed the foundation for the infant Puerto Rican
and Hispanic enclaves since the late nineteenth century. The commercial routes between San Juan and New York were well known
and among the most efficient of water routes. Certainly, during the
first decades of the twentieth century, these routes became increasingly available to passenger steamship trade. While the routes
between San Juan and the Gulf of Mexico or the southern ports of

the United States had been in use for contract labor contingents before, these offered a limited, more expensive first-class voyage for the private passenger, often beyond the means of most Puerto Ricans seeking to leave. On the other hand, the sea routes between the island and New York City offered several different class fares, were more efficient, and boasted the best facilities. Throughout the twenties and thirties, fares ranged between twenty-five and fifty-five dollars and travel time covered from three to five days. On faster ships direct travel time between New York and San Juan averaged 3½ days; others required from four to five days. By comparison, voyages undertaken by contract workers to the southwestern, western, or southern parts of the United States involved several stages totalling eighteen or more days.[57]

In 1926, for example, Rosa Roma left her native Mayaguez and headed for New York City completing a variety of transcontinental connections along the way:

> I came from Mayaguez to San Juan by train which cost five dollars and thirty-seven cents at that time in comparison with hiring a private car which was very expensive—twenty dollars. The train was for passengers and it was driven by coal. It left at 12:00 midnight from Mayaguez and arrived at the steamship terminal at 7:00 A.M. There, we immediately boarded the ship. I paid fifty-five dollars for the voyage to New York and the ship was the *Coamo*. We were seasick. I don't remember much about food service. But I do remember I was traveling second-class and there were some students traveling on first—Spaniards. We flirted with them, talked with them—they brought us pastries and fruits from first class.[58]

Fifteen years later, the journey offered more variety. For instance, Margarita Soto was twenty years old in 1940 when she made the trip from Puerto Rico to Cuba, then to Miami, and finally to New York City.

> We left Isla Grande, Puerto Rico by plane and flew directly to Santiago de Cuba. There were no direct flights to New York City at that time. From Cuba we changed planes because that

plane was scheduled to fly to South America. There we waited one day for a flight to Havana. Since we were almost at war, my aunt and uncle decided not to wait for a flight to Havana and instead took a bus. We left for Havana at 3:00 P.M. arriving the next day at 7:00 A.M. and took a flight to Miami. From there we rode a bus to New York.[59]

Around 1947 close to twenty-seven airlines, mostly from Miami, converged on San Juan Airport. With the increases in job opportunities after the Second World War, air travel became one of the greatest assets to the Puerto Rican migration, and regular air service commenced between New York City and San Juan. Many of the smaller wildcat lines originated with Army surplus planes purchased from the War Assets Administration by former G.I. pilots, but the commercial run was initiated by Eastern Airlines. In the late forties Puerto Ricans paid between thirty and fifty dollars, depending on which line they flew, for their trips north. The airplane cost about the same and could accommodate more passengers within a week's time than could the steamships. Moreover, airplanes made a radical improvement over ships as they were able to reach their destination in a matter of six hours. Throughout the late forties and fifties Puerto Ricans landed and departed frequently at the major airports at Newark and Teterboro in New Jersey, at La Guardia field in New York City, and in Miami, punctuating the airplane's contributions to the "great migration" from Puerto Rico.

Conclusion

Thus we have discussed the events which joined forces to push Puerto Ricans from the island and the opportunities which awaited them in New York City. Migration fluctuated according to the requirements of the labor market, drawing those facing critical futures on the island along with the family followers. In the words of the migrants themselves, almost all came in search of opportunity, the chance to make something for themselves and their families. They came on the steamship shuttles between San Juan and New York, ignoring closer destinations because New York represented familiarity and better resources. In time, they came by air, becoming the first airborne migration in history. And when they came, particularly to New York City, they formed communities and settlements frequently reflecting those left behind.

Notes

1. For an excellent account of eighteenth- and nineteenth-century contraband trade see: Arturo Morales Carrión, *Puerto Rico and the Non-Hispanic Caribbean: A Study in the Decline in Spanish Exclusivism* (Rio Piedras: University of Puerto Rico, 1952); and Loida Figueroa Mercado, *Breve historia de Puerto Rico,* 2 vols. (Rio Piedras: Ediciones Edil, 1970).

2. Robert Ernst, *Immigrant Life in New York City, 1825-1863* (New York: Kings Crown Press, 1949). See also Clarence Senior, *Puerto Rican Emigration* (Rio Piedras: University of Puerto Rico, 1948); and C. Wright Mills, Clarence Senior, and Rose K. Goldsen, *The Puerto Rican Journey* (New York: Columbia University Press, 1950).

3. History Task Force, Centro de Estudios Puertorriqueños, *Labor Migration Under Capitalism: The Puerto Rican Experience* (New York: Monthly Review Press, 1979). See also Angel Quintero Rivera, "Puerto Rico 1870-1940: From Mercantilist to Imperialist Colonial Domination" (paper presented at the Latin American Studies Association Conference, Pittsburgh, Pennsylvania, April 1979).

4. Carlos Buitrago Ortiz, *Los orígenes históricos de la sociedad precapitalista en Puerto Rico* (San Juan, 1976).

5. Olga Jimenez de Wagenheim, "Prelude to Lares," *Caribbean Review* vol. 8, no. 1 (January-March 1979), pp. 39-43. See also Figueroa Mercado, *Breve historia de Puerto Rico.*

6. Centro de Estudios Puertorriqueños, *Documentos de la migración puertorriqueña, 1879-1901,* no. 1 (New York: Centro de Estudios Puertorriqueños, Graduate Center, CUNY, 1977). In addition to the Centro's studies, several other groups have given the study of migration top priority. Among them are the Puerto Rican Migration Research Consortium in New York and the Centro del estudio de la realidad puertorriqueña (CEREP) in Puerto Rico.

7. History Task Force, *Labor Migration,* pp. 70-73.

8. Ibid. See also Morris Morley, "Dependence and Development in Puerto Rico"; Adalberto López and James Petras, *Puerto Rico and Puerto Ricans: Studies in History and Society* (New York: Schenkman Publishing, 1974), pp. 215-220.

9. History Task Force, *Labor Migration,* pp. 81-83.

10. Angel Quintero Rivera, "Background to the Emergence of Imperialist Capitalism in Puerto Rico," in López and Petras, *Puerto Rico,* pp. 87-102.

11. Ibid. See also Clarence Senior and Donald O. Watkins, "Towards a Balance Sheet of Puerto Rican Migration," in U.S.-P.R. Commission on Status of Puerto Rico, *Status of Puerto Rico: Selected Background Studies* (Washington, D.C.: Government Printing Office, 1966).

12. Quintero Rivera, "Puerto Rico, 1870-1940," pp. 12-20. See also Marcia Rivera Quintero, "Capitalist Development and the Incorporation of Women to the Labour Force" (paper presented at the Latin American Studies Association Conference, Pittsburgh, Pennsylvania, April 1979).

13. *La Correspondencia de Puerto Rico,* May 11, 1901, cited in Centro de Estudios Puertorriqueños, *Documentos,* p. 37.

14. This information appears in an interoffice memorandum addressed to the Secretary of War, Bureau of Insular Affairs, April 17, 1917.

15. Ibid.

16. Lawrence R. Chenault, *The Puerto Rican Migrant in New York City* (New York: Columbia University Press, 1938; reissue, Russell & Russell, 1970), pp. 28-30.

17. Oscar Handlin, *The Newcomers: Negroes and Puerto Ricans in a Changing Metropolis* (Cambridge: Harvard University Press, 1959), p. 49.

18. History Task Force, *Labor Migration,* pp. 103-106. This is also an important theme in Ricardo Campos and Frank Bonilla, "Industrialization and Migration: Some Effects on the Puerto Rican Working Class," *Latin American Perspectives,* vol. 3, no. 3 (1976).

19. Angel Quintero Rivera, "Puerto Rico 1870-1940," pp. 12-20, 87-110. Marcia Rivera Quintero, "Capitalist Development," pp. 9-11.

20. James Jennings, *Puerto Rican Politics in New York City* (Washington, D.C.: University Press of America, 1977), p. 32.

21. Campos and Bonilla, *Industrialization,* p. 79.

22. Senior and Watkins, "Towards a Balance Sheet," pp. 698-699. Marcia Rivera Quintero, "Capitalist Development," pp. 9-11.

23. Senior and Watkins, ibid.

24. Manuel Maldonado-Denis, *Puerto Rico: A Socio-Historic Interpretation* (New York: Random House, 1972), p. 312.

25. Morley, "Dependence and Development," p. 217.

26. Angel Quintero Rivera, "Puerto Rico 1870-1940," pp. 24-25.

27. Ibid., pp. 17-18.

28. Ibid., p. 23.

29. Marcia Rivera Quintero, "Capitalist Development," p. 23. See also: Caroline Manning, *The Employment of Women in Puerto Rico* (Washington, D.C.: U.S. Government Printing Office, 1934); and Isabel Picó de Hernández, "Estudio sobre el empleo de la mujer en Puerto Rico," *Revista de Ciencias Sociales,* vol. 19, no. 2 (June 1975).

30. Mills et al., *Puerto Rican Journey.* See also Harvey S. Perloff, *Puerto Rico's Economic Future* (Chicago: University of Chicago Press, 1950).

31. Senior and Watkins, "Towards a Balance Sheet," p. 705.

32. U.S. Department of Labor, *A Socio-economic Profile of Puerto Rican New Yorkers* (Bureau of Labor Statistics, Regional Report 46, July 1975), p. 9. See also Senior and Watkins, "Towards a Balance Sheet," p. 701; and History Task Force, p. 109.

33. Chenault, *Puerto Rican Migrant,* pp. 71-72.

34. History Task Force, *Labor Migration,* p. 109. See also: Centro de Estudios Puertorriqueños, Taller de Migración, *Conferencia de Historiografía* (New York: Graduate Center, CUNY, 1974), parts 1-3.

35. José L. Vázquez Calzada, "Demographic Aspects of Migration," in History Task Force, *Labor Migration,* pp. 223-238.

36. Constance M. Green, *The Rise of Urban America* (New York: Harper & Row, 1965).

37. Clara E. Rodríguez, "Economic Factors Affecting Puerto Ricans in New York," in History Task Force, *Labor Migration,* p. 199. See also: *The New York Times,* June 27, 1964.

38. José L. Vázquez Calzada, "Demographic Aspects," p. 231.

39. Rodríguez, "Economic Factors," p. 213.

40. Rita M. Maldonado, "Why Puerto Ricans Migrated to the United States in 1947-73," *Monthly Labor Review,* no. 9 (September 1976).

41. Lois S. Gray, "The Jobs Puerto Ricans Hold in New York City," *Monthly Labor Review,* no. 46 (October 1975).

42. The New York State Manuscript Census, 1925, Assembly Districts 16, 17, 18, and 19.

43. Senior and Watkins, "Towards a Balance Sheet," p. 707. See also: Clarence Senior, "Migration as a Process and the Migrant as a Person," *Population Review,* vol. 6, no. 1 (January 1962), pp. 30-41.

44. Senior and Watkins, "Towards a Balance Sheet," pp. 707-709. Gray, "Jobs," pp. 13-16. U.S. Department of Labor, *Socio-economic Profile,* pp. 16-17.

45. José L. Vázquez Calzada, "Demographic Aspects," pp. 228-230.

46. César Andreu Iglesias, ed., *Memorias de Bernardo Vega* (Rio Piedras: Ediciones Huracan, 1977), p. 40.

47. Interview with Homero Rosado, Brooklyn, New York, October 1980.

48. Interview with Antonio Rivera Hernández, Rio Piedras, Puerto Rico, August 1977.

49. Interview with Antonio Sánchez Feliciano, Aguada, Puerto Rico, July 1977.

50. Interview with Aurelio Cruz, Brooklyn, New York, October 1978.

51. Interview with Julia González, Rio Piedras, Puerto Rico, August 1977.

52. Interview with Elisa Baeza, Mayaguez, Puerto Rico, July 1977.

53. Interview with Rafael de León, Brooklyn, New York, October 1980.

54. Interview with Margarita Hernández, Mayaguez, Puerto Rico, July 1977.

55. *New York World Telegram,* May 1, 1947.

56. Ibid.

57. Centro de Estudios Puertorriqueños, *Conferencia de Historiografía,* pp. 16–19.

58. Interview with Rosa Roma, Santurce, Puerto Rico, August 1977.

59. Interview with Margarita Soto Alers, Aguada, Puerto Rico, July 1977.

Settlement Patterns and Community Development

Without doubt and contrary to the opinions of many researchers, there existed a pre-World War II communal structure within the Puerto Rican settlements, prepared to cushion the impact of the migration experience and to perpetuate essential characteristics designed to maintain that community intact.[1] Articulations in support of Latin customs and traditions coupled with a sense of communal responsibility found expression in more ways than one. Simple indicators of the existence of a Puerto Rican community were the facts that Puerto Ricans resided within clear geographical areas, had a common language, historical and cultural heritage, and shared common interests. Settlements formed on a physical level with the entrenchment and solidification of neighborhoods throughout the city. Through the proliferation of a business and professional sector, and the leadership and stability which these inspired, communities were easily identified as Puerto Rican. Moreover, early migrants continued to speak in Spanish as the language of communication and as the basis for a particular lifestyle in which traditions and customs were expressed.

The Meaning of Colonia

Two observers who identified such characteristics were Lawrence R. Chenault, who wrote of the Puerto Rican migration to New York City during the decade of the thirties, and José Hernández

Alvarez whose studies concentrated on the decade of the fifties. Chenault located the geographic boundaries of the early settlements in East Harlem, South Central Harlem, and in the Borough of Brooklyn, pointing out the main difference between the Puerto Ricans and other groups was that the former tended to come to particular areas of one large city, rather than to several cities.[2] Chenault furthermore demonstrated that these areas formed the heart of the entire Latin community in New York City with an abundance of restaurants, stores, theatres, and organizational activity. He described emerging institutions such as the regional societies and other associations of social and recreational interests.

Hernández Álvarez confirmed settlement patterns similar to those described by Chenault in his monumental study on the movement and settlement patterns of Puerto Ricans during the forties and fifties.[3] His work demonstrated the following:

1. Puerto Rican residents of the United States live in a *colonia* or urban nucleus marked by dense settlements, provision for manifestation of the Puerto Rican social identity and way of behavior and by frequency of internal activity and dependence.

2. These neighborhoods or *colonias* have constituted the primary context for migration and dispersal of the Puerto Rican population in New York City, which was in turn dependent on employment opportunities and the grapevine of information.

3. During the post-war period, 1945–1950, the migration flow from Puerto Rico was almost exclusively toward New York City and the basic social organization of the New York community was forged in the context of this initial movement.

4. Finally, the Puerto Rican migration was highly mobile. Many migrants were likely to return to the island and migrate to the mainland again within a five-year period. This phenomenon was the root of the close links which existed between the island and the mainland communities.

In writing about the *colonias* of the 1940s and 1950s, Hernández Álvarez introduced a model which isolated the distinct characteristics of a typical Puerto Rican community. The *colonias* were geographic, urban centers marked by dense settlement; they provided outlets for Puerto Rican interests, creating institutions which affirmed social identity and fostered internal activities while coping with problems stemming from contacts with the host society. The *colonias,* furthermore, attracted potential migration from Puerto Rico because they offered the migrant a familiar base in which to operate. In short, the migrant looked forward to settlement in an area where the language, customs, attitudes, interests, and traditions were similar to those he or she had left in Puerto Rico.

Although Hernández Álvarez wrote of Puerto Rican migratory patterns at mid-century, his model proved applicable to the earlier decades as well. Chenault had basically observed the same patterns of settlement among the Puerto Rican migrants of the mid-thirties. Indeed as early as the 1910s, there existed identifiable settlements, which not only created institutions and group associations, but kept active links with island society and broached communication on several levels with the non-Hispanic group as well. Moreover, these early settlements were held together by characteristics similar to the Hernández Álvarez model. They were:

1. The geographic location and distribution of Puerto Ricans in New York City.

2. The physical characteristics of Hispanic neighborhoods as evidenced by the growth of professional, commercial, and social enterprises and the types of leadership generated.

3. The persistence of the Spanish language, customs, and habits for the maintenance of a shared identity as Puerto Ricans.

4. Common interests and attitudes towards assimilation as expressed in popular culture.

Location and Characteristics of Puerto Rican Neighborhoods

The development of Puerto Rican neighborhoods coincided with the availability of jobs for Puerto Rican migrants. Thus, the earliest settlements flourished in those areas of the city where employment was readily accessible. The cigar-makers' migration at the turn of the century, for example, founded settlements in Manhattan's Lower East Side and Chelsea sections among Eastern European and Italian immigrants because close to five hundred Hispanic owned and operated tobacco factories located there. The Brooklyn community also developed along the Navy Yard area precisely because jobs along the waterfront were plentiful. During the 1920s, the Greenpoint section of Brooklyn similarly attracted Puerto Ricans.[4] Early settlers of that Borough affirmed the section was densely populated by Puerto Ricans who worked in several area factories such as the American Manufacturing Company, which specialized in making rope from Philippine hemp. Such companies were important to the development of Puerto Rican concentrations not only because they employed migrants already residing in New York City, but also because they directly recruited workers from the island, bringing them to live in the Borough and providing for their basic needs according to contractual agreements.

A case in point was the recruitment of 130 women directly from Puerto Rico by the American Manufacturing Company.[5] Their experiences, perhaps typical for other contractual workers as well, offer further insights into the relationship between settlement patterns and job opportunities.

The group was brought to Brooklyn by steamship, met by company representatives, and placed in company-owned, three-story buildings centrally located on a spacious thoroughfare. The shelters, considered modern for the period, used electric lighting rather than gaslight common in many buildings of the neighborhood. Two chaperones, from "well-known" respected Puerto Rican families looked after the women's welfare and completing the household, another group of four women were hired especially to provide domestic services such as cooking.

The rope factory, moreover, provided free bus transportation to and from work. This vehicle which accommodated forty persons was also available for recreational excursions in exchange for chauffeur's fees and the cost of gasoline. Through all of these company-sponsored activities, Puerto Rican workers had the opportunity to thoroughly familiarize themselves with city neighborhoods, transmitting this information in letters to friends and relatives in Puerto Rico.[6]

In addition, the settlement originally oriented around work opportunities soon attracted small businesses catering to specific migrant needs, particularly in the area of food consumption. While the appearance of restaurants, grocery stores, or rooming houses, the earliest types of commerce in Puerto Rican neighborhoods, was limited in the Greenpoint section at this time, some businesses were in operation. Workers employed in the American Manufacturing Company recalled the first businesses in the neighborhood concerned with the Puerto Rican consumer were *bodegas:*

> There was a small *bodega* on Franklyn Avenue near the factory which was owned by friends of mine and they sold hot lunches to the factory people. It took close to ten minutes to get there but once in a while we (me and my brother Carmito) ran like hell, got to the store and sat down to a steaming plate of rice and beans which we gulped down to get back to *"Las Sogitas"* on time.[7]

If the foundations of the earliest migrant settlements rested on a work-oriented base, the establishment of subsequent neighborhoods depended equally on cheap housing, good transportation, and accessible shopping. Motivated by these factors, the expansion of Puerto Ricans into other geographic areas and the conversion of these vicinities into *colonias* accelerated during the period of the late twenties and thirties.

While Puerto Rican *colonias* were simultaneously developing in various areas of the city, it was the Harlem community which would assume the lead as the largest and most significant of all the inter-wars settlements. Among the earliest descriptions of that neighborhood was that of Bernardo Vega, a young cigar maker who later committed his recollections to print.

In 1916, the year of Vega's arrival in New York, the section that was destined to become *"El Barrio,"* or the Spanish-speaking district, provided homes primarily for Jewish and Italian families. Recently arrived European immigrants mingled with first generations, creating a tapestry of vivid cultures, customs, and languages which fascinated the young cigar maker. Older, more experienced immigrant families lived along the spacious tree-lined Saint Nicholas and Manhattan Avenues while more recent arrivals occupied the easternmost section of the district.

The Jewish ghetto extended along Park Avenue between 110th and 117th Streets east of Madison Avenue. Professional centers

situated along 110th Street complemented the luxury and entertainment enterprises on Lenox Avenue while stores offering poorer
families lesser quality merchandise proliferated in the region east of
Eighth Avenue. Park Avenue also carried reasonably priced goods
in push carts bazaar-laden with bargain items. These formed an
open-air market under the trestle of the New Haven and New York
Central Railroad.[8] Nestled among all this confusion were some
fifty Puerto Rican families.

The *Marqueta,* the open-air market described by Vega, played an
important role in the everyday lives of early migrants because it
constituted the largest shopping center which sold Puerto Rican
items. Its location in the Harlem area in conjunction with available
cheap housing aided in attracting settlers into this region. It was
here that they could obtain essential consumer goods. Caribbean
foods and spices shared shelf-space with other ethnic favorites and
bargain hunters bought seasonal clothing, often irregulars and
second-hand, at a fraction of their original cost at other retail
stores. Early migrants were very familiar with the functionings of
the *Marqueta* and many dated their arrival in New York City
according to whether or not this landmark was indoors or open-air.
Recollections such as those of Raquel Rivera were common among
pioneer settlers.

> In the twenties and thirties the *Marqueta* was almost all Jewish.
> What happened was the Jews began to sell Puerto Rican
> products like *platanos* and other items. Eventually, Puerto
> Ricans took over the stalls but in the early times it was run by
> others, Jews, Italians. . . . Everyone communicated very well.
> I would see the "storekeepers" put your purchases in a little
> basket, weigh it and say, "un dollar" or "two dollars," (holding
> up two fingers) whatever it cost. Actually, I didn't do any
> shopping myself, but I accompanied my aunt who did shop.
> The Jewish vendors always knew a few words in Spanish: *si,*
> *bueno, barato* and so on.
>
> In addition to vegetables and other foodstuffs, everything
> was sold in *la marqueta:* I remember there was an area for
> selling stockings. Another for pocketbooks. Now I remember!
> One side, it was divided, one side, the right was reserved for
> those articles, stockings, pocketbooks, clothing. The left side
> was solely for, and I think it still is, for vegetables.[9]

Interestingly, the Brooklyn community also expanded geographically, but it lagged behind the Manhattan settlement particularly in the commercial and professional sectors. Throughout the first decades of the century, Brooklyn migrants looked towards Manhattan as the mecca for Latin entertainment, shopping, or professional services. Almost all of the important social and commercial institutions catering especially to Puerto Ricans operated in Manhattan. Families in need of medical care traveled to Manhattan, in some cases, forced to pay double fare. Moreover, the Brooklyn Puerto Rican neighborhoods were older, buildings more decrepit than those found in Manhattan. Coupled with inadequate housing conditions, the negative influences of run-down waterfront neighborhoods and related industries posed detrimental or inhibiting factors to that *colonia's* growth.[10] Before long, the leaders of the Brooklyn settlement, acutely aware of the disparities between both *colonias,* addressed themselves to these issues. One such individual angrily remarked:

> Sometimes I get angry with them (meaning the Puerto Rican professionals in Manhattan) because I do not see why when your kind arrives in Brooklyn from Puerto Rico, as soon as they leave the ship (steamships from the island often docked in Brooklyn piers), they run to Manhattan to operate there instead of staying in Brooklyn to help us. You can tell them that we resent their apparent disregard for us. You can tell them whenever you have a chance, that had they stayed in Brooklyn, and put up their businesses, established their law, medical and dental offices here things would have been more advantageous to them and to us. . . . I hope that as soon as possible something can be done to see that Brooklyn is the focal point of all Puerto Rican activities in New York.[11]

Were Brooklyn Puerto Ricans justified in their resentment of the rapid progress in the Manhattan *colonia*? In many ways they were. By 1926 the Porto Rican Brotherhood of America, a Manhattan-based community association, described the enormous geographic and numerical expansion of the city's Puerto Rican population, demonstrating Manhattan's superiority in numbers and resources. As depicted in their souvenir program for that year, the settlements throughout the city remained working class, but a small segment of the group participated visibly in the commercial and professional life of the *colonias*.[12] Whereas the migrant group had confined itself to geographical areas closely determined by work opportunities almost a decade before, neighborhoods now appeared in five distinct sections of the Manhattan and Brooklyn boroughs. Perhaps of greater significance, the report attempted to determine the actual numbers of Puerto Ricans living in New York City. The Brotherhood's report of 1926 estimated Puerto Rican residents throughout the city numbered close to one hundred thousand individuals—a debatable analysis if one considers the available research on the subject—and these were distributed as shown in Table 5.

Thus, 60 percent or the majority of the Puerto Rican migrant population lived in two areas of Manhattan: 90th Street to 116th Street between First and Fifth Avenues; and 110th Street to 125th Street between Fifth and Manhattan Avenues (see Map 3). These areas, recognized by the non-Hispanic as East Harlem and South Central Harlem, were known as *el Barrio* or *la colonia hispana* by the Puerto Rican migrants, both nomenclatures synonymous in the migrant mind.

"In New York City the *colonia hispana* was called Harlem and is still Harlem today. . . . The Puerto Rican colony . . . Harlem . . . was composed predominantly of Puerto Ricans and it has grown enormously throughout the decades," declared one resident. Similarly, others noted the expansion of such enclaves, referring interchangeably to the new geographic entities as East Harlem or Spanish Harlem. "The Puerto Rican settlement in the section of New York City known as East Harlem which covers the northeastern tip of Manhattan Island, grew up after the First World War," wrote journalist Dan Wakefield at mid-century.[13] These geographic boundaries, furthermore, were shared with a steadily diminishing Italian and Jewish population. Thus, within a decade *El Barrio's* fifty Puerto Rican families as described by Bernardo Vega in his recollections, had been joined by several thousands and these filled the living quarters vacated by other more upwardly mobile ethnic groups.

Additional insights may be obtained about the Puerto Rican families living in those areas from census data collected for four Harlem Assembly Districts for 1925. Of 7,322 individuals living in

1,535 households, practically all who were employed worked as operatives and unskilled workers in light industry, with smaller groups engaged in commerce or business, and a tiny fraction employed in the public service sector. These figures essentially coincided with the analysis of the distribution of Puerto Ricans in the city as reported in the Porto Rican Brotherhood program of 1926.

Moreover, Puerto Ricans in the four Manhattan Assembly Districts cited lived among other ethnic groups, particularly Jews, Italians, Russians, and Irish. These districts were rounded out with a smattering of black residents as well. But while some intermingling of Puerto Ricans and other ethnics within the same apartment house buildings appeared in the census, the incidence of blacks and Puerto Ricans sharing buildings was limited.[14] Finally, the census of 1925 indicated nine in ten heads of households were born in Puerto Rico. An average household evolved around a married couple with children. Lodgers or extended family members almost always completed the households. In short, during the twenties, the Puerto Rican *colonia* was characterized by family-based households, most of which were working class. (See Map 4.)

The thirties found limited changes in the settlement patterns of the Puerto Rican neighborhoods. "In Manhattan," declared Chenault, "Puerto Ricans lived in a district bounded from about 97th Street up to and along 110th around the northern part of Central Park, northward to about 125th Street and approximately from about Third Avenue on the East to Eighth and Manhattan Avenues

TABLE 5
Estimate of Puerto Rican Residents in New York City, 1926

DISTRICT	RESIDENTS
14th Street to 30th Street	10,000
90th Street to 116th Street	
First Avenue to Fifth Avenue	20,000
110th Street to 125th Street,	
Fifth Avenue to Manhattan Avenue	40,000
Washington Heights	5,000
Brooklyn	25,000
TOTAL	100,000

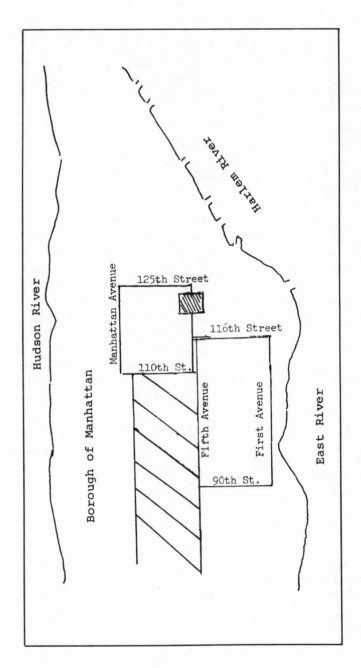

MAP 3 Largest Concentration of Puerto Ricans in Manhattan Based on Report of Porto Rican Brotherhood of America, 1926

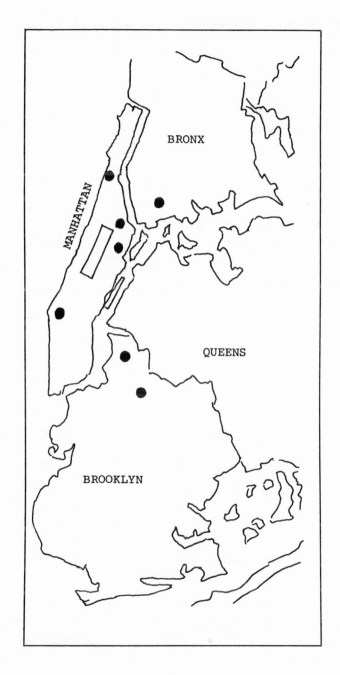

MAP 4 Geographic Location of Puerto Ricans in New York City Based on Report of Porto Rican Brotherhood of America, 1926

61

on the West." The largest concentration continued to develop in
the area around 115th and 116th Streets, further solidifying the
contours of the present-day *Barrio Latino*. At the same time, the
Brooklyn community expanded geographically along the water-
fronts south to the Gowanus Canal, extended inland to about Third
Avenue and included the Greenpoint section.[15]

The actual size of both settlements in numerical terms remained
debatable. As residents of a United States possession, migrant
Puerto Ricans did not figure in immigration counts, and calculations were based on private studies made by organizations such as
the Porto Rican Brotherhood or Catholic Charities. While the
Brotherhood's report estimated a total of 100,000 individuals in
1926, the *New York Times* and the New York Mission Society
arrived at figures between 150,000 and 200,000 persons for the
same period. By comparison, the growth of a commercial and professional sector in that sizeable community remained somewhat
limited.

The Growth of a Professional and Commercial Sector

If numerical increases among Puerto Ricans and the expansion
of settlement boundaries marked one aspect of community formation, the growth of a commercial and professional sector concur-
rent with a nascent type of leadership more clearly punctuated the
physical characteristics of the *colonia*. By the late 1920s the commercial sector had developed rapidly to include some two hundred
bodegas or grocery stores and about one hundred and twenty-five
restaurants. By 1926 newspaper articles confirmed the "rapid
influx of Latins and West Indians" who described themselves as
Puerto Rican and initiated the opening of their own businesses,
"patronizing no others."[16] It was precisely in the proliferation of
commercial and professional establishments—small businesses,
bodegas, botánicas, restaurants and boarding houses—that the
physical characteristics of the Puerto Rican community were most
sharply defined.

Since the early days of the Puerto Rican migration, the backbone
of the pioneer settlements had been formed by businessmen. The
ownership of barbershops and boarding houses represented the
first forms of entrepreneurship among the early settlers. More

important, pioneer enterprises lent an air of solidarity to the community offering consumer goods and services in familiar surroundings tailored to migrant needs. The *marqueta,* the open-air market described by early settlers, continued to supply consumer products but never assumed the "cultural" position of the neighborhood business for at least two reasons: First, the open-air market traded with all the ethnic groups residing in the Harlem area. Second, many of the shopkeepers of *La Marqueta* failed to involve themselves in the communal activities of the Puerto Rican *colonias.* It was in this capacity where many local businessmen and professionals assumed a degree of leadership. The owners of small businesses along with a handful of Puerto Rican professionals firmly held onto the reins of community leadership by spearheading the establishment of neighborhood clubs or organizations and making themselves available for advice or neighborhood activities. It was not unusual for Spanish-speaking customers to seek advice from the Puerto Rican pharmacist or the local *curandero* in health matters, from the neighborhood priest or spiritualist in matters of faith or from the community baker or barber on jobs, apartments, or other negotiations. These local leaders enjoyed a certain status in the community commensurate with their types of businesses or academic background. The pharmacist and the priest, for example, commanded greater admiration than the grocer because the former were better educated, thus more knowledgeable. However, all businessmen depended on the patronage and goodwill of the community. These sought to maintain customers by allowing credit and to attract new ones through advertising their Puerto Rican wares in the local community presses. In this regard, competition for migrant attention was stiff. All vehicles for conveying information were utilized and these included not only the local presses, but newspapers, newsletters, and journals popular within the community.

One hotel for example, *El Hotel Latino* located at 221 West 14th Street featured enticing Spanish foods—*Comidas Latinas*—as its main attraction. Another advertised in *El Heraldo* stressing its convenient location and easy access to public transportation:

> I have the pleasure once again of offering my home to my friends and to all travelers from the Antilles, Central and

South America. It is located at 440 West 23rd Street. It is one
of the most centrally located areas and can be reached by all
manner of public transportation. Dining is Creole style.

Ulises del Valle[17]

Throughout the early thirties, a growing number of restaurants
featured creole cuisines and on many occasions Puerto Ricans
patronized community restaurants, even though the home
remained the focal point for family meals. For those who cultivated
eating out as a popular leisure time activity, the choice of restaurants was varied as many continued to advertise in local presses.
The following ads were typical:

El Paraiso

Here you will find rice and *gandules verdes* and spare ribs,
codfish fritters and potatoes.
Open Tuesday and Wednesday, 12 noon to 4 A.M.
211 E. 116th St.[18]

Restaurant "El Louvre"

70 East 111th Street
Antonio Delgado—El hombre del dia
General Chef—Creole and Spanish
Specialty—Chicken and Rice with *mofongo*.[19]

Significantly, both of these restaurants, typical of the period,
addressed themselves to the Hispanic community in general, but
featured distinctive Puerto Rican specialties as their main attraction: *arroz con gandules verdes*—rice with pigeon peas, a dish traditionally reserved for the Christmas season when the peas were
harvested; *mofongo*—a plantain appetizer made with bacon, gar-
lic, and other spices.

In a personal interview, one migrant, niece of a *bodegero* in
Spanish Harlem, described dining out as a pleasant, reasonably
priced social experience:

What I recall most vividly was a restaurant called "Fuentes"
where they made *empanadas* with *tostones* for which they

charged a dollar or $1.25, but these *empanadas* were enormous and the *tostones* exquisite. Do you know it was there I met Tony (her husband to be) with his cousin Juan Antonio Corretjer. We went to eat there one night and I recall we ate very, very well. But observe (*fijate*) the restaurant was well-known! There was at the time a popular song which referred to Fuentes—well this was the celebrated *mozón* of the restaurant.[20]

This individual was representative of the younger Puerto Rican generation who were particularly active participants in many neighborhood activities. However, restaurants survived not only on the patronage of leisure dinnertime guests. Situated in predominantly working-class neighborhoods and catering primarily to an Hispanic clientele, restaurants often specialized in take-out trade. Hot lunches in three-tiered covered metal containers were prepared and sold to the workers residing in the community who continued to perpetuate the Latin custom of consuming a full midday meal. The containers often carried rice, beans, meat or poultry, salad and Puerto Rican bread—a large lunch by non-Hispanic standards.

Other *Barrio* residents recalled the growth of different types of businesses. Commercial enterprises like Valencia Bakery and Cofresi Travel Agency became synonymous with Puerto Rican business. During the thirties these not only advertised in local presses, but over Spanish-language radio stations as well. Valencia especially appealed directly to the Hispanic consumer by announcing weddings, birthdays, baptisms, and other celebrations over the airwaves for which special cakes were purchased.[21]

In addition to commercial ventures, a handful of Spanish-speaking professionals catered to the health and legal problems affecting the Puerto Rican community. According to the 1925 census, less than 3 percent of the 7,322 Hispanic individuals tabulated were professionals. However, one study proudly reported the professional community numbered about one hundred persons including "two Puerto Ricans engaged as Spanish instructors in the Department of the 'great' Columbia University."[22] Doctors, lawyers, and dentists also advertised their practices in the Hispanic press. For example, one newsletter carried an ad offering the services of a nurse/midwife: María F. Aparicio, *Enfermera y comadrona: gra-*

duada en Puerto Rico; 59 West 115th Street'' (graduated from Puerto Rico). Other ads announced the closing or resumption of specific practices. Such was the case of one physician who announced his return from Europe and his engagement once again in medical practice:[23]

Dr. Carlos G. Armstrong

Announces his return from Europe and the resumption of his medical practice.

Hours	*Telephone*	*Location*
1–2 p.m.	CAthedral 5578–7347	601 West 110th St.
6–7 p.m.		New York City

And another:

My best advertising is a satisfied clientele. Do you wish to be my best announcement? Come to see me and I assure you, you will be. In addition, so you will accept my offer, I'll make a special deal.[24]

By 1923 the listings in the *Guía Hispana,* a guide to the commercial and professional listing of the Spanish-speaking communities, reinforced the importance of Hispanic businesses. First, it made available the names, addresses, and telephone numbers of Spanish-owned businesses in much the same way that telephone directories did for other companies. Second, it advertised their existence. The *Guía* listed some one hundred and fifty professionals including physicians, dentists, and lawyers, and two hundred and seventy-five businesses. About forty restaurants completed the inventory.[25]

Interestingly, the Chenault study on the Puerto Rican migration during the mid-thirties shed doubts on the Puerto Rican commercial and professional entrepreneurship, maintaining that it was difficult to ascribe the ethnic origins of owners or professionals merely on the basis of a Spanish surname. Yet the majority of the Spanish-speaking residents of the city did come from Puerto Rico during the decades of the twenties, thirties, and forties, continuing to do so afterwards as well. The granting of American citizenship in 1917 contributed much to migration from the island without the restrictions necessarily placed on immigration from other Spanish-speaking countries. Furthermore, the census figures for the four sample districts in Harlem confirmed the predominance of Puerto Ricans among the city's Latin population.[26] Perhaps of greater importance, these early migrants were the ones who exerted considerable influence on the development of the commercial and professional sectors, as owners, as professionals, and as consumers. In many cases these individuals emerged in time as internal and/or external leaders within the *colonia hispana*.

Who were the handful of professionals who served the Puerto Rican community? One was Dr. José N. Cesteros, who lived and practiced medicine in his *barrio* apartment. He was equally respected by the Puerto Rican and non-Hispanic community as a physician and for his political activities during the thirties and forties (see Chapter 6). Another was Dr. José Julio Henna, Puerto Rican patriot and physician, one of the founders and deans of the Medical Board of French Hospital in Manhattan. Dr. Henna was born in Puerto Rico in 1853, the son of Joseph Henna of Plymouth, England and María del Rosario Pérez of Puerto Rico. As a young man Henna participated in the cause of Puerto Rican independence alongside Betances and Hostos, leading to his eventual banishment by Spain. The eighteen-year-old exile came to New York City, studied at the College of Physicians and Surgeons and obtained his medical degree in 1872. Following graduation, he traveled abroad, working for a time in Paris, London, and finally returning to New York. From 1880 until his death in 1924, Dr. Henna was one of the leading physicians connected with French Hospital, serving also on the staff of Bellevue Hospital.

Professional activities did not alienate Henna from life in the Puerto Rican settlements of New York nor from concern for events occurring in Puerto Rico. In 1895 he was chosen president of the Revolutionary Party which struggled for independence from Spain. After the Spanish-American War, he was twice elected as a delegate to appear before the Senate and House Committees on Civil Government in the island. Moreover, as founder and president of the Ibero-American Club, Dr. Henna participated at the forefront of many social and cultural activities in the New York *colonia* where he made his home for fifty-five years.[27]

As in the case of Dr. Henna, many individuals active in com-

merce or the professions participated in neighborhood associations, building a reputation as persons to whom the community
could turn in time of need. Some, like Dr. Henna or Dr. Cesteros,
were recognized by the host society as leaders or power brokers for
the early settlements. Others, like the Colóns, Jesus, Ramón, and
Joaquin, politically active community figures of the pioneer settlements of both Manhattan and Brooklyn, were considered leaders
primarily within the settlements by the residents of the *colonias.*
Thus, leadership operated on several levels. First, leaders were
prominent Puerto Ricans recognized by both the Latin and non-
Hispanic society as representing the pioneer settlements. Second,
leaders were those individuals like the local priest, pharmacist, or
curandera to whom the early migrants turned in times of stress.
Third, leaders were also individuals who distinguished themselves
as organizers or power brokers for the settlements, but not necessarily recognized as such by the host society.[28]

In the Brooklyn *colonia,* leadership emerged in much the same
way as in Manhattan. One leader, Carlos Tapia, was a storekeeper
by trade, but his experience at many different types of jobs and his
political involvement brought him into intimate communication
with the needs of the early migrants. Recognized as a leader among
his people in Brooklyn, Tapia held the distinction of being equally
respected by the residents of the Manhattan *colonia* as well. On several occasions he was called upon to aid the migrants of that
borough.[29] One incident involved the "Harlem Riot" of 1926,
when a group of more established Harlem residents engaged in
street fighting, arguments, and bottle throwing, protesting the
encroachment of Puerto Ricans and other Hispanics in the Harlem
area. Called upon by other Puerto Rican community leaders to
avenge the migrants, Tapia and a group of Puerto Ricans were
apprehended and dispersed by the police. This incident signaled a
critical moment in the life of the pioneer settlements and exemplified without a doubt the role of the community leader. In the minds
of the migrants this was especially defined as an individual who
placed himself between the *colonia* and the dominant host society.
Carlos Tapia fulfilled this role in the opinion of one migrant: "Carlos Tapia helped the Puerto Ricans in every way. He even used to
help them physically and economically. By physically I mean any

abuse the Puerto Ricans got they used to go to Carlos Tapia. And he and his people would correct everything. They didn't go to the police, they went to Carlos Tapia."[30]

Pura Belpré, folklorist and children's librarian by vocation, represented yet another type of leadership — one which strove to preserve the customs and cultural traditions of the Puerto Rican people, setting them apart as a distinctive identifiable group. The first Puerto Rican librarian in the New York Public Library system, Belpré initiated Latin community projects throughout several branches of the library system as early as 1921. Promoted to chief storyteller at the Seward Park Branch, she also volunteered her time as storyteller in the Union Settlement House, Madison House, and the Educational Alliance, all of which enjoyed considerable Puerto Rican patronage. Touched by the concern for cultural traditions among the early migrants, Belpré established children's programs which emphasized Puerto Rican traditions, games, and folk tales fostering through storytelling the internalization of positive language and cultural values. Under her supervision the Harlem branch to which she was assigned fulfilled community cultural needs by presenting Hispanic exhibitions and programs focusing on the many contributions of Latin writers and artists.[31]

Language as a Reinforcement of Community

As the migrant settlers became entrenched in various neighborhoods of New York City, those characteristics which singled them out as a distinct ethnic group became more visible to the non-Hispanic. Overall, these were (1) the use of Spanish as the language of communication and (2) the perseverance of island interests or customs as expressed in celebrations, close family associations, and attitudes toward assimilation.

Reserved as the language for the work place and business, English was also used as the means of communication with the host society. Spanish, on the other hand, remained in the home and the community. While authoritative institutions placed great emphasis on English language proficiency, these were not always priority concerns among the Puerto Ricans themselves.[32] Among the migrant population some desiring to improve their job prospects availed themselves of night school courses to perfect their command of vernacular English.[33] Others were more intent on structuring their new environments along the lines of those with which they were most familiar and were more concerned with instilling in their children the language and values which formed their cultural heritage. Still others intended to return to Puerto Rico once they had improved their economic situation. While economics and, to a lesser extent, education constituted important stimulae for learning English for the predominantly working-class communities, most Puerto Ricans did not envision themselves spending the rest of their lives as English-speaking "Americans."

The use of Spanish as the language of communication served as a bond which not only welded intercommunity relationships, but also secured the connections with the rest of Puerto Rico and Spanish-America. Puerto Ricans in New York City read Spanish language newspapers; saw Mexican and Argentinian films; listened to Spanish radio stations; formed associations which promoted Spanish language and culture; danced and listened to Latin music.

Since the late nineteenth century, for example, the growth and intellectual diversity of the Spanish-reading population in the city sought and found stimulation in a number of popular journals published abroad, in Puerto Rico and in New York. Among them were *El Buscapie* (1877), *América* (1883), *El Latino-Americano* (1885), *Las Novedades* (1887), *Revista de Literatura, Ciencias y Artes* (1887), *El Avisador Cubano* (1888), *El Economista Americano* (1887), and *La Juventud* (1889).[34] Similarly, novels and related reading material were available to the early migrant settlers during the first decades of the twentieth century. Among periodicals sold in New York were: *Cultura Proletaria,* which represented an anarchist political viewpoint; *El Heraldo,* a bilingual publication edited by the Autonomist leader Muñoz Rivera; and *La Prensa.* The latter began publishing in 1913 as a weekly, appearing on a daily basis by 1918. This newspaper was destined to become the most important journalistic endeavor for the city's Spanish-speaking population.[35]

La Prensa boasted the motto *"único diario español e hispano-americano en EEUU"* (the only Spanish and Hispano-American newspaper in the United States). It did not confine its services to reporting foreign and domestic news, but fully involved itself in community affairs. Besides advertising for local businesses, special sections reported the arrivals and departures of individuals to and from Spanish-America. Classified ads informed the Spanish-reading public of employment opportunities. Calendars of community events merited regular reporting as did the myriad activities of community groups throughout the city's *colonias*. Religious and educational affairs appeared in print including the weekly agendas of the Brooklyn and Manhattan Hispanic churches: *Nuestra Señora de Guadalupe, Nuestra Señora de la Esperanza, La Iglesia del Pilar,* and *La Milagrosa*. Finally, social or cultural news appealing directly to the small commercial and professional sector informed the public of events such as the series of literary seminars held at Columbia University directed by the well-known Spanish novelist Vicente Blasco Ibañez, the merger of two community associations, or a benefit dance for a church held at the Brooklyn Academy of Music.[36]

Direct community involvement centered on the sponsorship of Latin projects or activities appealing to Hispanics in general. In 1919, for example, *La Prensa* cosponsored a gala ball in conjunction with several community groups the proceeds of which were slated for building an Hispanic sanitarium. On another occasion, the paper's director, José Camprubi, participated at the initiation of a newly federated association composed of representatives of numerous neighborhood units. This liaison group proposed to represent the Spanish-speaking in matters relating to the wider non-Hispanic society. Finally, *La Prensa* frequently joined in fund raising for relevant neighborhood causes, concerts, contests, beauty pageants, and *los juegos florales*. The latter, consisting of competitive dramatic recitations, was significant because it perpetuated the cultural traditions of medieval Spain in the New York Latin *colonias*.[37]

Many less ambitious Spanish language *revistas* continued to appear periodically, oriented around fashionable causes or utilizing current fads, but these seldom retained the longevity characteristic of the older tabloids. Some were organs for the many diverse community organizations operating in the *colonia hispana*. Others, philosophically dedicated to the perpetuation of the language and culture, delivered their message to the Latin community in general. One of these was the magazine *Gráfico,* edited by Ramón LaVilla and later by Bernardo Vega. Published in New York City from

1926 to 1931, on a weekly basis, the motto of this worthy journal
was "Semanario Defensor de la Raza Hispana," a response to the
intrinsic mission of those who placed the preservation of both language and culture uppermost (see Figure 2).

Described by its creators as a satirical, comical, and literary journal, *Gráfico* appealed specifically to a working-class circulation
rather than the general Spanish-speaking population which read *La
Prensa*. It printed advertisements, an advice column, community
organizational news, general essays, and fiction. One typical issue
contained an editorial, a novella, a brief biography of the Mexican
philosopher José Vasconcelos, an autobiographical essay by the
Puerto Rican historian, Dr. Cayetano Coll y Toste, a sports article,
a movie review of *The Jazz Singer,* social and cultural news of
Puerto Rico, the New York *colonias,* and Spanish America.[38]

The editorial, in particular, was the vehicle for attacking significant issues affecting the Puerto Rican settlements. These covered a
wide range of ideas including views on the current political situation in New York, analysis of the meaning of key American holidays to Hispanics, discrimination against Puerto Ricans, and dis-
courses on class consciousness. An excellent example was the editorial of July 8, 1928, where the oppression of the working class,
which included most of the magazine's Puerto Rican readers, was
compared to the struggle for American independence:

> American people indulge today in celebration of the birth of
> their freedom forgetting they are no longer masters of their
> destiny. America is populated by economic slaves. The mas-
> ters of society are not only depriving their countrymen of
> their freedom but while engaging in celebration of the Fourth
> of July, the nation as a whole, is depriving some other unfor-
> tunate weak people of their liberty and pursuit of happiness.[39]

Another editorial questioned the value of American citizenship
in the protection of Puerto Rican civil rights. Here *Gráfico*
broached the subject of discrimination against Puerto Ricans in
New York, recommending the creation of a city agency authorized
to speak for these disadvantaged residents of the Spanish-speaking
settlements in the same manner that foreign consulates protected
their nationals:

The most vulnerable group of those which comprise the large family of Ibero-Americans (in New York City) is the Puerto Rican. Truly it seems a paradox that being American citizens these should be the most defenseless. While the citizens of other countries have their consulates and diplomats to represent them, the children of *Borinquen* have no one.[40]

The editorial highlighted, moreover, the inefficacy of the Puerto Rican resident commissioner, a United States congressional appointee charged with representing island interest in the North American congress, and other officials, to deal successfully with the everyday problems of the city's *colonias*. Regardless of how sympathetic they might be, these hard-working individuals fol-

SEMANARIO DEFENSOR DE LA RAZA HISPANA*

PUBLISHED EVERY SUNDAY

RAMON LA VILLA, Editor

ALBERTO O'FARRILL, Managing Editor
MARIO GARCIA, Business Manager
EMILIO PRENDES, Assistant to Publisher

Oficina: 108 West 115th Street :: Tel. Beekman 4419 :: New York City

*Weekly Defender of the Hispanic Race

Figure 2 Journal Masthead, *Gráfico,* 1927

lowed a different agenda oriented around island/mainland considerations, duties and obligations. But the problems of most Puerto
Ricans, as expressed in the editorial, took place in New York City
where they had established homes, faced racial and cultural discrimination daily from other ethnic groups, and dealt with menial,
undersalaried employment. *Gráfico's* recommendation was: "For
these reasons it is here (New York City) where Puerto Ricans
require a knowledgeable individual authorized to represent and
advise them in those relationships which, by virtue of the environment in which we, as aliens find ourselves, must be maintained with
other social groups." Calling attention to their perception of themselves as "aliens," the editorial issued a direct appeal to the Puerto
Rican worker, stressing unity, brotherhood, and understanding.
Gráfico intended to encourage support for their position on critical
issues on two levels: first, within the vertical class structure of
Puerto Rican society; second, by fostering an understanding of the
workers' struggle based on a one-to-one relationship: "Agrupare-
mos bajo una sola bandera: la de la fraternidad, y con ella en alto,
sostener los ideales y prestigios que nos son inherente" (We shall
unite under one flag: that of brotherhood and with it on high we
shall maintain those ideals and privileges which to us are inherent).[41]

While *Gráfico* exemplified a typical community journal for the
period of the late twenties, the *Revista de Artes y Letras* performed
a similar function for the community a decade later. Pledged to the
development and dissemination of Hispanic culture, this journal
also prided itself on a dedication to the preservation of the Spanish
language and a continuation of Latin traditions. It focused on
important issues relevant to the Spanish-speaking settlements,
social or educational affairs, and politics. Founded and edited by a
Puerto Rican woman, Dona Josefina Silva de Cintrón, an individual recognized for her involvement in the development of the interwar *colonias,* the monthly journal flourished from 1933 until 1945.
Revista de Artes y Letras published the writings of major literary
figures of Spain and Spanish America including notables like Julia
de Burgos and La Hija del Caribe. The former, best remembered
for her contributions as a lyric poetess, lived in New York during
the thirties and forties, an experience which sensitized her to the
particular situation of the migrant settler.

Artes y Letras frequently featured articles on family and child welfare, and its editorials centered on community issues such as the education of Puerto Rican children or the importance of preserving the Latin heritage. Community organizational news, advertising, interviews, and advice columns shared space with literary essays and fiction. The latter comprised close to 80 percent of the journal's format offering important exposure and communication for new Latin writers.

Through its emphasis on culture and literature *Artes y Letras* appeared to direct its efforts towards a more educated segment of the Spanish-speaking population. But while the journal did not openly address the working class as *Gráfico* had done before, *Artes y Letras* nevertheless strongly identified with the community in which it originated. It involved itself in the *colonias* by taking stands on relevant issues through its editorials and by concerning itself with the organizations of the early settlements. Announcements of all types of community activities appeared in print regardless of which groups were sponsoring the events. The political, religious, or social affairs of groups representing a wide range of interests were seldom ignored and as news items, failed to compromise the journal's original commitments to literary ideals.

The editorial of March 1936 signaled another example of the journal's community involvement as well as its preoccupation with the promotion of the Spanish language. Terming it the educational harassment of Spanish-speaking youngsters in New York City schools, the journal launched a crusade against the testing of Harlem school children by the city's Chamber of Commerce (see Chapter 6). Aroused by the journal's position on this issue, neighborhood groups, concerned also with the language issue, banded together to explore the situation.

For some time, migrant families believed their children suffered undue hardships in the school system because they were unable to speak fluent English. Youngsters transferring from Puerto Rico to New York City schools had commonly been placed one or two years behind the grade level previously completed on the island. In other cases, youngsters and secondary school students were assigned to classes for retarded or slow learners since school administrators could not adequately evaluate achievement levels for monolingual Spanish-speaking students. Equally disturbing, the repetition of grades on the secondary level discouraged many students from completing their course of studies.

The Puerto Rican *colonia* stood united on the language education issue, and several organizations spoke out against the city's educational policies. One such group, *Madres y Padres Pro Ninos Hispanos* sought to relieve the situation by offering an alternative. While they were not actively campaigning for the idealogical preservation of language and culture, they struggled for recognition of the Spanish academic achievements of their children. Acting as buffers between the school administrators, faculty and the *colonia's* schoolchildren, they proposed a rudimentary form of bilingual education in which the classrooms would be staffed with liaison-parents as well as teachers. While their ideas were not implemented, an attempt was made nevertheless, to aid the schools in evaluating the educational progress of Puerto Rican students more accurately.[42] Thus, the insistence on the preservation of Spanish as the language of communication emerges as a reaction to the rapid integration desired by the host society as well as a manner by which to keep an intact sense of identity.[43]

The importance of Spanish became apparent in other ways as well. One of these was in the area of entertainment. Movies and movie stars offered the working-class *colonias* Spanish escapism in a pre-television era. Argentina and Mexico, particularly the Mexican Estudios Churubusco, were the chief producers of Spanish comedies, melodramas, musicals, and westerns. The 1940s, termed the golden age of the Mexican cinema, produced between 130 and 140 Spanish language films a year, many under the direction of individuals like Buñuel, Julio Bracho, and Fernando Fuentes, all of whom would achieve international recognition in the coming decades.[44]

A subculture of Latin filmgoers responded to the Spanish cinema and promoted the popularity of such stars as María Felix, Mapi Cortez, Libertad Lamarque, Carlos Gardel, and Pedro Infante. Thrilled by the exploits of Jorge Negrete or Pedro Armendariz in Mexican westerns, audiences also eagerly applauded the comic antics of Cantinflas or Tin Tan. Community presses advertised current films and followed the professional and personal lives of the movie stars. Interviews with personalities like Dolores del Río or Arturo de Córdova, favorites among Latin filmgoers, frequently appeared in journals like *Gráfico* or *Artes y Letras*. Some, like

Dolores del Río, gained fame in American films as well. When this happened, as was also the case with a young Ricardo Montalbán, the Spanish language presses consistently emphasized the performer's Latin roots, as if to reclaim him or her for the community once again.[45]

Interests and Attitudes

The common interests and attitudes which coalesced the Puerto Rican settlements into a community were eloquently expressed in the popular culture of the period. Music proved remarkably vital for internalizing and externalizing the attitudes of the migrant population. As primary vehicles for expression combining Iberian, African, and Taino Indian influences within the Puerto Rican culture, music, song, and dance had undergone a long development on the island and were transported to the mainland along with the migrant settler. Thus, traditional rhythms such as *Bomba, Plena, Aguinaldo, Seis, Danza y Danzón* were found at the center of musical development in New York *colonias* as well as in Puerto Rico. Essentially summarizing the feelings and attitudes of frustration, nostalgia, unrequited love and homesickness of the Puerto Rican migrant, music also provided a crucial bridge between the island and the mainland communities. In the working-class *colonias* of New York, popular culture in many cases expressed migrant sentiments more poignantly than the written word.

Often a song gained popularity in the migrant settlements as well as in Puerto Rico, since it was played on the Spanish-language radio stations, carried back and forth by the migrant population itself, or played by musicians in groups of *trios* or *conjuntos*. Lyricists, arrangers, and musicians were well known to Puerto Rican audiences on both sides of the ocean and seldom did a piece gain popularity without the migrant community crediting the composer, the lyricist, and the musical group with the success of the song. These creative individuals ranked alongside movie stars or politicians in the minds of the people. One composer lyricist idolized on both sides of the ocean whose work evoked memories of Puerto Rico and the plight of the humble peasant was Rafael Hernández.

Owner of Almacenes Hernández, one of the first Puerto Rican music stores in Manhattan, Hernández composed the songs which became synonymous with the migration experience.

In the back of his store there was a piano which his sister, Victoria, used to teach aspiring musicians. Every time a student came for a lesson she would chase Rafael out of the rocking chair near the piano in which he was singing and strumming his guitar. Rafael would take his guitar and a tin can of black coffee out on the sidewalk, sit down near the edge of the curb and with his feet in the gutter, he would tune his guitar and begin to sing and write words to songs on little pieces of paper.[46]

In *Lamento Boricano,* Hernández succinctly captured the peasant's love for his homeland and the economic misfortunes underlying his move from the island. Along with *Preciosa,* another hymn to the island more nationalistic in tone, *Lamento Boricano* assumed the role of an informal national anthem in some circles of the interwar settlements precisely because it expressed wholehearted concern for the burdens under which the island existed. Moreover, migrants in New York identified with its message interpreting the *jibarito's* journey as the voyage from Puerto Rico to New York.

Popular music not only conveyed nostalgia for the lost homeland or concerns with the island's desperate situation; some songs like *Yo Me Vuelvo a Mi Bohío* satirized the difficulties of adjusting to living in New York City. In the song the protagonist comes to New York expecting to progress because things in Puerto Rico are so bad, only to find the situation in New York is worse. "Sometimes the heat and other times the damned cold, sometimes he resembles a mess ice skating through the snow"—the solution is he will return to his Puerto Rican home—his *bohío.*[47]

Still other songs like *¿Alo, Quien Llama?* expressed awareness of the working-class struggles taking place in Puerto Rico and immortalized an actual event which took place in the factories of Mayaguez. Both songs emerged at an important period in the development of the city's *colonias* following the end of the Second World War, when the Latin neighborhoods had increased dramatically in size. While agencies engaged in studies designed to deal with the problems of the city's newest neighbors and attempted to assimilate them into the dominant society, Puerto Ricans poked fun at themselves in their songs, asking if indeed they wanted to integrate into the system.

If gut feelings and reactions found expression in songs, music played other important roles as well. First, it enabled the migrant community to sing, listen to, and play the familiar songs associated with holidays or festive occasions in Puerto Rico. Second, it nurtured a continuation and bonding together of friends and relatives in the celebration of birthdays, weddings, baptisms, and other important life-cycle occasions in the migrant experience. Invariably, neighborhood musicians provided live music for these celebrations while invited guests danced or sang. These activities alternated with dramatic recitations or poetry declamations, all forming a natural part of the evening's entertainment, not unlike celebrations in Puerto Rico. Moreover, *trios* or *conjuntos* complete with vocalists often came together to entertain at weekend parties not necessarily confined to holiday celebration. These gatherings composed of friends, relatives, and neighbors encouraged intergenerational activities, and older participants interacted freely with children, infants, and young adults without friction.

Puerto Rican musicians played at house parties as well. Soon after his arrival, cigar maker Bernardo Vega noted the practice of holding rent parties, particularly in the Harlem settlement where spacious apartments lent themselves to this type of action. These parties were not confined to family participation (although family members frequently shared leisure time activities), but rather designed to attract paying customers. The underlying motive of a rent party was to sufficiently enrich the residents of the apartment so they could pay their rent. Vega observed: "In the more spacious Harlem apartments, the custom of celebrating parties on Saturdays and Sundays became established. These were not family parties but rather dances where people paid to get in."[48] Musicians were paid with profits from the sale of beer, *maví* (a native Puerto Rican soft drink) or Puerto Rican delicacies. Those families fortunate to include musicians as relatives appeared to be more economically secure during periods of hardships since these individuals often found house parties at which to play.

> During the 1930s a house party in the *Barrio* was a ball. The apartment and hallway reeked with the spicy aroma of garlic and oregano which emanated from the fresh hams in the oven. Thin slabs of *pernil* accompanied plates of steaming

arroz con gandules. The elders drank beer that flowed from a wooden keg kept in the kitchen sink on top of a twenty-five cent block of ice. The bathtub, filled with cracked ice, covered several flavors of soda pop that children drank. *Trios* or *quartets* which consisted of a lead vocalist, a maraca player, guitarist and sometimes a trumpeter provided live music in the living room . . . as the evening came to a close each musician was three dollars richer.[49]

As late as the 1950s these customs were still in practice. One young musician recalled similar parties taking place in the apartment which was his home. His mother was often the lead vocalist and music became an intimate, natural part of his upbringing. Live music and the special relationship surrounding musical expression flourished aided by a growing record industry catering to those very interests.

Two decades into the twentieth century *Danzas, Danzóns, Plenas,* and *Aguinaldos* had already been recorded by Columbia and RCA Victor Record Companies, finding a lucrative market of enthusiastic consumers among the city's Latin population. By the 1930s Latin bands played to packed houses in the *Teatro Hispano* or the *Campamor* Theatre at Fifth Avenue and 116th Street in the heart of Spanish Harlem. Dance halls like Hunts Point Palace, Tropicana Park Palace, and the Audobon Ballroom hired popular Latin bands to attract Hispanic dancers. However, record companies, above all, continued to bring popular music into the home.

By the late forties, the Latin music industry was thriving with record companies and labels. The first Puerto Rican-owned company recorded on the Dynasonic label. This was the Spanish Music Center on 110th Street and Fifth Avenue, where neighborhood trios and quartets recorded in the back of the store while records on the Decca or later the Tico labels were sold in the front. In addition to records, the Spanish Music Center sold piano rolls of Latin favorites and musical instruments such as the traditional Spanish guitar.[50]

As a business venture, the small music store spread quickly throughout the *colonia hispana* and came to symbolize the Latin settlements as the candy store had characterized other ethnic immigrant neighborhoods. Emanating from these establishments the rhythms of *el Son, la Guaracha,* Puerto Rican *Plenas* and *Aguinaldos* combined with the romantic *Boleros* and *Danzas* to serenade the Spanish-speaking neighborhoods day and night, nurturing a continuation of vital cultural expressions rooted in Puerto Rico and Spanish America. In time, other recording companies like Ansonia, Seeco, Mercury, and Alba also catered to Latin tastes especially after the enthusiastic response of non-Latin audiences to the introduction of the *Mambo.*[51]

In spite of the popularity of Latin music for the non-Hispanic host society, Latin music continued to be an integral part of the Spanish-speaking community, which not only set it apart, but served also to identify it as a distinctive unit. It was here that Puerto Ricans shared a common interest which more often than not, served as a community base, kept cultural communications open with the island, and even allowed a degree of interaction with the host society. Clearly, Latin music expressed the development of the *colonia* on two levels: The cultural, as an expression of Puerto Rican heritage and creativity; and the physical, as an example of Latin entrepreneurship.

Conclusion

That the pioneer Puerto Rican settlements prior to mid-century constituted communities is indisputable. We have traced the genesis of the Puerto Rican settlements in two dimensions: the geographic boundaries and settlement patterns as well as the physical characteristics emphasizing professional, commercial, and leadership development. Early *colonias,* or migrant neighborhoods, were urban centers marked by dense settlement patterns. Through the proliferation of a business, professional, and social sector, held solidly on a working-class base, settlements were easily recognized as Puerto Rican.

But the migrant settlements formed solid communities in other dimensions as well. These were the persistence of the Spanish language, customs, and habits for the maintenance of a shared identity as Puerto Ricans and a perpetuation of common interests and attitudes as expressed in life-cycle celebrations and popular culture.

Notes

1. Some of the studies which have debated communal development among Puerto Ricans include the following: Oscar Handlin, *The Newcomers: Negroes and Puerto Ricans in a Changing Metropolis* (Cambridge: Harvard University Press, 1959); Nathan Glazer and Daniel Patrick Moynihan, *Beyond the Melting Pot* (Cambridge: MIT Press, 1963); Alfred Kazin, "In Puerto Rico," in *Contemporaries* (New York: Little, Brown & Co., 1960); Daniel J. Boorstein, "Self Discovery in Puerto Rico," *Yale Review,* 1955.

2. Lawrence R. Chenault, *The Puerto Rican Migrant in New York City* (New York: Columbia University Press, 1938; reissue, Russell & Russell, 1970), p. 158.

3. José Hernández Álvarez, "The Movement and Settlement of Puerto Rican Migrants within the United States, 1950-1960," *International Migration Review,* vol. 2, no. 2 (spring 1968), pp. 40-51.

4. Interview with Ramón Colón, The Puerto Rican Oral History Project, 1973-1974, Long Island Historical Society, Brooklyn, New York. See also Ramón Colón, *Carlos Tapia, A Puerto Rican Hero in New York* (New York: Vantage Press, 1976), p. 44.

5. Octavo informe anual del negociado del trabajo, informe sobre la intervención e investigación realizada por el negociado del trabajo en relación con las trabajadores Portorriqueñas contratadas en Puerto Rico por la American Manufacturing Company de Brooklyn, New York (San Juan: Puerto Rico, 1920), pp. 10-18.

6. Ibid., p. 15.

7. Interview with Antonio Sánchez Feliciano, Aguada, Puerto Rico, July 1977.

8. César Andreu Iglesias, ed., *Memorias de Bernardo Vega* (Rio Piedras: Ediciones Huracan, Inc., 1977), pp. 45-46.

9. Interview with Raquel Rivera Hernández, Rio Piedras, Puerto Rico, August 1977.

10. Chenault, *The Puerto Rican Migrant,* pp. 104-107.

11. Colón, *Carlos Tapia,* p. 74.

12. The Souvenir Program of the Porto Rican Brotherhood of America, June 1926.

13. Daniel Wakefield, *Island in the City—The World of Spanish Harlem* (Boston, Houghton Mifflin Co., 1959).

14. The New York State Manuscript Census, 1925, Assembly Districts 16, 17, 18, 19. A partial tabulation of this census was done by the Center for Puerto Rican Studies, CUNY. See also History Task Force, Centro de Estudios Puertorriqueños, *Labor Migration Under Capitalism: The Puerto*

Rican Experience (New York: Monthly Review Press, 1979), pp. 148-151; and Peter Laslett, *Household and Family in Past Time* (Cambridge: Cambridge University Press, 1972).

15. Chenault, *The Puerto Rican Migrant,* p. 128. Handlin, *The Newcomers,* pp. 93-98.

16. *New York Times,* July 30, 1926, p. 29.

17. *El Heraldo,* August 3, 1901, classified ads.

18. *Gráfico,* March 27, 1927, p. 2.

19. Ibid.

20. Raquel Rivera Hernández interview.

21. Interview with Lillian López, New York City, May 1976. Interview with Evelina Antonetty, Columbia Oral History Project, Columbia University, New York City.

22. The Porto Rican Brotherhood of America, program.

23. Ibid.

24. *Gráfico,* February 27, 1927, p. 2.

25. Chenault, *The Puerto Rican Migrant,* p. 71. See also *Guía Hispana* (New York, Guía Hispana Publishing Co., 1934); *Polk's New York City Directory,* 1933-1934.

26. New York State Manuscript Census, 1925; Iglesias, *Memorias,* p. 193.

27. *New York Times,* February 3, 1924, p. 23; Iglesias, *Memorias,* pp. 184-185; History Task Force, *Labor Migration,* p. 83.

28. For an interesting interpretation of leadership in Puerto Rican communities, see John M. Goering et al., "An Examination of the Needs for Outreach Development in the Area of Hispanic Discrimination" (The Graduate School and University Center, CUNY, July 1977, unpublished manuscript). See also John W. Gotsch, "Puerto Rican Leadership in New York" (M.A. Thesis, New York University, 1966).

29. *New York Times,* July 27, 1926, p. 21; and July 30, 1926, p. 29. See also Iglesias, pp. 188-191; Ramón Colón interview.

30. Interview with Pedro Ruiz, Aguada, Puerto Rico, July 1977.

31. Interview with Pura Belpré, Brooklyn, New York, May 1979; and Columbia Oral History Project.

32. The following reports are examples of studies conducted on Puerto Ricans in New York City during the late forties and early fifties: C. Wright Mills, Clarence Senior, and Rose Goldsen, *The Puerto Rican Journey: New York's Newest Migrant* (New York: Harper & Bros., 1950) (this book was based on the Columbia Study of 1948, a research project conducted by the Bureau of Applied Social Research of Columbia University); New York City Board of Education, "A Program of Education for Puerto Ricans in New York City" (1947); New York City Board of Education, Bilingual

Committee of the Junior High School Division, "Tentative Report of the Committee on Classification," Bulletin no. 1 (1959). Welfare Council of New York City, "Puerto Ricans in New York City" (1948).

33. Ramón Colón interview; Raquel Rivera Hernández interview; Antonio Sánchez Feliciano interview.

34. Iglesias, *Memorias,* pp. 106–107. See also Iris M. Zavala and Rafael Rodríguez, *The Intellectual Roots of Independence* (New York: Monthly Review, 1980), pp. 12–30.

35. Iglesias, *Memorias,* pp. 96, 140, 148. Vega also cites the publication of the first Puerto Rican newspaper, *La Voz de Puerto Rico,* in 1874, and *Puerto Rico Herald,* a bilingual publication in 1901, on pp. 88 and 127.

36. Iglesias, *Memorias,* p. 140.

37. *La Prensa,* July 21, 1919, p. 2.

38. *Gráfico,* July 1, 1928.

39. Ibid., March 27, 1927, p. 2.

40. Ibid.

41. Ibid.

42. Interview with Fausta Mercado, Brentwood, New York, June 1976.

43. This information was conveyed in several interviews.

44. Interview with Rosa Roma, Santurce, Puerto Rico, August 1977; *Nuestro,* May 1980, pp. 26–27; *Gráfico,* July 8, 1928; *Artes y Letras,* January 1936.

45. See note 44.

46. Max Salazar, "The Perseverance of a Culture," in Clara E. Rodríguez, Virginia E. Sánchez Korrol and José Oscar Alers, eds., *The Puerto Rican Struggle: Essays on Survival in the U.S.* (New York: Puerto Rican Migration Research Consortium, 1980), pp. 77–78.

47. Miguel Angel Figueroa and Conjunto Típico Ladi, "Yo Me Vuelvo a Mi Bohío" (Verne Recording Corporation, V. 10006B).

48. Iglesias, *Memorias,* pp. 143–145.

49. Salazar, "The Perseverance," pp. 77–78.

50. Max Salazar, "Latin Music's Rivalries and Battles," *Latin New York,* January 1975, pp. 44–46.

51. Ibid., January 1976, pp. 36–38. Bandleader Pérez Prado is credited with introducing the mambo dance craze with his recording of "Mambo No. 5" in 1948.

The Other Side of the Ocean

Women held a special place in the early Puerto Rican settlements of New York City, often providing links between the island and mainland enclaves. Pivotal in retaining ethnicity through the transmission of language, customs, and cultural traditions within familial settings, women also functioned as part of an informal informational network. Referred to as "the family intelligence service" by Clarence Senior, and functioning very much like the Portuguese equivalent of "making a *cunha*," the network acclimated incoming migrants to the intricacies of the receiving society.[1] Over the factory sewing machines or on apartment house stoops, in the *bodegas* or in the privacy of their own homes, women exchanged information on housing, jobs, folk remedies, the best places to shop, their churches, and their children's schools. What has usually been classified as idle female chatter provided in essence the tools for handling the unfamiliar situation.

The women of the Puerto Rican *colonias* were charged with yet another responsibility—that of contributing to the creation of a Puerto Rican community rooted on traditional family units. This entailed maintaining Hispanic family values in the midst of an alien

An earlier version of this chapter appeared in *Caribbean Review,* January-March 1979, Vol. VIII, no. 1.

New York environment, establishing settlements where customs
and institutions mirrored those previously adhered to in Puerto
Rico, and within this context, contributing to the financial support
of the family.

Migrant Profiles

Who were the women of the *colonias*? A partial tabulation of
four Assembly Districts in the 1925 New York State Manuscript
Census revealed a modified social profile of the Puerto Rican
female migrant. The 1925 census enumerators listed all male and
female heads of household, children, extended relatives, and
boarders. Their ages, occupations, and lengths of stay in the United
States were also provided, indicating a partial but precise view of
the socioeconomic conditions of the early female migrants. Since
the Assembly Districts selected for tabulation were generally considered to shelter heavy Spanish-speaking concentrations, we can
speculate that the information provided in the census presented a
fairly typical profile for other boroughs as well as Manhattan. Out
of 7,322 Spanish-surnamed individuals living in Manhattan's Sixteenth, Seventeenth, Eighteenth, and Nineteenth Assembly Districts, almost half (3,496, or 47.7 percent) were female, leaving
3,815, or 52.1 percent, males and 11, or 0.2 percent, as unclassified
(see Table 6).[2]

The bulk of the female population was composed of housewives
and children; 1,474 or 52.2 percent of the females living in that area
listed their occupation as "housewife" in the manuscript census;
28.5 percent or 997 were female children, many of them students;
with the remaining 29.3 percent adult participants in the work
force. The group isolated under the categories of housewives and
children, furthermore, had spent a relatively short period residing
in the New York settlements. Forty-five percent of these had been
in the United States less than three years. Almost twenty-three out
of every one hundred women had been in the United States from
four to six years; 11 percent listed their term of residence at between
seven and ten years and about 6 percent admitted to eleven or more
years in New York City (see Tables 7 and 8). The majority of the
female population, 78.9 percent in the four sample districts, was
under thirty-five years of age; moreover, in the over-forty-five age
group, women substantially outnumbered men and there were ten

times as many grandmothers as grandfathers.[3] In short, the women migrants of the twenties and thirties were comparatively young, had not been residing in New York City for any length of time, and frequently listed their occupations as "housewives" in the census's occupational category.

TABLE 6
Gender Distribution of Hispanics in Assembly Districts 16, 17, 18, 19

	16		17		18		19	
	#	%	#	%	#	%	#	%
Female	294	48.1	1,770	47.3	928	48.0	504	48.6
Male	317	51.9	1,962	52.5	1,003	51.9	533	51.3
N.A.*	—	—	8	0.2	2	0.1	1	0.1
TOTALS	611	100.0	3,740	100.0	1,933	100.0	1,038	100.0

*No information available

Total Hispanic Population in Index Districts = 7,322.
Source: New York State Manuscript Census, 1925.

TABLE 7
Number of Years in United States as Reported by Hispanics in Assembly Districts 16, 17, 18, 19

YEARS	NUMBER	%
0–3.9	3,231	44.1
4–5.9	1,634	22.3
7–10.9	1,001	13.7
11–18.9	293	4.0
19	267	3.6
N.A.	896	12.2
TOTAL	7,322	100.0

Source: The New York State Manuscript Census, 1925.

TABLE 8
Number of Years in the United States by Gender Reported by Hispanics
in Assembly Districts 16, 17, 18, 19

YEARS IN U.S.	FEMALE		MALE	
	#	%	#	%
0–3.9	1,576	45.0	1,655	43.4
4–5.9	824	23.6	810	21.2
7–10.9	416	11.9	583	15.3
11–18.9	129	3.7	164	4.3
19	110	3.1	154	4.0
N.A.	445	12.7	449	11.8
TOTALS*	3,500	100.0	3,815	100.0

*Note: The total of 7,311 persons excluded the eleven individuals in Table 6 for
which gender information is unavailable.

Source: The New York State Manuscript Census, 1925.

With the exception of labor force participation, the male migrant
population compared favorably with the female. Of 3,815 individuals, 70.5 percent or 2,688 men were employed in the work force;
911 or 23.9 percent were listed as minors—children and students—
and 216 or 5.7 percent were retired, not working or not available
(see Table 9). Whereas 45 percent of the female migrant group had
resided in the United States for three years or less, 43.4 percent of
the males had lived in the mainland for that period of time.
Twenty-one male migrants out of every one hundred had been here
four to six years, and 15.3 percent estimated their residence at
between seven to ten years.

A homogeneous population such as that comprised by the
migrant group was extremely important for the perpetuation of traditional family patterns, which in turn would form the basis of the
early colonias. By comparison, it was somewhat different for the
Black West Indian immigrant population, for example, which also
came into the Harlem area about the same time. This immigration
followed the common European patterns in that West Indian males
outnumbered women in all but one (fifteen-to-twenty-four) adult

TABLE 9

Occupational Categories of Hispanics by Gender in Assembly Districts 16, 17, 18, 19

	FEMALE		MALE	
	#	%	#	%
PRIVATE SECTOR				
Owners, supervisors	16	.5	137	3.6
Production	600	17.2	1,604	42.1
Workers in circulation	118	3.4	466	12.2
Workers in services	156	4.5	390	10.2
PUBLIC SECTOR				
Supervisors	—	—	—	—
Production	—	—	1	—
Commerce	1	—	3	.1
Services	8	.2	87	2.3
OTHER				
Housewives	1,474	42.2	—	—
Children and students	997	28.5	911	23.9
Retired or not employed	55	1.6	126	3.3
N.A.	71	2.0	90	2.4
TOTALS	3,496	100.1	3,815	100.1

Source: The New York State Manuscript Census, 1925.

age bracket.[4] The relatively equal sex ratios among the Puerto Ricans, furthermore, encouraged the extension of island family composition patterns in the mainland settlements. These reflected an attempt in the pioneer settlements to preserve a traditional family structure where the male was the household head and the female's dominant role was reproduction, childcare, and household management.

Nevertheless, numerous migrant women were determined to combine jobs with traditional family life and initiated modifications in community living with this end in mind. One group composed predominantly of young wives and mothers, cherishing Hispanic family traditions which dictated women's place in society, preferred to remain in the home. Others formed an important segment of the city's labor force. Faced with the economic realities confronting the overwhelmingly poor, working-class *colonias,* this group found ways to combine traditional family life with gainful employment outside of the home. Finally, a small group found fulfillment participating in community affairs, in volunteer organizations, and working as professionals or in white-collar capacities. Based on census information and oral interviews, the majority of the migrant women fit into the first category.

THE TRADITIONALISTS

In New York, at least two factors unconsciously influenced Puerto Rican thinking in terms of women's roles. First, women were expected to fulfill their traditional role as wives and mothers in the new *colonias* as they had previously done in their island home. The fact that male and female migrant numbers remained relatively equal and stable in almost all age brackets, with the exception of the over-forty-five group, throughout the migration encouraged this dimension of community formation. Second, although women migrants in New York participated in a series of community and work-related enterprises, they remained conditioned to believe that motherhood and marriage expressed their primary functions in life. Those who did work for a living did so only because it was essential for their individual or collective survival. One migrant articulated typical sentiments regarding women's place in the work force when she stated:

> I do not criticize working outside the home because I did it myself in New York out of necessity and if it had not been out of necessity I would have never worked outside the home because I wanted to be with (to raise) my children. . . . If the husband earns enough to support his home, the wife *must* not work.[5]

However, the necessity to work in the home or outside of the home became such an integral part of Puerto Rican survival in general, both on the island and in the New York settlements, that women compromised and accepted wage-earning responsibilities as a natural extension of the homemaker role.

Clearly, the term "housewife" as it appeared in the census occupational category was misleading or open to interpretation when applied to Puerto Rican women. For while migrant females thought of themselves as *mujeres de la casa,* the traditional lady of the house, many found ways nevertheless to participate in activities designed to supplement and in some cases provide primary family incomes.

As necessity begets invention, many home-centered, money-making ventures emerged in response to the very real economic family needs of the working-class settlements. Among these, piecework ranked as one of the major forms of home enterprises. In New York this included the making or decorating of lampshades, hats, artificial flowers and jewelry, embroidery, crocheting, and garment sewing. Women commonly secured a work load or a "lot" from a local contractor or subcontractor for which the worker received payment per completed portion, virtually the same procedure practiced in Puerto Rico.

Women workers in Puerto Rico and in the New York settlements for the most part recognized the values and disadvantages of piece-working. This included an awareness that piecework, particularly home-based needlework, exemplified an exploitative enterprise designed to enrich the purses of the contractor, subcontractor and factory owner at the expense of the worker.[6] Moreover, piecework in Puerto Rico established a precedent for the forms it would take in New York *colonias.* Initially a cottage industry in Puerto Rico, wages in this economic sector were remarkably low. By 1934 a United States Department of Labor report on the employment of women on the island revealed the extent to which some workers were exploited in a number of industries, especially the home needlework area:

> Women worked extremely long hours, days and evenings. Hourly earnings in needlework were extremely low: for 31.4 percent of the women they were less than one cent, for 31.1 percent they were one and under 2 cents, and for 31.4 percent they were 2 and under 4 cents. . . . Unfair practices in home

needlework included payment in groceries, payment in keep;
delays in supplying work and payment, retention by agent of
wage increases.[7]

Since women's salaried labor was traditionally thought to be
merely supplementary and since any salary was better than none at
all, other benefits or conveniences were sought as compensation by
those who did piecework. Consequently, this type of work gained
popularity in New York precisely because of other adjustments: it
could be done in the home at one's own pace; made use of traditional sewing skills; and virtually eliminated the need for English
language proficiency or commutation throughout a strange city.

Not surprisingly, sewing and home piecework ranked among the
earliest and most popular work experiences of many women
migrants.[8] A significant number preferred this type of work rather
than securing outside employment because they had young children
who needed a mother's care. Some combined it with factory work
especially during critical periods such as the Depression. Others
turned to it sporadically, when faced with dependent family situations, language barriers, or simply the notion that women belonged
in the home. One woman, Doña María, ran a household in *El
Barrio* which included four children, elderly grandparents, and a
husband. Her major responsibilities, while the children were young
and her husband worked in the cigar industry, lay in the home.
There she made lampshades and other piecework items for several
years, but as her children matured, she began working in a local
factory, eventually becoming plant forelady.[9] Another migrant,
Doña Elisa, came to New York as a domestic, specifically to care
for the young children of a cousin. As the relative assumed personal responsibility for Doña Elisa's welfare, the young woman was
charged with childcare and household duties in exchange for room
and board. But Doña Elisa, requiring some degree of independence, took in piecework while at the same time fulfilling her end
of the agreement—remaining at home with her cousin's children.

In New York, few women complained about either the work or
low wages, perhaps because they failed to view their skills as valuable or perhaps because home work offered compensatory benefits,
as previously pointed out. Puerto Rican pieceworkers seldom described themselves as victims of exploitation. One migrant, typical

of the pieceworkers of the early settlements, emphasized the degree of independence and other advantages when she declared:

> At that time (1937) I started to hem handkerchiefs in the house while I awaited the birth of my first baby, to earn extra money. My husband worked for the Works Progress Administration, three weeks out of every month earning fifteen dollars a week. A Mexican lady had a small factory on Eighth Avenue and either me or my husband would go there to pick up packages of handkerchiefs once a week. I would work a little in the morning and some more at night. The rest of the time was devoted to housework, cooking and cleaning and that sort of thing. Later on, my spare time went to the baby.[10]

Similarly, several years later, Doña Clara, a newcomer from Cabo Rojo believed her most important function as a young mother was to raise her children, remaining at home with them and being at home when they returned from school. This decision motivated an interest in piecework.

> I had four children to care for so I only worked at home. In that instance, they gave out work to do in the house so I hemmed handkerchiefs or sewed blouse collars. I would get twenty dozen handkerchiefs a day for me and my sister-in-law, who also had young children at that time. They paid little—about thirteen cents a dozen but the cost of living was also less than now. A subway ride to pick up more piecework was only five cents. Later on, when my girls were young, I made blouse collars which was very easy for me to do on my machine at home. The children would all help me by counting the collars or turning them inside out. This type of work paid more—about twenty-five cents a dozen. You'd be surprised how that extra money helped us to buy little extras—or helped to stretch my husband's earnings.[11]

Doña Clara's recollections highlight two significant factors regarding piecework. First, she provides a realistic evaluation of the work in terms of wage earnings; and second, she reaffirms the benefits connected with the venture as viewed by the migrant work-

ers themselves. Throughout the late twenties and during the
Depression period, salaries for unskilled Puerto Rican workers
averaged about twenty-one dollars a week or less.[12] But during the
thirties, most Puerto Ricans fortunate enough to be employed
earned wages below WPA (Work Progress Administration) and
Home Relief Bureau levels. Unskilled WPA workers earned fifty-
five dollars for fifteen days of work each month and a family of
five on relief received between fifty and sixty dollars a month. Families often relied on the earnings of female workers, particularly
during crisis, when many heads of households were unemployed.

During the thirties migrants like Doña Clara or Doña Elisa estimated their earnings from piecework over the period of a week
fluctuated between five and ten dollars depending on how much
time they could devote to sewing. Moreover, increasing restrictions
placed on piecework by the New York State Department of Labor
and the minimum wage laws of the period failed to control the
growing numbers of bootleg illegal business ventures which
abounded in this business fostering a continuation of exploitative
practices. Employers paid little heed to minimum wage requirements, especially since few Puerto Ricans knew about or complained regarding their rights in this area. Thus, Puerto Rican
pieceworkers remained at the economic mercy of their employers.
Although piecework was believed to have declined considerably by
the mid-thirties, it continued well into the sixties and seventies
according to the women interviewed.

Similarly, needlework, which formed the basis of piecework in
the home, played an important role in the lives of migrant women.
Nurtured in a tradition of quality needlecrafts for generations,
Puerto Rican women almost always possessed skills in sewing,
crocheting, and embroidering. In fact, these skills were part of the
Puerto Rican school curriculum, taught as early as the second or
third grades. One migrant proudly explained she learned embroidery and lace working before her tenth birthday. Another described
her experiences in the factories of María Luisa Arcelay, a well-
known factory owner and industrialist in Mayaguez, crediting this
episode in her life as one responsible for learning the trade and
skills she brought with her to the New York garment factories:

> I worked with María Luisa Arcelay for ten years before com-
> ing to New York. I was always a great help to her since I could

work in the factories or in the home, doing piecework. This great and bountiful lady had such confidence in me that I often made bank deposits for her, walked her children to and from school, and would oversee the premises if she was busy somewhere else.

Our family was poor and my father was blind, so financial responsibilities rested on my shoulders, on my mother's, my sisters and brothers. Doña María Luisa Arcelay always had work for me and she understood the importance of it for our family's survival. In the beginning when I was still under age, do you know what she did? She would hide me in the bathroom when the investigators came. My earnings would appear as my mother's.

When I was older, a married woman and a mother myself, I never wanted for work because no sooner was my child born but there was a bundle of piecework for me to do. Do you know sometimes I made as much as forty dollars a week? (This was during the early forties.) That was a lot of money for those times. So everything I learned from this great lady made it easier for me to work when we moved to New York.[13]

Pura Belpré, writer and folklorist, noted the same resiliency among the migrant women of the early settlements, who relied on their needlework, in hard times, selling handicrafts from door to door. Others recalled highly intricate needlework decorations adorned their migrant homes particularly as doilies, tablecloths, and mantlepieces.

In addition to enhancing employment opportunities, needlecrafts, especially in piecework, provided a setting in mainland Puerto Rican homes for social interaction similar to that created by the North American custom of holding quilting bees or sewing circles. Young and old, grandmothers, aunts, mothers, and children all participated in this process, transmitting needlecraft traditions from one generation to the next in an almost exclusively feminine world. Working together in the home stimulated informational exchanges among adults while allowing children a glimpse into the adult work world as well as into a part of their heritage. The practical transmission of skills fortified cultural and community traditions while providing a degree of economic security. These practices, the combination of traditional needlecraft skills in the home and piecework as an income-producing venture, were followed by other enterprises with similar goals.

CHILDCARE PRACTICES

As Puerto Ricans entrenched themselves in the various *colonias* throughout the city, other income-promoting opportunities emerged enabling homebound women to secure supplementary or, in some cases, primary incomes for their dependents while upholding traditional family structures. Minding children and taking in lodgers represented two such opportunities. Although a few women in the city could rely on the ready availability of grandmothers, aunts, or *co-madres* (godmothers) to look after their families while they worked, others were forced to leave their children behind with relatives in Puerto Rico while they sought to secure a livelihood.[14] Many more developed alternative methods for the care of their children. For the most part, childcare responsibilities in the early community remained within the family whenever possible and the care of the young often delegated to unemployed household members. Yet, due to the unique Puerto Rican family composition in the early *colonias,* this was not always possible.

If, as the 1925 census suggested, the bulk of the Puerto Rican residences in South Central Harlem fell into the categories of "simple" or "nuclear family" households, then the "extended family" which had historically allowed women the peace of mind to work outside the home in Puerto Rico was somewhat limited in New York. An analysis of the 1925 census, moreover, indicated that "nuclear" or "simple families" and "simple families with lodgers," outnumbered "extended families," "extended families with lodgers" and "multi-family" dwellings during the decade of the twenties. Of the 7,322 Hispanics residing in the four key Assembly Districts cited, for example, 2,259 individuals or 30.9 percent lived in households classified as "simple families with lodgers"; 1,864 persons or 25.5 percent were designated as residents in "nuclear family" households; 1,079 individuals or 14.7 percent fit into the "extended families with lodgers" category; and 988 persons or 13.5 percent resided in "extended family households." The remaining 1,128 individuals or 15.4 percent were distributed among five other categories (see Table 10).[15]

Thus, 56.4 percent of the Puerto Rican households were headed

TABLE 10
Hispanic Household Types in Assembly Districts 16, 17, 18, 19

TYPE	16		17		18		19	
	#	%	#	%	#	%	#	%
Solitaries	6	1.0	58	1.6	37	1.4	13	1.3
Co-residents	14	2.3	141	3.8	103	5.3	40	3.9
Simple family	270	44.2	648	17.3	810	42.0	140	13.4
Simple family with lodgers	94	15.4	1,310	35.0	441	22.8	414	39.9
Extended family	119	19.5	430	11.5	325	16.8	114	11.0
Extended family with lodgers	65	10.6	807	21.6	143	7.4	64	6.2
Multiple family	39	6.4	150	4.0	48	2.5	15	1.4
Multiple, not related	—	—	174	4.6	26	1.3	224	21.6
N.A.	4	.7	24	.6	10	.5	14	1.3
TOTALS	611	100.1	3,742	100.0	1,943	100.0	1,038	100.0

Source: The New York State Manuscript Census, 1925.

by two parents (nuclear family) or consisted of married couples
without children (see Table 11).[16] Clearly, with the limitations of
extended family groups or multifamily households, coupled with a
scarcity of bilingual-bicultural daycare facilities, another system
for reliable childcare became essential for working Puerto Ricans.

TABLE 11
Hispanic Household Types

TYPE	#	%
Solitaries	104	1.4
Co-residents	298	4.1
Simple family	1,864	25.5
Simple family with lodgers	2,259	30.9
Extended family	988	13.5
Extended family with lodgers	1,076	14.7
Multiple family	252	3.4
Multiple family, not related	422	5.8
N.A.	56	.7
TOTALS	7,322	100.0

Source: The New York State Manuscript Census, 1925.

Childcare tasks previously undertaken by relatives defaulted to
friends and acquaintances outside the kinship network who provided the services in exchange for a prearranged fee. A grass-roots system of daycare was born from the merger of working mothers who
could ill afford to lose job security or union benefits and women
who remained at home. Working Puerto Rican mothers left their
children in the care of friends or relatives, and the arrangements
basically consisted of bringing child, food, and additional clothing
to the mother-substitute and collecting him after work. Women
who opened their homes to care for children found this a practical
means of increasing family earnings.

Although these arrangements fulfilled neither legal nor licensing
regulations, the system boasted several advantages not found in
established childcare institutions. In the first place, children were

often cared for in familiar neighborhood surroundings which especially benefitted the school-age youngster who could attend class with his neighborhood companions. Secondly, childcare operated on mutual trust and agreement between the adults involved. Very often this situation allowed for more flexibility than could be found in an institutionalized setting. If, for example, the parent(s) worked overtime or on the weekends, suitable arrangements beneficial to both parties were easily negotiated. Finally, and perhaps of most importance, the youngster was cared for within a natural family setting surrounded by adults and children of varying ages. This not only encouraged the child to interact in an atmosphere where his language, customs, traditions, and parental family values were constantly reinforced, but also fostered learning from one another among the children.

As late as 1948, a report issued by the Welfare Council of New York City deplored the situation wherein Puerto Rican children were being placed in unlicensed homes for care, but neglected to suggest alternative measures for minding Puerto Rican children of working mothers aside from requesting more daycare centers with bilingual personnel. The report posed the thesis that multitudes of working Puerto Rican mothers meant young children were often denied adequate care.[17] Furthermore, while many youngsters received care in nursery schools or settlement houses, these centers, often viewed as impersonal alien institutions by Puerto Ricans, could not accommodate all the children in need of such services. The lack of adequate bilingual, bicultural institutions which could deliver services without appearing intimidating further motivated the placement of Spanish-speaking children in neighborhood homes.

During the early periods of the twenties and thirties, women paid two or three dollars weekly per child for daycare, but by 1948 the Welfare Council speculated fees paid in private homes ranged between ten and twelve dollars a week. Almost all of the women interviewed placed their children in the homes of friends or relatives at some time throughout their working lives, and this system continued to offer more advantages than established centers. Moreover, women who did use public nurseries for their children found the institutions offered little flexibility, and they combined these services with home care as well.

Several migrant women shared the experience of being on both
sides of the system. Doña Julia's daughter, for example, was cared
for by her aunt; but after Julia's second child was born, she sometimes took care of other women's children. Another became a foster mother after she decided to remain at home with her three children. Doña Celina came to New York on the eve of the Second
World War with her infant daughter, whom she left in her sister's
care while she worked in a local factory. Five years later, the births
of a son and a daughter curtailed outside employment but permitted Doña Celina the opportunity to mind neighborhood children.
This practice continued for thirty-five years. Without a husband
and on public assistance during hard times, the woman nevertheless
managed to raise her own three children on the unpredictable earnings from piecework, selling her own handicrafts, and caring for
other people's children. Throughout the years the family prospered
moderately, and the income for her various enterprises made possible a long-awaited move to a more stable neighborhood with better
schools. Today, a senior citizen, Doña Celina cares for her grand-
chidren and devotes vast energies to Hispanic religious and community projects, but the familiar sign—*se cuidan niños*—(children
cared for) still adorns her front window from time to time.[18]

Certainly childcare practices as they emerged in the pioneer settlements were strongly influenced by the family customs and institutions of Puerto Rico. Among the cultural institutions brought by
Puerto Ricans to New York were those of ritual kinship—*compadrazgo*—and informal adoption, the rearing of *hijos de crianza*.
The former institution, based on Spanish roots, provided compan-
ion parents for the natural parents who in turn were godparents for
the child. Most often, these sponsored a child at baptism or confir-
mation, but the *compadrazgo* relationship could also form on the
basis of common interests or the intensification of friendships
which led men and women to consider themselves as more than
friends—*compadre* or *comadre*. The *compadres* were sometimes
relatives, but more often they were not. Within this relationship the
parties developed a deep sense of obligation, support, encouragement, commitment, and even financial assistance toward one
another.[19] The institution of informal adoption, on the other hand,
guaranteed that children within an extended family circle were
always assured of a home, food, and basic necessities regardless of

whatever misfortunes might befall the immediate family. Within this structure children were easily and frequently transferred from one family to another, often in attempts to relieve financial burdens.

Within these significant institutions in the family system, members of a nuclear family developed close bonds with non-kin individuals. These customs proved essential to the survival of the infant New York community. First, the attitudes regarding children and childcare customs aided the enlargement of family networks at a time when the numbers of nuclear family households in the city predominated and when these families were struggling to gain a foothold in the new environment. Second, childcare facilitated the formation of intimate friendships, if not ritual kinship. These personal contacts based on common language, heritage, and customs encouraged and maintained a social structure in the early settlements which perpetuated Puerto Rican values and interests. Third, with the enlargement of the family network and the cementing of relationships through ritual kinship, a support system was created for periods of crisis. During times of financial stress, job or housing scarcities, or family illness, there were now people to whom they could turn. The extended family unit which had been so important in Puerto Rico, and which would not appear en masse until the great migration, was being recreated in the New York settlements.

One migrant, Doña Eliza, for example, commented on the close relationships which frequently developed through the practice of minding children, an experience common for many who worked in this area. She arrived in New York in 1930 and spent most of her thirty-year residency caring for the children of others. Genuinely fond of children, her home was almost always equipped with the paraphernalia of her trade, which included extra cribs, high chairs or playpens. As a result of her childcaring, close to twenty youngsters were placed in her home, six of whom became her godchildren.

Doña Elisa remembers her home as a haven for unfortunate children, and in two extreme cases she became the adoptive parent of *hijos de crianza*. She recalls one incident which dramatically sums up the amount of responsibility inherent in the business of childcare as it developed among the New York Puerto Ricans:

José Luis was only two years old when he came to live with us—I remember because my own children were seven and two at the time. We lived in a four room apartment in the South Bronx; my husband had a good job and he never objected to my bringing in extra children to mind during the week. From the beginning Joselito was different. He and my little girl, Titi, made fast friends right away. At first, I took care of him and his brother on a weekly basis from nine until about six in the evening. His mother, María, was forced to work as she was their only support. As the time went by, life became harder for María. She was in and out of jobs and very depressed about her life. I found myself keeping the boys longer and longer without pay. The older boy did not like to be left with me when his mother went to work but the little one, Joselito, thought I was his mother and he soon started to call me Mami just like my two girls did.

Once, on a snowy winter night, my brother-in-law who worked the night shift found the boys scantily dressed hanging around the Jackson Avenue El Station at 2 A.M. He recognized them as the boys I took care of and brought them to my house. That night they stayed with us and the next morning I told María a thing or two for leaving the children alone. She pleaded with me to keep the little one while she and her other son went away for a while—to get herself together—and I consented. I don't know where she went but from time to time I'd get a letter and some money for Joselito. I raised him as my own for more than one year. When she returned for him, my heart broke. Of all the children I've taken care of, he was my first and very favorite but I vowed never to get so attached again.[20]

TAKING IN LODGERS

As childcare provided supplementary incomes and strengthened bonds among New York Puerto Ricans, so did taking in lodgers. Census enumerations often designated Puerto Rican women as heads of households composed primarily of lodgers. Within the lodger group many newly arrived migrants sought accommodations in the homes of friends, relatives, or hometown acquaintances, and married couples or family units also boarded with one another.

Lodgers often came from the same hometown as the head of the household. Through friends and relations, migrants quickly discovered, in many cases before coming to New York, where they could obtain lodgings. The informational network previously described in connection with women's roles, along with the Latin tradition of hospitality expressed in the saying, *mi casa es su casa* (my home is your home) contributed to many migrants' successful quest for housing. In some cases multifamily or extended family dwellings were classified as households with lodgers, since the census takers listed but one household head. In reality, several families shared living space and expenses equally. Doña Julia, for instance, recalls sharing an apartment with her husband, baby, and her brother and his family during the Depression.

Sharing households either as lodgers or as heads of households with lodgers appeared to be a common experience among the women interviewed. Almost without exception, those women who migrated from Puerto Rico lived in New York residences as lodgers while those who were born in New York related tales of woe regarding the not infrequent unannounced arrival of some relative or hometown acquaintance. One woman stated, "We never knew when we left for school in the morning if our bedrooms would still be ours in the evening. Sleeping arrangements were in constant flux depending on how many people lived with us at any given time."[21] Doña Celia evoked a scene of childhood memories worth noting:

> I remember as if it were yesterday. We lived on the first floor of a small apartment in the Bronx. We shared five rooms among the four of us—my parents and my younger sister, and myself, because a boarder, who was my father's cousin, Don Antonio, had just moved out after living with us for a number of years. That summer I was ten years old, starting to feel quite the young lady. My mother had recently decorated Don Antonio's old room for me in shades of pale blue. It was the tiniest room in the apartment but it was perfect for me.
>
> I was the first one to answer the buzzer that September afternoon. From our apartment's front door you could see directly into the downstairs vestibule with its double row of bright metal mailboxes on both sides. The sun shone brightly into the area but did not obscure the couple standing there

and the baby held in its mother's arms. They were an uncle I had never met, his wife, little more than a child herself, and their infant son. They had arrived without warning from Puerto Rico on the assumption that if there is room for one, there is always room for one more. My heart sank as I remembered my father's favorite value—you never turn away relatives, no matter how little you have for yourself. I knew instinctively they would be well received and my room with the matching blue spread and curtains would be given to them for as long as they needed it.[22]

Many women recalled meeting their future husbands as lodgers. Others became extremely attached to the friends they made in shared households continuing these relationships into the present often through ritual kinship systems. As early as 1925, 1,745 individuals or 23.8 percent out of 7,322 individuals listed in the census were classified as lodgers. Of these, males outnumbered females almost two to one. The majority of this population fell into the fifteen-through-forty-five age bracket as did 55.6 percent of the females and 64.2 percent of the males.[23] The lodger group, therefore, was in its most productive work years, often single, and represented the future household heads of the Puerto Rican communities. One interviewee, Doña Rosa remembered her experiences:

I came to live in my stepsister's house in 1926, when I was about twenty years old. Quite a few of my cousins were already there with wives and children—all living in my stepsister's house on 116th Street and Park Avenue. The household consisted of about fifteen people and each suitable bedroom was assigned to several of us. Most of us worked except for my stepsister who had youngsters and her sister who did all the cooking and cleaning for all of us. I started to work right away but never got used to the dirty winter darkness of the city. I earned about fifteen dollars weekly and paid six or seven dollars for my room out of that even though I hardly ate at the house. (This amount was for room and board.) On my days off, I'd go visit other relatives in the city and usually ate with them. I suppose now that I look back, that was an awful lot of money to pay for just a room but I was young with little responsibility and didn't know the value of money. Seven dollars went a very long way for me.

From this house I moved in with friends on 114th Street. At that time there were few Hispanics in this area. There was only one store which sold Hispanic articles. It was called Sefía and located on 113th Street and Fifth Avenue. As I recall there were few of us but we all lived in shared households until we married and set up our own homes. Then it was our turn to take in lodgers.[24]

It was not unusual for women migrants to make the ocean crossing alone, since they were met, for the most part, by relatives who had either invited them to come or were prepared to assume responsibility for them once they arrived. Doña Clara, a person who arrived almost a decade after Dona Rosa, recalled few changes in the customs and practice of lodgers. Her experience was similar to many others travelling the same road:

My brother sent for me as he had been in New York several years and we both lived with a cousin on 144th Street. New York didn't really seem too oppressive to me, perhaps because I arrived during the summer months and people socialized outdoors all of the time. Afterwards, I moved into the home of friends from my hometown of Cabo Rojo and when my brother married, I was invited to live with them. I stayed in his home until I was married myself. Then I moved to the West Side.[25]

One individual, Doña Perfecta, added yet another dimension to the functioning of boarders within a household. From her position as the wife of the household head, her New York home became the base for relatives, siblings, and friends who migrated from her hometown. These migrant lodgers, intent on carving a niche for themselves as soon as they were able, contributed financially to Doña Perfecta's household, eventually leaving to form households of their own. But the relationship between household heads and lodgers did not disintegrate with the latter's leaving. These remained within the extended family circle, frequently developing into *compadrazgos*. Both Perfecta and her husband often stood as godparents of the children born to their ex-lodgers. On many occasions the home and family life of the receiving host family served as models for the type of home the lodgers established. One migrant particularly recalled the type of household established by her godparents, the first home her parents lived in as lodgers upon their arrival in the city.

> I still remember growing up surrounded by caring family members. It was our custom to spend holidays and Sundays together usually at my godparents' home. Many of my aunts and uncles began their stay in New York by living with my godparents as boarders. To me their home represented a symbol of what my own should be. I was always impressed with its cleanliness, orderliness and I guess you might say, middle class values. To us, they had "made it." But my earliest memories about their home was that we were always served dessert after dinner—a custom which I in my youthful innocense considered extraordinary![26]

Thus, lodgers added important aspects within the household structures of the pre-World War II *colonias.* Sometimes they were hometown friends or acquaintances; more often they were close or extended family members. The functions of lodgers within these households were crucial not only for the general survival of the *colonias,* but for the individual families as well. Lodgers kept open the networks of communication between the island and mainland enclaves; they contributed to the financial support of the household; and they enabled women especially, who frequently carried the full burden of providing room and board, to supplement the family's income. Moreover, through ritual kinship, lodgers expanded the familial network at a time when the Puerto Rican *colonias* were at their most vulnerable both in size and in keeping traditional values intact.

The practice of taking in boarders based on the purchase of room, board, and domestic services within an established household was not limited to Puerto Rican communities. Lodgers had resided in Jewish and Italian households since the turn of the century. In some instances the desirability of the geographic area in which a family resided determined the abundance of lodgers. One

Jewish family, for example, decided to return to Manhattan "where they could get lodgers more readily and thus eke out their income of four hundred dollars by an addition of one hundred and twenty dollars a year. Out of the earnings of five hundred and twenty dollars, one hundred and eighty-six—that is, fifteen dollars and fifty cents a month—had to be paid for rent."[27]

Similarly, black Harlem settlements disclosed the existence of enlarged households often containing kin and unmarried lodgers in the census records of 1915 and 1925:

> A large number were lodgers. Nearly three in ten women aged fifteen and older, for example, were lodgers or lived alone. . . . In 1925, just one in three West Indian and two in five native black households were nuclear in composition. About half of all black households had one or more lodgers in them and about one in five households had one or more relatives other than members of the immediate families.[28]

Interestingly, the census records for East and South Central Harlem households convey a sense of community and mutual support among the many ethnic groups inhabiting those areas, since Puerto Ricans were found living as lodgers in European or South American homes, while the latter held similar positions in Puerto Rican homes. However, after the thirties when large numbers of Puerto Ricans resided in the city, ethnic mixtures within the households appear to diminish.

WORKING OUTSIDE OF THE HOME

If migrant women faced with the need to provide supplementary or primary incomes attempted to combine familial values with modified income-producing enterprises, many more also maintained regard for the traditional role of the family but integrated themselves into the city's labor force. Close to 25 percent of the female migrant population participated in the labor force as cigar makers and domestics; typists and stenographers; in the needle-trades industries as operators and unskilled workers; in the laundries or restaurants; and in the fields as agricultural workers. The first reports of female factory and field workers appeared in newspapers and government documents around the turn of the twentieth century. Puerto Rican women were part and parcel of the migrant labor force contracted to work in various parts of the Western Hemisphere, in the process establishing communities in which cultural traditions and institutions would flourish.[29]

The twenties witnessed an increase in the numbers of Puerto Rican women working in New York factories. Skilled labor predominated in at least two industries traditionally associated with Puerto Ricans—the needle trades and the tobacco industry. Women were well represented in the cigar-making industry, not only among skilled and unskilled workers, but as readers in many of the New York factories.

During the same period, Spanish language journals and newspapers vigorously advertised in their classified sections for both skilled and unskilled garment workers. Want ads frequently called for sewing machine operators, workers in embroidery, in crocheting and lace, as pieceworkers in the home or in the factory. Advertising attracted the attention of job-seeking women. The following ad, typical for the period, appeared in 1923: "se necesitan mujeres que sepan manejar máquinas de coser; 44 horas a la semana; $20.00; bordaderas, operarias en casa, crochet y abalorios."[30]

By mid-decade more women were employed in the production end of private industry than in any other sector. Of the 3,496 women listed in the four sample districts, 600 or 17.2 percent were involved in factory work of some sort, as operatives, dressmakers, or seamstresses. One hundred and fifty-six or 4.5 percent labored in services including laundries or restaurants while 118 or 3.4 percent worked in jobs requiring an exchange of money such as bookkeeping, sales, or as cashiers. About sixteen, or 0.5 percent, supervised or owned their own businesses, and a mere handful worked in the public sector, in the post office, or in other city agencies.[31]

However, participation in the labor force presented difficulties for many women workers. Among these were the necessity to communicate effectively in the English language and to negotiate the sometimes troublesome intricacies of transportation in the city. While many had been taught English in Puerto Rican schools, they were unprepared for the idiomatic, dialectical, and sometimes accented English encountered in New York. A command of English became essential for the Spanish-speaking working woman and many hoped to perfect their knowledge of the language by attending night school. One pioneer, Doña Petra, emphasized the importance of language in her early experiences in the city by stating:

> At first, I enrolled in high school to learn English but before graduating, I was forced to get a job. School was not difficult for me because as you know, in Puerto Rico we had been taught in English and Spanish, so I could understand a great deal when I came here. The greatest difference was in pronunciation because Americans usually slur their words. When I arrived there were pathetically few Hispanics living in the city. An Italian woman whom I had met in Puerto Rico but who was now in New York got me my first job. I became a packer in a candy factory and I soon realized I was the only Puerto Rican employee there. Can you imagine what a lonely feeling; to have people speak to you and not to understand and not be able to communicate in everyday situations? From that time I purposely set out to get a command of the language (a la brava aprendí el inglés). Within a short time I was able to defend myself in English and then it was I who took the newcomers all over the city in search of jobs, houses or whatever.[32]

Some women minimized language difficulties and emphasized appearance as the greatest deterrent to gainful employment. Discrimination against Puerto Ricans, especially if they were black, radically curtailed job opportunities. "If you looked Irish or German," explained one respondent, "it didn't matter how limited your English was. Most jobs were on assembly lines and it didn't take much talking to learn the procedure." Frequent descriptions of discrimination on the basis of color and language continued throughout the period. Almost all of the workers interviewed related tales of this nature.[33]

Transportation problems, on the other hand, presented relatively fewer problems since jobs were often found through the intercession of friends and relatives. One account, for example, suggested the typical pattern followed in seeking employment rested on a personal relationship where a fellow lodger or relative took the new

migrant to make the rounds. Some revealed there were jobs await-
ing them when they disembarked at the Brooklyn or Manhattan
piers. Others conceded they waited at least a week before working.

> My first job in 1926 was at a candy factory. Luis, a young
> man who lodged in my stepsister's house, took me to the fac-
> tory. It was located on Eleventh Street and Ninth Avenue. I
> remember I had to ride two trolleys to get there from where I
> lived. This is the kind of work I did. Do you know what
> Seven-Elevens were? Have you ever heard them mentioned
> before? This was a confection made out of peanuts with a
> caramel or sugar center and I would take this piece of candy,
> mold it in my hand, soak it in syrup then roll it in nuts again.
> Then we would weigh the pieces by hand. If it felt right we
> would package it; if not, we'd take a little off the end. I don't
> think that candy exists anymore.
>   After that I went to work in Washington—not D.C. but
> Washington Street in Brooklyn. What I did there was make
> parts for luggage or suitcases. It was difficult in the beginning
> to find jobs you really liked. We worked in that place for the
> money. Forty-four hours a week to earn six, seven or eight
> dollars a week. There were no unions to protect us and no
> taxes. And sometimes, we worked forty-eight hours a week
> for the same pay. After I became more skilled, I earned about
> thirteen dollars a week. Eventually I went to work in *costura*
> (the needle trades) but that was after I married in the thirties.[34]

Some interviewees, however, felt the period of the thirties and
especially the forties offered greater diversity in the kind of work
available to women, although mainly within the blue-collar occupations. In 1936, for example, Doña Mary worked as a seamstress
and later in a drapery factory for ten dollars a week. Within that
decade she also worked the evening shift in a defense plant and
again as a seamstress when the war ended.[35] In 1930 the Department of Labor of Puerto Rico established an employment service in
response to the growing number of migrants living in the city. Over
a six-year period, about six hundred women obtained job place-
ments through this agency.[36] Approximately 42 percent were employed as domestics while needleworkers, hand sewers and factory

workers comprised an almost equal percentage. Of all the Puerto Rican women workers who applied to this agency, roughly 80 percent found work as operatives or in domestic services. Although jobs were at a premium during this decade, the bureau's activities indicate the types of work available to Puerto Ricans, and these continued to be among the blue-collar sector.

Regardless of the type of work in which Puerto Rican women participated, the family remained uppermost in their minds, and work continued to be a necessity in order to maintain family unity. Women persisted in rationalizing their role in the work world as a natural extension of their home and family life. To work was not considered a luxury embarked upon to prove one's equality or to challenge or change in any way, traditional roles within the family. Doña Margarita, for example, best summed up this attitude in describing her experience in New York during the period of the forties. The first year of their New York residency found the family dependent on home relief due to her husband's unforeseen illness. As soon as she could confidently leave the home, after guiding her children into a familiar routine within the home structure, she returned to work. This woman took great pride in eventually repaying all the money the family had received from home relief.

> I accepted a job doing general factory work because I had to help my husband support us all. I folded handkerchiefs; I did everything that needed doing in the shop; I cleaned machines or cleaned the floor if it had to be done. My philosophy was that I would even clean latrines—because I did this in my own home—if I was getting paid. After a few months my husband returned to his job and I quit mine to stay at home with the children. But he wasn't able to make any more than seventy-five dollars to feed and dress six people. When our four children needed clothing, it presented hardships—four at one blow, without any outside help! Our children needed so much that I decided to return to work.
>
> My boys were getting older, more responsible and my girl was a tremendous help—very serious, honest and mature. They took care of one another. During the day when I was in the factory, I trusted them to look after one another. When I returned in the evenings, I took care of household duties. I

had Saturdays to clean house, buy groceries and wash clothes.
Then I had Sundays . . . Saturdays and Sundays to do my
things and Monday to return to work.[37]

WHITE COLLAR, PROFESSIONALS, AND VOLUNTEERS

While the majority of the female migrant community worked as
skilled or unskilled blue-collar laborers, a handful, usually skilled,
bilingual, or educated women wrested a foothold in other occupations. Some became known for their dedication to volunteer or
creative work necessary for shaping their community. Others
worked in clerical positions. The contributions of these few have
often been overlooked. Yet as professionals or as white-collar
workers, as *colonia* activists, as feminists, or as artists, this handful
appeared before the public eye, serving as spokespersons, as role
models, or as objects of emulation for the broader, working-class
base. These were the women who held jobs which required some
degree of academic preparation; who made possible the functioning of community organizations which in turn helped structure the
early settlements; who wrote for the magazines read in the *colonia*.
Within the latter group, many maintained contacts with their peers
in Puerto Rico or Spanish America, essentially linking class interests across the ocean. Thus, in spite of their limited numbers, the
group played a part in the formation of perspectives and predelec-
tions of the overall community.

Sister Carmelita Bonilla, a case in point, represented Puerto
Rican womanhood among the religious, as the first Trinitarian nun
from Puerto Rico. She arrived in the city as a teenager enroute to
Georgia where she took her vows. As a nun she was assigned to a
Brooklyn convent. Her new responsibilities required involvement
in social welfare, housing, educational and vocational counseling,
public health, and religious education. Her recollections evoke
memories of a poor community, where she was frequently called
upon as a translator and as an intermediary between the Spanish-
speaking settlement and the wider, non-Hispanic society. Youngsters of that period credit Sister Carmelita with directly encouraging their academic growth and aspirations. Her own education
included earning a bachelor's and a master's degree. As one of the
founders of the early settlement house, Casita María, she continued
to direct and influence the social, cultural, and educational welfare
of the early migrants.[38]

Doctora Eloísa García Rivera, on the other hand, made her mark in politics and in higher education. A university graduate upon her arrival in the city, Doña Eloísa completed graduate work in Spanish literature and dedicated herself to community services. Firmly adhering to the traditional philosophy that women should be helpmates to their spouses, she contributed time and energy to her husband's bid for the Albany legislature by campaigning and directing voter registration drives on his behalf.[39]

Yet a different perspective appears in the case of Honorina Irizarry who came to live in her brother's comfortable Brooklyn home during the twenties. An accomplished secretary with B.F. Goodrich in Puerto Rico, Doña Honorina had studied and perfected her clerical skills before undertaking the move. Once in the Brooklyn *colonia,* determined to work, use her mind and skills, she sought employment against the wishes of her family who considered working "unladylike." In her own words she recalls:

> One day I saw an ad in the newspaper for a bilingual secretary/ stenographer. I applied for the position but withheld this information from my sister and brother. The office was located across from City Hall. The trolley cars used to pass City Hall from Brooklyn so I had no trouble finding the office building and the company which placed the ad. When I arrived, they gave me an interview and dictation in both Spanish and English and asked me to translate for them. I got the position without any difficulty and that's how I started my work career in New York.[40]

Doña Honorina was an exceptional woman for her time. She studied at Erasmus Hall High School at night while she continued to work days, mastered five languages fluently, and eventually earned a liberal arts degree. Clearly, Doña Honorina's past experiences in Puerto Rico directly molded her subsequent activities in New York, as was the case with many of the women found in this category. In time Doña Honorina participated also in the political organizations of the Brooklyn settlement where her position within the community afforded her a degree of leadership as well.

Finally, one individual who epitomizes the professional, organizational, and well educated woman was Doña Josefina Silva de Cintrón. She began her career as an elementary school teacher in

Puerto Rico. Distinguished as a community leader in the island, Doña Josefina was also credited with establishing the first Post Office in Hato Rey, Puerto Rico, working with the Red Cross and with various other organizations. In the journalistic field, she collaborated with feminist Mercedes Sola in the publication of a journal, *La mujer en el siglo XX,* and contributed to the literary arena as a writer.[41]

Successful enterprises also followed in New York where Doña Josefina pursued similar intellectual inclinations and took part in a variety of social, political, and cultural community organizations. Among the latter were the *Unión de mujeres Americanas* and the League of Spanish-speaking Democrats. But perhaps her foremost contribution was the creation of the monthly journal, cited in previous chapters, *Revista de Artes y Letras.*

Conclusion

The integration of Puerto Rican women into the economic mainstream of the United States and particularly in New York City requires more intensive exploration and interpretation not merely in terms of their relationship to the non-Hispanic world, but also in their relationship to their respective communities. Migration and work did not produce major changes in their roles within Puerto Rican society, for the image of dutiful wives, loving mothers, and respectful sisters and daughters remained paramount to their way of thinking. Neither did changes occur in the work world to which they were committed, since they neither demanded nor were given the opportunity to control strategic resources or educational facilities.

Only a handful became factory foreladies or union representatives, and fewer owned their own establishments. A small group assumed the reins of community leadership, volunteer work, professional, or clerical endeavors. Through group work and involvement, they were frequently in the public eye, their actions reported in the presses of the early *colonias.* In most fields, however, decision making remained male-dominated and organizations male-oriented. Yet subtle messages were filtering down to younger generations. Women worked; women were wives and mothers; women were involved.

Notes

1. Estelle M. Smith, "Network and Migration Resettlement: Cherchez la Femme," *Anthropological Quarterly* vol. 49, no. 1 (January 1979), pp. 20–27. See also Clarence Senior and Donald O. Watkins, "Towards a Balance Sheet of Puerto Rican Migration," in U.S.–P.R. Commission on the Status of Puerto Rico, *Status of Puerto Rico: Selected Background Studies* (Washington, D.C.: Government Printing Office, 1966), p. 706.

2. New York State Manuscript Census, 1925, Assembly Districts 16, 17, 18, 19. New York City Hall of Records, Municipal Building. See also History Task Force, Centro de Estudios Puertorriqueños, *Migration Under Capitalism: The Puerto Rican Experience* (New York: Monthly Review Press, 1979), pp. 147–149.

3. New York State Manuscript Census, 1925.

4. Herbert Gutman, *The Black Family in Slavery and Freedom, 1750–1925* (New York: Pantheon Press, 1979), p. 153.

5. Interview with Margarita Hernández, Mayaguez, Puerto Rico, July 1977.

6. In Puerto Rico women became essential to the labor force particularly as piece workers and in the needle-trades industry as early as 1910. A decade later they constituted close to 25 percent of the island's work force. See Celia Fernández Cintrón and Marcia Rivera Quintero, "Bases de la sociedad sexista en Puerto Rico," *Revista/Review Interamericana* vol. 4, no. 2 (summer 1974), pp. 239–249. See also Marcia Rivera Quintero, "Capitalist Development and the Incorporation of Women to the Labour Force" (paper presented at the Latin American Studies Association Conference on April 6, 1979, Pittsburgh, Pennsylvania). Isabel Picó de Hernández, "Estudio sobre el empleo de la mujer en Puerto Rico," *Revista de Ciencias Sociales* vol. 19, no. 2 (June 1975), pp. 141–144.

7. Rivera Quintero, p. 16. See also Caroline Manning, *The Employment of Women in Puerto Rico* (Washington, D.C.: Government Printing Office, 1934).

8. Lawrence R. Chenault, *The Puerto Rican Migrant in New York City* (New York: Columbia University Press, 1938; reissue, Russell & Russell, 1970), p. 76. See also Rinker Buck, "The New Sweat Shops: A Penny for Your Collar," *New York* vol. 12, no. 5 (January 29, 1979), pp. 40–46.

9. Interview with María Bonilla, New York City, summer 1976.

10. Interview with Julia González, Rio Piedras, Puerto Rico, July 1977.

11. Interview with Clara Rodríguez, Cabo Rojo, Puerto Rico, July 1977.

12. Chenault, *The Puerto Rican Migrant,* pp. 69–88. In 1914 the average "real" weekly wages in the United States was $10.73. This rose to $13.14 in 1926. For unionized trades during the same period, it increased from $8.22 to $23.94; miners, from $11.56 to $15.03; printers, from $19.67 to $21.63.

See Samuel Eliot Morrison, *The Oxford History of the American People,* vol. 3 (New York: New American Library, 1972), pp. 234–237.

13. Margarita Hernández interview.

14. Lourdes Miranda King, "Puertorriqueñas in the United States," Commission of Human Rights, *Civil Rights Digest* (Washington, D.C., spring 1974), p. 23. See also Rosemary Santana Cooney and Alice Colón Warren, "Work and Family: The Recent Struggle of Puerto Rican Females," in Clara E. Rodríguez, Virginia Sánchez Korrol, and José Oscar Alers, eds., *The Puerto Rican Struggle: Essays on Survival in the U.S.* (New York: Puerto Rican Migration Research Consortium, 1980), pp. 58–73.

15. New York State Manuscript Census, 1925.

16. Gutman, *The Black Family,* pp. 455–456. These findings are comparable with black households in central Harlem where the typical Afro-American family consisted of two-parent households. "The two-parent household was not limited to better-advantaged Afro-Americans," wrote Gutman in his study.

17. Welfare Council of New York City, *Puerto Ricans in New York City* (New York, 1948).

18. Interview with Celina Santiago, Brooklyn, New York, summer 1976.

19. Joseph P. Fitzpatrick, *Puerto Rican–Americans* (Englewood Cliffs, N.J.: Prentice-Hall, 1971), pp. 81–82. See also Kal Wagenheim, *Puerto Rico: A Profile* (New York: Praeger Press, 1970), pp. 189–190.

20. Interview with Elisa Baeza, Mayaguez, Puerto Rico, July 1977.

21. Interview with Celia Santiago, Brooklyn, New York, 1977.

22. Celia Santiago interview.

23. New York State Manuscript Census, 1925.

24. Interview with Rosa Roma, Santurce, Puerto Rico, August 1977.

25. Clara Rodríguez interview.

26. Celia Santiago interview.

27. Irving Howe, *The World of Our Fathers* (New York: Harcourt, Brace, Jovanovich, 1976), p. 132.

28. Gutman, *The Black Family,* pp. 453–4.

29. *New York Times,* "The Porto Rican Exodus," April 4, 1901, cited in History Task Force, Centro de Estudios Puertorriqueños, *Documentos de la migración Puertorriqueña, 1879–1901* (New York: Centro de Estudios Puertorriquenos, Research Foundation of the City University of New York, 1977), p. 32.

30. *La Prensa,* vol. 8, July 21, 1919, p. 463.

31. Interviews with Antonio and Raquel Hernández Rivera, Rio Piedras, Puerto Rico, August 1977. Also Julia González interview.

32. Interviews with Petra and Valentín Negrón, Rio Piedras, Puerto Rico, August 1977.

33. Rosa Roma interview.

34. Ibid.

35. Interview with Mary Geraldini, Levittown, Puerto Rico, July 1977.

36. Chenault, *The Puerto Rican Migrant,* pp. 79–84.

37. Margarita Hernández interview. See also Nancie L. González, "Multiple Migratory Experiences of Dominican Women," *Anthropological Quarterly* vol. 49, no. 1 (January 1979), pp. 36–43, for a comparative view toward work and family life in New York City.

38. Interview with Sister Carmelita Bonilla, Puerto Rican Oral History Project, Long Island Historical Society, Brooklyn, New York. See also Anthony Stevens Arroyo, "Puerto Rican Struggles in the Catholic Church," in Clara E. Rodríguez, Virginia Sánchez Korrol, and José Oscar Alers, eds., *The Puerto Rican Struggle.*

39. Interview with Eloísa García Rivera, New York City, 1977.

40. Interview with Honorina Weber Irizarry, Puerto Rican Oral History Project.

41. Interview with Josefina Silva de Cintrón, New York City, 1977. See also Virginia Sánchez Korrol, "Between Two Worlds—Educated Puerto Rican Migrant Women of the Early Settlements" (paper presented at the 14th Annual Conference of Caribbean Historians, San Juan, Puerto Rico, April 1981).

Plates

PLATE 1 Puerto Rican migrant woman, New York City, circa 1927. Courtesy of Mrs. Helen Guzman Steffens, Centerreach, New York.

PLATE 2 Formal portrait of woman migrant, circa 1927.
Author's private collection.

PLATE 3 Woman and children on board the Borinquen, circa 1930. Courtesy of Mrs. Clara Rodriguez, Cabo Rojo, Puerto Rico.

PLATE 4 Family group on board ship, late 1930s. Courtesy of
Mrs. Clara Rodriguez, Cabo Rojo, Puerto Rico.

PLATE 5 Formal portrait of Antonio Sanchez Feliciano, New York City, circa 1930. Author's private collection.

PLATE 6 Formal portrait of Elisa Santiago Baeza in New York City, circa 1930. Author's private collection.

PLATE 7 Puerto Rican children on Manhattan rooftop, circa 1930. Courtesy of Mrs. Helen Guzman Steffens, Centerreach, New York.

PLATE 8 Mother and first-born child in New York City's
Central Park, circa 1940. Courtesy of Mrs. Clara Rodriguez,
Cabo Rojo, Puerto Rico.

PLATE 9 Family gathering in Central Park, circa 1940. Also courtesy of Mrs. Clara Rodriguez.

PLATE 10 Musical trio entertaining at a house party, circa 1945.
Courtesy of Mrs. Helen Steffens, Centerreach, New York.

Organizational Activities Among Puerto Ricans in New York City Settlements

For Puerto Ricans in New York City, the first decades of the twentieth century provided a significant degree of group involvement which reinforced and redefined the community image of the Spanish-speaking neighborhoods. Associations formed which acclimated incoming migrants to their new environments, allowed them to participate in group activities based on common interests, and represented the *colonias* before the host society. Group formation proliferated as the settlements increased in population aiding both the structure and survival of the early communities as identifiable Puerto Rican entities and confronting those issues which most affected them. Some groups concerned themselves with education, culture, or social service needs within a continental context; others functioned as buffers between the wider non-Hispanic society and the Spanish-speaking enclaves, seeking to represent the *colonias* during critical periods or on a city-wide basis.

Yet the issue of the existence of organizational structures among Puerto Ricans has often been debated; the value of such community networks, as well as the potential leadership with they fostered, was a controversial point. Some scholars, such as Elena Padilla or Lawrence Chenault, who wrote about New York Puerto Ricans before and after the Second World War, observed group activity among Puerto Ricans, but failed to explore the subject in depth.[1] While social scientists argue the pros and cons of Puerto Rican organizational structure, most agree it is a topic about which little has been written.

A Review of the Literature on Puerto Rican Organizations

Perhaps Moynihan and Glazer best typify those fostering a concept of limited communal development. In their popular work the authors repeatedly not only call attention to an apparent shortcoming in cultural organizational action on behalf of the migrant community, but allude as well to what they interpret as a lack of leadership. Lacking information for the pre-World War II period, Moynihan and Glazer begin their discussion with the post-war period: "In 1948, only six percent of the migrants belonged to Puerto Rican organizations, somewhat more men than women and more of the older migrants than recent arrivals." Moreover, the authors refer to "many social organizations, based on places of origin," but judge these to be less important and inferior when compared with the associations of earlier immigrant groups.[2] Moynihan and Glazer believed the relative weakness of neighborhood organization and community leadership was characteristic of Puerto Ricans in New York. The working-class composition of the pre-World War II migration, furthermore, encouraged the alienation of the community's few professionals from their fellow Puerto Ricans, inhibiting also the creation of associations or emergence of leadership among the early groups. On these themes Glazer and Moynihan raised more questions than they answered, and they failed to grasp the significance of the groups which they did observe. Among these were the neighborhood or hometown groups which served as orientation facilitators for incoming migrants. Their structure was often not unlike that of the hometown societies in operation among the Jews and Italians of the earlier period.[3] More important, the authors ignored completely other types of organizations in existence at that time.

Similarly, Donald Stewart's short history of the Harlem community which appeared in 1972, supported the Glazer and Moynihan thesis.[4] While acknowledging a rapid intensive concentration of Puerto Rican migrants in Spanish Harlem, the belief continued to be that Puerto Ricans had not progressed to the point of effectively organizing for any purpose. The author reported, "Except for the

Jewish-Italian Socialist movement in the twenties and thirties, the black and Hispanic communities were not represented by organized politically oriented committees until the 1950s."[5]

More recently, historian Adalberto López recognized the existence and potential of early Puerto Rican associations, but admittedly lacked sufficient evidence on their structure and modes of operation to evaluate their roles effectively within the Spanish-speaking settlements. Lopez believed groups emerged to cope with some of the social and economic problems affecting early *colonias,* but these units "rarely drew national attention or funds and ordinarily limited themselves to asking for small and inadequate funds from urban government."[6] López, however, offered one possible suggestion to explain the apparent lack of organizational involvement. "Throughout the 1950s more and more Puerto Rican workers joined labor unions but within these unions they were discriminated against and rarely enjoyed any power or influence."[7] While López skillfully assessed the situation for the period under scrutiny, he makes no mention of union organization among Puerto Ricans before the 1950s. How much experience did Puerto Ricans have with unions or labor movements before coming to New York City and to what degree was this reflected in the early associations?

Significantly, an important source for the early period used by many researchers was Lawrence Chenault's study on the Puerto Rican migrant. His work, considered groundbreaking for the period before the Second World War, offered valuable insight into communal organizational activity. Although he neglected to draw a connection between organizations in Puerto Rico and associations in the migrant settlements, or between Latin and non-Latin groups in the city, his description of Puerto Rican societies is among the first to appear in print. Referring to the hometown or neighborhood clubs, Chenault observed numerous social organizations were in operation for a variety of reasons ranging from groups favoring independence for Puerto Rico to others operating as social outlets for small groups of people from particular cities or towns on the island. Many of these sponsored dances in a number of halls suitable for this purpose. Of the smaller groups, few appeared to be permanent and many were constantly broken up to be formed again into new units.[8] The fact that associations were constantly being broken up suggests either that the groups were rather immature in the ways of maintaining an organization; that members were not committed enough; or that the group's membership needs were not satisfied.[9] While we may speculate on the motivation behind Chenault's observation, it remains clear that new associations *were* constantly being formed. Did the new groups rely on new leadership as well or were they composed of the same membership under a new name? What degree of organizational experience existed among the early migrants and what connection, if any, was kept with island counterparts? While Chenault viewed organizational activity as either socially or politically oriented, he failed to investigate the wide range of purposes for which groups formed and he was unable to provide insights into community leadership within an organizational structure.

However, Rosa Estades, a sociologist, does address the issue of leadership within the *colonias* throughout the decade of the thirties.[10] Examining group structure, she describes socially, culturally, and politically active settlements, particularly in the East Harlem section of Manhattan. Here groups formed based on common interests and/or experiences. Financing came from membership dues. Most of the organizers met in members' living rooms, with the exception of a few who met in hotel suites. Estades lists thirty-three organizations composed predominantly of Puerto Rican membership, even though other Spanish-speaking individuals finding familiarity and communalism based on language and culture were also welcomed.[11] Estades does draw a connection between club leaders and local non-Hispanic political groups, stating that the Spanish-speaking leaders were often sought out as contacts with the early *colonias*. With regard to the connections between island and mainland Puerto Rican groups, Estades believed a connection indeed existed based on issues, styles, and experiences, but that the New York groups did not depend on Puerto Rico either in terms of finances nor in bargaining for their political situation with the New York political leaders.[12] Was this the case with all types of New York Puerto Rican associations? Estades focused mainly on political participation and her descriptions of social, cultural, or civic groups offered limited historical reconstruction and analysis.

One report which not only recognized the significance of social and cultural associations confirming also their existence in the New York area over several decades was *A Study of Poverty Conditions in the New York Puerto Rican Community.*[13] Although references are made to group activity during the mid-sixties, the report's descriptions of hometown associations provided excellent examples of Puerto Rican social units and are not unlike descriptions found for the pre-World War II period. For example:

> On Sunday in New York one can wander into hundreds of "Hometown Club" meetings, where members gather from every part of the city to spend their leisure day together, eating, playing cards, making plans for future activities, or talking over old—and new—times. These and other similar groups have helped the family in its role to cushion the individual in the face of adversity. There are many church clubs that have various extra-religious functions, a small number of private social agencies and federated citizen's groups.[14]

Here, the role of the organization as broker between Hispanic resident and the wider society becomes obvious. With few exceptions, the groups in operation during the late fifties and early sixties were extensions of similar associations of an earlier period.

Models of Puerto Rican Organizations

An examination of group formation between the turn of the century and the decade of the forties revealed many organizations emerged based on common interests or relevant issues. Within this period at least three types of associations predominated. The first, the mutual aid societies of the early decades, patterned themselves on island counterparts, addressing migrant needs in New York as enthusiastically as they had previously served the community in Puerto Rico. In time, these attempted to organize the working-class *colonia* into trade unions affiliated with those on the island and on the mainland.

By the mid-twenties another type of organization emerged representing migrant settlements before the non-Hispanic community. These groups, exemplified by the Porto Rican Brotherhood of America, embodied some of the characteristics of the earlier mutual aid groups, but equally emphasized cultural values and traditions and responded to more immediate issues and concerns affecting Puerto Ricans in New York or in Puerto Rico. Yet another type of association characterized the decades of the thirties and forties. These were societies appealing to common interests of subgroups within the *colonias* and often lacked a cultural or community vision. Based on professional or occupational needs, these emerged as special-interest or single-issue associations. An example of this third model was the Post Office Workers' Organization. What were the issues which concerned the different types of organizations in operation over a period of several decades and how did they respond? As important, why did these groups come into being and how did they operate? A survey of several representative organizations provides some answers.

The earliest groups to function in New York Puerto Rican settlements were the mutual aid societies established by pioneer migrant tobacco workers in Manhattan's Lower East Side and Chelsea district. Based on similar groups operating among the urban artisans of Puerto Rico, the concept of self-help organizations came into New York harbor along with the first working-class representatives. When the *Federación Libre de Trabajadores,* tacitly recognized as the island's first central craft union, came into being in 1899, artisan group organizations based on common needs and interests had already been in existence on the island for several decades.[15] *Gremios,* patterned on the Spanish guild system, limited competition, regulated artisan markets, controlled conditions of employment, and provided fairs for the exchange of merchandise. *Cofradías* and *Hermandades* provided medical and hospital aid, raised dowries or ransoms, supplied burial, social, or religious services for its members. It was the *Hermandades,* for example, which supplied the monies to emancipate the slaves during the last third of the century. Based on occupational common interests, the groups dealt with the material needs of their members. In tragedy, death, or illness, the *Cofradías* and *Hermandades* both pledged support for the stricken family. Vying with one another in the grandiosity of the celebrations honoring their patron saints, the groups combined religious purposes with social services.[16]

The experience of skilled workers on the island, particularly in fostering labor movements, promoting strikes, and forming guild-like associations would stand to benefit the early workers' organizations in the New York *colonias.* Included in their collective history were the initiation of militant labor movements begun well before 1898, the strike and syndicalist ideology. Strikes, the most effective working-class weapon, became an integral part of labor movements in Puerto Rico well before the Spanish-American War. About the same time, urban artisans including printers, tinsmiths, carpenters, cigar makers, painters, typesetters, and shoemakers became influenced by European radical, anarcho-syndicalist ideas. Within this climate, study circles formed to analyze and propagate the new ideology based on working-class solidarity. Radical newspapers appeared and regional federations of the workers' international movement motivated the conversion of guild-like organizations into trade unions in the island's three or four principal urban centers.[17] These then incorporated within the larger *Federación Libre de Trabajadores* and subsequently affiliated with the American Federation of Labor.

The labor-related activities of the Puerto Rican workers were further enriched by familiarity with and knowledge of North American and international labor movements. It was precisely in the arena of labor organization and participation as well as in the commitment to socialist ideas that Puerto Ricans most resembled European and South American workers. Affiliation with the American Federation of Labor brought Puerto Ricans into contact with North American labor issues while information shared through the practice of *la lectura,* the traditional reading period in the island's tobacco factories, highlighted international workers' struggles within an organizational context. Concern for the problems of all of the working people as a class, regardless of national origin, would foster a degree of camaraderie between the various workers' groups in New York City. Thus when the Puerto Rican workers became the migrants of the early *colonias,* they were adequately prepared to continue working-class struggles in New York City. As skilled workers, especially cigar makers, were well represented among the city's earliest migrants, it was not unusual that groups such as mutual aid societies and trade unions associated with this segment of the working population in Puerto Rico would also flourish in the New York settlements.

The trade unions most patronized by the early Puerto Rican migrants in New York City were *La Internacional,* affiliated with the American Federation of Labor, and *La Resistencia*. Most of the

Spanish-speaking tobacco workers belonged to the latter. *La Internacional*'s membership closely followed the basic guidelines set forth by North American trade unionism including collective bargaining, better working conditions, and wages, but excluded support for social revolution or the formation of a worker's party. *La Resistencia,* on the other hand, considered itself more revolutionary, favoring principles of Latin American anarcho-syndicalist organization. In a pre-welfare environment, these unions became instrumental in fostering benefits for the Spanish-speaking working class. They also succeeded in nurturing the formation of mutual aid societies and cultural units similar in operation and purpose to those which coexisted alongside or within trade unions on the island.[18]

Based in New York City and responding to pioneer migrants' material and supportive needs, *La Aurora, La Razón,* and *El Ejemplo* were three such organizations. Cigar maker Bernardo Vega asserted that these groups along with the trade unions were the only active Hispanic associations in New York City following the decline of Antillean immigration at the conclusion of the Spanish-American War. He based his assertion on personal community involvement, observation, and on conversations held with senior workers in the industry. One interview taken with a fellow tobacco worker who had resided in New York since 1913 yielded the following information:

> There did not exist exclusively Puerto Rican societies but the tobacco workers had mutual aid organizations such as *La Aurora, La Razón, El Ejemplo*. . . . The educative circles were always of anarchist ideology with the exception of the *Círculo de trabajadores* in Brooklyn which admitted workers of diverse ideologies. The trade unions were the *Internacional* of Tobacco Workers and the *Resistencia*. . . . In my neighborhood there was a club called *El Tropical* which sponsored dances and celebrated conferences from time to time. . . . On the West Side, I remember that Dr. Henna presided over the Club *Ibero-americano*.[19]

The *Círculo de Trabajadores* mentioned in the interview suggests that some socialist-oriented Puerto Rican affiliation may have existed between tobacco workers and others of related ideologies. This organization, originating in the nineteenth century, was supposed to be the exception "which admitted workers of diverse ideologies." It is not known whether this group was founded by Spanish-speaking cigar makers, along the lines of the mutual aid societies, or patterned after the popular Jewish Workmen's Circle, supported by working-class socialists, as the name implies. If it was indeed modeled after the Jewish Workmen's Circle, did this mean a degree of reciprocity existed between Puerto Ricans and non-Hispanics? While answers are merely speculative, one cigar maker who frequented the *Círculo* described it as an Hispanic association patronized predominantly by tobacco workers of that period, regardless of ethnic background, who shared common interests as the working class of the trade (see chapter 6 for discussion of political groups of that period).[20]

Another group frequented by Puerto Rican tobacco workers and functioning similarly to the Workmen's Circle was the *Círculo de Tabaqueros*. Originating in Brooklyn around the turn of the century, the *Círculo* along with the Francisco Ferrar y Guardia School located at 107th Street near Park Avenue, provided a meeting center for tobacco workers and their families. It operated like a European casino, a mixture of social organizations and philosophical forum. Many who frequented that organization favored progressive or radical ideas, openly identifying themselves as anarchists, socialists, or leftist republicans. A typical gathering at the headquarters of this association found individuals participating in recreational group activities, playing chess, dominoes, or conversing in small groups. Topics of interest ranged from discussions of current events to the planning of forthcoming projects. On a typical Sunday afternoon, visitors might be treated to a series of formal presentations, for example, Spanish language interpretations of Russian playwrights such as Chekov and Gorky, or informal presentations including lectures and workshops. Refreshments and light snacks were also available. One afternoon in particular, the following series of lectures were presented, a testimony to the great variety of an afternoon's entertainment:

The particular day which I am remembering, Carlos Tresca, director of the newspaper *Il Martele,* spoke in Italian on

"Anarchism and Darwinian Theory"; Elizabeth Gurley
Flynn spoke in English on "Utopian Communities and Free
Will"; Pedro Esteves spoke in Spanish on "War and Peace
and the Role of the Proletariat"; and Frank Kelly, a Catholic
anarchist, spoke also in Spanish on "Jesus Christ, the First
Communist." Discussions were followed by a question and
answer period.[21]

In presenting lecture series and discussions on a variety of social
issues, the *Círculo de Tabaqueros* was following an international
pattern long established among Puerto Rico's skilled workers, as
well as among other immigrant groups in New York. First, the
study circles connected with the birth of the island's labor movement and the subsequent foundation of the trade union, *Federación Libre de Trabajadores,* used the lecture and discussion model
in much the same way as the presentations of the *Círculo.* Second,
the Latin practice of employing a reader in the tobacco factories of
Puerto Rico and New York similarly engaged the lecture and discussion method. Here readers devoted the morning's session to the
dissemination of factual material, news of the day, and cablegraph-
ic information. The afternoon's reading session included literary or
philosophical studies followed by a lively period of discussions.
Third, passion for lectures similarly infused the earlier immigrant
residents of the Lower East Side, setting a precedent in ethnic settlements for this type and method of communication. In New York
City scores of lectures were advertised in the local presses, in many
languages, and on a variety of topics. Historical or literary themes
often followed lectures on trade unionism or religion. Many were
scheduled for weekends in consideration for the working-class
composition of the audience. Sometimes a fee of ten or fifteen
cents was charged for the evening. That this method of sharing
ideas and communication was not unique to any one ethnic group
or Puerto Ricans in particular is exemplified by the recollections of
a Jewish worker recalling his experiences just after the turn of the
century.

I began to buy newspapers and watch for the notices. There
were scores of lectures every week. . . . One night it was Dar-
win and the next it might be the principle of air pressure. On a

Saturday night there were sometimes two meetings so arranged that both could be attended by the same audiences. I remember once going to a meeting at Cooper Union to protest against the use of the militia in breaking a strike somewhere in the West, and then retiring with a crowd of others to the anarchist reading room on Eldridge Street to hear an informal discussion on "Hamlet Versus Don Quixote."[22]

It was no accident that tobacco workers' associations, mutual aid groups, and trade unions should be among the first to emerge in the Puerto Rican *colonia*. For the first decades of the century, tobacco workers and their families predominated among the Puerto Rican working class. Small in numbers, these workers recreated the organizations which they had known in Puerto Rico and which were most beneficial to their trade and welfare. Since they were based on island counterparts articulating familiar ideologies and modes of operation, they helped to ease the migrant's adjustment to the mainland settlements. Groups like *La Aurora, El Ejemplo,* or *La Razón* provided essential supportive services for their membership while *La Resistencia* and the *Internacional* brought contact with other ethnic groups through their affiliation with anarcho-syndicalist or socialist associations.

By the mid-twenties the Puerto Rican settlements experienced significant changes producing limitations in the effectiveness of these pioneer organizations. Precipitated by a numerical growth of the Spanish-speaking settlements, now estimated to number around one hundred thousand individuals, the *colonia* expanded beyond the original nucleus of tobacco workers. At the same time, their influence was further reduced by critical changes in the tobacco industry. Throughout this period, the effects of mechanization in cigar manufacturing coupled with an increase in cigarette consumption resulted in a reduction in the employment of skilled cigar makers. Since the nineteenth century, these individuals had manufactured cigars using their hands and simple tools, but the newly mechanized industry of the twentieth century could now stimulate the employment of less skilled and less experienced persons.[23] This factor contributed to a geographic dispersal of Puerto Rican cigar makers and drew them into competition with other ethnic groups for unskilled jobs in other sectors. A reduction of tobacco workers meant also a reduction in the membership of those associations previously connected with the office. Therefore, declining membership and failure to recruit new dedicated individuals combined to diminish the popularity of the mutual aid societies. By mid-decade other groups emerged which incorporated some of the elements of the mutual aid groups but expanded their scope to become more representative of the entire community.

ORGANIZATIONS DURING THE TWENTIES

The very growth of the Spanish-speaking settlements in New York City and the recognition of the existence of a community with urgent needs and varying interests prompted the appearance of other types of organizations. These included more social units such as the hometown or regional clubs; groups pledged to support island or continental political persuasions; Latin cultural societies or civically oriented associations. By the mid-1920s at least forty-three three Hispanic organizations operated in the heart of the Latin *colonias* in Brooklyn and Manhattan. Group formation and the effective use of organizations became topics of frequent discussion. These commentaries often appeared in print. One group, considered a key organization during the period of the twenties, expressed its position on that issue (see Figure 3 and Maps 5, 6, and 7).

> In the city of New York the Puerto Rican community is today undoubtedly the largest among the Spanish-speaking. Its organization into a strong and powerful nucleus would produce incalculable results, not only for the residents of the continental communities but for the island as well. We speak English and are citizens of the United States, valuable attributes for the defense of our individual and collective interests. Organization is mandatory. It is an urgent imperative and truly patriotic necessity. If the task is a task of heroes— difficult and crude—it is not impossible. Let us begin at least by joining existing societies. Perhaps it will be easier later on to accomplish the complete consolidation of the community.[24]

If the organizations and their leadership, aware of their potential impact, sought to consolidate and mobilize the community behind an associational network, the *colonias* also looked to the organizations for leadership. Newspapers and journals which frequently

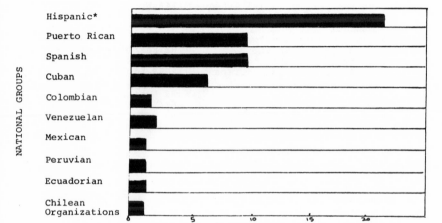

*Note: Hispanic organizations were those groups which were composed of Spanish-speaking membership but whose name did not imply orientation to a specific national group.

Source: Based on information provided by the Souvenir Program of The Porto Rican Brotherhood of America, June, 1926 and 1927.

Figure 3 Distribution and Ethnicity of Organizations in Operation in 1926

Club Estrella de Borinquen	134 West 112th Street
Centro de Amigos	100 West 113th Street
Peruvian Social & Sporting Club	197 Lenox Avenue
South American Sporting Club	33 West 113th Street
Rialto Social & Sporting Club	197 Lenox Avenue
Centro Equatoriano	101 West 87th Street
Club Patriótico Social Cubano	144 West 132nd Street
Asociación de Maestros de Español	419 West 117th Street
Alianza Obrera Puertorriqueña	38 West 117th Street
Ateneo Obrero Hispano	62 East 106th Street
Casa de las Espanas	247 Park Avenue
Fraternidad Hispano-Americano	2059 Eighth Avenue
Asociación Cubana	2061 Broadway
Porto Rican Brotherhood	36 West 120th Street
Club Esperanza	624 West 156th Street
Beneficiencia Cubana	50 West 122nd Street
La Razón, Inc.	233 East 75th Street

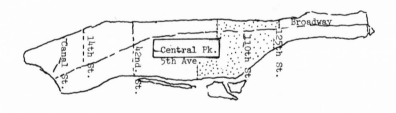

Source: Based on the Souvenir Program of the Porto Rican
Brotherhood of America, 1926-1927

MAP 5 Hispanic Organizations in Operation in Upper Manhattan,
1926-1927

Centro Hispano-Americano	353 West 17th Street
Galicia Sporting Club	108 West 14th Street
Casa Galicia	108 West 14th Street
Comité Pro-Cuba	Hotel Waldorf Astoria
Centro Vasco-Americano	77 Catherine Street
Sociedad Mutualista Americana	City Hall Station
Sada y Sus Contornos	311 Water Street
Logia Teosófica "Mayflower"	255 West 14th Street
Sociedad Naturista Hispana	255 West 14th Street
Instituto de las Espanas	2 West 45th Street
Club Excelsior	218 E. 19th Street
Chilean Social & Sporting Club	420 West 23rd Street
Club Colombia	17 Battery Street
La Cosmopolita	239 West 14th Street

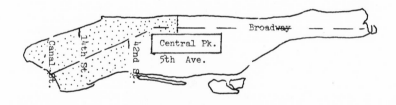

Source: Based on the Souvenir Program of the Porto
          Rican Brotherhood of America, 1926-1927

MAP 6 Hispanic Organizations in Operation in Mid and Lower
Manhattan, 1926-1927

Club Reflejo Antillano	310 Adams Street
Centro Andaluz	59-61 Henry Street
Centro Montañes	166 Pacific Street
Centro Asturiano de New York	50 Willow Street
Centro Social Venezolano	140 Adams Street
La Nacional	1153 Fulton Street
Unión Obrera Venezolana	4 Willow Street
Centro Asturiano de la Habana	50 Willow Street
Segura Football Club	27 State Street

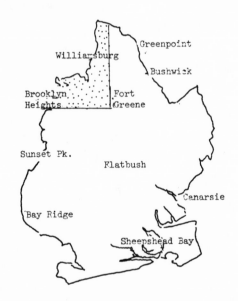

Source: Based on the Souvenir Program of the Porto
          Rican Brotherhood of America, 1926-1927

MAP 7 Hispanic Organizations in Operation in Brooklyn, 1926-1927

advertised the activities of the settlements' organizations were
quick to criticize them for failing the community in this direction
from time to time. In 1928 an editorial in *Gráfico* openly chided the
associations currently in operation for failing to unite, enlighten, or
prepare the migrants "so our living conditions would improve."[25]
This was followed by a series of editorials postulating plans for
converting "our fraternities and social groups into useful instruments to achieve our economic goals and political betterment."
Organizations of the twenties and thirties were expected to act not
only in the interests of their membership or a particular interest
group, but also on behalf of the community at large. Such a group
was The Porto Rican Brotherhood of America *(Hermandad Puertorriqueña);* another was *La Liga Puertorriqueña e Hispana.*

Founded in 1923, The Porto Rican Brotherhood emerged as one
of the most significant organizations of the period. The purposes
for incorporation, as stated in its charter several years later, offered
only a partial indication of what the group's actual functions were:

> The promotion of sociability and friendship among its mem-
> bers, their social and intellectual advancement, and with this
> end in view, to provide a club house, or club rooms by lease
> or purchase or otherwise for the use and benefit of its mem-
> bers. The above objects are voluntary and the club is not
> organized for profit.[26]

Between the time of its appearance in 1923 and its incorporation
in 1927, the Brotherhood covered a wide range of activities. It
labored toward promoting unity, brotherhood and mutual aid
among Puerto Ricans according to the consent of its members.
While it strove to achieve the maturity necessary to properly describe itself as a true brotherhood, the group purposely deleted politics from its agenda. A letter which appeared in San Juan's *El
Imparcial* described the Brotherhood in positive and realistic terms
for the island's readers.[27] It also suggested a degree of interest in
the affairs of the migrant community on the part of Puerto Ricans
in Puerto Rico:

> The Brotherhood founded two years ago has had its ups and
> downs: situations in which enthusiasm has been feverish and
> others where its frigidity has placed it in danger of extinction.

Actually, it is a Puerto Rican organization with a large following—in the month of February it listed fifty members. To
unite the Puerto Rican *colonia* here is a Herculean task. It
must first attack the indifference with which we greet everything Puerto Rican and the feverishness with which we follow
all the exotic. Within this limitation, the Brotherhood has
developed a plausible organization, not only because of its
ideology but also for the harvest of its results.

What was its ideology? While it was not stated as part of its purposes for incorporation, the Brotherhood's platform certainly
demonstrated an expanded sense of commitment which did not lim-
it itself to one segment of the Spanish speaking *colonias* as the
mutual aid groups had done in the past. Included among their principles were:

1. An awareness concerning the working-class base of the
   organization's membership.

2. An awareness of the importance of mutual assistance and
   defense of the Puerto Rican *colonias* within the frame-
   work of the city's political structure.

3. Involvement in island political issues and a commitment to
   the advancement in the United States of the cause of Puerto
   Rico.

4. An awareness of issues concerning United States politics
   abroad, particularly in Latin America and most of all, the
   Caribbean.

5. A belief that Puerto Ricans themselves will define their
   problems and needs and devise their own remedies.[28]

The Brotherhood sought to be the type of group which could
defend the Puerto Ricans within the political structure of New
York City while maintaining links with Puerto Rico and acting as
watchdog in issues involving the United States and Spanish America. While these commitments appeared to be overambitious for a
young and relatively small group, an analysis of their activities over
a period of several months documents the association's integral
role in the community and dedication to its principles.[29]

One example of the Brotherhood's involvement took place when the group was called upon as advocate for four Puerto Ricans erroneously detained at Ellis Island as aliens, unable to prove their American citizenship. With the aid of the Puerto Rican resident commissioner in Washington, D.C., the Brotherhood acted in defense of Puerto Rican civil rights, successfully clearing the individuals.[30] On other occasions the Brotherhood set aside funds for needy Puerto Rican families, assisting them during critical periods in much the same way the earlier mutual aid societies had done. The annual report of 1926 to 1927 mentioned two instances in which the organization extended itself to cover the burial expenses of indigent Puerto Ricans, not necessarily members of the organization.

Throughout that year, the Brotherhood organized various social and cultural activities. These included *jaranas,* social gatherings, dances, and several youth-oriented celebrations supervised by the women's auxiliary. The work of the women's auxiliary was vital for the general survival of the organization. Their committee, patterned on the constitution and bylaws of the larger Brotherhood, provided for the election of officers and a board of directors. It was the women's auxiliary, for example, which generated publicity and propaganda for the Brotherhood, supervised fund raisers and bake sales, directed youth groups, and performed charitable works. Fund raisers secured monies to cover the year's activities and functions, but a small amount was also set aside for miscellaneous social services.

Another important activity sponsored by the Brotherhood during that period took place in conjunction with the Romance Language Department of Columbia University, the *Centro de Estudios Históricos de Madrid* and the *Instituto de las Españas.* This was a conference honoring illustrious Puerto Rican patriots. Among those honored were Luis Muñoz Rivera and Dr. José Celso Barbosa, both connected with the island's political development, and the historical playwright and essayist Alejandro Tapia y Rivera.[31] Muñoz Rivera led the island's autonomist movement in the nineteenth century and was instrumental in securing the Charter of Autonomy from Spain in 1897. Celso Barbosa, on the other hand, was a physician who served in the cabinet of the autonomous government and later formed the island's Statehood Republican Party.

For the most part the Brotherhood's activities fulfilled specific social service, cultural, or political community needs. But the increasing numerical growth and geographical expansion of the migrant population produced changes even beyond the scope of the Brotherhood's control. The everyday adjustment problems faced by *colonia* residents still undergoing the psychological effects inherent in the migration experience included such difficulties as providing a livelihood, securing adequate housing, or enduring frequent bouts of discrimination, hostilities, or suspicions on the part of the more established immigrant groups. These worries far outdistanced the efforts of the best community organizations. While the Brotherhood continued to act as caretaker for the Puerto Rican settlements, incidents based on migrant adjustment problems arose which provoked *colonia* residents to take matters into their own hands.

Such a situation took place in July 1926 when migrants engaged in a series of confrontations with other non-Hispanic area dwellers. Following a heat wave of several weeks' duration, the residents of Spanish Harlem had begun to literally live in the streets, hoping to gain relief from the torridness of their tenement dwellings. People slept on rooftops, fire escapes, and in Central Park where light breezes blew across the lake with the onset of evenings. The Puerto Rican *piragueros,* peddlers of cupfuls of scraped ice drenched in sweet syrups *(piraguas)* were much in demand by thirsty customers.

The conflicts were described as "Harlem Riots" by the *New York Times* and supposedly stemmed from "ill feeling of recent weeks between young Porto Ricans and others of Spanish blood who have been moving into Harlem in large numbers recently and the older residents of the district."[32] Sporadic street fights, arguments, and bottle throwing from the rooftops had characterized the relations between the "old settlers and the new residents" for over a week. These encounters culminated in the arrests of three Puerto Rican youths, all under the age of sixteen, charged with disorderly conduct. In retaliation, groups of Puerto Ricans descended upon 115th Street and Lenox Avenue armed with "staves wrapped in paper," but these were scattered by the reserves of four police precincts who then proceeded to disperse crowds of onlookers estimated to number in the thousands.

According to the reports of several migrants who lived through

the episode as well as spokespersons of several Puerto Rican organizations, the riots were caused primarily by irritations over the
steady encroachment of Spanish-speaking merchants in commercial areas predominantly controlled in the past by Jewish merchants. The situation was further complicated by repeated harassment against Puerto Rican men and women residing in the area,
finally ending in violence, destruction, and the overthrowing of
peddlers' pushcarts as well as a general boycott of both Jewish and
Spanish-owned stores in the vicinity. Added to the fear of losing
business, the old residents' distrust of Puerto Ricans and other
West Indians was compounded by the fact that Puerto Ricans were
racially mixed, perhaps provoking fantasies of future alliances with
nonwhites, along racial lines.

One narrative described this particular incident as a surprise
attack by hordes of individuals armed with sticks. Several Puerto
Rican-owned stores were vandalized. Broken glass, mixed with
rice, beans, plantains, and *yautias* (Puerto Rican root vegetable) lit-
tered the sidewalks and gutters in front of neighborhood *bodegas*.
All of this was viewed by the observer as purposely directed against
the *Barrio Latino:*[33] "It was not until much later that we found out
with certainty what had happened. The first attacks resulted in over
fifty wounded, some seriously. Upon learning what had transpired,
Puerto Ricans reacted taking to the streets to avenge the wrong. It
was then that the police arrived."[34]

In accordance with this version, the *Times* subsequently reported, "the bad feeling is said to have been caused by the rapid influx
of Latin and West Indian negroes who describe themselves as Porto
Ricans. The newcomers have opened their own stores and patronize
no others. The old residents of the district have resented the inva-
sion."[35]

> The ill-feeling between the Spanish-speaking people and the
> old residents of the section it was declared by one speaker,
> was due to rivalry between the Jewish and Spanish residents.
> Speaking on behalf of the Jewish people, Joseph N. Schultz,
> a former President of the Liberty Republican Club, declared
> there were no real grounds for ill-feeling and called upon the
> factions to forget their differences and remember that they
> were all residents of the United States.[36]

If the Harlem riots were any indication, the problems and issues confronting the *colonias* of the mid-twenties were indeed a far cry from those facing the tobacco workers of the past decade.

Faced with an expanding and visible Puerto Rican population, the surrounding ethnic groups resented their presence on the competitive job market and in the Spanish Harlem tenements. The fact that Puerto Ricans were also citizens of the United States, allowed to travel without restrictions at a time when European immigration was legally curtailed, did little to eradicate feelings of cultural and racial discrimination on the part of the older immigrants. The Porto Rican Brotherhood set forth to deal with the more complex situation on both a communal and a national level. The Harlem conflict, for example, was handled on several fronts. First, the Brotherhood selected and sent a representative committee to the local police precincts to request protection for the innocent citizens and punishment for the guilty, regardless of ethnic origin. Second, the Brotherhood secured *La Prensa's* cooperation in unleashing a vigorous campaign calling for a return to normalcy in the *colonias*. *La Prensa* by this time enjoyed a certain degree of prestige as it was considered a major newspaper for the Spanish-speaking population throughout the city. Third, the Brotherhood telegraphed Mayor Walker, Governor Smith, the resident commissioner, and other federal authorities, demanding the reestablishment of order and protection in general for the entire community.

Although the Brotherhood was somewhat successful in coping with this particular incident, the need for a comprehensive group composed of representatives from all of the active organizations became apparent. Instigated primarily by the Brotherhood the development and planning of such a group was soon undertaken and an organization created to act on behalf of the community emerged before the end of the year.

Thus, throughout this period the Porto Rican Brotherhood succeeded in its caretaker role by confronting the large non-Hispanic society; by representing the individual members of the *colonia;* by carrying out charitable works; promoting cultural and social activities designed to strengthen the Puerto Rican identity; and by assuming a position of leadership. Was the Brotherhood a unique organization, or was it characteristic of other groups of the period? How was the Brotherhood able to achieve so many of its goals in so short a period? Certainly one reason for its success was that few groups fulfilled the many needs and functions which the Brotherhood did. Indeed, the Brotherhood was among the earliest organizations to recognize the fact that the *colonia* needed groups to represent them before the host society, to handle particular problems, such as discrimination, affecting all Puerto Ricans and to categorically articulate the *colonia*'s position on the many issues which concerned them. The recurrence of situations which disadvantaged the migrant community and affected its expansion in general prompted the creation of a group specifically structured to assume these responsibilities and to share in its composition the input of most of the Hispanic community through the representation of different groups. Recognizing the importance of such a move and secure in the endorsement of other *colonia* organizations, the Brotherhood took the lead in the establishment of *La Liga Puertorriqueña e Hispana* for this purpose.

The idea of a federation of organizations had surfaced four years before when community leaders first attempted to form *La Liga Puertorriqueña* in 1923.[37] These individuals issued a call for a nonpartisan, diverse membership to represent the settlements at large. *La Prensa* reported the new association's goals as: "to widen the bands of confraternity among the city's Puerto Rican residents and to sustain the integrity of the Puerto Rican community; its moral and intellectual prestige, to foster its economic interests and protect its progress and welfare."

This organization appears to have disintegrated over a political issue, but its principles reemerged in *La Liga Puertorriqueña e Hispana,* a group deeply traumatized by the Hispanic-Jewish confrontations of the recent past. Taking credit for the group's formation, the Porto Rican Brotherhood dutifully reported the undertaking in its annual report explaining the functions and bylaws of the new unit.

The *Liga Puertorriqueña e Hispana* intended to serve the interwar settlements as an association whose constituency came from other groups already in existence. As such, it benefited from the past community organization experience of its leadership. The new leadership and their affiliations were: president—Blas Oliveras, president of the Porto Rican Brotherhood of America; vice-presidents—Joseph V. Alonso, president of the Caribe Democratic

Club, and Pedro San Miguel, president of *Alianza Obrera Puertorriqueña.*[38] The remaining officers were all voting members of
other organizations as well. In short, the first set of *La Liga*'s directors were remarkably well equipped to represent the Puerto Rican
community.

The announcement of the group's formation at the Harlem
Casino declared the general purposes for organizing were "obtain-
ing civic defense and promoting the general welfare of United
States citizens of Porto Rican and Spanish birth."[39] Included
among its specific goals were:

1. To unite all Hispanics without national distinctions
2. To represent the community before the authorities
3. To be a benevolent society
4. To provide an education center
5. To provide an information (referral) center
6. To propagate the vote among Puerto Ricans
7. To work toward the economic, political and social betterment of Puerto Ricans and Puerto Rico
8. To refrain from partisan politics[40]

As with the Brotherhood before it, *La Liga Puertorriqueña e
Hispana* worded its purposes for incorporation almost a year after
its actual creation. These appeared in the certificate of incorporation as:

> The promotion of sociability and friendship among its mem-
> bers, their social and intellectual advancement, and with this
> end in view, to provide a club house or club rooms by lease or
> purchase or otherwise for the use and benefit of its members.
> The above objects are voluntary and the club is not organized
> for profit.[41]

While there is little conflict between the purposes as stated in the
incorporation document and the goals of the group as expressed in
the press, it is clear from the issues which the group confronted that
the association accepted very seriously its militant mandate to act

on behalf of the community. Within a relatively short period they were indeed representing the *colonia* before the non-Hispanic society as they sought to better the social and political situation of the migrants.

Outstanding among the first incidents attracting *La Liga*'s attention as an organization which stood for Puerto Rican interests was the situation immediately following a highly publicized visit to Puerto Rico by the nation's first lady, Eleanor Roosevelt.[42] In an attempt to stimulate national concern toward granting federal aid for the people of Puerto Rico after a series of natural disasters, Mrs. Roosevelt called attention to the island's poor health and living standards. Stressing as inexcusable the high incidence of tuberculosis among the people, Mrs. Roosevelt innocently cautioned Americans against contracting the disease through contacts with Puerto Ricans in the United States. The inference that most Puerto Ricans therefore carried the contagious disease placed the migrant community in a precarious and prejudicial situation, according to *La Liga,* especially as large numbers of the New York migrants were employed as waiters or countermen in the hotels and restaurants of the city. In a vigorous campaign, *La Liga* pointed out the dangerous repercussions of Mrs. Roosevelt's statement focusing on the unintentional damage it would create. Launching a defense of the migrant working class, *La Liga* presented its position in the community's newspapers, and while it appeared the issue was forgotten after a while, it reappeared in a matter involving the children of the migrant communities.[43]

The Federation of Protestant Welfare Agencies had customarily sponsored a series of nondenominational summer camping programs for the city's underprivileged children. Until the summer of 1934, close to six thousand Puerto Rican children had participated among the campers, but that year the funding foundation failed to provide for the inclusion of Puerto Rican children and advised the Federation of its action. *La Liga* responded rapidly, interpreting this action on the part of the Foundation and the Federation as discriminatory, a direct result of the tuberculosis episode.[44] In their role as community representatives and to publicize their position on the issue, *La Liga* called for a mass meeting in which the matter was debated. A council of twenty-three representatives of Hispanic workers and religious organizations denounced the actions of the

Federation and called for retraction of the questionable policy. An intensive publicity campaign within the *colonia* brought the issue before the non-Hispanic public as well, and through the intercession of various religious groups, the situation was resolved in favor of the *colonias,* allowing the reinstatement of camping privileges.

Yet another incident in which *La Liga* marched at the forefront of community organizations took place the following year. It was in 1935 that the New York City Chamber of Commerce administered and interpreted the results of an experiment in which 240 Puerto Rican children were given an intelligence test. Numerous organizations, newspapers, and community newsletters indignantly greeted the Chamber's report that scores of Puerto Rican children were mentally deficient and intellectually immature. Following *La Liga*'s lead, community journals, newspapers, and group associations viewed the Chamber's findings as blatantly irresponsible and inflammatory. Associations and area leaders fanned communal wrath by addressing the incident as an important community issue. This particular episode, for example, became one of the East Harlem politician Vito Marcantonio's battle cries on behalf of his Puerto Rican constituency. The congressman from the Twentieth District advocated in support of Puerto Rican children whom he viewed as victims of subtle discrimination resulting from adverse classifications based on IQ tests. In administering these tests, Marcantonio contended, Puerto Rican children were placed in unfavorable positions because of inadequate allowances for social, economic, linguistic, and environmental factors.[45]

One journal, *Revista de Artes y Letras,* added its voice to the furor against the Chamber's actions. Josefina Silva de Cintrón's editorial called for community unity on this issue, Hispanic community representation among the examining committee, and the administration of the questionable examinations to a control group of non-Puerto Rican children living under similar socio-economic conditions.[46] Unequivocably believing the Chamber of Commerce's mode of operation was unfair and the results of interpretations inconclusive, *La Liga* agreed with the recommendations set forth in *Artes y Letras.* Adding yet another recommendation to the *Revista's, La Liga* suggested the creation of a Spanish-speaking teachers' committee and offered a list of suitable candidates for that purpose. These recommendations were apparently ignored by the non-Hispanic community.

In addition to the more publicized activities in which *La Liga* participated, the association sponsored numerous cultural acts and festivities. Determined to serve the Spanish-speaking *colonias* as a resource center, the group took the lead in matters affecting the future of Puerto Rican children, established courses for them and for the education of adults in Spanish on political and sociological topics, and sponsored the celebration of literary and artistic endeavors through conferences or *veladas.*

If groups like the *Liga Puertorriqueña e Hispana* and the Porto Rican Brotherhood personified sentinel associations, concerned with the representation, protection, and perpetuation of the city's Spanish-speaking, other groups also formed based on subgroup or individual interests. Responding to different needs, defining other issues, these groups drew a varied constituency. The *Club Ibero-Americano* and *La Asociación Latino Americana,* for example, appealed to the small group of well-educated elites and emphasized cultural heritage, language, Hispanic traditions, and professionalism.[47] Others, like the *Ateneo Obrero* and the *Alianza Obrera,* drew their membership primarily from the working class. The first proposed the expansion of Hispanic literary and artistic expression focusing on the educational development of the new Puerto Rican generation, most of whom had been born in New York. The second group promoted class awareness and related to the workers' syndicalist movements in the city. Similarly, groups such as *Puerto Rico Literario* catered to the special interest of Puerto Rican writers. Finally, the hometown or regional clubs responded to more basic needs, providing both social and recreational activities for the incoming migrant.

Among the earliest hometown clubs, the *Club Caborrojeño* was founded during the early twenties especially for migrants from the town of Cabo Rojo. Its purposes included providing social, civic, cultural, and recreational activities for its membership. The club depended on dues whenever possible and on fund raising for its budget. Originally envisioned as a nostalgic endeavor where migrants from the same geographic location could interact within a familial setting, the hometown clubs grew in membership and in importance until they became integral units of the Spanish-speaking neighborhoods.[48] Within a short period, clubs like *Mayaguezanos Ausente, Hijos de Penuelas* or *Hijos de Camuy* dominated the social organizational network.

These groups progressed from social clubs to more sophisticated units when they began to provide social services along with their informal activities. Tasks designed to alleviate the migrant's feelings of alienation covered a wide range depending on the specific association. It was not unusual among the older clubs to offer job-related information; to visit the sick, aiding with monetary contributions; composing and typing letters or other correspondence in English; resolving problems with written contracts; organizing demonstrations for protesting the myriad incidents which made up the migrant's condition; and other similar tasks. The club's rent and other utilities, stationery, and miscellaneous needs were paid from activities conducted among the members, and collections were often taken to meet emergency expenditures.[49]

The neighborhood clubs or hometown groups of the twenties and thirties evolved at a time when the survival of the individual and the community was at its most tenuous. The hometown club provided migrants with an oasis in an otherwise hostile territory, served to link the New York environment with the village or island town they had left behind, and in general cushioned the inevitable adjustment. Already composed of a membership which knew one another either directly or by word of mouth, the clubs also served as a substitution for the extended family and friends left in Puerto Rico. In years to come, these would mark the highlight of grass-roots involvement among Puerto Ricans and, united under the Federation of *El Congreso de los Pueblos,* constitute the backbone of the Puerto Rican Day Parade in New York City.

SPECIAL INTEREST GROUPS

By the last half of the decade of the thirties, other groups emerged to rival the veteran associations of the twenties. Some continued to form in the patterns of federation. *La Confederación de Sociedades Puertorriqueñas,* for example, founded under the directorship of José Camprubi, editor of *La Prensa,* attempted to function as an umbrella agency representing several community groups, but this type of organization would not be as effective as those which came before.[50] At least three factors mitigated against the success of federations during this period. First, *La Liga Puertorriqueña* was still in operation and other federated groups would serve to splinter and duplicate its functions; second, social service agencies which became more intensive in their response to the Depression communities duplicated many of the services provided by the older Hispanic units; third, many of the groups which bridged the period of the thirties and early forties appeared to be more professionally or occupationally oriented, not expanding their concerns to the community at large, but rather limiting their purposes to their own interests, issues, and survival. One exception was the community settlement house, Casita María, which provided social services for over twenty-five thousand Puerto Ricans since its establishment by the Trinitarian nun Sister Carmelita in 1934.[51]

Similarly, groups like the Club Eugenio María de Hostos, part of whose membership came from *La Liga Puertorriqueña* and the Puerto Rico Civic Club, exemplified societies which focused on internal issues. The Club de Hostos termed itself a cultural or educational association, and its purposes for coming together included stressing Hispanic culture, offering classes in Spanish, and sponsoring literary conferences and *veladas.* The Puerto Rico Civic Club, on the other hand, sought to: "further, promote and foster the sociability and friendship between the members of its association; to volunteer aid and assist the said members in times of sickness and distress; and in general, to do all the things a social civic group would do."[52]

Perhaps the best example of a successful organization oriented around special needs and specific interests was the Spanish Grocer's Association. Cited by Fitzpatrick as one of the oldest groups to operate in the Spanish-speaking community, the association began in 1937 as the Spanish Merchants' Association and continues to function to the present.[53] Founded at a time when the growth of the small businesses within the community paralleled the physical growth of the early settlements, its purposes for incorporation testified to its concern with the welfare of the merchants. Covering several areas of importance for the merchant membership, the group formed to:

1. Unite all Hispanic merchants in the City of New York, socially, fraternally, and commercially

2. Better their living conditions through better social and business ethics

3. Assess and assist effectively the problems facing the Hispanic merchant

4. Protect the close union of all Hispanic merchants established in the State of New York

5. Organize and maintain a center for information and advice[54]

This interest group succeeded in bringing together the owners of numerous small *bodegas* or *colmados* which dotted many Puerto Rican neighborhoods in the *colonias*. The Merchants' Association became a significant group in aiding the advancement of Puerto Ricans into small private businesses.[55] They published a newsletter which became a sophisticated enterprise entitled *FUERZA: Órgano Informativo de los Comerciantes y la Comunidad*. Here the *colonias'* merchants publicized and photographically illustrated their many activities, advertised their products, and kept the merchants informed of events in Puerto Rico and in the United States. Furthermore, the association served to police its own ranks, operating as an internal better businessmen's bureau and also guiding its membership in dealing with the business and banking institutions of the city.[56]

While the Merchants' Association functioned as an orientation point for the businessmen of the Spanish-speaking settlements, the civil service workers forged their own groups to provide social and civic direction. The Puerto Rican Veteran's Welfare Postal Workers' Association became incorporated in 1951, but the connection between the Puerto Rican worker and civil service dated to the twenties. Post office employees, schoolteachers, and social workers included Puerto Ricans among their ranks. By 1926 the Brotherhood's report charged, "400 (four hundred), more or less Porto Ricans are holding different ranking positions with the Postal Service and about six are with custom house service in the city of New York."[57] Within a decade, *Revista de Artes y Letras* listed an organization named *Asociación de Empleados Civiles de Correo* whose purpose for joining together was both civic and social in nature.[58]

With the onset of the Second World War, Puerto Ricans were hired as postal workers in greater numbers. Many filled essential positions as censors in that agency's departments. Bernardo Vega, who worked as a censor during the war years, affirmed that over one thousand Puerto Ricans were employed in that division, many of whom held university or advanced degrees, were college professors, distinguished writers, and artists. All were required to pass a civil service examination which demonstrated their proficiency in at least two languages as well as other subjects.[59]

Another migrant employed by the censorship department at that time was Raquel Rivera Hernández. A recent college graduate, Doña Raquel's first job consisted of intercepting civilian mail en route to Spain, Latin America, and the Spanish Caribbean. Rivera Hernández believed her work with the Post Office was essential to the war effort. Her goals were to perform her responsibilities as efficiently as possible and to support the workers' group which coalesced around the Spanish-speaking employees. This group sponsored recreational activities, fund raisers for important causes or for the group's own projects, cultural events, and extravaganzas in which the talents of the employees themselves were the main attraction. Doña Raquel often marveled at the numbers of talented and well-educated Puerto Ricans who, through unforeseen circumstances, found themselves working together in the city's Post Office. Had the Puerto Rican community harnessed the potential leadership and ability displayed within this setting, it would have made a tremendous impact at a crucial period in the development of Puerto Rican settlements, according to Doña Raquel.[60] But this group alienated itself from political or leadership situations and failed to assert itself as a community representative. Their reasons for uniting were probably not unlike those expressed in the certificate of incorporation of 1951. These were:

> To promote friendship and encourage social and intellectual intercourse among veterans born in Puerto Rico employed in the service of the United States of America; to disseminate among its members and families knowledge and practices for health advancement in civic spheres, and in their call; to sponsor social activities among them, all to the exclusion of political subjects, said corporation being non-sectarian and non-political, and in general, to promote the general and social well-being of its members in a social and civic manner.[61]

Conclusion

Thus the Puerto Rican community of the period before the Second World War was defined in yet another perspective—its organizational structure. Groups evolved to meet the needs of the pioneer settlements based on common interests and in response to changes within the migrant situation. The first groups, mutual aid societies and trade unions, served the needs of a relatively small community of skilled workers who lived close to the tobacco factories of Chelsea and the Lower East Side. These continued to follow the patterns of counterpart active groups on the island, identified with the workers' struggles on an international level, but formed for the specific benefit of their New York members. With the numerical growth of the *colonia* and its eventual concentration in East Harlem and Brooklyn, two other types of groups predominated: the fraternal, which represented the community on a city-wide basis; and the hometown group which began simply as a place where migrants from the same hometown, feeling lost in the unfamiliar city, came together. Thus, where one group concentrated on the external issues affecting the early settlements, the other focused on the internal needs of the migrants in an alien environment.

By the mid-thirties and into the war years, many groups appeared to turn inward, once again satisfying the special needs of their specialized membership. Here again we can see a return to the organizational patterns of the earlier decades, this time decidedly motivated by the creation of city government agencies designed to smooth the adjustment of the newcomers. One prime example was the Migration Division of the Labor Department of Puerto Rico, established in New York in 1948 to clear migrants for jobs, provide them with proper identification, and refer those needing help to appropriate public agencies.[62] Another was the Mayor's Committee on Puerto Rican Affairs established by William O'Dwyer in 1949. These groups proposed to investigate problems associated with the migration and provide leadership and supervision in solving them. These agencies thus aided in duplication and eventual eradication of many grass-roots groups which had previously provided social services.

Clearly the issue is not whether or not a communal organizational network existed within the pioneer settlements, but rather how such a network managed to survive at all. The predominantly working-class nature of the *colonias* prohibited many migrants from becoming active members of any group. We can only speculate then on how many individuals could actually afford to spend their time supervising or planning activities, fund raising, publicizing group events, attending meetings, and recruiting membership after an eight-hour day[63] at the factory. That groups functioned as they did and received the support from the community which they did is a tribute to the Puerto Rican community structure and to the individual's own sense of commitment. As social and civic associations grouped around occupations or special interests and non-Puerto Rican city-wide agencies became more dominant, other groups would emerge to deal with the host society. To an extent the political units which had been in operation since the turn of the century would help provide models in this direction.

Notes

1. Elena Padilla, *Up from Puerto Rico* (New York: Columbia University Press, 1958). See also Lawrence R. Chenault, *The Puerto Rican Migrant in New York* (New York: Columbia University Press, 1938; reissue, Russell & Russell, 1970).

2. Nathan Glazer and Daniel Patrick Moynihan, *Beyond the Melting Pot* (Cambridge: MIT Press, 1968), pp. 101–107.

3. Irving Howe, *World of Our Fathers* (New York: Simon and Schuster, 1976), pp. 183–184. See also Puerto Rican Forum, *A Study of Poverty Conditions in the New York Puerto Rican Community* (New York: Puerto Rican Forum, Inc., 1964); Carlota Suárez, "Don Ralph Rosas, Puerto Rico en Nueva York: Visión y Práctica" (unpublished manuscript, Department of Educational Services, Brooklyn College).

4. Donald Stewart, *A Short History of East Harlem* (New York: Museum of the City of New York, 1972), pp. 49–50.

5. Ibid., p. 52.

6. Adalberto López and James Petras, *Puerto Rico and the Puerto Ricans: Studies in History and Society* (New York: Schenkman Publishing Co., 1974), pp. 328–329.

7. Ibid. See also Clara E. Rodríguez, "Puerto Ricans in the Melting Pot," *The Journal for Ethnic Studies,* vol. 1, no. 4 (winter 1974), pp. 89–97; Herbert Hill, "Guardian of the Sweatshops," in Lopez and Petras, pp. 384–416.

8. Chenault, *The Puerto Rican Migrant,* p. 149.

9. The phenomenon of constant reformation of organizations was not

limited to the Puerto Rican community. Roy V. Peel comments on it among non-Hispanic groups as well. See Roy V. Peel, *The Political Clubs of New York City* (New York: G.P. Putnam & Sons, 1935), pp. 138-147.

10. Rosa Estades, "Patterns of Political Participation Among Puerto Ricans in New York City" (New School for Social Research, Ph.D. Dissertation, 1974), chapter 3.

11. Ibid., p. 71.

12. Ibid., p. 72.

13. Puerto Rican Forum, *Study of Poverty Conditions,* p. 12.

14. Ibid., p. 12.

15. Miles Galvin, "The Early Development of the Organized Labor Movement in Puerto Rico," *Latin American Perspectives,* vol. 111, no. 3 (summer 1976), pp. 17-33. See also Angel Quintero Rivera, "La clase obrera y el proceso político en Puerto Rico," *Revista de Ciencias Sociales,* nos. 1-4, 1974; Juan Carreras, "Bandera Roja," in Jose Ferrer y Ferrer, *Los ideales del siglo XX,* pp. 125-134.

16. Galvin, "Early Development," pp. 17-33.

17. Ibid., p. 24. Luisa Capetillo, "Recuerdos a la Federación Libre de Trabajadores," in Angel Quintero Rivera, *Lucha Obrera en Puerto Rico* (Rio Piedras: CEREP, 1971).

18. César Andreu Iglesias, ed., *Memorias de Bernardo Vega* (Rio Piedras: Ediciones Huracan, Inc., 1977), p. 123.

19. Ibid., p. 147.

20. Howe, p. 184 and p. 311 for reference to functions and growth of the Workmen's Circle during the early decades of this century. Also interview with Homero Rosado, Brooklyn, New York, October 1980. This individual was active in socialist organizations and affirms there was ethnic integration within this group.

21. Iglesias, *Memorias,* pp. 144-147.

22. Howe, *The World,* p. 239.

23. W. D. Evans, "Effects of Mechanization on Cigar Manufacturing," *Works Progress Administration Report No. B-4* (Washington, D.C.: Government Printing Office, 1934).

24. The Porto Rican Brotherhood of America, "Puerto Rico in New York," Brotherhood Newsletter, 1926.

25. *Gráfico,* September 2, 1928 and August 12, 1928.

26. Porto Rican Brotherhood of America, Certificate of Incorporation, File No. 05660-27C, March 23, 1927, New York City County Clerk's Office, Municipal Building, New York City. See also Peel, *The Political Clubs,* p. 141.

27. *El Imparcial,* cited in the Porto Rican Brotherhood of America Souvenir Program, June 1926. It is not clear if the reference to fifty members

meant additional new members for the month or for the organization's entire membership roster.

28. Taller de Migración, Centro de Estudios Puertorriqueños, *Cuaderno de la migración* (New York: Centro de Estudios Puertorriqueños, Graduate Center, CUNY), April 1974.

29. Porto Rican Brotherhood of America, Annual Report, June 1926. See also Iglesias, *Memorias,* p. 178.

30. Porto Rican Brotherhood of America, Annual Report, June 1926. The Resident Commissioner was the nonvoting, nonspeaking observer in the U.S. Congress who represented the interests of Puerto Rico.

31. See Antonio S. Pedreira, *Un hombre del pueblo: José Celso Barbosa* (San Juan: Instituto de Cultura, 1965); Philip Sterling and María Brau, *The Quiet Rebels* (New York: Doubleday, 1968).

32. *New York Times,* July 27, 1926, p. 21.

33. Iglesias, *Memorias,* p. 188.

34. Ibid.

35. *New York Times,* July 30, 1926, p. 29.

36. Ibid., August 9, 1926, p. 5.

37. *La Prensa,* January 15, 1923, p. 1.

38. *New York Times,* August 9, 1926, p. 5.

39. Ibid.

40. *Gráfico,* April 3, 1927, p. 13.

41. La Liga Puertorriqueña e Hispana, Certificate of Incorporation, File No. 056-59-27c, March, 1928, County Clerk's Office, Municipal Building, New York City.

42. Iglesias, *Memorias,* pp. 223–225.

43. Ibid.

44. Ibid., p. 224.

45. *Revista de Artes y Letras,* March 1936. See also The Marcantonio Collection, New York Public Library, Archival Division, Boxes 2, 3, 4; Salvatore La Gumina, *The People's Politician* (Iowa: Kendall Hunt Publishing Co., 1969), p. 48.

46. *Revista de Artes y Letras.*

47. *New York Times,* February 3, 1924, p. 23. See also Iglesias, *Memorias,* pp. 137, 147.

48. Rosa Estades, "Symbolic Unity: The Puerto Rican Day Parade," in Clara E. Rodríguez, Virginia Sánchez Korrol, and José Oscar Alers, eds., *The Puerto Rican Struggle: Essays on Survival in the U.S.* (New York: Puerto Rican Migration Research Consortium, 1980), pp. 82–89. See also Carlota Suárez, "Don Ralph Rosas."

49. Puerto Rican Forum, *Study of Poverty Conditions,* p. 60.

50. Iglesias, *Memorias,* p. 242.

51. *New York Times,* November 19, 1961. Interview with Sister Carmelita Bonilla, Puerto Rican Oral History Project, 1973–1974, Long Island Historical Society, Brooklyn, New York. See also Anthony Stevens Arroyo, "Puerto Rican Struggles in the Catholic Church," in Rodríguez, Sánchez Korrol, and Alers, pp. 129–139.

52. The Puerto Rico Civic Club, Certificate of Incorporation, File No. 10884-33c, September 15, 1933, County Clerk's Office, Municipal Building, New York City.

53. Interview with Antonio Moreau, secretary, Hispanic Merchants' Association, Bronx, New York, July 1976.

54. *Fuerza,* August–September 1975.

55. Joseph P. Fitzpatrick, *Puerto Rican-Americans* (Englewood Cliffs, N.J.: Prentice-Hall, 1971), pp. 62–63.

56. Antonio Moreau interview.

57. Porto Rican Brotherhood of America, Souvenir Program.

58. *Revista de Artes y Letras,* cited in Estades, *Patterns,* p. 72.

59. Interviews with Antonio and Raquel Rivera Hernández, Rio Piedras, Puerto Rico, August 1977. See also Carlota Suárez, "Don Ralph Rosas," p. 2; Iglesias, *Memorias,* pp. 255–256.

60. Raquel Rivera Hernández interview.

61. Puerto Rican Employees Association, Certificate of Incorporation, File No. 68070-36c, 1936, County Clerk's Office; Puerto Rican Veteran's Welfare Postal Workers' Association, File No. 5440-70-3, 1951, County Clerk's Office.

62. Carlota Suárez, "Don Ralph Rosas," pp. 7–12.

63. Homero Rosado interview. It is estimated that although the actual active membership of an average organization might not number more than one hundred individuals, the functions given by organizations, dances, conferences, etc. might draw additional membership and guests numbering well over two hundred. Based on oral interviews with persons active in early settlement organizations, this appears to be the case for most of the groups.

Politics, Issues, and Participation in Puerto Rican Colonias

If the movement toward sociocultural, social service, and fraternal organizations structured the internal dynamics of the Puerto Rican communities, their political associations went one step further. These provided the rubric for interacting with the host society, for solidifying their identity as a community, and for addressing the relevant political issues of the period. Bostered by a long tradition of political activity in Puerto Rico, political units were among the earliest to emerge in the New York *colonias*. But while the island-related groups formed in the late nineteenth century focused on the colonial relationship between Spain and Puerto Rico, those appearing in New York after 1898 provided communal leadership and facilitated interaction between the settlements and the dominant political system.

Before the Spanish-American War in 1898, Puerto Rican political organizations in New York represented an extension of island politics for the handful of migrants living in the city. The first Puerto Rican political units formed in New York were composed of exiles fighting for independence from Spain. In 1895 they created the Puerto Rican branch of the Cuban Revolutionary Party. Highly organized and working along with the respected Cuban leader José Martí were Puerto Rican patriots such as Sótero Figueroa or Julio J. Henna. Other survivors of the ill-fated Lares insurrection like Juan de Mata Terraforte and Antonio Vélez Alvarado attracted

Latin American supporters, also forced exiles from their countries,
to the cause of Antillean freedom. This type of revolutionary fer-
vor and activity, basically unconnected with New York non-Hispanic political patterns, was instrumental in the formation of other
Latin supportive associations. One of these was the *Club Borinquen* led by Sótero Figueroa, aimed at propagating the cause of
Cuban and Puerto Rican liberation through community newsletters
and organs like *El Porvenir* and *La Revolución*. Another was *La
Liga Artesanos* and its sister organization, *La Liga Antillana*.

Founded initially as a cultural and civic association, *La Liga
Artesanos* disseminated propaganda and raised funds for independence. Among the names of its founding members were active,
organizationally minded individuals who were repeatedly represented on the rosters of numerous early associations. *La Liga Are-
sanos,* for example, listed the aforementioned Sótero Figueroa
along with Flor Braega and Felipe Rodríguez as members. *La Liga
Antillana,* on the other hand, held the distinction of being a racially
integrated women's group, composed predominantly of working-
class women. It was considered among the first of its kind within
the Hispanic settlements, and besides supporting Spanish and
Caribbean independence, focused much of its attention on fund
raising and cultural presentations. Because of the group's interra-
cial composition, however, the association was often denied access
to many meeting places in the city, thus they held their reunions in
the Masonic Temple, Hardman Hall, or the meeting rooms of the
Socialist Party. Here distinguished guests gathered including José
Martí, Figueroa, and Pachín Marín. Active revolutionaries, both
Marín and Martí gained recognition as poets and essayists as well.[1]
Others, including Lola Rodríguez de Tío, poetess and author of the
island's revolutionary anthem, and Arturo Schomberg, specialist in
black Caribbean and Spanish-American history, also took part in
the group's activities. Both *Ligas* were believed to have been frequented predominantly by tobacco workers, skilled laborers, and
their families, who were among the earliest Puerto Rican settlers in
Brooklyn and Manhattan.[2]

Besides the groups already cited, other organizations, political,
social and civic in orientation, fleshed out the communal structure of
the turn-of-the-century Puerto Rican settlements in both boroughs
(see Map 8 and Table 12). Many of these turned toward events hap-

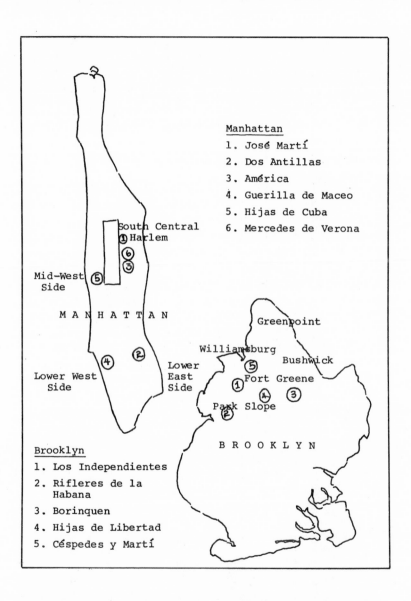

MAP 8 Geographic Location of Hispanic Organizations in Brooklyn and Manhattan

TABLE 12
Geographic Location and Officers of Active Hispanic Associations in Brooklyn and Manhattan, circa 1895

NAME	LOCATION	OFFICERS
Manhattan		
1. José Martí	1642 Park Avenue Manhattan	B. H. Portuondo Sotero Figueroa Felipe Rodríguez
2. Dos Antillas	1758 Third Avenue Manhattan	Roseando Rodríguez Arturo A. Schomberg
3. América	231 E. 61st Street Manhattan	J. R. Álvarez E. M. Amoros
4. Guerilla de Maceo	146 W. 24th Street Manhattan	Juan B. Beato Juan Fernández
5. Hijas de Cuba	116 W. 64th Street Manhattan	Angela R. de Quesada Carmen Matillas

6. Mercedes de Verona	235 E. 75th Street Manhattan	Inocencia M. de Figueroa Emma Betancourt

Brooklyn

1. Los Independientes	839 Fulton Street Brooklyn	Juan Frago Genero Baez
2. Rifleres de la Habana	2141 Pacific Street Brooklyn	Antonio Camero Adelaido Marín
3. Borinquen	129 McDougal Street Brooklyn	J. M. Torreforte Domingo Collazo
4. Hijas de Libertad	1115 Herkimer Street Brooklyn	Natividad R. de Gallo Gertrudis Casano
5. Céspedes y Martí	2012 Fulton Street Brooklyn	Petrona Calderón Juana Rosario

Source: Based on César Andreu Iglesias (ed.), *Memorias de Bernardo Vega.*

pening in Puerto Rico, and while they served to unite the exiled population of the small *colonias,* it was understood that their concerns were for the homeland and not for the future of the pioneer settlements in New York. In fact, the existence of a permanent community outside of Puerto Rico was not within their frame of reference. With the culmination of the Spanish-American War, these groups became inactive, but the example set by the associations and their leadership was not easily forgotten by the early migrant settlers. Inasmuch as some community leaders like Dr. Henna and the Figueroa brothers continued to exert direction in the New York settlements after 1898, they were instrumental in the foundation of new groups now concerned with the stabilization of Puerto Rican migrant status within a North American orbit.[3]

Thus the influences of the pre-twentieth-century political organizations on the infant Puerto Rican settlements were significant. First, groups composed of a Spanish-speaking membership existed and operated as politically oriented units in New York City, setting a precedent for this type of activity. Second, many of the original leaders of these units exerted similar dynamics in the new post-1898 associations, bringing together a small but effective cadre of experienced organizers within the pioneer settlements.

Political Groups After the Spanish-American War

The new units to appear after 1900 responded to the political and economic pressures faced by the migrants in New York as well as the political issues affecting the island. Responding also to the internal insecurities inherent in the massive relocation of a people struggling to survive in alien surroundings, the new political associations provided supportive units which reaffirmed migrant values and interests. It was not unusual for such groups to set aside funds for needy Hispanic families, offer advice on housing and job inquiries, perform charitable deeds, and provide social and recreational outlets. Migrant interviews attest to the direct involvement of organization members in the everyday problems of the migrant community. This involvement ranged from playing on baseball and other sport teams to removing the furniture of evicted tenants from city sidewalks back into their apartments. The latter activity reinitiated lengthy eviction proceedings which allowed the migrants to accumulate the necessary rents in the interim. Thus the relationship between the groups and the *colonia* rested firmly on personal considerations from the very start.

Utilizing a paternalistic approach, the clubs assumed a familiar role in settlement structure, not unlike the *hacendado-agregado* relationship still in effect within the island's predominantly agrarian society. The *hacendado,* or landowner, by virtue of his social and economic status, traditionally protected and provided for the welfare of his workers. The *agredados,* landless peasants or sharecroppers, sought the favors and protection of the *hacendado,* usually through their good work and loyalty. Based on a rigid class structure, deference, and personalism, Puerto Rican workers were conditioned to respond best to those relationships rooted in personal contact.

As early as 1918, the first Puerto Rican political clubs patterned on a paternalism-patronage model and connected with the New York City political party system took shape. These were the *Club Demócrata Puertorriqueño* in Brooklyn headed by Joaquin Colón and J. V. Alonso; the Harlem Branch of the Manhattan Democratic Party whose leaders J. C. Caballero and Domingo Collazo had participated in the organizations of the turn of the century; and the Puerto Rican Committee of the Socialist Party which included among its founders the community activists Bernardo Vega, Jesus Colón, and Homero Rosado.[4] Following the examples set by other immigrant groups and Hispanic associations before them, the Brooklyn clubs offered a wide range of activities and sponsored dances, sports programs, and social services. The clubs made provision for health referrals, legal aid, and advice on housing and employment as well as counseling on other working-class problems. Credited with spearheading political organization in that borough, Carlos Tapia and Luis F. Weber became the power brokers between the Brooklyn Democratic Party and the Puerto Rican *colonia.* As such, they commanded respect as informal intercommunity leaders while at the same time receiving a degree of acknowledgment as intermediaries from the borough's wider Democratic organization leaders, Frank V. Kelly and John H. McCoy.[5]

During the twenties and early thirties, political activity continued to increase as did the migrant population. One individual outlined the borough's Puerto Rican political history in the following manner:

> It is to be noted that up to the year 1927 when the Liberty Republican Club was organized in "El Barrio" (then part of Harlem's 14th Assembly District, Manhattan) by Puerto Ricans all the Puerto Rican political organizations in the city of New York originated in Brooklyn. The Puerto Rican Democratic Club, Inc.—1923—operated in the 1st Assembly District, as did the later—1928–1932—De Hostos and Guaybana Democratic Clubs. The Betances Democratic Club, Inc., founded by Carolos Tapia and other Puerto Ricans in 1918, operated in the 3rd Assembly District. The Baldorioty Democratic Club, Inc.—1932—operated in the Navy Yard area in those days in part of the 4th Assembly District and the Tompkins and Marcy Avenues, then part of the 6th Assembly District. The Guarionex Democratic Club, Inc.—1929—operated in the Greenpoint area then part of the 15th Assembly District and densely populated by Puerto Ricans.[6]

Almost all the clubs listed incorporated under the names of past Puerto Rican political figures, honoring the memory of patriots like Betances, de Hostos, or Baldorioty or indigenous persons like Guarionex or Guaybana. In this way the club originators appealed to the migrants' dual sense of pride and patriotism. In actuality, these were subsidiary political clubs some of which were but loosely connected with the Brooklyn Democratic Party machinery. It was also significant that the major part of political action among Puerto Ricans centered in Brooklyn rather than Manhattan.

As the first seat of Puerto Rican settlement, the Brooklyn *colonia* developed along the same lines as did the Manhattan settlement, but more of the Brooklyn Puerto Rican clubs outrightly admitted their political orientation than did the other. Incorporated into the city of New York in 1898, Brooklyn along with the Bronx and Staten Island maintained less rigid patterns of political participation. Conversely, political growth in Manhattan dominated by Tammany Hall, was stunted along racial, ethnic, and geographic lines. The Harlem area in which the Spanish-speaking population predominated had been divided into four Assembly Districts to discourage the political ascendency of Jewish or black District leaders.[7] While a proliferation of Hispanic political clubs was not evident in Manhattan, there did exist a concentration of sociocultural and fraternal associations, many of which appeared frequently in political affairs or expressed their positions on political issues.

While funding for the functioning of political organizations often depended on the meager dues of their working-class membership, dances, pageants, contests, and other fund raisers added to the club treasury. Significantly, much of the outside funding for the Brooklyn clubs during the first decades of the century came from the *colonias' boliteros,* or numbers-game operators. As an assistant secretary to the Puerto Rican Democratic Club and later as president of the Baldorioty Democratic Club, Ramon Colón recalled raising money in the offices of the local Puerto Rican *bolitero.* These individuals were in no way regarded as lawbreakers within the *colonias,* and several migrants testified that the people involved in the numbers rackets were often thought of as modern-day Robin Hoods. Alluding to the outside funding, Colón remarked:

> The principal donors were the numbers game *bolita* operators at that time. Their response was always prompt and generous. It seemed that the financial help given by them to the Puerto Rican Democratic organizations paid off in the form of political "protection" for their numbers game operation.[8]

Luis Felipe Weber, a Puerto Rican migrant recognized by both the Spanish-speaking community and the non-Hispanic society as a leader among Puerto Ricans in Brooklyn, was involved in the numbers rackets as well as in the political organizations of the twenties and thirties. Weber's sister, Doña Honorina, admittedly scorned the rackets in which he was linked, but conceded that community attitudes toward Weber's role as a *bolitero* were seldom negative or condemning. Her recollections of her brother's role in the Brooklyn settlement emphasize instead his contributions rather than his involvement in the numbers game. More important, Doña Honorina's remembrances present a picture of the operation of both clubs and leaders which solidly fit the Puerto Rican clubs into a paternalistic mold:

Luis was the one who took care of the unfortunate Puerto Ricans. In fact, he was called the father of the Puerto Ricans. He made a little fortune and whenever anybody needed help either because of illness or lack of employment he was ready to give his help or to get it through politics. He had three political clubs. None of the members paid any dues. Luis funded the clubs himself. One on Adams Street—Agueybana; Betances on Sackett Street and Hostos on Jefferson Street. These were all Democratic Clubs. I remember that during the holidays they donated over two hundred baskets of groceries, toys and confections to needy families.[9]

Clearly Weber's role as a bolitero in Brooklyn partly laid the financial groundwork for working-class migrant political activities. As a prominent *colonia* leader and patron, Weber was credited with building playgrounds for neighborhood recreation, donating food baskets, and extending a helping hand when needed. In many ways this justified his internal community leadership role. Weber, moreover, represented the Puerto Rican community outside of the Brooklyn settlement, acting as an intermediary or power broker between the migrants and the dominant political party structure. Yet his involvement in *la bolita* raised more questions than acceptance. How legitimate was Weber in his role as community leader, under these circumstances, and to what extent were the Brooklyn neighborhoods gaining from the arrangement?

For the most part, Puerto Ricans viewed the numbers game as a harmless pastime not connecting nickel and dime bets with illegal racketeering. Betting on numbers or combinations of numbers significant to the bettor, perhaps based on dreams or premonitions, the migrants sought to realize their fantasies. A winning bet yielding perhaps $150 to $200 meant a return trip to Puerto Rico, or new furnishings and clothing, or monetary gifts for family members and a tip for the *bolitero,* who made it all possible in the first place. The *bolitero,* on the other hand, symbolized someone who had succeeded, to a degree, in conquering the new environment, who beat the system, but remained true to his people in the community. He was also, on occasion, the neighborhood connection, visiting a series of homes or stores on his collection rounds. Commanding respect based on his economic and social status in the *colonia,* the *bolitero* also lived comfortably, able to afford such luxuries as cars or telephones.

Nevertheless, by the mid-1930s the Puerto Rican Democratic clubs made a conscious effort to sever the association with the numbers game. At a meeting of all the Brooklyn Hispanic branch officers it was decided to rely solely on membership dues and other more acceptable means of fund raising. In a speech delivered by community leader Carlos Tapia to this assembly, he praised the unique working relationship in the past between the clubs and the boliteros recognizing that the alliance had been a necessary evil for both parties:

> Without it, these clubs, perhaps would not have been possible, but we cannot continue this way, because there is a feeling among our people that neither the regular party leaders nor the community would have any respect for our organizations as long as these situations continue. Luis and I (referring to Luis Felipe Weber) have talked about the problem and he agrees with me that it is about time we get due political recognition and respect from the regular party leaders.[10]

If "due political recognition and respect from the regular party leaders" concerned Carlos Tapia, just what was the relationship between the New York City political party system and the Puerto Rican clubs? Some researchers believe Puerto Ricans were not at all considered politically by the dominant Democratic or Republican party organizations. Others insisted Puerto Ricans failed to integrate themselves into city politics because they were not organizationally mature enough to do so.[11] But some felt a limited relationship did exist and that it was decidedly more beneficial for the dominant parties than for the Puerto Rican clubs. Based on this premise, the Puerto Rican community was given a semblance of political representation through the intercession of two non-Puerto Rican bosses, Jimmy Kelly and George McCure. Throughout the early thirties, these two individuals saw to it that any contact between Puerto Ricans and dominant party politics existed through them and because of this, Puerto Ricans were kept aloof from politics.[12]

Dominant Party Politics and the Puerto Rican Organizations

Along with minority party participation, especially the Socialist and Communist parties, Puerto Rican political club activity was indeed connected to dominant party politics. The concern for migrant welfare on the part of *colonia* organizations required a working relationship between the Puerto Rican associations and the political units of the larger non-Hispanic society. The Democratic party organization, traditionally the party of immigrants and the working class, functioned on paternalism and patronage patterns remarkably similar to the Puerto Rican clubs and familiar to the migrants themselves. Moreover, while Puerto Ricans would not be directly drawn into the city's political arena until the late forties and early fifties, the group as a potential voting bloc did not escape the notice of the New York politicians, particularly Democrats whose clubs outnumbered Republicans throughout the earlier decades.[13]

An association between European immigration and New York politicians can be traced to the mid-nineteenth century when Irish contractors connected with Tammany Hall brought over thousands of their countrymen on indenture, renting them out to canal builders in return for passage money.[14] Toward the last decades of the century when the Society of Tammany gained control of the Democratic Party in New York City and State, the immigration of Southern Italians and East European Jews was at its peak. These immigrants would participate in an association with Tammany Hall based on patronage and paternalism, the latter symbolized by the boss system. The boss or leader of the party organization on the borough or county level managed party affairs, often with an eye to his own private advantage. It was this individual, the party boss, along with the Assembly District leaders and the party faithful of the districts or neighborhood clubs throughout the city, who established the first contacts between the immigrant and American society. Meeting the boats at Ellis Island, the boss and his supporters assumed paternal responsibility for guiding the newcomer from alien status to citizenship, providing legal, housing and/or health aid, jobs, and even entertainment, for which the immigrant paid by loyal party support, party funding, and more important, the votes which kept the party in power. In exchange for their votes, the immigrants could turn to the local political machine when in need; party politicians and district clubs responded with holiday food baskets, annual picnics and clambakes.[15]

In the absence of a competitive civil service the boss system provided patronage on another level—jobs on the public payroll. The borough boss could reward a follower with a job as an office clerk, night watchman, garbage collector, street inspector, or policeman. For a price, saloons and gambling house owners in the city's ghettoes were protected from penalties on law violations; traffic tickets and jury notices were fixed; reduced tax assessments were procured; and building and sanitary code violations were overlooked. Theoretically, the party boss dealt with political matters only, but practically he was the economic overlord, social arbiter, unofficial government agent, and community patron.[16] All services rendered to the community by the district party were credited directly to him. Moreover, it was the party machine so closely connected with immigrant support and bossism which fostered political careers and influenced legislation through elected officials.

The unofficial union of party members into a cohesive self-governing society composed the city's "regular" Democratic or Republican clubs. These groups served as intermediaries between their constituency—the man on the street—and the city or state elected office holders. While the party's continued political entrenchment depended on votes, its objectives were to:

1. maintain political and financial control of the city and state.
2. advance the political fortunes of leaders, organizers of the group who exercised leadership functions.
3. improve political opportunities of the party membership.
4. develop loyalty to the party and as a result to serve the political interests of its membership.[17] With this end in mind, the clubs promoted social, civic, political, and welfare activities financed by private donations, fund raisers, and membership dues.

Leadership at the national level formed the apex of the party structure followed by leadership at the state, sectional, and regional levels. Among these were the County or Borough leaders. Their functions included the administration of party affairs through state and city-wide fund raising, collaboration, and consensus among themselves on political issues and supervising the election activities of their representatives on the local or district level, the Assembly District leaders. In the mid-thirties, seventy-six Assembly District leaders fulfilled their obligations as heads of the dominant clubs in sixty-two Assembly Districts. (Some districts had more than one leader.[18]) These individuals concerned themselves with "getting out the vote" and were charged with selecting captains and co-captains for each election district. These numbered from thirty to two hundred and fifty depending on the size of the Assembly District. Finally, the captains and co-captains supervised block captains, apartment house captains, and members of the election district committee (see Figure 4). Thus, when Tapia, Weber, and Ramón Colón became the power brokers between their clubs and county or district leaders, they were fulfilling roles in this capacity.

The political steps taken by Puerto Ricans in New York City during the late twenties and early thirties were intended to further the stability and ensure the permanence of the pioneer settlements. Puerto Rican political club leaders sought to trade welfare and social benefits for the migrant vote, and in turn aspired to deliver the votes to non-Hispanic politicians in exchange for patronage and protection. In this respect, the functions and objectives of these local units were similar to other political groups throughout the city; but while most of the latter constituted regular clubs within the dominant party structure, the Puerto Rican organizations fell into the category of subsidiary or "nationality" clubs.[19]

The clubs which occupied an undetermined or subsidiary status were categorized as: ordinary; nationality; racial or religious; or antisocial. These formed independently of the regular Assembly District leader, but often sought and received the recognition of the county, borough, or Assembly District leader. Recognition symbolized the acknowledgment by those above the local level, of the claims made by the clubs upon the rewards and resources of the party. A few groups existed without recognition, completely independently, and only the club name itself identified them with a particular party:

> The so-called "national" clubs are technically not part of the regular organization at all but they and other aristocratic

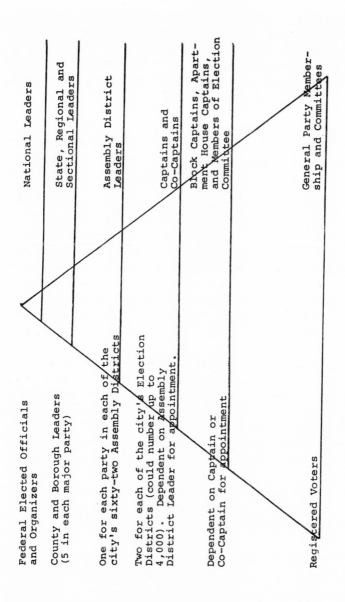

Figure 4 Party Structure and Function of Party Officials in New York, 1936

Federal Elected Officials
and Organizers

County and Borough Leaders
(5 in each major party)

One for each party in each of the
city's sixty-two Assembly Districts

Two for each of the city's Election
Districts (could number up to
4,000). Dependent on Assembly
District Leader for appointment.

Dependent on Captain or
Co-Captain for appointment

Registered Voters

National Leaders

State, Regional and
Sectional Leaders

Assembly District
Leaders

Captains and
Co-Captains

Block Captains, Apart-
ment House Captains,
and Members of Election
Committee

General Party Member-
ship and Committees

clubs may participate very frequently and significantly in normal political club activities. Another class comprises the nationality clubs whose local units may, or may not be integral parts of the Assembly District organization, but are affiliated with each other on a county-wide, city-wide, state-wide or national basis.[20]

Of the three categories, it was the nationality type to which the Puerto Rican clubs belonged. Nationality clubs embodied contradictory purposes. While they performed useful services in uniting heterogeneous groups into municipal, state, or national party politics, the organization also served as a disruptive force by upholding the particular traditions, language, and leadership of the ethnic group. The Puerto Rican locals did just that. Utilizing Spanish as the principal language of communication, the clubs were, after all, named for Puerto Rican historical and patriotic figures and perpetuated island heritage through the celebration of traditional holidays. Nevertheless, the necessity to support a city-wide political system through the electoral process, for the rewards garnered in terms of patronage, brought the group into contact with mainland politics. On the other hand, regular party leaders had no fixed purpose in stimulating the organization of nationality clubs for any reason other than the immediate one of harnessing votes. In fact, one of the financial obligations which the district leader agreeably accepted was the provision of payment of a few dollars for Puerto Rican poll watchers on election day.[21] One observer commented:

> The Czech, Armenian, Greek, French, Syrian, *Porto Rican,* Jewish, Ukranian and Hungarian clubs are generally affiliated with the Democratic Party but, since they are usually *starved for patronage,* their loyalty is uncertain. Most of them are "recognized" by the Tammany leaders only during campaigns.[22]

Subsidiary clubs including the nationality groups formed in several different ways. Some were organized on the initiative of the Assembly District Leader himself, who would invite members of a particular ethnic group to join him in the creation of such a club. Here, the leader would aid in securing club headquarters and would recognize his cofounders as captains or marshals in the city-wide party structure. Others came about on the initiative of the nationals themselves. These might have begun as social or civic groups which achieved political status when singled out by the regular party leaders for political purposes. A third method depended on the local club leaders assembling their compatriots as outright Democrats or Republicans. This was the case when Ramón Colón formed the Puerto Rican Republican Party Club in Brooklyn in 1935. After its formation, the club then seeks the support and affiliation of the regular party leaders. Finally, there were quasi-political units, such as social, fraternal, civic, or recreational groups, which in time acquired political interests and attitudes, reinforcing common heritage and traditions among their members and taking stands on relevant political issues.

The Puerto Rican Vote

If the recognition of Puerto Rican subsidiary groups rested on the potential voting bloc pledged to the regular party county or district leader, just how important was the Puerto Rican vote and how frequently did they, citizens since 1917, exercise this franchise? The answers to these questions are merely preliminary, since research on the political attitudes and the degree of participation in the *colonias* of the twenties, thirties, and forties is still scanty. Many Puerto Ricans obviously did not vote, for they were kept directly and indirectly from joining regular political clubs dominated by old-line Irish and Italians, and from participating in voter-connected activity.[23] Discouraged also by the unnerving experience of registration and submission to an English literacy test, a significant number of Puerto Ricans felt they had nothing to gain from electoral participation. As one migrant political activist who participated in community organizations during the period remarked:

> Many Puerto Ricans did not exercise their right to vote. In addition, it was not an easy matter to vote at that time. The officials submitted the aspirant to an interrogation with the purpose of frightening them and making them abandon their original political persuasions. This only served to keep Puerto Ricans away from the polls. But they [Puerto Ricans] also believed that they had nothing to look for in American politics.[24]

Yet as early as 1927, Fiorello La Guardia, congressman from East Harlem from 1923 to 1933 and subsequent Mayor of New York City, had courted the potential Puerto Rican vote. "Could you send me a list of Puerto Rican organizations located in my Congressional District?," he petitioned an aspiring Puerto Rican organization leader. "I would like to hear your plans as to the best way of getting Puerto Ricans interested. Do you know if they are interested in any particular legislation in Congress?"[25] However, it was always assumed by researchers like Chenault or Moynihan and Glazer that few Puerto Ricans responded to these overtures and that it was not until the mid-thirties that Hispanic and non-Hispanic politicians emerged who captured the imagination of the migrant voter.

Interestingly, the available evidence suggests the Puerto Ricans of the interwar years were far more politicized than previously assumed. One estimate is that over seven thousand registered Puerto Rican voters participated in the 1918 election of New York State Governor Alfred E. Smith. Most of these voters aligned themselves with the Democratic clubs of Brooklyn and Manhattan. A decade later, during the mid-twenties, the organizational report of the Porto Rican Brotherhood of America stated: "In the last general election of 1926, two thousand Porto Rican voters were credited to the 19th Congressional District while the entire registration for the city was over five thousand."

The next period in which a surge of electoral participation would occur among Puerto Rican voters was in the forties. Over 30,000 voters registered in Hispanic districts. Of these, 80 percent supported Franklin D. Roosevelt for the presidency and Vito Marcantonio for the East Harlem congressional seat.[26]

More personal indications of political activity appear in the migrants' own recollections of their experiences. Residents of the early Brooklyn community reported tremendous interest among the migrants in political organization and participation. One in particular, Guillerma Echevarria, devoted a good part of her time to political activities. Arriving in Brooklyn as a child in the early twenties from her native Vieques, most of Doña Guille's concerns were for the growth and integration of Puerto Ricans into the American political system. With an excellent command of both English and Spanish, she acted as an interpreter whenever Spanish-speaking individuals faced legal or bureaucratic entanglements. As a poll watcher, she was knowledgeable of the electoral processes, lecturing her neighbors on the power of the ballot and admonishing them not to abuse the privilege of casting their vote.[27]

In addition to electoral participation, at least two other factors guaranteed dominant party interest in cultivating Puerto Rican support. First, the decline in European immigration necessitated party support from other bases; second, the Seabury investigations' exposure of graft and corruption within the Democratic ranks reduced the power of the party in New York City.

Beginning with the twenties, European immigration began to decline at a time when the Puerto Rican settlements were both numerically and geographically expanding. While early-twentieth-century Jewish and Italian immigrants had found *Landsmanschaften* or regional associations already in existence upon their arrival, it had been the Democratic Party machinery which offered itself as political broker between the new immigrants and their new environment. Tammany Hall had traditionally given daily attention and assistance to the immigrant community through the boss system. But the First World War coupled with the first immigration restriction laws placed unfavorable quotas on Southern and Eastern European immigration, radically reducing the numbers of aliens coming to New York City.[28] The district political clubs, conditioned to transforming immigrants into ardent supporters and voting citizens, needed a new immigration to replace second and third generations of Europeans whose ties to the political machine were based more on convenience than necessity.

The Seabury investigations consisted of three separate probes running consecutively from 1930 to 1932, which included a full-scale exposure of corruption within the entire city government and resulted in virtually shattering the strength and credibility of the Democratic Party in New York. Moreover, by mid-decade President Franklin D. Roosevelt's New Deal program generated job-creating agencies such as the Works Progress Administration, Public Works Administration, Civil Conservation Corps, as well as social security and unemployment insurance programs on a nationwide scale, radically undermining the traditional paternalistic role of the city's party machine.[29]

Thus it was in the interest of the dominant party to court Puerto

Rican support. The Puerto Rican voter of the mid-twenties and thirties represented a replacement for the declining numbers of Italian and Jewish immigrants so important for the continued entrenchment of the party. Similarly, the Puerto Rican migrant leaders, dependent on patronage and protection for their community, sought due political recognition and respect from the regular party leaders and projected concerns which suggested the overriding importance of remaining within the Democratic party orbit. It was this organization, after all, which would provide the benefits, patronage, and protection for the Puerto Ricans as it had for immigrant groups before, forming bonds between city politics and the pioneer settlements not easily broken.

In the opinion of Puerto Rican community leaders, the relationship between the borough-wide Democratic party and the Puerto Rican local clubs was crucial for the survival of the Hispanic settlements. For example, in a perceptive dialogue with his colleagues, Carlos Tapia revealed practical and far-reaching ideas not only on the future of Puerto Ricans in New York's political affairs, but also on their own political future as a people. To achieve these aims, the working relationship between the city's politicians and the *colonias* remained top priority. Tapia explained the underlying basis for keeping an intact connection when he stated:

> So that when some unfortunate Puerto Rican is arrested by the police I can ask some politicians to talk to the judge on his behalf. So that I can ask the same politician to help some poor Puerto Rican who needs medical attention in some municipal hospital. . . . I am looking ahead for my people in Puerto Rico also and that is what every one of us should have in mind. The only way for our island to get political recognition is through the Puerto Ricans here in New York and in other states of the Union. Someday the Puerto Ricans in New York and in many other states of the United States, will by their political power get what our brothers on the island will never get, congressmen who in exchange for our help to elect them will have to help our beloved Puerto Rico. Someday our island will be a state like New York, or a republic like Cuba. Besides very soon we should be able to elect right here in New York, to begin with, some "Puerto Ricans" as aldermen.

Once we start doing that, the rest like electing Puerto Rican
district leaders and Puerto Rican assemblymen, etc., would
come as a matter of course.[30]

Tapia knew the importance of making personal contacts to
ensure the continuation of political favors which repaid loyal party
support. Among these were the eventual election of Puerto Rican
aldermen, district leaders, and assemblymen. More important, in
Tapia's opinion, these officials represented the vehicles through
which the political status of the island would be resolved. In this
way, the paternalistic relationship which had formerly existed
between the party politicians and other ethnic groups continued to
operate in the Puerto Rican settlement. Able to deal with district or
county politicians on a personal basis, a trait highly prized among
Puerto Ricans who functioned best within a network of personal
relationships, Tapia fostered associations designed to produce
immediate benefits for his people in the community.

Throughout the thirties and forties, political paternalism, personalism and concern for the Puerto Rican community in New
York and on the island continued to be integral factors in the political actions of *colonia* migrants. While the decade before was characterized by the domination of Democratic Party politics and its
conditioning on the Puerto Rican local clubs, succeeding decades
brought increased activity from rival political party contenders.
Moreover, both Hispanic and non-Hispanic political figures
emerged as representatives of the pre-World War II settlements and
these continued to base their performance on traditional paternalistic patterns.

Political Leadership

Few non-Hispanic politicians captured the imagination and the
vote of Puerto Ricans as did Vito Marcantonio, congressional representative from Manhattan's Twentieth Assembly District. Born
and raised in a Harlem tenement, Marcantonio was educated in
New York schools, receiving his law degree from New York University in 1926. A protégé of Fiorello La Guardia, Marcantonio
became a charismatic politician whose public speaking, knowledge,
and familiarity with East Harlem and highly developed ability at

organization merged to form the necessary leadership qualities to which people were drawn. After almost a decade of political experience as a lawyer, and as La Guardia's campaign manager in the district, Marcantonio ran for Congress in 1934, opposing the Democratic incumbent, J. J. Lanzetta. Marcantonio gained the endorsement of the Fusion and Republican parties, the Knicker-bocker Democrats and the Liberal party.

Marcantonio relied on the patterns of paternalism and personal contact, *personalismo,* so vital to the Puerto Rican migrant. In tune with the Depression needs of his district, the congressman staffed his Harlem office with Spanish-speaking personnel, law-yers, and secretaries who advised on legal and bureaucratic affairs or relief rolls. Bernardo Vega's position as a community activist afforded an opportunity to assess Marcantonio's rapport with the Puerto Rican settlement, and he wrote:

> His office and campaign headquarters located at 247 East 116th Street were practically full of people at all hours of the day or night. People spoke in no less than six languages: Italian, Spanish, Polish, Yiddish, Hungarian and English. They were men and women, young and old with citizenship, health or relief problems, accidents, housing, immigration and the hundred and one preoccupations of the poor.

The relationship between the migrant community and the con-gressman centered on bread-and-butter issues, and the support given Marcantonio would in time supersede that given to any other non-Hispanic politician. It was solidly based on the personal atten-tion paid to community situations as well as his firsthand experi-ence and knowledge in attacking *colonia* problems. Personal migrant accounts repeatedly described the individual care given their problems. One woman, wrongly accused of not paying her rent, sought Marcantonio's help. Another denounced the local butcher for overcharging. No problem was too insignificant. The fact that Marcantonio and his representatives concerned themselves in this manner on basic daily issues assured him community sup-port in times to come and in a very real sense filled the void left by the old-style Democratic party connections.[31]

One migrant and long-time resident of the Spanish-speaking

community conveyed the sentiments of other working-class Puerto Ricans with regard to Marcantonio. As a representative of neighborhood clubs and a confirmed supporter of the congressman, his description expressed a devotion rooted in the fatherly leadership which Marcantonio personified:

> Marcantonio was the best. People said he was a communist, may the Lord rest his soul, but he was the best New York ever had. At that time he was a congressman but he aspired to become mayor of New York but because people thought he was a communist, well, he couldn't accomplish his goal. Marcantonio would say to us when we would get together, always, he would say, "we will struggle so that New York would not become a disaster." I would always remember those words. He would say, "do you see you are paying five cents in the subway today. If New York doesn't look to where it's going it will soon be sixty cents a fare" and we are already seeing that. And there is very little that Marcantonio said which did not come true.[32]

A spokesperson for the working class, Marcantonio sat on the committees on Territories, Civil Service, and Labor, instrumental vehicles for passing legislation affecting his Puerto Rican constituency both in New York City and on the island. At mid-decade, he was the undisputed political leader of the area. He gained fame for defending the Puerto Rican nationalist leader, Don Pedro Albizu Campos, who was convicted and incarcerated for political acts against colonialism in Puerto Rico. He commanded respect for opposing a proposed change in the Fair Labor Standards Act which would exempt the island from minimum wage provisions. These and many more stands endeared him to the Puerto Rican community. Moreover, in city politics, he was equally concerned with the plight of the Puerto Ricans in his district, denouncing as discriminatory the New York City Board of Education's classification of Hispanic students based on biased testing.[33]

Marcantonio's presence within the Puerto Rican political orbit signaled the start of a new era for the political aspirations of the pre-World War II settlements. Understandably, the community offered him their unlimited support, particularly through clubs and organizations. *La Mutualista Obrera Puertorriqueña,* the Communist Party, *Centro Obrero Español, Unión Industrial de Tabaqueros* and the Committee Against Facism and the War, all endorsed Marcantonio. In addition, small churches, some leftist intellectuals, and the working class also came out in his favor. But some Puerto Rican community leaders, loyal Democratic Party endorsers, opposed Marcantonio's candidacy, preferring instead his opponent the Democratic incumbent. These were clearly influenced by the widespread belief that Marcantonio used the Puerto Rican community for his own advantage, gaining support from the group by declaring his sympathy for Puerto Rican independence, condemning the treatment of the island by the United States, and vigorously pressing for concessions for the distressed people living in the Harlem area.[34] Certainly, the ties between the Puerto Rican community and the Democratic party were not yet severed.

Perhaps the best example of a Puerto Rican political leader during the same period was Oscar García Rivera. He was the first Puerto Rican to run for the New York State Legislature in the elections of 1937. A lawyer by training and at first a Republican, García Rivera later ran on the American Labor Party ticket in 1938, but was defeated the following year during a Roosevelt Democratic landslide. At that time it was not unusual for a Puerto Rican candidate running on a Republican ticket to gain the endorsement of Puerto Rican Democrats. First, as in the case of García Rivera, Puerto Ricans readily crossed party lines to support a candidate or an issue which directly affected them.[35] Second, the Republican party appeared in a remarkably favorable light after the Seabury investigations succeeded in crippling Democratic control. Although a Republican, García Rivera preached a social reform program more akin to socialist ideology than to a conservative stance. Third, the Republicans had also courted the Puerto Rican vote, aligning themselves early in the century with sympathizers for Puerto Rican independence. The Liberty Republican Club had operated in Manhattan since the end of the twenties with migrant representation. Moreover, in 1935, the first Puerto Rican Republican party local had been founded in Brooklyn by Ramón Colón in an attempt to offer the Puerto Rican voter a two party system.[36]

García Rivera's candidacy was heartily endorsed by Puerto Rican voters for yet another reason. In a personal interview, his widow, Dr. Eloísa García Rivera, confirmed the Spanish-speaking community turned out en masse, relentlessly campaigning in his behalf as a result of the super organization of his party headquarters. Campaigners knocked on doors, distributed propaganda, personally escorted potential voters to the polls, arranged for babysitting, and launched intensive voter registration drives in the neighborhoods of Spanish Harlem.

Aware of the special needs of the Harlem migrants, and particularly of the intimidation of facing a voter registration board, Doña Eloísa herself designed a program to prepare potential voters for registration. Along with a trained cadre of political supporters which included bilingual-bicultural high school and college students, Doña Eloísa commandeered a small office adjacent to campaign headquarters where she tutored residents in the intricacies of the literacy test and registrational procedure. In her opinion, this task force did more to secure García Rivera's seat in the State Legislature than any other maneuver.[37]

While in office, García Rivera spoke often in support of his Harlem tenement constituency, proposing reforms and endorsing legislation sometimes in conflict with Republican party priorities. Maintaining his law offices on 116th Street, García Rivera also concerned himself with the immediate problems affecting Puerto Ricans in the metropolitan area. One example in particular centered on a series of investigations and subsequent reports issued on the exploitation and crude work experiences of Puerto Rican seasonal migrant agricultural laborers in the states of New York and New Jersey. Legal representative for local businesses and private residents of the *colonia,* Oscar García Rivera also represented many of the Puerto Rican associations of the period.

Yet, in spite of the show of support exhibited in the elections of 1937 and 1938, Puerto Ricans for the most part apparently continued to identify with the Democratic party. "Between the two major political parties, the Puerto Rican is almost without exception Democrat," declared one researcher on the topic.[38] Throughout the thirties and forties, the Democratic party and related associations continued to court Puerto Rican favor. After close to two decades of participation, the Puerto Rican political clubs appeared to have become increasingly dominated by a handful of professionals within the *colonia*. Instead of grass-roots politicians like Tapia or Weber, the new leaders were doctors, lawyers, or other professionals. Rosters of prominent community leaders appeared on club stationery along with secretarial and public relations personnel. In 1932, for example, a letter written on letterhead stationery of The League of Spanish Speaking Democrats demonstrated the growing tendency among professionals to engage in politics. Written in Spanish, the communication alludes to a void in the directorship of the public relations committee offering the post to one Dr. Gabriel E. Álvarez, a chiropractor based in New York City. The offer, made in recognition of Dr. Álvarez's continued and enthusiastic service in association activities, carried the authorization of the publicity committee members.[39] This particular organization numbered among its board of directors six doctors, one lawyer, a clergyman, a professor, and four women, all recognized for their dedication and support of the Hispanic community.

An example of a professional who distinguished himself as a political leader within the Puerto Rican *colonias* as well as with the host society was Dr. José Negrón Cesteros. A native of Bayamón, Puerto Rico, Cesteros came to the United States in 1913 at the age of nineteen, where he studied at the University of Iowa, graduating also from Howard University Medical School. After coming to New York, he received staff privileges at Manhattan General Hospital. Dr. Cesteros lived and practiced medicine in that borough, was vice chairman of the Mayor's Committee on Puerto Rican Affairs, and a member of the Hispanic Medical Association.[40]

Dr. José N. Cesteros became one of the political representatives of the Harlem community during the late thirties and forties. Assuming leadership during the difficult period of the Depression, he quickly rose through the political ranks, serving on such committees as the Emergency Unemployment Relief Committee and the South Harlem Committee Headquarters. These committees represented a cross-section of the Puerto Rican and Hispanic leadership. Through civic participation, Dr. Cesteros promoted Democratic party goals. Appointed chairperson of the Puerto Rican Division of the Democratic National Committee by 1936, Cesteros formed a coalition which included Robert F. Wagner, United States senator from New York, Dennis Chavez, senator from New Mexico, and Representative Adolph J. Sabath from Illinois as honorary members. Moreover, thirteen coordinators from New York City, a 150-member advisory committee, and twenty-seven members of a ladies' committee, the majority of whom were Puerto Rican, also sat on this body. Cesteros continued participating in the political arena until his death in 1958 at the age of sixty-three.

Thus, on the one hand, Cesteros fulfilled one of the major goals articulated by Tapia decades before as part of the underlying reasons for Puerto Rican involvement in party politics—that of key placement of Puerto Rican political figures. On the other hand, as a professional, Cesteros was not quite typical of those Puerto Rican major party supporters of the late thirties and forties, who were overwhelmingly working class. Who spoke for the migrants? Those too preoccupied with job and family responsibilities, with survival in a Depression era, to dedicate themselves to party politics? Who spoke for the issues most relevant to the Spanish-speaking *colonias*? At least two alternative developments during the interwar years partially answer these questions. One was, of course, the emergence of populist politicians like García Rivera or Vito Marcantonio, already discussed, who continued the paternalistic pattern of party politics evident before the thirties; the other was the creation of numerous politically oriented community groups which spoke in the name of the *colonias* (see Appendix II).

Politically oriented associations or quasi-political groups demonstrated political involvement in several different ways. One was through the sponsorship of particular candidates whom they permitted to address their groups. Another was through the support given to certain political issues. Yet another was through the creation of or participation in organizations which aligned themselves to specific political stands. The latter often endorsed minority party politics such as socialist, communist, or liberal. Because of the unique migratory patterns between Puerto Rico and the settlements in the United States, those issues which most affected the island either of a political, social, or work-related nature affected the New York settlements as well.

The nature of the migration was such that ties between the island and the continental communities were never severed and constantly reinforced by the circular migration. Puerto Ricans traveled freely between both points, keeping abreast not only of domestic interests but of organizational and political issues as well. It was not surpris-

ing then that the relationship between Puerto Rican politics in
Puerto Rico and electoral behavior among the migrants of the New
York settlements had more in common than just methods of electioneering, campaigning, or voter registration drives. Frequently,
island politicians and elected officials appeared before migrant
organizations soliciting their support and goodwill on behalf of
continental office-seekers.[41]

In the 1930s, for example, the Puerto Rican politician Antonio
Barceló came to *El Barrio* to speak in support of Vito Marcantonio. Similarly, during the 1940s Gilberto Concepción de Gracia,
founder of the island's Independence party did the same. One
migrant's personal account affirmed that between 200 and 250 individuals would turn out to hear Concepción de Gracia. Similarly,
Santiago Iglesias Pantín, active in Puerto Rican union organizing
and one of the founders of the *Federación Libre de Trabajadores*
commanded a large audience. He actively campaigned against Marcantonio. Muñoz Marín, founder of the *Partido Popular Demo-
crata* and the first elected governor of the island, did the same. In
the 1940s the incumbent mayor of New York City, William
O'Dwyer, reaped the benefits of endorsement from the Mayoress
of San Juan, Doña Felisa Rincón de Gautier. A familiar figure in
the political scenario on both sides of the ocean, Doña Felisa continued to influence the political behavior of the migrant community
well into the fifties. So too did New York-based politicians look
toward the Puerto Rican social and political organizations as the
vehicles through which they could win Hispanic support. The fact
that this type of electioneering and campaigning was almost always
carried out within the confines of *colonia* organizations points out
once again the importance of the network within the Spanish-
speaking communities.

Minority Party Politics and Puerto Rican Organizations

The Puerto Rican political clubs or quasi-political organizations
which aligned themselves along minority party politics were almost
always socialist or communist in outlook. Many were distinctly European or Latin American in their interpretations of and dedication
to respective political ideologies. However, neither the Socialist nor
Communist parties in New York City benefited from the thorough

organization—from local neighborhood to district to county level—that characterized the major or dominant parties. In 1929, for example, there were only forty-three regular organizations operating within the city's sixty-two Assembly Districts and an additional eighteen special organizations catering specifically to the various ethnic groups.[42] Nevertheless, the minority parties functioned to check the secondary (Republican) party, provided more forums for open discussion, and encouraged the participation of the city's ethnic or national groups on a larger scale than did the majority parties. Those attracted to minority parties worked collectively for a more systematic reorganization of government and society rather than for the tangible individual rewards based on the patronage of dominant party structure. Moreover, among the priorities of the Puerto Rican minority-oriented locals, there existed an unconditional concern for the welfare of the working class in Puerto Rico as well as in New York City.

The Puerto Rican *Alianza Obrera* exemplified a quasi-political unit because it supported the political parties which best represented the interests of its membership. Founded in 1922, the group operated as a class-conscious community organization which forged links with the Socialist party. Through its newspaper, *The Socialist Call,* the city's Spanish-speaking population was kept informed of the group's activities. *Alianza Obrera* not only lent its backing to socialist causes; it provided a forum in which candidates and party members could present their ideas. Furthermore, among the membership of the *Alianza* were individuals who belonged to the Socialist party. One of these, Jesus Colón, was a founding member of the first New York committee of the Puerto Rican Socialist party in 1918, and secretary of the *Alianza Obrera Puertorriqueña* in 1922.[43] As one of the *colonia's* leading writers, Colón bridged the gap between the island and the continent, helping to popularize socialist causes and *Alianza* activities. As a correspondent, he wrote for the socialist press, *La Justicia.* Along with his brother Joaquin and his cousin Ramón, Jesus Colón figured in the founding of several newspapers in Brooklyn with the purpose of informing readers on both sides of the ocean about their respective community issues and events. Of these, *Curioso* was intended to relay political propaganda.

During the 1920s another group, *La Liga Puertorriqueña,* shifted its objectives from its foundation as an apolitical federation of community associations to an affiliation with the regular Democratic party. At that time, Gonzalo O'Neill, the *Liga*'s president, justified this action in the following manner:

> If we are to live within the North American orbit, if we are to form part of the Great Republic, we do not wish, given our aspirations, to vegetate within this atmosphere, like automatons, but instead act like conscientious beings—demonstrating that we possess qualities worthy of valuable workers.[44]

While the *Liga* was not founded specifically with political objectives in mind, other groups combined both social and political goals in their charters of incorporation. The Porto Rican Political and Social League, incorporated on March 31, 1936, vowed to promote political participation among its members in spite of its nonpartisan stand:

> This is a non-partisan political and social organization for the following purposes: to create, promote and develop social and civic activities among its members; to develop a better understanding and political unity among Puerto Ricans and Spanish-American individuals who are eligible to vote within the confines of the city of New York; to hold gatherings at different periods of the year for the recreation of members and their guests; to provide opportunities and places for the expression of social acts and to hold social affairs; nothing in this constitution shall be construed as a limitation on the part of the membership to adhere to any political party who will give recognition to our association and will assist in benefitting its members and will accept our candidates for election, or of the powers of this organization, which shall exercise all those implied and necessary prerogatives to carry on and conduct them within enumerated powers.[45]

In the same year the Puerto Rican Democratic and Social Union stated similar objectives in its certificate of incorporation:

> To maintain an organization for the social and mental uplift of all its members; to take an active and civic interest in gov-

ernmental affairs and to have helpful recreation. These activities shall be carried out without pecuniary profit to the corporation or to any of its members. This organization shall be financed from the collections of dues and voluntary contributions.[46]

The issues which most concerned the quasi-political organizations were: a combination of internal community problems; issues beyond the geographic confines of the *colonias* such as the Spanish Civil War; concerns over Puerto Rico's political status; emergency relief funds, and identification with social and political developments throughout Spanish-America.

One case in point, nationalism and support for the island's independence movement, commanded substantial interest in the New York settlements. Nationalist campaigns for independence, including the formation of groups for this purpose and fund raising, were evident in the settlements during the mid-thirties.[47] A hotly debated issue, the cause for independence was firmly supported in New York with the eruption of the Ponce Massacre in Puerto Rico.

The Ponce Massacre took place on Easter Sunday in 1937 in the Puerto Rican city of the same name. Following a series of sporadic confrontations between Nationalist and anti-Nationalist forces over a period of several years, the former had requested and been given permission to assemble peacefully in Ponce on March 21. At the final hour, the permit to march was revoked, too late for the Nationalists to cancel their procession. Ignorant of the last-minute changes, those who marched were greeted by armed resistence as the police fired into the marchers, wounding and killing hundreds of Nationalists and innocent bystanders.

Thousands of Puerto Ricans in New York City demonstrated against the situation in Ponce. Over ten thousand Puerto Rican members of scores of political and social clubs assembled in Central Park and then paraded through the streets of Spanish Harlem in protest, as they had done the year before over the arrests, trial, and conviction of the island's Nationalist leaders. Their intention, clearly illustrated by the speeches made and placards on exhibition, was to denounce the attitudes and actions of "Imperialist America" in Puerto Rico. Critical issues such as this one united Puerto Ricans of all political persuasions.

Certainly the politics of the island continued to interest early set-

tlement migrants. As groups turned out in support of the Nationalist movement, so did they uphold other avenues of political
thought. As early as the 1920s, for example, Antonio R. Barceló
had articulated a preference for a type of autonomy called the
Estado Libre Asociado (Associated Free State) modeled after the
Irish Free State, as the solution to Puerto Rico's legal status. Aware
of the island's strategic importance to the United States, and
accepting the relationship between the two, Barceló suggested the
formation of a government equally beneficial to both interests. As
Barceló was a frequent visitor to the New York settlements, his
ideas found favor as one viable alternative for the island's political
future.[48]

Finally, groups like the Porto Rican Political and Social League
and the Puerto Rican Democratic and Social Union encouraged the
practice of good American citizenship indirectly condoning the
reality of the Puerto Rican existence within the North American
political orbit. These units would have articulated conformity with
the status quo, conditioning migrants in this direction.

Of equal interest and importance, particularly for those who had
relatives in Latin American countries or in Spain, were the political
and social affairs of those countries. Puerto Rican groups took
political stands opposing the Machado and the Gómez dictator-
ships in Cuba and Venezuela and against the rise of Fascism in
Spain. They supported the Sandinistas in Nicaragua and continued
to closely observe political developments in the Dominican Republic. "We defend the aspirations of Puerto Rico and combat the
tyranny of Juan Vicente Gómez in Venezuela and Gerardo Machado in Cuba," wrote Bernardo Vega in the pages of *Gráfico* during
the thirties.[49]

Commitment was not merely in words, but included practical
action as well. The pioneer settlements demonstrated their support
through relief units and emergency committees, all formed in connection with the existing *colonia* organizations. The Nicaraguan
Sandinistas, for example, received aid from the associations, which
included clothing, food, and medical supplies. In this particular
incident, Sandino's brother, a long-time resident of the New York
Spanish-speaking *colonia*, was able to muster additional support by
personally appealing to neighborhood groups and inviting them to
send a representative, fact-finding committee to Nicaragua, to

observe conditions firsthand. A central committee, *Manos Fuera de Nicaragua,* was formed, medical supplies sent, and communication firmly established between Nicaraguan Sandinistas and the New York settlements.[50]

Similarly, the Spanish Civil War effort generated volunteer services, providing medical aid and ammunition from New York. Puerto Ricans were almost always in support of the Loyalists, but the issues surrounding the war were nevertheless endlessly debated. Many Puerto Ricans had relatives in Spain, and with the bombardment of Madrid in the summer of 1936, thousands of men, women, and children paraded through the streets of New York in protest.

Finally, national issues also garnered attention among Puerto Rican political units. The emigration of Puerto Rican agricultural workers proposed by private corporations in Arizona was soundly denounced by *colonia* groups and presses. One such group, the Workers Alliance, or *Alianza Obrera,* frequently raised human rights issues for both action and discussion. These ranged from the plight of the Oakies in the West, the Chicago riots, and city and national politics, to the importance of activating student unions.[51]

Conclusion

Surely, political awareness and participation among Puerto Ricans in New York was far greater than previously assumed. We have traced political consciousness and action beginning with those foundations laid before the turn of the century to the period just before the Second World War. The earliest groups nurtured leadership as well as a preoccupation with the island's status within the context of Puerto Rican political development. Against the background of the United States occupation, the migration accelerated, taking root in New York *colonias* where political activity also underwent changes commensurate with the growth and predilections of the pioneer settlements. By the twenties, an awareness of the importance of functioning within a North American political orbit intensified causing political or quasi-political clubs to give priority to the problems of the migrants and their community. Aligned with dominant and minority party politics, Puerto Rican groups attempted to exchange the vote for social welfare benefits, as many others had done before them. Based on patronage, paternalism, and personalism, a new cadre of political figures commanded the loyalties of the Puerto Rican voter.

Without doubt, the political organizations served as roadways toward the larger surrounding society, Spanish America and Spain, and Puerto Rico. Through political associations, Puerto Ricans kept abreast of the issues and events affecting their Spanish-speaking compatriots on a global scale. Absent from the homeland, they expressed their sentiments on numerous topics impacting on Puerto Rico, but especially the political status of the island. As migrants they used political groups as buffers between non-Hispanics and the *colonias*. Moreover, politics embodied a recognition among the migrants of their true situation in America, as settlers in an unfamiliar territory, as an identifiable ethnic group, and as members of the working class.

Notes

1. Ricardo Campos and Juan Flores, "National Culture and Migration: Perspective from the Puerto Rican Working Class," *Centro Working Papers,* Centro de Estudios Puertorriquenos (New York: CUNY, 1978), pp. 8-9. See also César Andreu Iglesias, ed., *Memorias de Bernardo Vega* (Rio Piedras: Ediciones Huracan, Inc., 1977), pp. 77-85.

2. Iglesias, *Memorias,* pp. 106-107.

3. Julio José Henna continued his work in community organizations participating in Groups like the Club Latinoamericano and the Democratic Party associations in the city. Figueroa similarly appeared on the rosters of several groups. See Appendices I and II.

4. Iglesias, *Memorias,* pp. 155-156. Also interview with Homero Rosado, Brooklyn College, Brooklyn, New York, November 1980. Interview with Ramón Colón, Puerto Rican Oral History Project, 1973-1974, Long Island Historical Society, Brooklyn, New York.

5. Ramón Colón, *Carlos Tapia, A Puerto Rican Hero in New York* (New York: Vantage Press, 1976), p. 44. Also Ramón Colón interview; James Jennings, *Puerto Rican Politics in New York City* (Washington, D.C.: University Press of America, 1977), p. 24. *Note:* Jennings refers to the Democratic politicians as Jimmy Kelly and George McCure.

6. Colón, *Carlos Tapia,* p. 44; Jennings, *Puerto Rican Politics,* pp. 24-25.

7. Wallace S. Sayre and Herbert Kaufman, *Governing New York City* (New York: W.W. Norton & Co., 1965), pp. 11-18. See also Warren Moscow, *The Last of the Big-Time Bosses* (New York: Stein & Day, 1971).

8. Colón, *Carlos Tapia,* p. 45.

9. Interview with Honorina Weber Irizarry, Puerto Rican Oral History Project.

10. Colón, *Carlos Tapia,* p. 45.

11. Among the researchers who share this point of view are: Patricia Cayo Sexton, *Harlem Español* (Mexico: Editorial Diana, 1966), p. 133; Nathan Glazer and Daniel P. Moynihan, *Beyond the Melting Pot* (Cambridge, Mass.: MIT Press, 1963), p. 107.

12. Jennings, *Puerto Rican Politics,* pp. 24, 85, 138.

13. *Brooklyn Daily Eagle Almanac,* Brooklyn Eagle Press, 1924 through 1937. Throughout this period the *Almanac* consistently listed a predominance of Democratic Party organizations. See also Wallace S. Sayre, *Governing New York City,* p. 463; Roy V. Peel, *The Political Clubs of New York City* (New York: G.P. Putnam & Sons, 1935), pp. 22–45; Hugh A. Bone, "Political Parties in New York City," *American Political Science Review,* vol. 40 (April 1946), pp. 272–282.

14. Page Smith, *The Shaping of America,* vol. III (New York: McGraw-Hill Book Co., 1980), p. 748. See also Peel, *The Political Clubs,* pp. 56–57.

15. Peel, *The Political Clubs,* pp. 64–68. See also Jack Alexander, "District Leader: Profile of James J. Hines," *The New Yorker,* vol. 12, July 25, 1936, pp. 21–26, August 1, 1936, pp. 18–23.

16. Peel, *The Political Clubs.*

17. Sayre and Kaufman, *Governing New York City,* pp. 70–73. See also Citizens Union, "Party Organization in New York City," *The Searchlight,* vol. 41, May 1951; Marilyn Gittell, "Administration and Organization of Political Parties in New York City" (New York University, Masters Thesis, 1953).

18. Peel, *The Political Clubs,* p. 65.

19. Ibid., pp. 251–267.

20. Ibid., p. 65.

21. Interview with Homero Rosado; Ramón Colón interview.

22. Peel, *The Political Clubs,* p. 258. Emphasis added.

23. Clara E. Rodríguez, "Puerto Ricans in the Melting Pot," *The Journal for Ethnic Studies,* vol. 1, no. 4 (winter 1974), pp. 89–97.

24. Homero Rosado interview.

25. Arthur Mann, *La Guardia—A Fighter Against His Times: Vol 1, 1881–1933* (New York: J.B. Lippincott, 1959), p. 246.

26. Iglesias, *Memorias,* p. 155.

27. References to Guillerma Echevarria recur in the interviews found in the Puerto Rican Oral History Project.

28. Samuel Eliot Morrison, *The Oxford History of the American People, Vol. III* (New York: New American Library, 1972), p. 234. See also

Terry L. McCoy, "A Primer for U.S. Policy on Caribbean Emigration," *Caribbean Review,* vol. 8, no. 1 (January-March 1979), pp. 10-15. The Johnson Act of 1921 limited the numbers of aliens admitted annually to 3 percent of the number of foreign born of that nationality already in the United States according to the census of 1910. The total allowed was 358,000 of which 200,000 were allotted to Northern European countries and 155,000 to those of Southern and Eastern Europe.

29. Rosa Estades, "Patterns of Political Participation of Puerto Ricans in New York City" (New York, New School for Social Research, Ph.D. Dissertation, 1974), p. 65. See also Moscow, *The Last of Big-Time Bosses,* pp. 24-29; Sayre and Kaufman, *Governing New York City,* pp. 535-581.

30. Ramón Colón interview.

31. Numerous interviews discuss the devotion felt for Marcantonio among Puerto Ricans, and many commented favorably on the way he related to the community. Among them were Ramón Colón, Bernardo Vega, Homero Rosado, Antonio Rivera Hernández, Eloísa García Rivera, and Margarita Soto Alers.

32. Interview with Pedro Ruiz and Margarita Soto Alers, Aguada, Puerto Rico, July 1977.

33. The Vito Marcantonio Collection, New York Public Library, Archival Division, Boxes 2, 3, 4, 17. See also Annette T. Rubenstein and Associates, *I Vote My Conscience—Debates, Speeches and Writings of Vito Marcantonio, 1935-1950* (New York: The Vito Marcantonio Memorial, 1956).

34. Lawrence R. Chenault, *The Puerto Rican Migrant in New York* (New York: Columbia University Press, 1938; reissued, Russell & Russell, 1970), p. 155.

35. Interview with Dr. Eloísa García Rivera, New York City, May 1976; Margarita Soto Alers interview; Ramón Colón interview.

36. Iglesias, *Memorias,* pp. 194-195; Ramón Colón interview.

37. Eloísa García Rivera interview. Moreover, in the mid-fifties Ralph Rosas, former director of the Community Organization Division of the Office of the Commonwealth of Puerto Rico, instituted a program of voter registration similar in operation to Dr. García Rivera's, in conjunction with the Council of Hispanic Organizations. See Carlota Suárez, "Don Ralph Rosas, Puerto Rico en Nueva York: Visión y Práctica" (Brooklyn College, 1980, unpublished manuscript).

38. Chenault, *The Puerto Rican Migrant,* p. 155; Iglesias, *Memorias,* p. 187.

39. Correspondence of the League for Spanish-speaking Democrats, October 24, 1932.

40. *New York Times,* February 9, 1958, p. 88.

41. Iglesias, *Memorias,* pp. 183-184. See also Adalberto López, "An

Italian-American's Defense of Puerto Rico and Puerto Ricans," *Caribbean Review,* vol. 8, no. 1 (January-March 1979), pp. 16–21.

42. Peel, *The Political Clubs,* pp. 299–300.

43. Campos and Flores, "National Culture," pp. 40–41; Iglesias, *Memorias,* p. 156; Ramón Colón Interview.

44. *La Prensa,* January 15, 1923, p. 1. See also Iglesias, *Memorias,* pp. 174–175.

45. The Porto Rican Political and Social League, Certificate of Incorporation, File No. 3091-360, March 13, 1936, New York City County Clerk's Office, Municipal Building, New York City.

46. Puerto Rican Democratic and Social Union, Inc., Certificate of Incorporation, File No. 00923-35C, January 17, 1935.

47. Chenault, *The Puerto Rican Migrant,* pp. 153–154.

48. López, "An Italian-American's Defense," pp. 16–21. See also Kal Wagenheim, *Puerto Rico: A Profile* (New York: Praeger Press, 1974), p. 71.

49. Iglesias, *Memorias,* p. 196; interview with Lillian López, New York City, May 1976.

50. *Gráfico,* July 8, 1928.

51. Interview with Evelina Antonetty, Columbia Oral History Project, Columbia University, New York City.

Reflections and Considerations

The primary purpose of this study has been to present an interpretation of the Puerto Rican experience in New York City, early settlement patterns, and the formation of a distinctive Puerto Rican community. Historically situated in the period between the two world wars, this phenomenon was both complex and multifaceted. Rooted on the steady migratory stream from the island to the mainland, and against the interplay of a colonial relationship, the dispersal of countless Puerto Ricans was decidedly influenced by a series of individual and collective factors. People came for economic considerations, for better opportunities, and for adventure. Once in New York City, they set about reconstructing neighborhoods solidly modeled on those they had known in Puerto Rico. In the process, they transported distinct sets of ideas, values, practices, and traditions, which shaped and distinguished their Puerto Rican *colonias* from all the others.

The nature of the migration was such that movement between both geographic points was constant. Reinforcing Hispanic communal development, this circular movement of people served also in a sense to inhibit the adjustment and assimilation of the migrant community, so evident in other ethnic groups. Some expected to leave once their economic positions were secure; others could never return. If the twin torchlights of language and cultural identity played a dominant role in early settlement considerations, complete

North American assimilation was frequently outside of the migrants' frame of reference. "I think we have to recognize in this long-standing rejection of a quick transfer of identity a profoundly political act that is decidedly life-affirming and non-suicidal," wrote one spokesperson of the second generation, mirroring, as it were, the sentiments expressed by many of his ancestors while shaping the pre-World War II community.[1]

Almost from the start, formal and informal coping institutions emerged to structure the early settlement. Childcare systems, household sharing, taking in boarders, and working in the home partly attest to women's undisputed role in community development, laying to rest former stereotypes which curtailed Latin women's involvement in the economic mainstream. The hand that rocked the cradle invariably participated in the work force and nurtured community organizations and activities designed to preserve culture, language, and heritage, among other goals. Moreover, we now recognize the importance of an organizational network which was far more extensive than previously suspected by earlier researchers. Sustaining internal communal growth and dynamics while confronting daily struggles on behalf of the pioneer migrants, these groups forged connections with the surrounding non-Hispanic world, fostered and adjusted methods of coexistence, and initiated dialogue with their island home and other Spanish-speaking communities.

Concerned also with the survival of the infant settlements as an intact, solid Puerto Rican community, social, cultural, and fraternal groups worked alongside political organizations to reaffirm civil rights while modifying values and practices in the best interests of the *colonia*. Significantly influenced by paternalistic tendencies, patronage, and personalism, these patterns of behavior set the style for future interaction between the city's dominant political party system and the Puerto Rican clubs. In addition, some Puerto Rican groups aligned themselves with minority party politics, establishing the rubric through which they could best vent their sympathies on worldwide issues. The concerns of Puerto Rican Socialists, liberals, independence supporters, or Communists, deeply rooted in nationalism or class consciousness, were not limited to the island or the New York settlements.

Therefore, the importance of this study is threefold: first, it presents a rare view of the Puerto Rican experience in New York—the creation of an identifiable community with its formal and informal institutions, leadership capabilities, businesses and professionals, and common cultural interests—which served to cushion the impact of the "Great Migration" following the Second World War. Second, the account stems from the recollections and experiences of those who lived through the early migration as well as from biographical and documentary materials not available in earlier studies. Third, it paves the way for future intensive studies in this direction, for comparisons with other Latin population movements, and for comparisons with the developments of other Puerto Rican communities throughout the United States.

In spite of the growth of the Puerto Rican population in New York City since the turn of the century and especially in the years following the First World War, the presence of a distinctive community and the foundations it created for the post-World War II migration have for the most part been overlooked. While this study does not claim to present a definitive history of Puerto Ricans in New York City, it nevertheless describes their beginning, opening the way for more detailed research in this area. Surveying the limited and often one-dimensional aspect of accepted materials relating to the early Puerto Rican experience, we have chosen to heed the voices of the early migrants and their descendants and to convey a seldom acknowledged portrait of the *Colonia Hispana*. "If Puerto Ricans . . . are interested in the history of Puerto Rico . . . they are primarily interested in the history of the Puerto Rican migration to the United States, in the history of the Puerto Rican communities in this country, and in the problems which continue to face those communities," declared Adalberto López in his summary of literature on Puerto Ricans in English.[2] Seeking historical roots, the children of the early migration were too often surprised to find themselves as statistics on the city's welfare rolls, school dropouts, truants, health and correctional hazards, a rootless people, devoid of a history and a culture, according to published reports and sound research.

Of exceptional importance, the problems faced by migrants and their community were seldom glossed over in the works produced during the early fifties and sixties. C. Wright Mills, Clarence Senior, and Rose Goldsen presented good insights into the motivations of the migration of the forties in *The Puerto Rican Journey: New York's Newest Neighbors.* Similarly, Elena Padilla's *Up from Puerto Rico,* Dan Wakefield's *Island in the City: The World of Spanish Harlem,* and Patricia Cayo Sexton's *Spanish Harlem: Anatomy of Poverty* delved deeply into the social and economic hardships engulfing Puerto Ricans.[3] Personal, literary, and biographical accounts like Piri Thomas's *Down These Mean Streets* and Nicolasa Mohr's *Nilda* provided poignant, realistic views of childhood and adolescence in Spanish Harlem.[4] But if the problems inherent in the massive relocation of people from island to mainland attracted attention, reference to the more positive aspects of early community development, the self-help associations, family structure and values, the role of women, the community in other boroughs, and other guidance apparatus hardly received notice. Among the many scholars interested in the topic of Puerto Ricans, a few attempted to present the experience from an historical and comparative perspective, but the Puerto Rican case frequently fell short.[5]

Regarding the mechanisms of early Puerto Rican community formation in New York, misconceptions abounded. Some observers commented on the apparent lack of leadership and communal institutions within the settlements. Interpreting the concept of community in terms of host society leadership and organization patterns, Puerto Rican leadership and the many civic, social, and religious associations, significant to the shaping of the pioneer settlements, were obscured.[6] Others followed suit, proposing the erroneous thesis that since Puerto Ricans on the island possessed neither a strong familial support network nor important cultural, social, or political coping institutions, those who came to the mainland lacked the experience to establish communities as other ethnic groups had done before them.

> Aside from storefront churches, organization life is not strong among Puerto Ricans. There are many social organizations based on place of origin on the island, but they do not have the importance of the immigrant societies among earlier immigrants. . . . One can always find functions for an organization if one is organizationally minded, but Puerto Rico, just as the rest of Latin America, had always been weak in spontaneous grass-roots organizations.[7]

The existence of cultural and associational networks was highly desirable, for these enhanced and improved an immigrant settlement, allowing it to channel resources in unfamiliar situations, to organize, to encourage pride and effort among its members, and even to Americanize. Among Puerto Ricans, the absence of these networks was deemed regrettable. Early migrant families were thought too unsophisticated to build strong community units, and more important, the failure to generate grass-roots entities stemmed directly from an inherent weakness among those of Latin culture. The significance of regional or neighborhood clubs, those social groups which did in fact operate, was negatively perceived.

If Puerto Ricans failed to mold a solid community, they did so inadvertently, according to other studies, since they lacked a cultural base on which to act. How could Puerto Ricans seek any real attachment to the American culture as symbolized by an organizational network designed to mimic the host society's, if their past experience precluded strong local traditions or articulated and positive ideals in their history for which expression and fulfillment were sought in their new environment?

> In Puerto Rico itself one discovers . . . that these cultural institutions have never existed, and so cannot arbitrarily be created in New York. As many a school teacher in East Harlem has learned, Puerto Rican kids are often as illiterate in Spanish as they remain in English; and judging from the frenzied missionary effort of the Catholic Church to reclaim Puerto Ricans in New York for the faith, they often arrive without any real religious traditions at all.[8]

How accurate were these observations? Once again, the comparative approach rendered the Puerto Ricans vulnerable and short-changed. Seeking similarities between the Puerto Rican experience and the settlement patterns of other ethnic groups, Puerto Ricans were judged on a level which imposed the experience, time period, and Americanization goals of other immigrants as criteria.

Thus, the study becomes significant from yet another aspect. Recognizing the disparities apparent in the existing literature, it reconstructs and reinterprets the story of a community and its people from within, through the eyes of those who lived through the experience. Moreover, this interpretation raises the following questions. What were the links between the post- and pre-World War II communities, and how would social service government agencies affect the former? What became of many community organizations? Were they perhaps rendered impotent in light of the class differences and growing numerical superiority of the postwar migration? Did the breakup of neighborhoods under the guise of urban renewal result in the disintegration of the Hispanic community? It is left to a new generation of Puerto Rican scholars and those interested in the Puerto Rican experience to analyze, criticize, and reevaluate our past.

Notes

1. Frank Bonilla, "Beyond Survival: Por que Seguiremos Siendo Puertorriquenos," in Iris M. Zavala and Rafael Rodríguez, eds. *The Intellectual Roots of Independence* (New York: Monthly Review Press, 1980), p. 365.

2. Adalberto López, "Some of the Literature on Puerto Rico and Puerto Ricans in English," in Adalberto López and James Petras, eds., *Puerto Rico and Puerto Ricans: Studies in History and Society* (New York: Schenkman Publishing, 1974), p. 477.

3. C. Wright Mills, Clarence Senior, and Rose Goldsen, *The Puerto Rican Journey: New York's Newest Migrants* (New York: Harper & Bros., 1950); Elena Padilla, *Up From Puerto Rico* (New York: Columbia University Press, 1958); Daniel Wakefield, *Island in the City: The World of Spanish Harlem* (Boston: Houghton Mifflin, 1959); Patricia Cayo Sexton, *Spanish Harlem: Anatomy of Poverty* (New York: Harper & Row, 1965).

4. Piri Thomas, *Down These Mean Streets* (New York: Alfred Knopf, 1967); Nicolasa Mohr, *Nilda* (New York: Bantam Books, 1975).

5. Lawrence R. Chenault's *The Puerto Rican Migrant in New York,* (New York: Columbia University Press, 1935) is one of the few books to deal with the Puerto Rican experience in detail.

6. Oscar Handlin, *The Newcomers: Negroes and Puerto Ricans in a Changing Metropolis* (Cambridge: Harvard University Press, 1959), pp. 61–118.

7. Nathan Glazer and Daniel P. Moynihan, *Beyond the Melting Pot* (Cambridge: MIT Press, 1963), p. 107.

8. Alfred Kazin, "In Puerto Rico," in *Comtemporaries* (New York: Little, Brown & Co., 1960), pp. 34–37.

Appendixes

APPENDIX I:
Organizations in Operation in Puerto Rican Communities, 1900–1950

NAME	PURPOSE FOR ORGANIZING	MEMBERS OR TYPES OF MEMBERSHIP
1900–1919		
Unión Internacional de Tabaqueros	union activity	tobacco workers
La Resistencia	union activity	tobacco workers
Asociación Latino-Americana	fund raising for needy Spanish-speaking families	Dr. Antonio González Dr. Manuel Castillo Vilar Dr. Arturo Font Sr. Alberto León Sr. Francisco L. Pla Sr. Ricardo E. Manrique
Unión Benéfica Español	unknown	unknown
La Aurora, La Razón, El Ejemplo	Mutual Aid Societies	tobacco workers
El Tropical	social activities, fund raising for membership	Gonzalo Torres
Club Ibero-Americano	social activities, cultural purposes	Dr. Henna

NAME	PURPOSE FOR ORGANIZING	MEMBERS OR TYPES OF MEMBERSHIP
1920–1930		
Trabajadores Amalgamado de la Industria del Tobaco	educational; published newspaper *The Tobacco Worker*	Non-Puerto Ricans and Puerto Ricans: W. Rico, Sam Sussman, Cayetano Loria, Bernardo Vega, J. Brandon
La Asociación Puertorriqueña	unknown	Manuel Negrón Collazo
Club Caborrojeño	neighborhood social club; provided meeting grounds for migrants from Cabo Rojo	Ramón Pabón Aviles
Casa de Puerto Rico	to promote Hispanic culture, customs and traditions	Dr. Ruiz Arnau, Martin Travieso, R.M. Delgado, Manuel Argueso, Dr. Lopez Antongiorgo, F. González Acuna, Dr. Janer, Ulises García Sandov, Gonzalo O'Neill, Ledo. Pedro Rodríguez, Dr. Arturo Martínez
Puerto Rico Literario	literary, cultural and social. Promoted desire to learn among Puerto Rican youth.	Pura Belpré, Francisco Acevedo, Lorenzo Pineiro, Max Vázquez, Bartolo Malavé, Rafael Mariotta, René Jimenez Malaret, Juan Bautista Pagan, Luis Hernández Aquino, Erasmo Vando

Organization	Purpose	Members
Liga Puertorriqueña e Hispana	unite Hispanics regardless of national origins. Cultural, educational and mutual aid.	Juan Villanueva, Blas Oliveras, J.V. Alonso, Pedro San Miguel, J.M. Vivaldi, José González Benítez, J.M. Antonmarchi, Tomás Gares, Carlos L. Fernández, Cayetano Arieta, Rafael Pérez
La Alianza Obrera	sponsored syndicalist ideas; a common center for defense of Puerto Ricans regardless of political affiliations.	Lupercio Arroyo, Jesus Colón, Eduvigis Cabán, Guillermo Vargas, Catalino Castro, Luis Muñoz Marín
Porto Rican Brotherhood of America	promoted sociability and friendship; social and intellectual advancement; sponsored civic, social, cultural and educational activities; represented Puerto Ricans.	Antonio Dávila, Eusebio Cruz, Juan Carreras, Aurelio Betancourt, Jacinto Paradis, Faustino Dorna, Juan I. Mares, A. Rivera Hernández
Junta de Defensa de Puerto Rico	attempted to safeguard legal rights of Puerto Ricans	Domingo Collazo, J. Monge Sánchez, Ernesto Andino Cespe, Luis Battistini, J.A. González, Antonio Gotay
Ateneo Obrero	cultural, literary and educational. Promoted the needs of second generation	Bernardo Vega, Sabino Vázquez, Juan Rovira, Manuel Flores Cabrera, Juan Bautista Pagán, Emilio Fariza

APPENDIX 1 (continued)

NAME	PURPOSE FOR ORGANIZING	MEMBERS OR TYPES OF MEMBERSHIP
Club Videro	social and political	unknown
New York Sporting Club	sports, recreational and social activities	unknown
Club Esperanza	benevolent and charity	unknown
Puerto Rican Employee's Association	social, cultural, athletics and recreational	Carmelo Colón, Bide Jesus, Rafael Rivera, Tomás Gares, Ruperto Ruiz
1930–1940		
Comisión Pro Centenario de Hostos	cultural and social	unknown
Club Claridad Humanitaria	charity	women's group
Club Eugenio María de Hostos	cultural, political and educational	Jesus Colón, Alberto Rivera, Manuel Flores Cabrera, Bernardo Vega, Isabel O'Neill, María Alamo Cerra, Juan Rovira
International Ladies Garment Workers Union, Local 22	union activity	Spanish-speaking workers
Liga Anti-imperialista Puertorriqueña (Centro Obrero Español)	attempted to organize against U.S. imperialism in Latin America	unknown

Organization	Purpose	Members
La Confederación de Sociedades Puertorriqueñas	alliance of all community groups; social and cultural	José Camprubi, J.M. Vivaldi; Oscar García Rivera, J. Cabán Soler, Cesar G. Torres, José Santiago, Laura Santiago, Isabel O'Neill, Tomás Gares, Angel Vidal, García Angulo
Círculo Cultural Cervantes	cultural and literary	unknown
Pan American Women's Association	social and cultural	Latin women
Emergency Unemployment Relief Committee; South Harlem Committee Headquarters	welfare, political and civic	unknown
Spanish Association for the Blind	charity	unknown
Asociación de Empleados Civiles de Correo	civic and social	Postal workers
Sociedad de Mujeres Puertorriqueñas	cultural and social	women's group
Hispanic Merchants' Association	social, commercial	small businessmen
Asociación de Escritores y Periodistas Puertorriqueños	literary, cultural and social	Rafael Torres Mazzor, Angel M. Arroyo, Gonzalo O'Neill, Antonio J. Colorado, Erasmo Vando, Jose Enamorado Cuesta, Max Vázquez, Max Ríos, María Mas Pozo, Clotilde Betances

APPENDIX 1 (continued)

NAME	PURPOSE FOR ORGANIZING	MEMBERS OR TYPES OF MEMBERSHIP
Puerto Rican Civic Club	civic, social, and mutual aid	Joseph R. Pacheco, Pedro Vega, Jr., Octavio y Garavidez, Prudencio L. Vicente, Joseph Hoppe, Sr.
1940–1950 Porto Rican Athletic Club	social, recreational, athletics	unknown
Puerto Rican Cultural Society, Inc.	welfare, civic and political	Manuel Torres, Cesar Gouverniuer, Eusebio Pérez
Puerto Rican Veterans Welfare Postal Workers Association, Inc.	social, cultural and civic	Juan I. Matos, Luis J. Ramirez, Dario González, Luis A. Vidal, Rafael Villalobas, Angelo Becerra, James A. Figueras, Gerardo Torres, Luis Castro, Miguel Bisbal
Club Artes y Letras	cultural and literary	Josefina Silva de Cintrón
Spanish Correspondence for Soldiers	civic and patriotic	unknown
Comite Hispano-Americano Pro Defensa de America	civic and patriotic	unknown

Sources: Certificates of Incorporation
Memorias de Bernardo Vega, César Andreu Iglesias (ed.)
Group Participation of Migrants as related in interviews

POLITICAL CLUBS AND ORGANIZATIONS	MEMBERSHIP AND FUNCTIONS
1900–1919	
Club Demócrata Puertorriqueño	J.V. Alonso and Joaquin Colón Puerto Rican Local of New York City – Democratic Party
Harlem Branch	J.C. Cebollero and Domingo Collazo
Puerto Rican Committee of the Socialist Party	Lupercio Arroyo, Jesus Colón, Bernardo Vega, Eduvigus Cabán, Valentin Flores – founding members
Asociación Nacionalista	Vicente Balbas Capo; organization pledged to secure Puerto Rican independence
El Corserio	Anarchist. Some Puerto Rican membership. Mostly Merchant Marines. Published a newspaper.
Alianza Puertorriqueña	Composed of Puerto Rican intellectuals. Founding members: Gonzalo O'Neill, Rafael Torres, Luis G. Muñiz, Domingo Collazo, Fiol Ramos, J. Curzado, Radeo Pico
Club Latinoamericano	J.J. Henna
Club Betances	Tapia and Weber; Democratic Party Local

NAME	MEMBERSHIP AND FUNCTION
Liga Puertorriqueña	A federation of Latin societies. Founding members: G. O'Neill, J. Rodríguez Sanjurjo, R. Pabón Aviles
Club Demócrata Hispanoamericano	unknown
Federation of Puerto Rican Clubs in New York City	Joaquin Colón and J.V. Alonso
Alianza Obrera Committee to Support Robert M. La Follette	Presented activities in support of candidates. Fiorello La Guardia, Jesus Colón, Luis Muñoz Marín, Bernardo Vega, Lupercio Arroyo, Felix León, Valentin Flores, Cabán
El Caribe Democratic Club	Carlos Tapia and Luis Weber
Brooklyn Democratic Club	Founding members: Jesus Colón, Ramón Colón, Julio Díaz, Luis Weber. Active in legal aid and social work.
De Hostos Democratic Club	Functions similar to Brooklyn Dem. Club
Baldorioty Democratic Club	same as above
Guaybana Democratic Club	same as above
Guarionex Democratic Club	same as above
Puerto Rican Republican Organization	Founding members: R. Villar, Juan B. Matos, Fernando Torres, Frank Torres, F.M. Rivera, F. Gómez

1920–1930

Legión de la Flor Roja	Clandestine Cuban and Puerto Rican organization to combat Machado regime in Cuba
Hispanic Branch — Fusionist Party	Founding members: J.M. Vivaldi, Enrique Torregrosa, Victor Fiol, Antonio González, Florencio Ruiz, Felix Caro, J.D. López, Miguel Collazo, Luis Caballero, Salguero Font
Puerto Rican Political and Social League	membership unknown
League of Spanish Speaking Democrats	Chairman: Dr. J.A. López, Secretary: Adelia Pérez Ravelo
Brooklyn Branch of the Puerto Rican Republican Club	Founder: Ramón Colón
Puerto Rican Democratic and Social Union	membership unknown

Sources: César Andreu Iglesias, (ed.) *Memorias de Bernardo Vega*
Ramón Colón, *A Puerto Rican Hero in New York City*
Certificates of Incorporation
Personal Interviews

Officers and Voting Members of the Porto Rican Brotherhood of America, 1923, 1925, 1927

	1923	1925	1927
President	Rodrigo del Manzano	Blas Oliveras	Carlos L. Fernández
Vice-President	Tomás Gares	Carlos L. Fernández	Rafael Pérez
Secretary	Juan Carreras	Román Mínguez	Antonio González
Treasurer	Vincente Rolón	Julio Delgado	Fernando Navas
			Samuel Roig
Under-Secretary	Julio Pietratoni	Antonio González	José González Benítez
Auditor	Felipe Gómez	Juan A. Natali	Juan A. Natali
Voting Members (Vocales)	Antonio Dávila	Guillermo Patino	William L. Martínez
	Eusebio Cruz	Antonio Mark, Jr.	José M. Vivaldi
	Juan Valderrama	Jaime Gutierrez	Cirilo Pérez
	Aurelio Betancourt	Alfonso R. Quinones	Felipe Gómez
	Jacinto Paradis	Felipe Gómez	Jaime Gutierrez
	Juan I. Matos	Jorge L. Oller	Blas Oliveras
	Faustine Dorna	José R. Silen	Erasmo Vando, Jr.

Sources: César Andreu Iglesias, (ed.) *Memorias de Bernardo Vega*, p. 178.
Souvenir Program, Porto Rican Brotherhood of America, June, 1926
Certificate of Incorporation, Porto Rican Brotherhood of America, #05660-27C, March, 1927

Note: The exact posts held by Julio Pietratoni and Felipe Gómez in 1923 are not known but Vega declares both officers succeeded del Manzano as president.

Glossary

agregado	landless peasant, sharecropper
arroz	rice
barato	cheap, inexpensive
barrio	district or neighborhood, ward
bodega	grocery or general store
bolita	numbers racket or numbers game
bolitero	one who takes bets, numbers runner
Borinquen	indigenous name for Puerto Rico
botánicas	stores specializing in religious articles or plants
campesinos	rural, rustic, a countryman or woman
chiripeo	marginal employment
colmado	grocery or general store
colonia	subdivision of a city, colony, neighborhood, settlement
colonia hispana	Spanish settlement
comadre	godmother
compadrazgo	ritual kinship, the relationship between the natural parents and the godparents of a child
compadre	godfather, benefactor or protector
conjuntos	instrumental musical group
costura	sewing or needlecrafts
cuñha	a bed, a niche or a nest (Portuguese)
curandera	healer
empanadas	breaded meats or vegetables, meat pies
fíjate	observe, take notice
gandules verdes	pigeon peas

hacendado	landowner, owner of an hacienda
hacienda	landed property, large, self-sufficient farm
hijos de crianza	foster children
ingenio	sugar plantation
jaranas	a party, spree or scuffle, binge or revelry
juegos florales	dramatic or poetic competitions for troubadours
marqueta	market
maví	Puerto Rican drink made with fermented ginger root
mofongo	appetizer made with plantains, pork rind and spices
mozón	waiter, male attendant at a restaurant
mujeres	women
pernil	roast ham
personalismo	patron-client relationship based on personal contact
piragua	scraped ice drenched in sweet syrup
piraguero	one who sells piraguas
plátanos	fruit of plantain tree
se cuidan niños	children cared for
tostones	plantain fried chips
trio	musical group composed of three individuals
velada	evening party or gathering, conference
yautía	root vegetable

Bibliography

Books

Braverman, Harry. *Labor and Monopoly Capital: The Degradation of Work in the Twentieth Century.* New York: Monthly Review Press, 1974.

Buitrago Ortiz, Carlos. *Los orígenes históricos de la sociedad precapitalista en Puerto Rico.* San Juan: Ediciones Huracan, 1976.

Brooklyn Daily Eagle Almanac. Brooklyn: Brooklyn Eagle Press, 1926–1939.

Carroll, Henry K. *Report on the Island of Porto Rico.* Washington, D.C.: Government Printing Office, 1899.

Centro de Estudios Puertorriqueños. *Documentos de la migración puertorriqueña, 1879–1901.* New York: Centro de Estudios Puertorriqueños, Graduate Center, CUNY, 1977.

———. *Taller de migración, conferencia de historiografía.* New York: Graduate Center, CUNY, Centro de Estudios Puertorriqueños, 1974.

Chenault, Lawrence R. *The Puerto Rican Migrant in New York City.* New York: Columbia University Press, 1938; reissued, Russell and Russell, 1970.

Colón, Jesus. *The Puerto Rican in New York and Other Sketches.* New York: Arno Press, 1975.

Colón, Ramón. *Carlos Tapia, A Puerto Rican Hero in New York.* New York: Vantage Press, 1976.

Erickson, Charlotte. *American Industry and the European Immigrant, 1860–1885.* Cambridge: Harvard University Press, 1957.

Ernst, Robert. *Immigrant Life in New York City, 1825-1863*. New York: Kings Crown Press, 1949.

Figueroa Mercado, Loida. *Breve historia de Puerto Rico*. 2 vols. Rio Piedras: Ediciones Edil, 1970.

Fitzpatrick, Joseph P. *Puerto Rican-Americans: The Meaning of Migration to the Mainland*. Englewood Cliffs, N.J.: Prentice-Hall, 1971.

Glazer, Nathan, and Moynihan, Daniel. *Beyond the Melting Pot*. Cambridge: MIT Press, 1970.

Green, Constance M. *The Rise of Urban America*. New York: Harper & Row, 1965.

Gutman, Herbert C. *The Black Family in Slavery and Freedom, 1750-1925*. New York: Pantheon Press, 1976.

Handlin, Oscar. *The Newcomers: Negroes and Puerto Ricans in a Changing Metropolis*. Cambridge: Harvard University Press, 1959.

History Task Force, Centro de Estudios Puertorriqueños. *Labor Migration Under Capitalism: The Puerto Rican Experience*. New York: Monthly Review Press, 1979.

Howe, Irving. *The World of Our Fathers*. New York: Harcourt, Brace, Jovanovich, 1976.

Iglesias, César Andreu, ed. *Memorias de Bernardo Vega*. Rio Piedras: Ediciones Huracan, 1977.

Jennings, James. *Puerto Rican Politics in New York City*. Washington, D.C.: University Press of America, 1977.

Kanrowitz, Nathan. *Ethnic and Racial Segregation in New York Metropolis*. New York: Praeger Publishers, 1973.

La Gumina, Salvatore. *The People's Politician*. Iowa: Kendall Hunt Publishing Co., 1969.

Laslett, Peter. *Household and Family in Past Time*. Cambridge: Cambridge University Press, 1972.

López, Adalberto, and Petras, James, eds. *Puerto Rico and the Puerto Ricans: Studies in History and Society*. New York: Schenkman Publishing Co., 1974.

Maldonado-Denis, Manuel. *Puerto Rico: A Socio-Historic Interpretation*. New York: Random House, 1972.

Mann, Arthur. *La Guardia—A Fighter Against His Times, 1881-1933*. New York: J.B. Lippincott, 1959.

Manning, Caroline. *The Employment of Women in Puerto Rico*. Washington, D.C.: Government Printing Office, 1934.

Mills, C. Wright; Senior, Clarence; and Goldsen, Rose. *The Puerto Rican Journey: New York's Newest Migrants*. New York: Harper & Bros., 1950.

Morales Carrión, Arturo. *Puerto Rico and the Non-Hispanic Caribbean*. Rio Piedras: University of Puerto Rico, 1952.

Morrison, Samuel Eliot. *The Oxford History of the American People. Vol. 3.* New York: New American Library, 1972.

Moscow, Warren. *The Last of the Big-Time Bosses.* New York: Stein & Day, 1971.

Nieves Falcón, Luis. *El emigrante puertorriqueño.* Rio Piedras: Editorial Edil, 1975.

Padilla, Elena. *Up From Puerto Rico.* New York: Columbia University Press, 1958.

Peel, Roy V. *The Political Clubs of New York City.* New York: G.P. Putnam & Sons, 1935.

Perloff, Harvey S. *Puerto Rico's Economic Future.* Chicago: University of Chicago Press, 1950.

Picó, Fernando. *Libertad y servidumbre en el Puerto Rico del siglo XIX. Rio Piedras: Editorial Huracon, 1979.*

Rodríguez, Clara E. *The Ethnic Queue in the United States: The Case of Puerto Ricans.* San Francisco: R.&E. Research Associates, 1973.

_____; Sánchez Korrol, Virginia; and Alers, José Oscar, eds. *The Puerto Rican Struggle: Essays on Survival in the U.S.* New York: Puerto Rican Migration Research Consortium, 1980.

Rubenstein, Annette, et al. *I Vote My Conscience—Debates, Speeches and Writings of Vito Marcantonio, 1935-1950.* New York: The Vito Marcantonio Memorial, 1956.

Sayre, Wallace S., and Kaufman, Herbert. *Governing New York City.* New York: W.W. Norton & Co., 1965.

Senior, Clarence. *Puerto Rican Emigration.* Rio Piedras: Social Science Research Center, University of Puerto Rico, 1947.

_____. *The Puerto Ricans: Strangers then Neighbors.* Chicago: Quadrangle Books, 1965.

Shorter, Edward. *The Historian and the Computer.* New York: W.W. Norton & Co., 1971.

Smith, Page. *The Shaping of America. Vol. 3.* New York: McGraw-Hill Book Co., 1980.

Stewart, Donald. *A Short History of East Harlem.* New York: Museum of the City of New York, 1972.

Swierenga, Robert P. *Quantification in American History.* New York: Atheneum, 1970.

Toro, R. de Jesus. *Historia Económica de Puerto Rico.* Cincinnati, Ohio: South-Western Publishing Co., 1982.

Wagenheim, Kal. *A Survey of Puerto Ricans in the U.S. Mainland in the 1970s.* New York: Praeger Publishers, 1975.

_____. *Puerto Rico: A Profile.* New York: Praeger Publishers, 1975.

Wakefield, Daniel. *Island in the City: The World of Spanish Harlem.* Boston: Houghton Mifflin Co., 1959.

Articles and Periodicals

Alexander, Jack. "District Leader: Profile of James J. Hines." *The New Yorker,* vol. 12 (1936).

Berrol, Selma C. "School Days on the Old East Side: The Italian and Jewish Experience." *New York History.* New York Historical Association (April 1976).

Bone, Hugh A. "Political Parties in New York City." *American Political Science Review,* vol. 40 (April 1946).

Boorstein, Daniel J. "Self Discovery in Puerto Rico." *Yale Review* (1955).

Campos, Ricardo, and Bonilla, Frank. "Industrialization and Migration: Some Effects on the Puerto Rican Working Class." *Latin American Perspectives* vol. 3, no. 3 (1976).

―――― and Flores, Juan. "National Culture and Migration: Perspectives from the Puerto Rican Working Class." *Centro Working Papers.* New York: Centro de Estudios Puertorriqueños, Graduate Center, CUNY (1978).

Cintrón Fernández, Celia, and Rivera Quintero, Marcia. "Bases de la sociedad sexista en Puerto Rico." *Revista/Review Interamerican,* vol. 4, no. 2 (summer 1974).

Citizens Union. "Party Organization in New York City." *The Searchlight,* vol. 41 (May 1951).

Dyos, H. J., and Baker, A.B.M. "The Possibilities of Computerizing Census Data." In H. J. Dyos, *The Study of Urban History,* London: Edward Arnold Publishers, Ltd., 1968.

Estades, Rosa. "Symbolic Unity—The Puerto Rican Day Parade." In Clara E. Rodríguez, Virginia Sánchez Korrol, and José Oscar Alers, eds., *The Puerto Rican Struggle: Essays on Survival in the U.S.* New York: Puerto Rican Migration Research Consortium, 1980.

González, Nancie L. "Multiple Migratory Experiences of Dominican Women." *Anthropological Quarterly,* vol. 49, no. 1 (January 1979).

Gráfico, 1926–1928.

Gray, Lois. "The Jobs Puerto Ricans Hold in New York City." *Monthly Labor Review,* no. 46 (October 1975).

Hernández Álvarez, José. "The Movement and Settlement of Puerto Rican Migrants Within the U.S., 1950–1960." *International Migration Review,* no. 2 (spring 1968).

Hill, Herbert. "Guardians of the Sweatshop: The Trade Union, Racism and the Garment Industry." In Adalberto López and James Petras, eds., *Puerto Rico and Puerto Ricans: Studies in History and Society.* New York: Schenkman Publishing, 1974.

Kazin, Alfred. "In Puerto Rico." In *Contemporaries.* New York: Little, Brown & Co., 1960.

King, Lourdes Miranda. "Puertorriqueñas in the United States." In Commission of Human Rights, *Civil Rights Digest.* Washington, D.C.: U.S. Commission of Civil Rights, spring 1974.

La Correspondencia de Puerto Rico, 1901.

La Prensa, 1919–1924.

López, Adalberto. "Vito Marcantonio." *Caribbean Review,* vol. 8, no. 1 (January–March 1979).

_____. "The Puerto Rican Diaspora." In Adalberto López and James Petras, eds., *Puerto Rico and Puerto Ricans: Studies in History and Society.* New York: Schenkman Publishing, 1974.

_____. "Some of the Literature on Puerto Rico and Puerto Ricans in English." In Adalberto López and James Petras, eds., *Puerto Rico and Puerto Ricans: Studies in History and Society.* New York: Schenkman Publishing, 1974.

Maldonado, Rita M. "Why Puerto Ricans Migrated to the United States in 1947–73." *Monthly Labor Review,* no. 9 (September 1976).

McCoy, Terry L. "A Primer for U.S. Policy on Caribbean Emigration." *Caribbean Review,* vol. 8, no. 1 (January–March 1979).

Morley, Morris. "Dependence and Development in Puerto Rico." In Adalberto López and James Petras, eds., *Puerto Rico and Puerto Ricans: Studies in History and Society.* New York: Schenkman Publishing, 1974.

New York Times, 1926–1955.

New York World Telegram, 1945.

Pantoja, Antonia. "Puerto Rican Migration." Preliminary Report to the U.S. Commission on the Civil Rights of Puerto Ricans (1972).

Picó de Hernández, Isabel. "Estudio sobre el empleo de la mujer en Puerto Rico." *Revista de Ciencias Sociales,* vol. 19, no. 2 (June 1975).

Quintero Rivera, Angel. "Background to the Emergence of Imperialist Capitalism in Puerto Rico." In Adalberto López and James Petras, eds., *Puerto Rico and Puerto Ricans: Studies in History and Society.* New York: Schenkman Publishing, 1974.

Revista de Artes y Letras, 1934–1946.

Rinker, Buck. "The New Sweatshops: A Penny for Your Collar." *New York,* vol. 12, no. 5 (January 1979).

Rodríguez, Clara E. "Economic Factors Affecting Puerto Ricans in New York." History Task Force, Centro de Estudios Puertorriqueños. *Labor Migration Under Capitalism: The Puerto Rican Experience.* New York: Monthly Review, 1979.

_____. "Puerto Ricans in the Melting Pot." *The Journal of Ethnic Studies,* vol. 1, no. 4 (winter 1974).

Salazar, Max. "The Perserverance of a Culture." In Clara E. Rodríguez, Virginia Sánchez Korrol, and José Oscar Alers, eds., *The Puerto Rican Struggle: Essays on Survival in the U.S.* New York: Puerto Rican Migration Research Consortium, 1980.

————. "Latin Music's Rivalries and Battlers." *Latin New York,* January 1975.

Santana Cooney, Rosemary, and Warren Colon, Alice. "Work and Family: The Recent Struggle of Puerto Rican Females." In Clara E. Rodríguez, Virginia Sánchez Korrol, and José Oscar Alers, eds., *The Puerto Rican Struggle: Essays on Survival in the U.S.* New York: Puerto Rican Migration Research Consortium, 1980.

Senior, Clarence. "Migration as a Process and the Migrant as a Person." *Population Review,* vol. 6, no. 1 (January 1962).

————, and Watkins, Donald. "Toward a Balance Sheet of Puerto Rican Migration." In U.S.-Puerto Rico Commission on the Status of Puerto Rico, *Status of Puerto Rico: Selected Background Studies.* Washington, D.C.: Government Printing Office, 1966.

Shedd, William B. "Italian Population in New York." Bulletin No. 7, Casa Italiana Educational Bureau. New York: Columbia University, 1930.

Smith, Estelle M. "Networks and Migration Resettlement: Cherchez la Femme." *Anthropological Quarterly,* vol. 49, no. 1 (January 1979).

Stevens-Arroyo, Anthony. "Puerto Rican Struggles in the Catholic Church." In Clara E. Rodríguez, Virginia Sánchez Korrol, and José Oscar Alers, eds., *The Puerto Rican Struggle: Essays on Survival in the U.S.* New York: Puerto Rican Migration Research Consortium, 1980.

Vázquez Calzada, José. "Demographic Aspects of Migration." In History Task Force, Centro de Estudios Puertorriqueños, *Labor Migration Under Capitalism: The Puerto Rican Experience.* New York: Monthly Review Press, 1979.

Wagenheim, Olga Jimenez de. "Prelude to Lares." *Caribbean Review,* vol. 8, no. 1 (January-March 1979).

Documents and Reports

Cayce Morrison, J. *The Puerto Rican Study, 1953-1957.* New York: Board of Education, 1957.

Evans, W.D. "Effects of Mechanization on Cigar Manufacturing." Works Progress Administration, Report No. B-4. Washington, D.C.: Government Printing Office, 1934.

New York State Manuscript Census, 1925. New York City Municipal Archives.

Octavo informe anual del negociado del trabajo. San Juan, 1920.

The Porto Rican Brotherhood of America. Annual Report, 1926-1927.

Puerto Rican Forum. *A Study of Poverty Conditions in the New York*

Puerto Rican Community. New York: Puerto Rican Forum, Inc., 1964.

U.S. Commission on Civil Rights. *Puerto Ricans in the United States: An Uncertain Future.* Washington, D.C., 1976.

_____. *Civil Rights Digest,* vol. 6, no. 3 (spring 1974).

U.S. Department of Labor, Bureau of Labor Statistics. "The New York Puerto Rican: Patterns of Work Experience." Regional Report no. 19. Poverty Area Profiles. New York, 1972.

_____. "A Socio-Economic Profile of Puerto Rican New Yorkers." Regional Report no. 46. New York, 1975.

U.S.-Puerto Rico Commission on the Status of Puerto Rico. *Status of Puerto Rico.* August 1966.

Welfare Council of New York City. *Puerto Ricans in New York City.* New York: The Welfare Council, 1948.

Welfare and Health Council of New York City. Population of Puerto Rican Birth or Parentage. New York City, 1950.

_____. Brooklyn Council for Social Planning. "Report on Survey of Brooklyn Agencies Rendering Services to Puerto Ricans." (June 1953).

Unpublished Materials and Dissertations

Amaral, Daniel Joseph. "Family, Community and Place: The Experience of Puerto Rican Emigrants in Worcester, Massachusetts." Ph.D. Dissertation, Clark University, 1978.

Estades, Rosa. "Patterns of Political Participation of Puerto Ricans in New York City." Ph.D. Dissertation, New School for Social Research, 1974.

Gittell, Marilyn. "Administration and Organization of Political Parties in New York City." Master's Thesis, NYU, 1953.

Gotsch, John W. "Puerto Rican Leadership in New York." Master's Thesis, NYU, 1966.

Gray, Lois. "Economic Incentives to Labor Mobility: The Puerto Rican Case." Ph.D. Dissertation, Columbia University, 1966.

Quintero Rivera, Angel. "Puerto Rico, 1870-1940: From Mercantilist to Imperialist Colonial Domination." CEREP, Rio Piedras, Puerto Rico, 1979.

Rivera Quintero, Marcia. "Capitalist Development and the Incorporation of Women to the Labour Force." CEREP, Rio Piedras, Puerto Rico, 1979.

Sánchez Korrol, Virginia E. "Settlement Patterns and Community Development Among Puerto Ricans in New York City, 1917-1948." Ph.D. Dissertation, SUNY at Stony Brook, 1981.

Index

contemporary
HOME PLANS
SECOND EDITION

235
sleek designs
for
modern lifestyles

Design HPT820002, see page 8

Photo by Oscar Thompson Photography, Design by The Sater Design Collection, Inc.

HOME PLANNERS

Home Planners, LLC
Wholly owned by Hanley-Wood, LLC

C o n t e m p o r a r y   H o m e   P l a n s

Published by Home Planners, LLC

Wholly owned by Hanley-Wood, LLC

3275 West Ina Road, Suite 110

Tucson, Arizona 85741

Distribution Center:

29333 Lorie Lane

Wixom, Michigan 48393

Jayne Fenton, President

Jennifer Pearce, Vice President, Group Content

Linda B. Bellamy, Executive Editor

Jan Prideaux, Editor In Chief

Marian E. Haggard, Editor

Ashleigh Stone, Plans Editor

William Knight, Graphic Production Artist

Sara Lisa, Senior Production Manager

Fariba Crawford, Production Manager

Photo Credits

Front Cover: Andrew D. Lautman, Design by Home Planners

Back Cover: Larry E. Belk Designs, Design by Larry E. Belk Designs

Library of Congress Catalog Card Number: 2001097491

ISBN softcover: 1-931131-02-3

On the front cover: Design HPT820199, with its stucco walls, multitude of windows and delightful angles, displays plenty of contemporary style. For more information about this design, please see page 207.

On the back cover: Design HPT820072 offers soaring ceilings and crisp details to brighten up anyone's day. For more information about this design, please see page 80.

Table of Contents

Design HPT820027, see page 35

Anthropologists say that you can tell a lot about people by the type of homes they choose to live in. Contemporary architecture certainly tells a lot about some people's lifestyles. A style that consciously strives for modernity and an artistic expression, contemporary architecture borrows heavily from Modernist and International styles. The emphasis on the future rather than the past is one of this style's principal characteristics.

Concrete, smooth-faced stone, large glass openings, geometric shapes and vivid colors define the style and give it a special flavor. Elements from Europe and even Early American sometimes combine with Cubism and Modernist/ International styles to produce dramatic results. Mix these styles with traces of Tudor, Georgian, Salt Box and Cape Cod, and you get an elegantly eclectic design known as today's contemporary.

The popular slogan "form follows function" has been transformed to the more recent "form and function are one," and is expressed in the way the indoor/outdoor relationships are defined. Typical features include terraces, patios, large glass viewing areas and private balconies—all designed neatly in private rear and side yards. The fronts are reserved for window space that provides plenty of natural light to interior rooms.

Indoors, contemporary design caters to the pace of today's more frenetic lifestyle. With open spaces, efficient kitchens, many large bathrooms and multi-purpose rooms to provide the space for a variety of activities, contemporary style adds adaptability to its impressive description.

While found throughout the United States, contemporary architecture is prevalently rooted in the Pacific Northwest, California, the Southwest, and the Midwest. Evolutions of contemporary design vary from region to region.

In the Northwest particularly, designers, builders and especially consumers showed early preference for contemporary design. Today, Northwest contemporary architecture reflects its woodsy surroundings and

adaptation to the climate and materials of the region. A futuristic effect is achieved through combining the use of extended wood beams, exposed rafter tails, heavy shake roofs, dark-stained exteriors and wide overhangs with a simplified and streamlined form. As with all successful architecture, Northwest contemporaries fit their settings and are built with materials readily available in the area. A

good example of this can be seen with Design HPT820054 (page 62).

Generally, the composite contemporary homes of the Southwest are simple, open, comfortable and informal. They incorporate Spanish and Native American design with contemporary styling. Adobe, concrete block or masonry—often washed with a stucco finish to protect the surface—are usually employed. Southwestern contemporaries often incorporate porches, sheltered "ramada" terraces, shady overhangs and large blank walls that face west away from the burning sun. Floors are often tile, quarry or scored concrete to

weather the heat. Terraces and patios frequently feature fountains, pools and plants. Design HPT820199 (page 207) exhibits these features well and combines them with the flavor of International style.

Design HPT820031 (page 39) incorporates all the elements when it comes to the Midwest contemporary ranch: long, low lines, a sense of mass- or self-enclosure with rambling buildings of various rooflines and pitches all leaning toward a central point. Emphasis is place on aesthetic values over disciplined art forms in quest of space, freedom, peace and the outdoors. Introduced after World War II, the Midwest ranch house combines design elements from east and west with practical substitution of Midwest materials.

The influence of early American architecture is highly evident in the Northeast contemporaries. Once-simple Cape Cod cottages of few rooms and basic needs have been expanded to larger, more complex homes. The openness, gathering space to the rear and multiple accesses to the terrace all point toward contemporary design in Design HPT820127 (page 135), while still evidencing the flavor of yesterday so popular in the Northeast.

A compromise is demonstrated in Southern contemporary style. Elements of traditional styling are smoothed into modern lines. Traditional-style columns, balconies and cupolas are combined with sleek lines and interesting angles on Design HPT820072 (page 80). Originally designed for a sloping site, the home incorporates multiple levels inside, furthering the futuristic ambience.

The homes presented here represent a look toward tomorrow. They're a fine, new collection of the many forms and variations of what contemporary design has become and encompass the potential for what it is yet to be. Ranging from ground-hugging, one-story ranches to lavish multi-level homes, the designs in this book provide the lover of contem-porary style with a vast choice of sizes and looks. So, peruse, compare and enjoy!

Design HPT820072, page 80
Photo by Larry E. Belk Designs

This home contains elements that will shape new-home design and construction in the years ahead. The home resembles a village, with compelling destinations—a greenhouse for herb gardening, an overnight port for kid sleepovers, and a masters retreat with a glass roof for stargazing. Flexible to the utmost, the plan features a drive-in motor court that doubles as a hardscape playground, a garage that serves as a sports court, and a parlor that could one day become an in-law suite. The flexibility culminates in a great room with movable walls, sliding Shoji-like doors and modular furniture. It can be reconfigured at will and within minutes. Dual casitas, connected to and yet separate from the main house, provide tantalizing living possibilities. Designed as an art studio and guest suite today, they could become home to a small import business, a boomerang child or a workshop tomorrow. A practical and efficient kitchen is a must for the busy homeowner. In this design, dual ovens allow cooks to prepare multi-course meals. Lit by a corner window, the built-in desk provides a handy spot for menu planning or letter writing. Special spaces in

this house lend themselves to creative escapism for parents as well as children. A domed retreat off the master suite provides valuable getaway space to contemplate the stars, watch the seasons pass or escape with a good book. A bridge leads to the children's wing, where a two-story circular port makes sleepovers a memorable event for kids. This home is an attempt to reconcile competing and intensifying family demands for work, play, entertainment, sleep and refuge. It's a home that accommodates myriad pursuits—painting, Internet surfing, movie watching, craft making, sports, and gourmet cooking. Yet it never loses sight of a home's main function: to unite a family, no matter how varied their interests, all under one roof.

A practical and efficient kitchen is a must for the busy homeowner.

Second Floor

First Floor

HPT820001

First Floor: 2,266 square feet
Second Floor: 1,633 square feet
Total: 3,899 square feet
Width: 62'-5" Depth: 95'-11"

Photos by Oscar Thompson

6559

Double doors lead into the lavish master

bath that boasts an impressive tub.

Luxurious dreams and contemporary style combine to give this home striking appeal. A stunning courtyard entry welcomes you inside. Two guest suites with pampering private baths flank the foyer. The gathering room features an impressive bar. The right wing of the home offers a gourmet kitchen, which is open to the leisure room and nook—the dining room connects close by. Stairs lead up to a bonus room with a private deck. The left wing of the home is devoted to the master suite, which features steps up to a private sitting retreat. Double doors lead into the lavish master bath that boasts an impressive tub, separate shower, twin vanities, a compartmented toilet and His and Hers walk-in closets. Private access to the study is a convenient touch. An extensive wraparound deck surrounds the pool. A bridge leads over the pool to an outdoor kitchen enhanced by skylights.

HPT820002

Square Footage: 5,887
Bonus Room: 570 square feet
Width: 137'-4" Depth: 103'-0"

The gourmet kitchen features dual islands and warm wood cabinets to offset black appliances and a stainless range hood.

9

This striking Floridian plan offers

a classy contemporary design.

This striking Floridian plan offers a classy contemporary design for entertaining. A large, open floor plan provides soaring, sparkling space for planned gatherings. The foyer leads to the grand room, highlighted by a glass fireplace, a wet bar and wide views of the outdoors. Both the grand room and the formal dining room open to a screened veranda. The first floor includes two spacious family bedrooms and a secluded study which opens from the grand room. The second-floor master suite offers sumptuous amenities, including a private deck and spa, a three-sided fireplace, a sizable walk-in closet and a gallery hall with an overlook to the grand room.

HPT820005 [L]

First Floor: 2,066 square feet

Second Floor: 810 square feet

Total: 2,876 square feet

Bonus Space: 1,260 square feet

Width: 64'-0" **Depth:** 45'-0"

Light and bright, the kitchen features a snack-bar island and bright windows overlooking a fabulous view.

Second Floor

First Floor

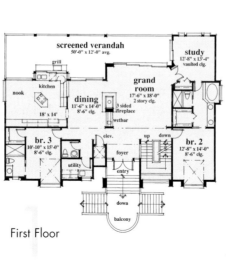

Basement

First Floor

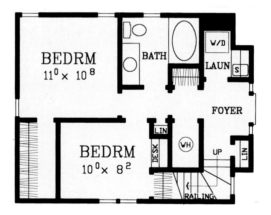

BEDRM
11⁰ × 10⁸

BATH

W/D

LAUN S

FOYER

BEDRM
10⁰ × 8²

LIN

DESK

WH

UP

LIN

RAILING

Combine a shingled exterior and an upstairs deck, and you can recall the joy of seaside vacations. Let breezes ruffle your hair and ocean spray settle on your skin in this comfortable two-story home. Unique window treatments provide views from every room. The lifestyle is casual, including meals prepared in a kitchen separated from the living room by a snack-bar counter. A powder room and a wet bar complete the second floor. The first floor houses two bedrooms, a full bath and a laundry room. A walk-in closet enhances one of the bedrooms that could serve as the master suite. Built-ins make the most of compact space.

REFG

PANT

S

WET BAR

STOR

RANGE

S

KITCHEN

SNACK BAR

LIVING
11⁸ × 16⁰

DECK

DW

RAILING

PDR

DESK

DN

RAILING

Second Floor

QUOTE ONE®

Cost to build? See page 246 to order complete cost estimate to build this house in your area!

HPT820004

First Floor: 507 square feet
Second Floor: 438 square feet
Total: 945 square feet
Width: 20'-0" *Depth:* 26'-0"

A level for everyone! This home is sure to please every member of the family. On the first floor, there's a study with a full bath, a formal dining room, a grand room with a fireplace, and a fabulous kitchen with an adjacent morning room. The second floor contains three suites—each with walk-in closets—two full baths, a loft and a reading nook near the laundry room. A lavish master suite on the third floor is full of amenities, including His and Hers walk-in closets, a huge private bath and a balcony. In the basement, casual entertaining takes off with a large gathering room, a home theater and a spacious game room.

HPT820003

Main Level: 2,347 square feet

Second Level: 1,800 square feet

Third Level: 1,182 square feet

Total: 5,329 square feet

Finished Basement: 1,688 sq. ft.

Width: 75'-5" Depth: 76'-4"

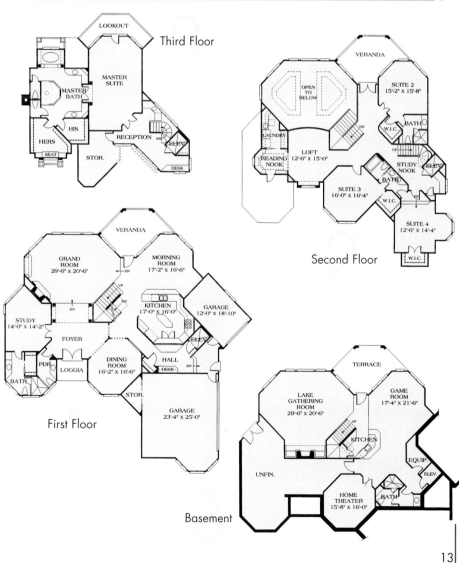

Third Floor

LOOKOUT

MASTER SUITE

MASTER BATH

HIS

HERS

SEAT

STOR.

RECEPTION

DN

ELEV.

DESK

Second Floor

VERANDA

OPEN TO BELOW

SUITE 2
15'-2" x 15'-8"

BATH

W.I.C.

LAUNDRY

LOFT
12'-6" x 15'-0"

READING NOOK

STUDY NOOK

BATH

ELEV.

SUITE 3
16'-0" x 16'-4"

W.I.C.

SUITE 4
12'-6" x 14'-4"

W.I.C.

First Floor

VERANDA

GRAND ROOM
29'-6" x 20'-6"

MORNING ROOM
17'-2" x 16'-6"

DN

KITCHEN
17'-0" x 16'-0"

GARAGE
12'-0" x 18'-10"

ELEV.

STUDY
14'-0" x 14'-2"

DN

FOYER

BATH

PDR.

LOGGIA

DINING ROOM
16'-2" x 16'-6"

HALL

DESK

DN

STOR.

GARAGE
23'-4" x 25'-0"

Basement

TERRACE

LAKE GATHERING ROOM
29'-6" x 20'-6"

GAME ROOM
17'-4" x 21'-6"

UP

KITCHEN

EQUIP.

UNFIN.

ELEV.

HOME THEATER
15'-8" x 16'-0"

BATH

13

Second Floor

First Floor

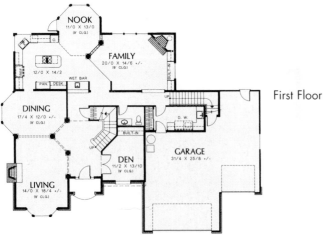

A dramatic entry beckons visitors and family into this elegant home. The entry contains a curved staircase and leads to a formal living room with a fireplace and bay window, and to a den with built-in bookshelves. The dining room also has a bay window—this room connects to the island kitchen and the breakfast nook, which overlook the family room with its corner fireplace. A rear staircase leads to the second-floor sleeping area with four bedrooms. The master suite is especially appealing with a spa tub, bay window and huge walk-in closet. One of the secondary bedrooms has its own bath; the other two feature window seats.

HPT820006 L

First Floor: 1,940 square feet
Second Floor: 1,578 square feet
Total: 3,518 square feet
Bonus Room: 292 square feet
Width: 70'-6" Depth: 59'-6"

Here's an upscale multi-level plan with expansive rear views. The first floor provides an open living and dining area, defined by decorative columns and enhanced by natural light from tall windows. A breakfast area with a lovely triple window opens to a sun room, which allows light to pour into the gourmet kitchen. The master wing features a tray ceiling in the bedroom, two walk-in closets and an elegant private vestibule leading to a lavish bath. Upstairs, a reading loft overlooks the great room and leads to a sleeping area with two suites.

Second Floor

First Floor

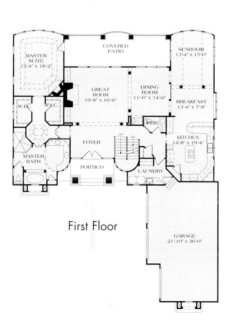

Basement

HPT820007

First Floor: 2,391 square feet

Second Floor: 922 square feet

Total: 3,313 square feet

Bonus Room: 400 square feet

Finished Basement: 1,964 sq. ft.

Width: 63'-10" Depth: 85'-6"

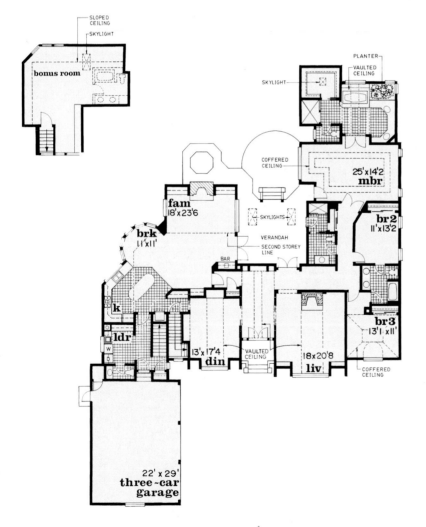

SLOPED CEILING

SKYLIGHT

bonus room

PLANTER

SKYLIGHT

VAULTED CEILING

COFFERED CEILING

25'x14'2 **mbr**

fam 18'x23'6

SKYLIGHTS

brk 11'x11'

VERANDAH

SECOND STOREY LINE

BAR

br2 11'x13'2

k

ldr

w

13'x17'4 **din**

VAULTED CEILING

18x20'8 **liv**

br3 13'1'x11'

COFFERED CEILING

VAULTED CEILING

22' x 29' **three~car garage**

Decorative latticework and circle-head windows combine to make the exterior of this home unique. The long entry hall is flanked by the living and dining rooms. An island kitchen acts as a hub for the circular breakfast area and the family room with a fireplace. Bedrooms are at the right of the plan with the luxurious master suite at the back and two family bedrooms sharing a hall bath. Bonus space above the kitchen could be developed as an office, guest bedroom or studio.

HPT820008

Square Footage: 3,555
Bonus Room: 568 square feet
Width: 80'-0" Depth: 109'-6"

Classic columns, circle-head windows and a bay-windowed study give this stucco home a wonderful street presence. The foyer leads to the formal living and dining areas. An arched buffet server separates these rooms and contributes an open feeling. The kitchen, nook and leisure room are grouped for informal living. A desk/message center in the island kitchen, art niches in the nook and a fireplace with an entertainment center and shelves add custom touches. Two secondary suites have guest baths and offer full privacy from the master wing. The master suite hosts a private garden area, while the master bath features a walk-in shower that overlooks the garden, and a water-closet room with space for books or a television. Large His and Hers walk-in closets complete these private quarters.

HPT820009 [L]

Square Footage: 2,794
Width: 70'-0" Depth: 98'-0"

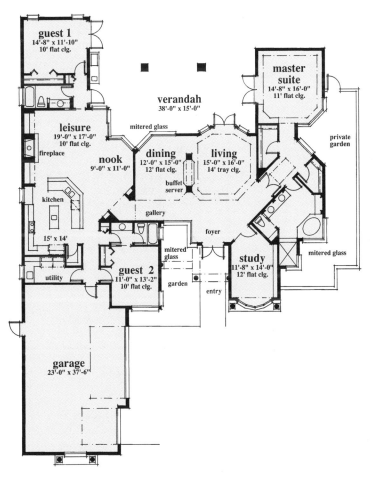

guest 1
14'-8" x 11'-10"
10' flat clg.

master
suite
14'-8" x 16'-0"
11' flat clg.

verandah
38'-0" x 15'-0"

leisure
19'-0" x 17'-0"
10' flat clg.

mitered glass

private
garden

fireplace

dining
12'-0" x 15'-0"
12' flat clg.

living
15'-0" x 16'-0"
14' tray clg.

nook
9'-0" x 11'-0"

kitchen

buffet
server

15' x 14'

gallery

foyer

utility

guest 2
11'-0" x 13'-2"
10' flat clg.

mitered
glass

study
11'-8" x 14'-0"
12' flat clg.

garden

mitered glass

entry

garage
23'-0" x 37'-6"

HPT820010

The raised foyer and living room bring an interesting change of levels to this ingenious plan. The family room, with a twelve-foot wall of sliding glass doors, brings the outside in, and the entertainment/fireplace wall wows visitors. The efficient kitchen features a pantry and easy access to the sunny breakfast nook. Three secondary bedrooms are conveniently separated from the master suite. The rear bedroom doubles as a guest or in-law suite and shares the pool bath. The open and airy master suite, located off the nook, accesses the patio. The master bath holds a corner soaking tub, an oversized shower, a large double vanity with a make-up area, and double walk-in closets.

Square Footage: 2,221
Width: 65'-0" Depth: 50'-0"

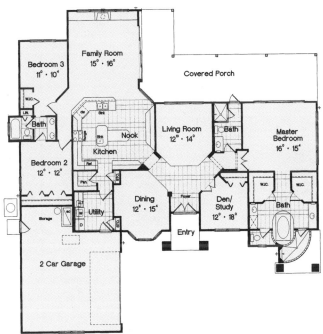

HPT8200111

Square Footage: 2,530
Width: 71'-10" Depth: 72'-8"

Multi-pane windows provide plenty of light for this sensational stucco home. A wall of glass in the living room provides unlimited vistas of the rear grounds, while the nearby dining room completes the formal area. The kitchen, breakfast nook and family room comprise the family wing, coming together to create the perfect place for casual gatherings. Two secondary bedrooms share a bath and provide complete privacy to the master suite, located on the opposite side of the plan. The master bedroom is full of amenities, including His and Hers walk-in closets. The lavish master bath, which pampers with a sumptuous soaking tub flanked by a step-down shower and compartmented toilet, is sure to please.

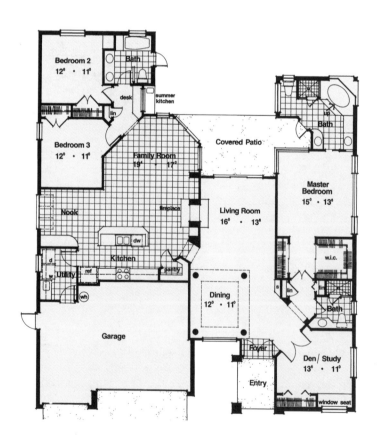

A three-car garage gives this home large-scale appeal in less than 2,400 square feet. The casual areas of the home remain open to each other for lots of family time. The kitchen features a pantry and island work surface and works well with the nearby nook. Nearby secondary bedrooms enjoy a built-in desk and a roomy bath. Formal living and dining areas flow into a den or study. The master bedroom delights with lots of windows, two closets and a custom bath. Off the covered patio, a summer kitchen facilitates added pool-time fun.

HPT820012

Square Footage: 2,398
Width: 57'-6" Depth: 66'-0"

J.N. HANSEN P.T.L.

Grand arched windows create a classic look for this sensational stucco home. A magnificent view from the living room provides unlimited vistas of the rear grounds through a wall of glass. The kitchen, breakfast nook and family room comprise the family wing, coming together to form the perfect place for casual gatherings. Two secondary bedrooms share a bath and provide complete privacy to the master suite located on the opposite side of the plan. The master bedroom sets the mood for relaxation and the lavish master bath impresses with a soaking tub flanked by a stepdown shower and a compartmented toilet. Bonus space may be completed at a later date to accommodate additional space requirements.

HPT820013

Square Footage: 2,322

Bonus Room: 370 square feet

Width: 60'-0" Depth: 76'-8"

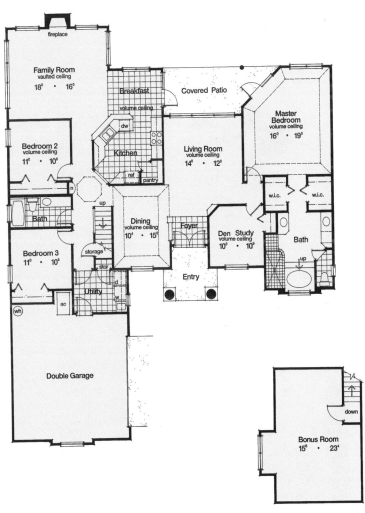

PATIO

DEN
12/0 X 10/8
(9' CLG.)

NOOK
9/2 X 10/0

VAULTED
FAMILY
16/6 X 21/4

LIVING
16/0 X 16/4
(13'-4" CLG.)

MASTER
15/8 X 15/8
(9' CLG.)

BR. 2
11/6 X 12/0

DESK

PANTRY

REF.

DINING
11/0 X 16/8

(13'-4" CLG.)

15/8 X 9/6

LIN.

BR. 3
12/8 X 11/0

GARAGE
20/6 X 19/8

25/2 X 11/0

HPT820014

Square Footage: 2,755
Width: 84'-0" Depth: 73'-0"

Squared columns flank an appealing entrance to this three-bedroom home. Columns continue inside, helping to define the formal dining room and formal living room, and separating the family room/nook area from the kitchen. The gourmet cook of the family will be ecstatic when presented with this amenity-filled kitchen. The living room and the vaulted family room share a through-fireplace. A cozy den opens through double doors just off the nook area. To the left of the plan, two family bedrooms share a full bath between them. Located at the opposite end of the home, the master bedroom suite is sure to please with a double-door entry, walk-in closet, sumptuous bath and private access to the rear yard.

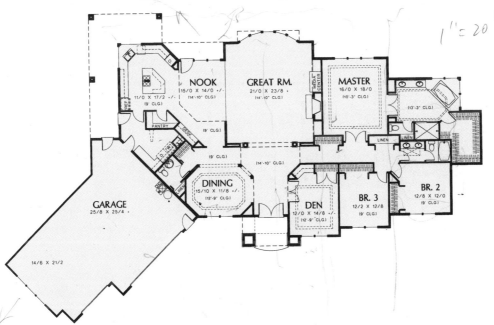

HPT820015

Square Footage: 3,242
Width: 118'-0" Depth: 74'-0"

A grand entrance leads through double doors into a foyer flanked by a formal octagonal dining room and a cozy den with a tray ceiling. The huge great room lies just ahead and features a fireplace, a built-in media center and a bowed window-wall. The island kitchen tempts the cook to stay all day, enjoying the corner sink with its window, the walk-in pantry and the nearby nook which offers access to the rear yard. Two family bedrooms share a full bath that includes a dual-bowl vanity and a large hall linen closet. The master suite is sweet indeed, with a double-door entry, a tray ceiling, a walk-in closet and a lavish master bath.

A two-story entry, varying rooflines and multi-pane windows add to the spectacular street appeal of this three-bedroom home. To the right, off the foyer, is the dining room surrounded by elegant columns. Adjacent is the angular kitchen, which opens to the bayed breakfast nook. The family room includes plans for an optional fireplace and accesses the covered porch. The master bedroom is tucked in the back of the home and features a walk-in closet and full bath with a dual vanity, spa tub and oversized shower. Two additional bedrooms share a full bath.

HPT820016

Square Footage: 1,831
Width: 59'-0"   Depth: 55'-4"

Italianate lines add finesse to the formal facade of this home. Strong symmetry, a soaring portico and gentle rooflines are the prized hallmarks of this relaxed, yet formal design. To the right of the foyer, columns and a stepped ceiling offset the dining room. A plant shelf heralds the living room, which also has a twelve-foot ceiling. An angled cooktop counter adds flair to the kitchen, which includes a desk and a walk-in pantry and serves the breakfast nook. A corner fireplace, high ceiling and patio enhance the family room. An arch opens the entry to the lavish master suite. Two additional bedrooms come with separate entries to a full bath.

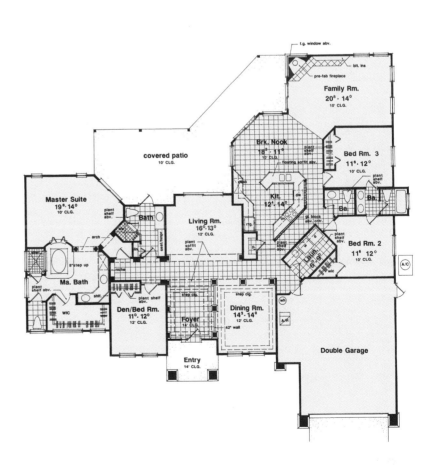

HPT820017

Square Footage: 2,691

Width: 78'-6" Depth: 73'-10"

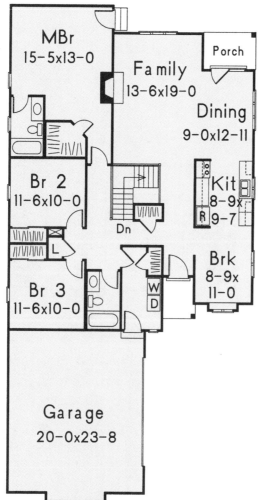

MBr
15-5x13-0

Family
13-6x19-0

Porch

Dining
9-0x12-11

Br 2
11-6x10-0

Dn

Kit
8-9x
9-7

R

Br 3
11-6x10-0

L

W
D

Brk
8-9x
11-0

Garage
20-0x23-8

This stunning stucco design features a three-bedroom layout with plenty of living space for a comfortable family lifestyle. Enter inside—a breakfast room is located to the immediate right. The compact kitchen is conveniently set between the breakfast room and the formal dining area. The dining room accesses a petite rear porch that's perfect for outdoor grilling. A fireplace warms the family room, which combines with the open dining area. The master bedroom is located at the rear of the plan and offers a walk-in closet and private bath. Two additional family bedrooms share a hall bath. A laundry room connecting to the garage completes the floor plan.

HPT820018

Square Footage: 1,624
Width: 38'-0" Depth: 74'-4"

Quote One®

Cost to build? See page 246
to order complete cost estimate
to build this house in your area!

HPT820019 LD

Square Footage: 2,916
Width: 77'-10" Depth: 73'-10"

Intricate details make the most of this lovely one-story design. Besides the living room/dining room combination to the rear, there is a large conversation area with a fireplace and plenty of windows. The kitchen is separated from the living areas by an angled snack-bar counter. Three bedrooms grace the right side of the plan. The master suite features a tray ceiling and sliding glass doors to the rear terrace. The dressing area is graced by His and Hers walk-in closets, a double-bowl vanity and a compartmented toilet. The sunken shower area is highlighted with glass block. A garden whirlpool tub finishes off this area.

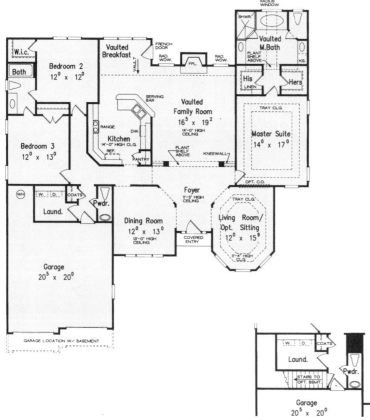

Optional Basement Staircase

Contemporary accents and captivating interior spaces dazzle this perfect family floor plan. The spacious foyer is flanked on either side by formal living and dining rooms. Beyond, the vaulted family room offers a spacious casual area warmed by a fireplace. The kitchen opens to the vaulted breakfast nook. The luxurious master suite features His and Hers walk-in closets and a vaulted bath with an enticing whirlpool tub. Two additional family bedrooms offer access to a Jack-and-Jill bath. A laundry room connects to the two-car garage. Please specify basement or crawlspace foundation when ordering.

HPT820020

Square Footage: 2,201
Width: 59'-6" Depth: 62'-0"

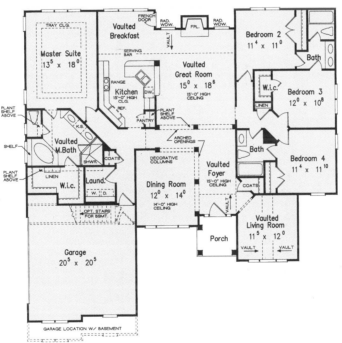

HPT820021

Square Footage: 2,279
Width: 59'-6" Depth: 58'-0"

Spacious quarters for a large family comprise the one floor in this four-bedroom family design with Country French and contemporary accents. The master suite occupies the left side of the plan, while the right side contains family bedrooms and a vaulted living room. The hub of this home is the vaulted great room with a fireplace. The kitchen, breakfast nook and dining room are nearby. Please specify basement or crawlspace foundation when ordering.

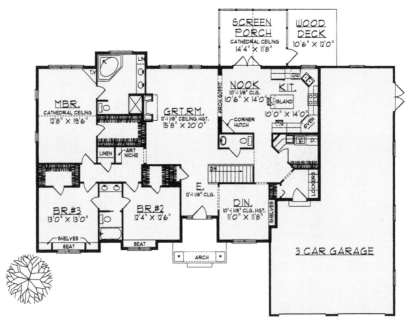

SCREEN PORCH
CATHEDRAL CEILING
14'4" X 11'8"

WOOD DECK
10'6" X 12'0"

NOOK
10'-1 1/8" CLG.
10'6" X 14'0"

KIT.
ISLAND
10'0" X 14'0"

MBR.
CATHEDRAL CEILING
12'8" X 19'6"

GRT.RM.
12'-1 1/8" CEILING HGT.
15'8" X 20'0"

CORNER HUTCH

ART NICHE

LINEN

E.
12'-1 1/8" CLG.

BR #3
13'0" X 13'0"

BR #2
12'4" X 12'6"

DIN.
10'-1 1/8" CLG. HGT.
11'0" X 11'8"

SHELVES

SEAT

SEAT

ARCH

LOCKERS

3 CAR GARAGE

HPT820022

The stucco facade of this home lends dramatic and contemporary accents to the exterior. An arched entrance welcomes you inside. The spacious great room provides backyard views and is warmed by a fireplace. The U-shaped kitchen sports an island countertop and a casual family nook. Double doors open from the nook to the screened porch— a perfect relaxing escape for seasonal temperatures. The master suite features a walk-in closet and a private bath with a whirlpool tub. Two additional bedrooms located at the front of the home share a Jack-and-Jill bath, and each bedroom offers its own walk-in closet.

Square Footage: 2,224
Width: 78'-0" Depth: 64'-0"

Simplicity is the key to the stylish good looks of this home's facade. Inside, the kitchen opens directly off the foyer and contains an island and a work counter with eating space on the living area side. The master bedroom sports sliding glass doors to the terrace. Its dressing area is enhanced with double walk-in closets and lavatories. A whirlpool tub and seated shower are additional amenities. Two family bedrooms are found on the opposite side of the house.

HPT820023 L

Square Footage: 2,189
Width: 56'-0" Depth: 72'-0"

Rear View

HPT820024

This modern country cottage reveals both European and contemporary influences. A covered front porch opens inside, where formal rooms greet the entry. To the left, the great room features a fireplace and access to the side wrapping porch. The island kitchen is open to an eating nook and connects to the formal dining room nearby. The right side of the plan contains the family bedrooms. The master suite offers a private bath and walk-in closet, while Bedrooms 2 and 3 share a full hall bath. The rear porch is accessed through the dining room and utility room. A three-car garage completes this plan.

Square Footage: 2,314
Width: 81'-0" Depth: 72'-0"

Don't let the small size of this home fool you. It serves both formal and informal occasions. The living room and dining room are found to the right of the plan and are open to one another. The well-planned kitchen is nearby and also serves a nook eating area and the casual family room. The master suite is filled with amenities not usually found in a smaller home, such as French doors, a walk-in closet and a luxurious spa bathroom. One secondary bedroom has a full bath nearby.

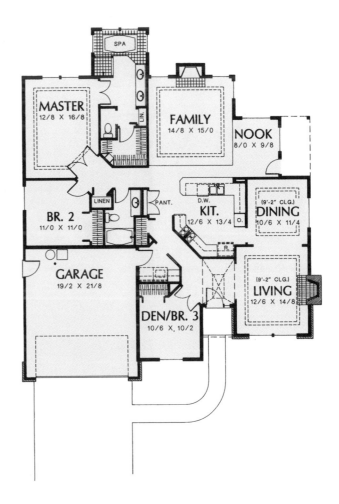

HPT820025 L

Square Footage: 1,865
Width: 50'-0" Depth: 59'-0"

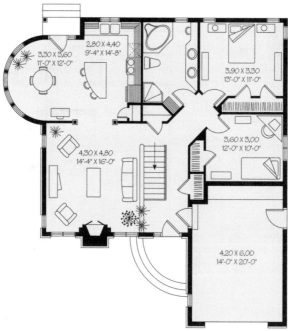

3.30 X 3.60
11'-0" X 12'-0"

2.80 X 4.40
9'-4" X 14'-8"

3.90 X 3.30
13'-0" X 11'-0"

4.30 X 4.80
14'-4" X 16'-0"

3.60 X 3.00
12'-0" X 10'-0"

4.20 X 6.00
14'-0" X 20'-0"

HPT820026

Contemporary style and European influences shape this lovely brick exterior. The entry opens to a living room warmed by a fireplace—flanking windows illuminate the interior. The island snack-bar kitchen combines with a circular bayed breakfast room for casual family meals. The two family bedrooms share a hall bath that includes a corner tub, separate shower and double-bowl vanity. The master bedroom features ample closet space. A garage completes the floor plan. This home is designed with a basement foundation.

Square Footage: 1,175
Width: 44'-0" Depth: 46'-0"

This unique contemporary design features large illuminating windows throughout that bathe the entire design in sunlight. Double doors open inside to a spacious foyer. To the right, a bay-windowed area surrounds the living room, which extends into the formal dining room. The U-shaped kitchen is placed between this combined area and a casual family area at the rear of the plan. The master suite boasts ample closet space and private access to the exercise room. Two additional bedrooms share a full hall bath and a huge walk-in storage closet with the master bedroom. A front garage completes this one-story plan.

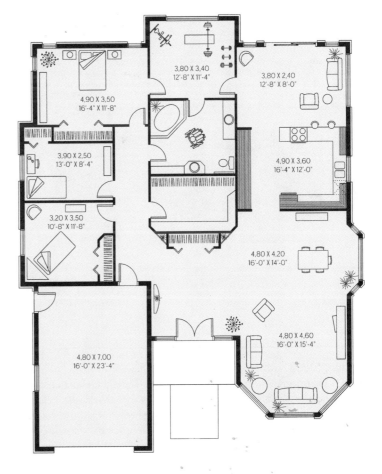

HPT820027

Square Footage: 2,263
Width: 48'-0" Depth: 64'-0"

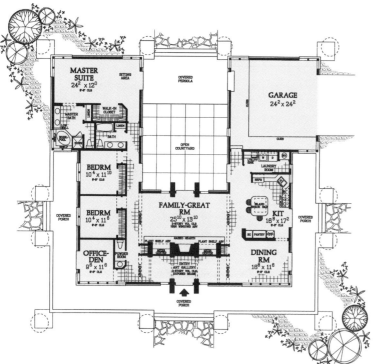

QUOTE ONE®
Cost to build? See page 246
to order complete cost estimate
to build this house in your area!

Rear View

Square Footage: 2,626
Width: 75'-10" Depth: 69'-4"

Frank Lloyd Wright had a knack for enhancing the environment with the homes he designed. This adaptation reflects his purest Prairie style complemented by a brick exterior, a multitude of windows and a low-slung hip roof. The foyer introduces a gallery wall to display your artwork. To the right, an archway leads to a formal dining room lined with a wall of windows. Nearby, the spacious kitchen features an island snack bar. The two-story family/great room provides an ideal setting for formal or informal gatherings. If philosophical discussions heat up, they can be continued in the open courtyard. The left wing contains the sleeping quarters and an office/den. The private master suite includes a sitting area, a walk-in closet and a lavish master bath with a corner whirlpool tub.

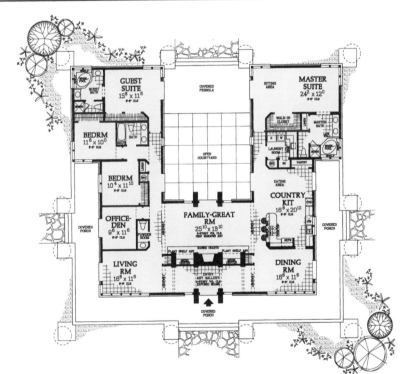

QUOTE ONE®
Cost to build? See page 246
to order complete cost estimate
to build this house in your area!

HPT820029 L

Square Footage: 3,278
Width: 75'-10" Depth: 69'-4"

Form follows function as dual gallery halls lead from formal areas to split sleeping quarters in this Prairie adaptation. At the heart of the plan, the grand-scale great room offers a raised-hearth fireplace framed by built-in cabinetry and plant shelves. Traditional formal rooms blend into more open, casual living areas through classic archways. Open planning combines the country kitchen with an informal dining space and adds an island counter with a snack bar. A lavish master suite harbors a sitting area with private access to the covered pergola. The secondary sleeping wing includes a spacious guest suite with an angled whirlpool tub. A fifth bedroom or home office offers its own door to the wraparound porch.

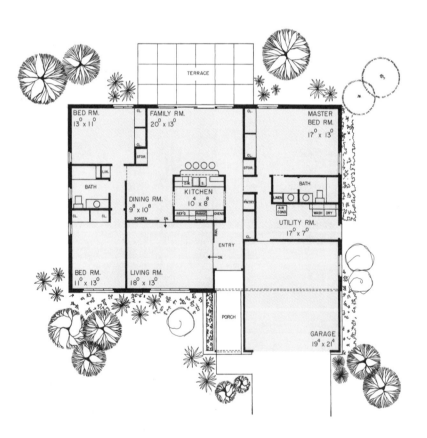

The extension of the wide overhanging roof of this distinctive home provides shelter for the walkway to the front door. A raised brick planter adds appeal to the outstanding exterior design. The living patterns offered by this plan are delightfully different, yet extremely practical. Notice the separation of the master bedroom from the other two bedrooms. While assuring an extra measure of quiet privacy for the parents, this master bedroom location may be ideal for a live-in relative. Locating the kitchen in the middle of the plan frees up valuable outside wall space and leads to interesting planning. The front living room is sunken for dramatic appeal and need not have any cross-room traffic. The utility room houses the laundry and the heating and cooling equipment.

HPT820030

Square Footage: 1,862
Width: 56'-10" Depth: 48'-10"

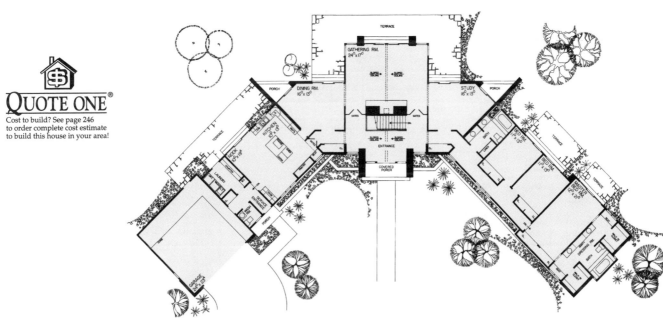

HPT820031 L

Square Footage: 3,262
Width: 144'-8" Depth: 71'-7"

Reminiscent of the original low-slung ranch house from the Spanish Southwest, this is one wonderful one-story—from the magnificent double-door entryway, to the gargantuan gathering room (400 square feet and a mammoth fireplace), to the roomy master suite with a cozy private terrace. Other attractive features include an angular study and dining room, a large rear terrace off the gathering room, a spacious L-shaped kitchen with a prep island and a breakfast nook, and loads and loads of extra storage.

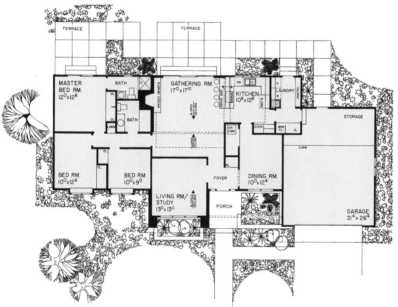

This outstanding contemporary design features a recessed front entry with a covered front porch. The rear gathering room has a sloped ceiling, a raised-hearth fireplace, sliding glass doors to the terrace, and a snack bar with a pass-through to the kitchen. In addition to the gathering room, there is the living room/study. This room could be utilized in a variety of ways depending on your family's choice. The formal dining room is convenient to the kitchen. Three bedrooms and two closely located baths are in the sleeping wing. This plan includes details for the construction of an optional basement.

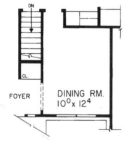

Optional Basement Staircase Location

QUOTE ONE®

Cost to build? See page 246
to order complete cost estimate
to build this house in your area!

HPT820032 LD

Square Footage: 1,566
Width: 76'-0" Depth: 34'-4"

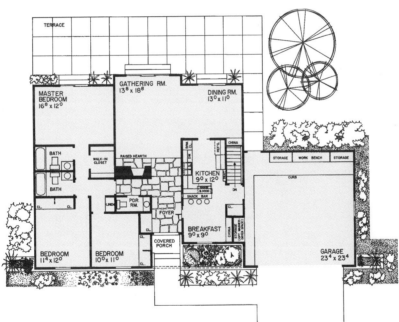

Quote One®

Cost to build? See page 246
to order complete cost estimate
to build this house in your area!

HPT820033 LD

Square Footage: 1,589
Width: 68'-0" Depth: 40'-5"

The rustic exterior of this one-story home features vertical wood siding. The flagstone entry foyer leads to the three areas of the plan: the sleeping area, the living area and the work center. The sleeping area features three bedrooms. The master bedroom utilizes sliding glass doors to the rear terrace. The living area, consisting of the gathering room and a dining room, also enjoys access to the terrace. The work center is efficiently planned. It houses the kitchen with a snack bar, the breakfast room with a built-in china cabinet, and stairs to the basement. This is a very livable plan exemplified by such special amenities as a raised-hearth fireplace in the gathering room and a walk-in closet in the master bedroom.

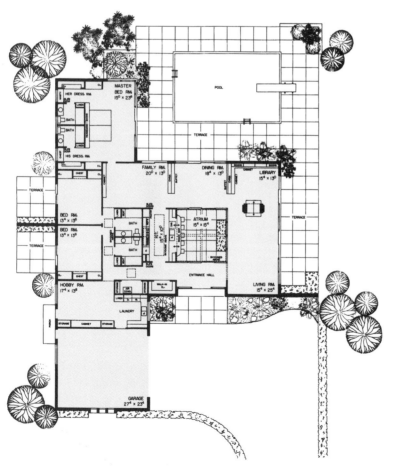

Containing over 3,500 square feet, space for living in this home is abundant. Each of the various rooms is large. Further, each major room accesses the outdoors. The efficient kitchen is strategically located near to the family and dining rooms. Observe how it functions with the enclosed atrium to provide a snack bar. Functional room dividers separate various areas. A two-way fireplace divides the spacious living room and the cozy library highlighted by built-in cabinets and bookshelves. A hobby room with a laundry adjacent will be a favorite family activities spot.

HPT820034

Square Footage: 3,578
Width: 92'-0" Depth: 114'-1"

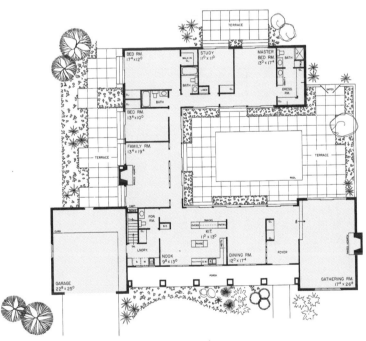

HPT820035

Square Footage: 3,110
Width: 95'-8" Depth: 74'-4"

If you have a growing, active family, the chances are good that they will want their new home to relate to the outdoors. This distinctive design puts a premium on private outdoor living. And you don't have to install a swimming pool to get the most enjoyment from this home. Developing the garden court will provide the indoor living areas with a breathtaking awareness of nature's beauty. Notice the fine zoning of the plan and how each area has sliding glass doors to provide an unrestricted view. Three bedrooms plus a study are served by three baths. The family and gathering rooms provide two great living areas, while the kitchen is very efficient. Of special note is the master suite with a dressing room, two sinks and a linen closet.

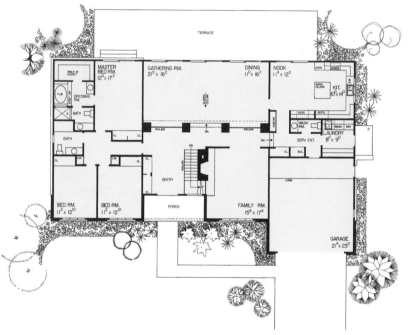

This impressive one-story home has numerous fine features that will ensure the best in contemporary living. The sunken gathering room and dining room share an impressive sloped ceiling; a series of three sliding glass doors provides access to the terrace. The family room, with a cozy fireplace, is ideal for informal entertaining. The kitchen features an efficient work island, pantry and built-in desk. The master suite opens to the rear terrace, and the bath offers a separate step-up tub and shower. Two additional bedrooms are located at the front of the home.

HPT820036 LD

Square Footage: 2,652
Width: 78'-0" Depth: 48'-0"

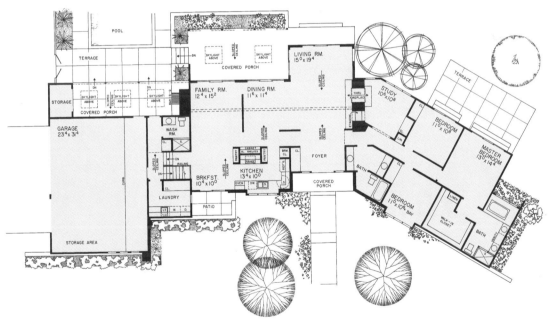

HPT820037 D

Square Footage: 2,459
Width: 121'-5" Depth: 57'-4"

Indoor/outdoor living will be enjoyed to its fullest in this rambling one-story contemporary plan. Each of the rear rooms in this design, excluding the study, accesses a terrace or porch. Even the front breakfast room accesses a private dining patio. The covered porch off the living areas—family, dining and living rooms—has a sloped ceiling and skylights. A built-in barbecue and storage room are found on the second covered porch. Inside, there is exceptional livability. The master suite is especially nice, with a huge walk-in closet and grand bath. Note the through-fireplace that the living room shares with the study. There is even extra storage in the three-car garage.

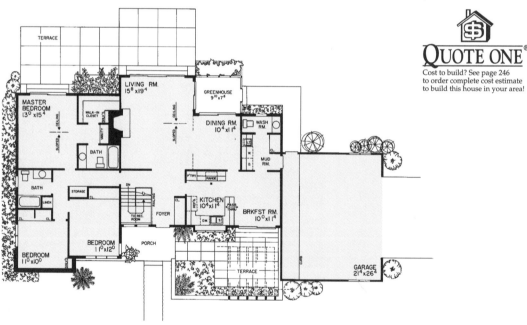

HPT820038 D

A greenhouse area off the dining room and living room provides a cheerful focal point
for this comfortable three-bedroom home. The spacious living room features a cozy fireplace and a sloped ceiling. In addition to the dining room, there's a less formal breakfast room just off the modern kitchen. The kitchen and breakfast area look out onto a
front terrace. Stairs just off the foyer lead down to a recreation room in the basement.
The master bedroom suite opens to a terrace. A mudroom and a washroom off the
garage allow rear entry to the house during inclement weather.

Square Footage: 1,824
Width: 80'-4" **Depth:** 43'-0"

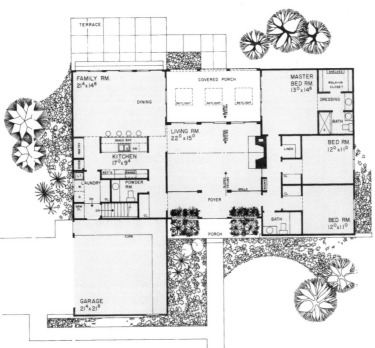

HPT820039

Square Footage: 2,075
Width: 66'-0" Depth: 56'-4"

Enter this contemporary home through the double doors and you'll immediately appreciate the slope-ceilinged living room with a fireplace. Sliding glass doors lead to the covered porch at the rear, brightened by skylights above. The family room also has sliding glass doors—they lead to a rear terrace. A galley-style kitchen shares a snack bar with the family room and its dining space. The laundry is adjacent to the service entrance and to stairs leading to the basement. Sleeping quarters consist of two family bedrooms and a master suite. The master bath features a walk-in closet and a bath with a dressing area. Family bedrooms share a full bath—note the walk-in linen closet. A two-car garage is accessed through the service area near the kitchen.

HPT820040

This sun-oriented design was created to face the south, allowing the morning sun to brighten the living and dining rooms and the adjacent terrace. During the winter, a glass roof and walls on the garden room will provide solar heat—and relief from high energy bills. Solar shades allow you to adjust the amount of light allowed in. The kitchen has a snack bar and a serving counter to the dining room. The breakfast room and laundry area are convenient to the kitchen. The master bath includes a skylight, garden tub and separate shower. Two nearby family bedrooms share a full bath.

Square Footage: 2,231
Width: 62'-5" Depth: 62'-0"

This elegant one-story contemporary home is designed for sites that slope slightly to the front. As a consequence, the major rooms of the home are sunken just a few steps from the grand entry foyer. The large gathering room is in line with the entry doors and has sliding glass doors to the terrace and a through-fireplace to the study. The nearby dining room offers sliding glass doors to a covered porch. The L-shaped kitchen and breakfast nook share the use of a patio just outside the nook. For real convenience, the study has built-ins and a powder room close at hand. Amenities in the master suite include a walk-in closet, spa tub and double sinks. Family bedrooms share a full bath that includes a garden tub and double sinks.

HPT820041 LD

Square Footage: 2,732
Width: 85'-10" Depth: 72'-4"

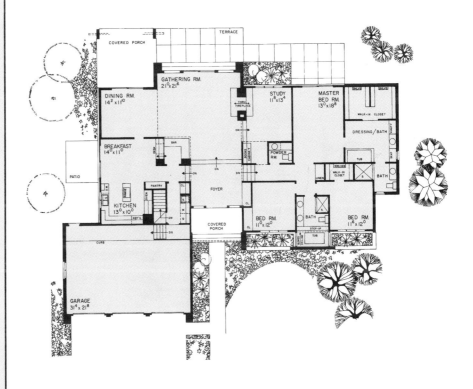

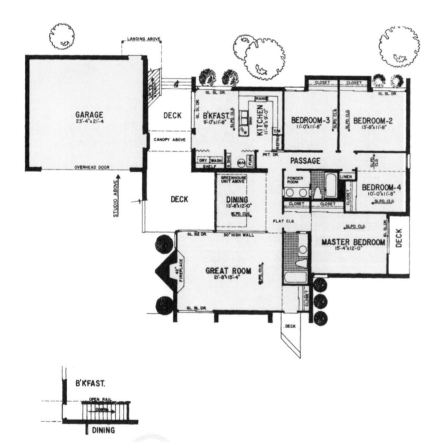

GARAGE
23'-4"x21'-4

DECK

LANDING ABOVE

B'KFAST
9'-0"x11'-8"

KITCHEN
11'-8"x9'-0"

CLOSET   CLOSET

BEDROOM-3
11'-0"x11'-8"

BEDROOM-2
13'-8"x11'-8"

CANOPY ABOVE

OVERHEAD DOOR

STUDIO ABOVE

DRY   WASH

SHELF

PASSAGE

PKT. DR.

DECK

GREENHOUSE
UNIT ABOVE

DINING
13'-8"x12'-0"

SLPD CLG.

POWDER
ROOM

LINEN

CLOSET   CLOSET   CLOSET

BEDROOM-4
10'-0"x11'-8"
SLPD. CLG.

FLAT CLG.

GL. SL. DR.   30" HIGH WALL

42"
FIREPLACE

GREAT ROOM
21'-8"x15'-4"

GL. SL. DR.

SLPD. CLG.

MASTER BEDROOM
15'-4"x12'-0"

DECK

CLOSET

DECK

B'KFAST.

OPEN RAIL

DINING

Optional Basement Staircase Location

Nothing is excluded in this delightful contemporary one-story design. Enter the home from a deck to the oversized great room. A fireplace and sliding glass doors are nice accents here. The dining room is separated from this area by a divider wall, and it is embellished with a greenhouse unit and sloped ceiling. The breakfast area and kitchen access the rear yard as well as a side deck. Four bedrooms include three family bedrooms (two with sliding glass doors) and a master suite with a private deck.

HPT820042 L

Square Footage: 1,885
Width: 78'-10" Depth: 50'-10"

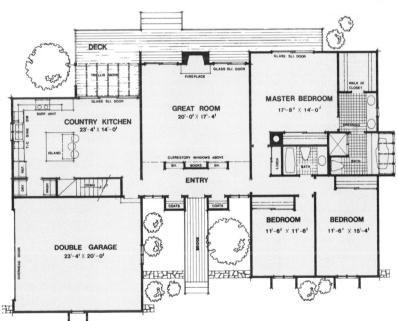

DECK

TRELLIS ABOVE

GLASS SLI. DOOR

SURF. UNIT

COUNTRY KITCHEN
23'-4" X 14'-0"

ISLAND

REF. T/C SINK DW

DRY WASH DOWN

OVERHEAD DOOR

DOUBLE GARAGE
23'-4" X 20'-0"

GREAT ROOM
20'-0" X 17'-4"

fireplace

GLASS SLI. DOOR

CLERESTORY WINDOWS ABOVE

SH. BOOKS SH.

ENTRY

COATS COATS

BRIDGE

GLASS SLI. DOOR

MASTER BEDROOM
17'-8" X 14'-0"

WALK IN CLOSET

DRESSING

LINEN BATH BATH

BATH

BEDROOM
11'-6" X 11'-8"

BEDROOM
11'-6" X 15'-4"

HPT820043 D

Square Footage: 1,873
Width: 71'-0" Depth: 44'-4"

Simple lines and a balanced sense of proportion dominate the look of this compact design. Approach over a welcoming bridge to an entry flanked by coat closets. The open great room, with clerestory windows, offers a fireplace and sliding glass doors to the rear deck. A country kitchen with an island work area features plenty of space for a table and chairs. The deluxe master suite is complete with a walk-in closet, dressing area, pampering bath and sliding glass doors to the rear deck. Two family bedrooms to the front of the home access a full bath.

Alternate Elevation

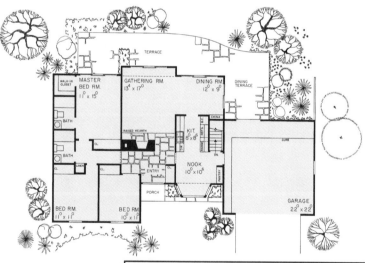

Alternate Elevation

This design offers you a choice of three distinctively different exteriors. Blueprints show details for all three optional elevations. A study of the floor plan reveals a fine measure of livability. In less than 1,400 square feet, you'll find amenities often found in much larger homes. In addition to the two eating areas and the open planning of the gathering room, the indoor/outdoor relationships are of great interest. The basement may be developed later for recreational activities.

QUOTE ONE®

Cost to build? See page 246
to order complete cost estimate
to build this house in your area!

HPT820044 LD

Square Footage: 1,366
Width: 65'-0" Depth: 37'-4"

Attractive, contemporary split-bedroom planning makes the most of this plan. The master suite pampers with a lavish bath and a fireplace. The living areas are open and easily access the rear terrace. Note, in particular, the convenient snack bar between the kitchen and the gathering room/dining room. A large laundry area and washroom separate the main house from the garage. A balcony overlook on the second floor allows views to the gathering room or to the entry foyer.

Second Floor

QUOTE ONE®
Cost to build? See page 246
to order complete cost estimate
to build this house in your area!

HPT820045

First Floor: 1,414 square feet

Second Floor: 620 square feet

Total: 2,034 square feet

Width: 53'-0" **Depth:** 51'-8"

First Floor

© 1984 Donald A. Gardner Architects, Inc.

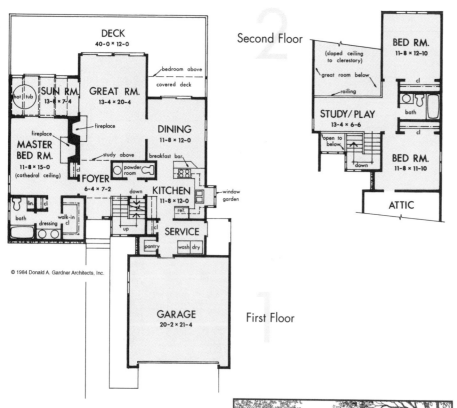

Second Floor

DECK
40-0 × 12-0

bedroom above

covered deck

SUN RM.
13-8 × 7-4

hot tub

GREAT RM.
13-4 × 20-4

fireplace

fireplace

MASTER BED RM.
11-8 × 15-0
(cathedral ceiling)

study above

DINING
11-8 × 12-0

breakfast bar

FOYER
6-4 × 7-2

powder room

down

KITCHEN
11-8 × 12-0

window garden

ref.

bath

lin. cl

walk-in cl

dressing

up

SERVICE

pantry

wash dry

© 1984 Donald A. Gardner Architects, Inc.

(sloped ceiling to clerestory)

great room below

railing

BED RM.
11-8 × 12-10

cl

bath

STUDY/ PLAY
13-4 × 6-6

open to below

down

BED RM.
11-8 × 11-10

ATTIC

First Floor

GARAGE
20-2 × 21-4

Rear View

An elegant exterior combines with a functional interior to offer an exciting design for the contemporary-minded. Notice the cheery sun room that captures the heat of the sun. The master suite and great room both access this bright space through sliding glass doors. Note how the great-room ceiling with exposed wood beams slopes from the deck up to operable clerestory windows at the study/play area on the second level. A U-shaped kitchen contains a window garden, a breakfast bar and ample cabinet space.

HPT820046

First Floor: 1,345 square feet
Second Floor: 536 square feet
Total: 1,881 square feet
Width: 45'-0" Depth: 69'-4"

© 1984 Donald A. Gardner Architects, Inc.

Because this home's sun room is a full two stories high, it acts as a solar collector when oriented to the south. Enjoying the benefits of this warmth are the dining and great rooms on the first floor and the master suite on the second floor. A spacious deck further extends the outdoor living potential. Special features include: a sloping ceiling with exposed wood beams and a fireplace in the great room; a cathedral ceiling, fireplace, built-in shelves and ample closet space in the master bedroom; a balcony overlook in the upstairs study; and convenient storage space in the attic over the garage.

Rear View

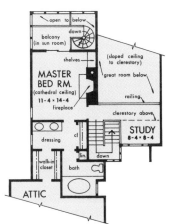

Second Floor

© 1984 Donald A. Gardner Architects, Inc.

First Floor

HPT820047

First Floor: 1,340 square feet
Second Floor: 547 square feet
Total: 1,887 square feet
Width: 45'-4" **Depth:** 60'-0"

First Floor

Second Floor

QUOTE ONE®

Cost to build? See page 246
to order complete cost estimate
to build this house in your area!

HPT820048 LD

The street view of this contemporary design features a small courtyard entrance as well as a private terrace off the study. Inside, the livability is outstanding. This design features spacious first-floor activity areas that flow smoothly into each other. In the gathering room, a raised-hearth fireplace creates a dramatic focal point. An adjacent covered terrace, featuring a skylight, is ideal for outdoor dining and could be screened-in later for an additional room.

First Floor: *1,370 square feet*
Second Floor: *927 square feet*
Total: *2,297 square feet*
Width: *52'-0"* **Depth:** *48'-0"*

Second Floor

2

First Floor

1

HPT820049 L

First Floor: 1,590 square feet

Second Floor: 756 square feet

Total: 2,346 square feet

Width: 66'-8" Depth: 62'-4"

Entering this home will be a pleasure through the sheltered walkway to the double front doors. And the pleasure and beauty does not stop there. The entry hall and sunken gathering room are open to the upstairs for added dimension. There's even a built-in seat in the entry area. The kitchen/nook is very efficient with its many built-ins and the adjacent laundry room. The two upstairs bedrooms offer their own baths, while the first-floor master suite is designed to pamper with a lavish bath, walk-in closet and access to a private terrace. There are fine indoor/outdoor living relationships in this design. Note the spacious rear terrace with access from the gathering room, dining room and nook.

© 1990 Donald A. Gardner Architects, Inc.

B. NATHAN

First Floor

DECK

SUN RM.
13-8 x 7-4
skylights

GREAT RM.
15-4 x 23-2

DINING
15-4 x 12-4

MASTER
BED RM.
15-4 x 13-0

fireplace

balcony above

KITCHEN
13-4 x 11-6

walk-in
closet

FOYER

up down

lin.

pd. rm.

cl

BRKFST.
13-4 x 8-8

master bath

storage

cl

wash dry

sto.

UTILITY
7-6 x 9-4

© 1990 Donald A. Gardner Architects, Inc.

GARAGE
20-6 x 21-4

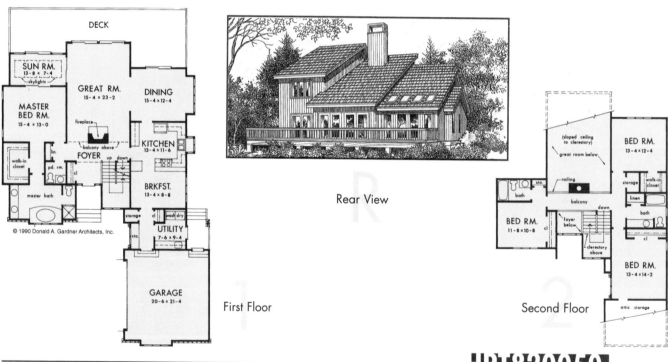

Rear View

Second Floor

(sloped ceiling
to clerestory)

great room below

sto.

BED RM.
13-4 x 12-4

bath

railing

storage

walk-in
closet

balcony

linen

BED RM.
11-8 x 10-8

down

foyer
below

bath

clerestory
above

cl

BED RM.
13-4 x 14-2

attic storage

HPT820050

First Floor: 1,837 square feet
Second Floor: 904 square feet
Total: 2,741 square feet
Width: 51'-0" Depth: 80'-0"

Stone and vertical wood siding add a touch of the rustic to this clever contemporary design. Its shed roof allows soaring heights inside and plenty of glass for sunny spots. The first floor contains an entertainment-sized great room with a fireplace and sliding glass doors to the rear deck. It connects directly to the dining room on the right. The U-shaped kitchen has an attached breakfast room and loads of counter space. On the first floor for convenience, the master suite features a sun room and pampering bath. Family bedrooms on the second floor include two sharing a full bath and one with its own private bath. The balcony connecting the three bedrooms overlooks the great room and the foyer.

© 1986 Donald A. Gardner Architects, Inc.

This home's sun room will delight all with its spiral staircase leading to a balcony and the master suite. The great room enjoys a fireplace and two sets of sliding glass doors leading to the deck. In the kitchen, a U shape lends itself to outstanding convenience. Three bedrooms include two secondary bedrooms and a glorious master suite. Located on the second floor, the private bedroom has a fireplace, a generous dressing area with a skylight, and a lavish bath.

HPT820051

First Floor: 1,434 square feet

Second Floor: 604 square feet

Total: 2,038 square feet

Width: 47'-4" Depth: 69'-0"

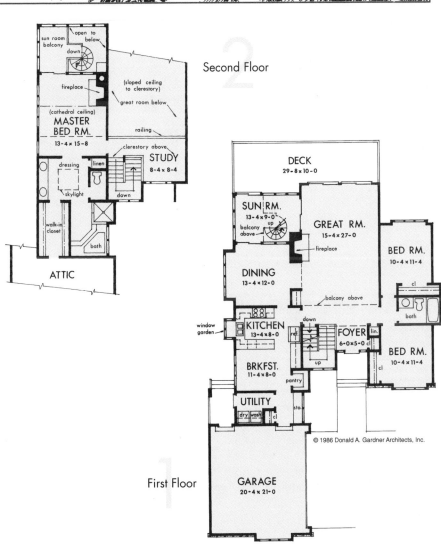

Second Floor

First Floor

© 1986 Donald A. Gardner Architects, Inc.

Second Floor

4,200 x 5,200
14'-0" X 17'-4"

OPEN TO
BELOW

Contemporary style and modern interior spaces lend this great design dramatic character. The open two-story living room is warmed by a country fireplace. The warmth extends to the island snack-bar kitchen, which is open to the eating area. The large wraparound deck will provide plenty of outdoor entertainment possibilities. Two first-floor family bedrooms share a hall bath that offers laundry facilities. Upstairs, the master bedroom loft features a private shower bath and a roomy walk-in closet. This home is designed with a basement foundation.

2,90 X 3,10
9'-8" X 10'-4"

3,20 X 4,00
10'-8" X 13'-4"

2,75 X 3,00
9'-2" X 10'-0"

2,50 X 3,80
8'-4" X 12'-8"

5,20 X 3,90
17'-4" X 13'-0"

First Floor

HPT820052

First Floor: 1,062 square feet
Second Floor: 454 square feet
Total: 1,516 square feet
Width: 40'-0" Depth: 28'-0"

© 1985 Donald A. Gardner Architects, Inc.

What a grand plan for contemporary family living! Beyond the handsome exterior are some excellent features that complement today's lifestyles. Of special note: the two-story sun room with access to the great room, the dining room, and the master bedroom; a slope-ceilinged great room with clerestory windows; two first-floor bedrooms and a third second-floor bedroom that could double as a study; a delightful rear deck; and ample storage space over the garage. If contemporary living is your style, this may be the plan for you.

Rear View

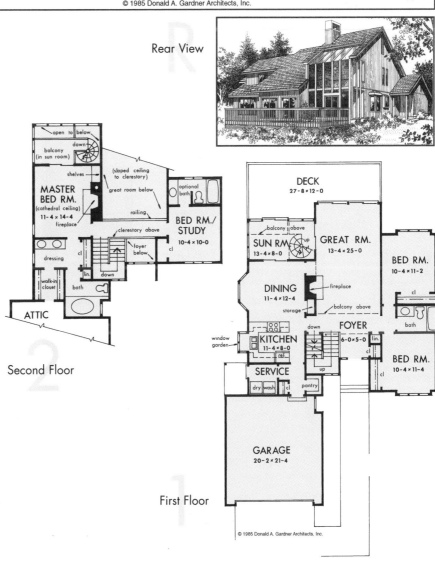

HPT820053

First Floor: 1,340 square feet
Second Floor: 651 square feet
Total: 1,991 square feet
Width: 45'-4" Depth: 60'-0"

Second Floor

First Floor

© 1985 Donald A. Gardner Architects, Inc.

© 1989 Donald A. Gardner Architects, Inc.

seat

DECK
55 - 4 × 14 - 6

GREAT RM.
14 - 4 × 17 - 10

(sloped ceiling to clerestory)

fireplace

SUN RM.
15 - 2 × 10 - 0

skylights

DINING
12 - 0 × 14 - 0

loft above

MASTER
BED RM.
13 - 0 × 14 - 0

cl

pd. rm.

wash dry

UTILITY
9 - 8 × 8 - 0

storage

FOYER
7 - 0 × 6 - 6

cl

master bath

whirlpool

KITCHEN
12 - 0 × 15 - 0

up

GARAGE
21 - 0 × 20 - 0

© 1989 Donald A. Gardner Architects, Inc.

First Floor

(sloped ceiling to clerestory)

great room below

railing

BED RM.
12 - 8 × 15 - 0

cl   cl

LOFT
14 - 4 × 6 - 2

foyer below

down

BED RM.
12 - 0 × 12 - 4

cl   cl

linen

bath

Second Floor

Rear View

Sleek contemporary lines, plenty of windows and a combination of textures give this home a lot of curb appeal. Great for entertaining, the formal dining room has a pass-through to the kitchen for ease in serving. The adjacent great room offers a fireplace, built-ins and access to both the rear deck and the sun room. Located on the first floor for privacy, the master suite features many luscious amenities. Two bedrooms, a full bath and a loft complete the second floor.

HPT820054

First Floor: 1,514 square feet
Second Floor: 642 square feet
Total: 2,156 square feet
Width: 64'-4" Depth: 46'-4"

© 1989 Donald A. Gardner Architects, Inc.

Find a sunny spot to relax in this contemporary design—it isn't hard as there are sun-filled rooms everywhere. It begins in the dining room with a wall of windows. Continue to the family room with an attached sun room and an octagonal breakfast room. Even the living room allows passage to the rear deck. Two bedrooms on the first floor share a full bath. Upstairs, the master suite offers a sun room/balcony. The study overlooks the living room and leads to an additional bedroom with a full bath.

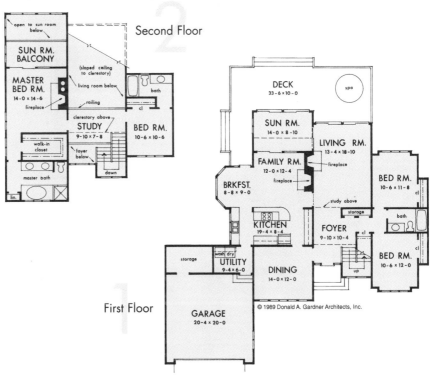

Second Floor

First Floor

© 1989 Donald A. Gardner Architects, Inc.

HPT820055

First Floor: 1,657 square feet

Second Floor: 845 square feet

Total: 2,502 square feet

Width: 62'-0" Depth: 57'-4"

Rear View

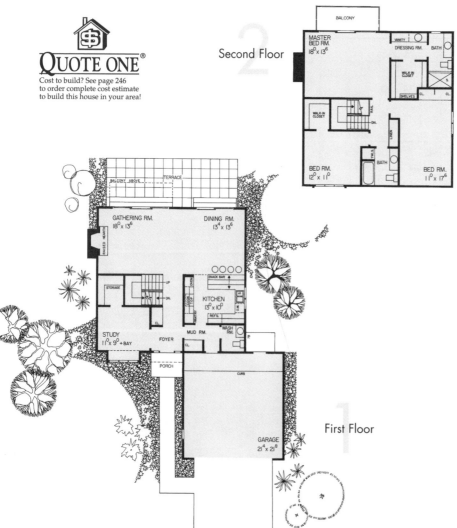

Second Floor

2

BALCONY

MASTER
BED RM.
18⁰ x 13⁶

VANITY

DRESSING RM.

BATH

WALK-IN
CLOSET

SHELVES   CL.   CL.

WALK-IN
CLOSET

RAIL.

DN.

LINEN

BED RM.
12⁰ x 11⁰

BATH   TWLS.

BED RM.
11⁰ x 17⁶

BALCONY ABOVE   TERRACE

GATHERING RM.
18⁰ x 13⁶

DINING RM.
13⁴ x 13⁶

RAISED HEARTH

STORAGE

UP

DN.

SNACK BAR

COOK TOP / OVEN

PANTRY

KITCHEN
13⁰ x 10⁰

REF.

CL.

STUDY
11⁰ x 9⁰ +BAY

FOYER

MUD RM.

WASH RM.

CL.

P.

PORCH

CURB

GARAGE
21⁴ x 21⁸

First Floor

1

Sleek, modern lines define this two-story
contemporary home. Open planning in
the living areas creates a sense of spaciousness found in much larger plans.
The formal dining area and informal
eating counter, both easily served by the
U-shaped kitchen, share the cozy
warmth of the centered fireplace and
views to the rear grounds offered by the
gathering room. Amenities abound in
the second-floor master suite with a private balcony, walk-in closet, separate
dressing area and knee-space vanity.
Two secondary bedrooms and a full
bath complete this floor, perfect for
guests or visiting relatives—or make one
room a study or hobby room.

HPT820056 LD

First Floor: 1,024 square feet

Second Floor: 975 square feet

Total: 1,999 square feet

Width: 40'-4" Depth: 52'-0"

88 Donald A. Gardner Architects, Inc.

DECK
32 - 2 × 12 - 0

down

DINING
12 - 6 × 13 - 0

GREAT RM.
13 - 4 × 19 - 10

fireplace

balcony above

BED RM.
11 - 0 × 11 - 0

cl

covered deck

dry
wpsh

storage

ref

UTIL.
6 - 8 × 10 - 0

KITCHEN
12 - 6 × 10 - 4

lin.

cl

bath

GARAGE
20 - 0 × 20 - 4

SUN RM.
12 - 6 × 11 - 0

balcony above

FOYER

down

up

BED RM.
12 - 4 × 10 - 6

cl

First Floor

© 1988 Donald A. Gardner Architects, Inc.

Second Floor

master bath

(sloped ceiling to clerestory)

great room below

cl

**MASTER
BED RM.**
12 - 6 × 14 - 8

railing

STUDY
11 - 4 × 5 - 6

walk-in closet

clerestory above

BALCONY
10 - 0 × 6 - 8

foyer below

open to below

down

HPT820057

First Floor: 1,395 square feet
Second Floor: 581 square feet
Total: 1,976 square feet
Width: 60'-10" Depth: 48'-2"

Here is a design for folks who want to combine outdoor living with the comforts of home. A sun room and banks of large windows bring the outdoors in, while a large back deck will tempt you to relax outside. The great room, with a corner fireplace, and the dining room provide an open area for entertaining, with an efficient L-shaped kitchen nearby. Two family bedrooms and a shared bath complete the first floor. Upstairs, the sumptuous master suite boasts a walk-in closet, pampering bath and private study.

Quote One®

Cost to build? See page 246 to order complete cost estimate to build this house in your area!

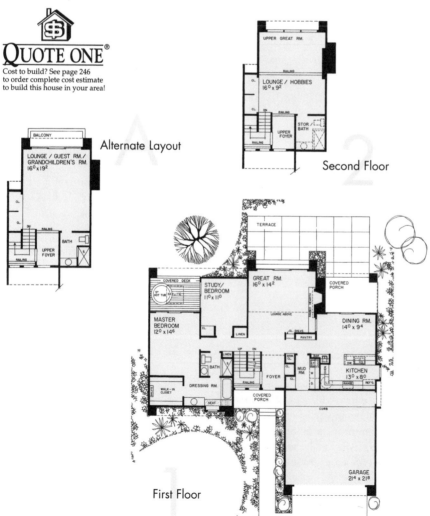

Alternate Layout

BALCONY

LOUNGE / GUEST RM. / GRANDCHILDREN'S RM. 16⁰ x 19²

CL.

CL.

DN.

RAILING

BATH

UPPER FOYER

RAILING

UPPER GREAT RM.

RAILING

CL.

LOUNGE / HOBBIES 16⁰ x 9²

DN.

RAILING

STOR. / BATH

UPPER FOYER

RAILING

Second Floor

TERRACE

COVERED DECK

HOT TUB

FLUE

STUDY/ BEDROOM 11⁰ x 11⁰

GREAT RM. 16⁰ x 14²

COVERED PORCH

MASTER BEDROOM 12⁰ x 14⁶

CL.

LINEN

LOUNGE ABOVE

CL. SHLVS.

PANTRY

DINING RM. 14⁰ x 9⁴

BATH

UP DN

MUD RM.

KITCHEN 13⁰ x 8⁰

DW

RANGE

REF.

WALK-IN CLOSET

DRESSING RM.

RAILING

FOYER

CL.

W

D

SEAT

COVERED PORCH

CURB

GARAGE 21⁴ x 21⁸

First Floor

Tailor-made for small families, this is a one-level design with second-floor possibilities. The bonus room upstairs (please see alternate layout) can be nearly anything you want it to be: lounge, guest room, playroom for the kids—partitioned or open. Downstairs, a little space goes a long way: an extensive great room with an extended hearth, a formal dining room with a private covered porch, and a master wing that includes a study and a spacious bath with a dressing area, walk-in closet and access to a hot tub/spa.

HPT820058 L

First Floor: 1,363 square feet
Second Floor: 351 square feet
Total: 1,714 square feet
Width: 54'-8" Depth: 54'-0"

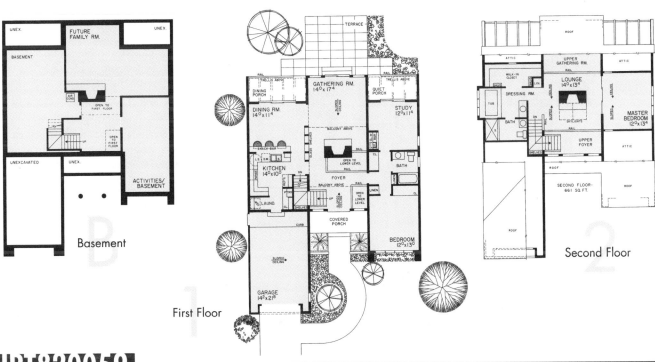

Basement

First Floor

Second Floor

HPT820059

First Floor: 1,338 square feet

Second Floor: 661 square feet

Total: 1,999 square feet

Finished Basement:

1,321 square feet

Width: 42'-0" Depth: 56'-0"

This attractive contemporary 1½-story home offers an optional basement to provide a family room. On the main level, the kitchen features a snack bar for quick meals. In addition to the large dining room, there's an adjacent dining porch. An exciting feature is the gathering room's centered fireplace that extends up to the second floor and down to the basement. The first floor also offers a study with a wet bar and sliding glass doors that open to a private porch. Adjacent to the study is a full bath followed by a bedroom. The master suite takes up the entire second floor. It features a bath with an oversized tub and shower, a large walk-in closet with built-ins and an open lounge with a fireplace. Both the lounge and master bedroom, along with the gathering room, have sloped ceilings.

Second Floor

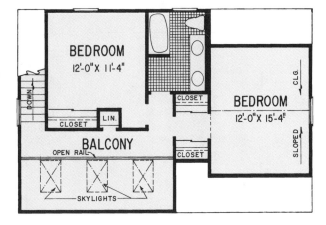

BEDROOM
12'-0" X 11'-4"

DOWN

CLOSET

LIN.

CLOSET

BEDROOM
12'-0" X 15'-4"

CLG.

SLOPED

CLOSET

BALCONY
OPEN RAIL

SKYLIGHTS

The rectangular shape of this design will make it an economical and easy-to-build choice for those wary of high construction costs. The first floor benefits from the informality of open planning: the living room and dining room combine to make one large living space. The partitioned kitchen is conveniently adjacent yet keeps the cooking process out of the living area. Also downstairs is the master suite. The second floor houses two large bedrooms, a full bath and a balcony overlooking the living room.

UP
OPEN RAIL

DINING
9'-8" X 11'-4"

KITCHEN
11'-0" X 10'-0"

RANGE

REF'G.

SINK

D/W

FURN.

W.H.

WASH

DRY

COATS

LIVING ROOM
LINE OF BALCONY ABOVE
18'-8" X 12'-0"

MASTER BEDRM.
12'-0" X 15'-0"

STOOP

STEP

CLOSET

CLOSET

STONE

First Floor

HPT820060 [LD]

First Floor: 893 square feet
Second Floor: 549 square feet
Total: 1,442 square feet
Width: 36'-0" Depth: 26'-4"

What makes this such a distinctive four-bedroom design? First of all, the formal gathering room and informal family room share a dramatic raised-hearth fireplace. Other features of the sunken gathering room include high sloped ceilings, a built-in planter and sliding glass doors to the front entrance court. A study off the entrance hall offers a built-in bar. The kitchen has a snack bar, many built-ins, a pass-through to the dining room and easy access to the large laundry/washroom. The master bedroom is located on the main level for privacy and convenience. The upper level contains three more bedrooms, a bath and a lounge looking down into the gathering room.

HPT820061 D

First Floor: 2,060 square feet

Second Floor: 897 square feet

Total: 2,957 square feet

Width: 80'-8" Depth: 40'-4"

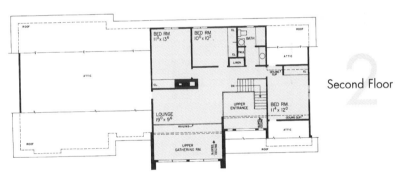

Second Floor

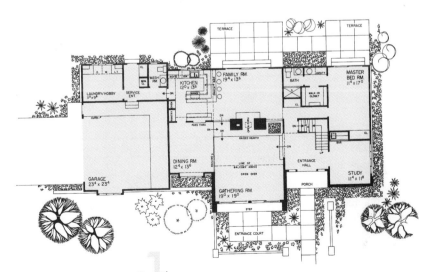

First Floor

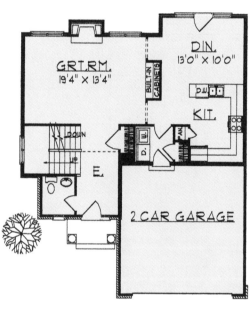

GRT.RM.
19'4" X 13'4"

DIN.
13'0" X 10'0"

BUILT-IN CABINETS

KIT.

DOWN

UP

2 CAR GARAGE

First Floor

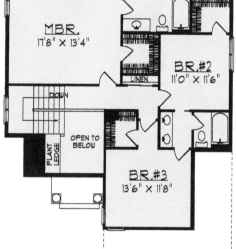

MBR.
17'8" X 13'4"

BR.#2
11'0" X 11'6"

LINEN

DOWN

OPEN TO BELOW

PLANT LEDGE

BR.#3
13'6" X 11'8"

Second Floor

This transitional home features sharp features outlined in contemporary accents. The exterior is enhanced by a mixture of brick and siding, while the interior features spacious living on a smaller scale. The two-story entry leads to a great room warmed by a cozy fireplace. The U-shaped kitchen shares access to built-in cabinetry with the dining area. A laundry room leads to the two-car garage. Upstairs, the master bedroom contains a private bath and walk-in closet. Two additional bedrooms sport walk-in closets as well, along with access to a Jack-and-Jill bath.

HPT820062

First Floor: 880 square feet
Second Floor: 906 square feet
Total: 1,786 square feet
Width: 36'-0" Depth: 43'-0"

With two end gables and five front gables, this design becomes an updated "house of the seven gables." Meanwhile, brick veneer, the use of horizontal siding, radial head windows and interesting roof planes add an extra measure of charm. The attached side-opening, two-car garage is a delightfully integral part of the appealing exterior. Designed for a growing family with a modest building budget, the floor plan incorporates four bedrooms and both formal and informal living areas. The central foyer, with its open staircase to the second floor, looks up to the balcony. The spacious family room offers a high ceiling and a dramatic view of the balcony. In the U-shaped kitchen, a snack bar caters to quick on-the-run meals.

Quote One®
Cost to build? See page 246 to order complete cost estimate to build this house in your area!

Second Floor

First Floor

HPT820063 LD

First Floor: 1,617 square feet

Second Floor: 725 square feet

Total: 2,342 square feet

Width: 62'-0" Depth: 41'-0"

First Floor

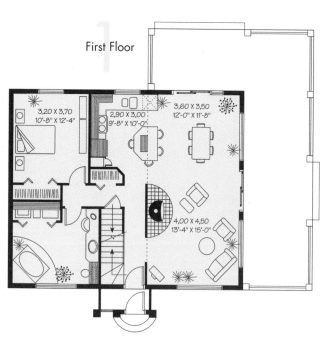

3,20 X 3,70
10'-8" X 12'-4"

2,90 X 3,00
9'-8" X 10'-0"

3,60 X 3,50
12'-0" X 11'-8"

4,00 X 4,50
13'-4" X 15'-0"

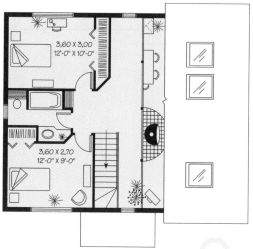

3,60 X 3,00
12'-0" X 10'-0"

3,60 X 2,70
12'-0" X 9'-0"

Second Floor

Skylights illuminate the interior of this attractive contemporary design. A large wrap-around porch welcomes outdoor activities for warm seasonal events. Inside, the living room, dining room and island/snack-bar kitchen are open to each other. The living room is warmed by a fireplace. The first-floor master suite features ample closet space and is placed just across the hall from a spacious bath with a laundry closet. Upstairs, two family bedrooms share a full hall bath. This home is designed with a basement foundation.

HPT820064

First Floor: 984 square feet
Second Floor: 560 square feet
Total: 1,544 square feet
Width: 34'-0" Depth: 28'-0"

Rustic design invades contemporary detailing. The result? This fine two-story home. The front porch is expected and appreciated as a cozy outdoor retreat. Its mate is found at the back in another porch. The foyer leads to an immense great room with a fireplace and cathedral ceiling, and to its attached formal dining space. This area is open to the U-shaped kitchen and cornered breakfast area. A private bedroom and a bunk room are found to the left of the first floor and share the use of a full bath. You might also turn the bunk room into two separate bedrooms; the choice is yours. The master suite sits on the second level near an attached study loft that overlooks the great room. ©1996 Donald A. Gardner Architects, Inc.

HPT820065

First Floor: 1,750 square feet

Second Floor: 604 square feet

Total: 2,354 square feet

Width: 64'-0" **Depth:** 42'-8"

Alternate Layout

Second Floor

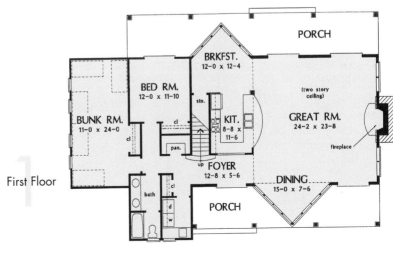

First Floor

© 1988 Donald A. Gardner Architects, Inc.

Rear View

This striking contemporary home retains some traditional flavor at the front exterior. Inside, the mood is modern and efficient. The formal dining room and the great room open to the sun room, which has four skylights for passive solar heating. A spacious kitchen allows for a breakfast bar or separate table. The sun room, great room and master bedroom offer direct access to the deck, which provides space for a hot tub. The luxurious master bath features a double-bowl vanity, shower and whirlpool tub. The second level contains two spacious bedrooms sharing a full bath and a loft area overlooking the great room below. Ample attic storage space is provided over the garage.

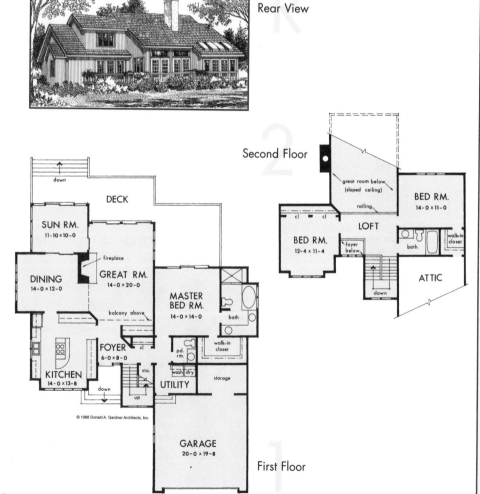

Second Floor

great room below
(sloped ceiling)

railing

BED RM.
14-0 x 11-0

cl   cl

LOFT

BED RM.
12-4 x 11-4

foyer
below

bath

walk-in
closet

ATTIC

down

DECK

down

SUN RM.
11-10 x 10-0

fireplace

DINING
14-0 x 12-0

GREAT RM.
14-0 x 20-0

MASTER
BED RM.
14-0 x 14-0

bath

balcony above

FOYER
6-0 x 8-0

cl

pd.
rm.

walk-in
closet

KITCHEN
14-0 x 13-8

sto.

wash dry

storage

down

UTILITY

up

© 1988 Donald A. Gardner Architects, Inc.

GARAGE
20-0 x 19-8

First Floor

HPT820066

First Floor: 1,479 square feet
Second Floor: 576 square feet
Total: 2,055 square feet
Width: 52'-8"   Depth: 60'-6"

2,90 X 4,40
9'-8" X 14'-8"

4,00 X 4,30
13'-4" X 14'-4"

3,40 X 3,60
11'-4" X 12'-0"

First Floor

4,10 X 2,70
13'-8" X 9'-0"

5,30 X 3,20
17'-8" X 10'-8"

Second Floor

HPT820067

First Floor: 711 square feet

Second Floor: 539 square feet

Total: 1,250 square feet

Width: 26'-4" Depth: 26'-4"

This contemporary mountain-cottage design is just right for a vacation home or a retired couple. A side-entry welcomes you inside to the foyer. A two-story bay window brightens the interior. The living room is warmed by a country fireplace and connects through double doors to the dining room. The compact kitchen features an abundance of counter and cabinet space. The second-floor landing overlooks the living room. Two family bedrooms are located upstairs and share a full hall bath. This home is designed with a basement foundation.

3.80 X 3.80
12'-8" X 12'-8"

4.20 X 3.90
14'-0" X 13'-0"

3.90 X 3.80
13'-0" X 12'-8"

4.50 X 4.10
15'-0" X 13'-8"

4.20 X 6.10
14'-0" X 20'-4"

4.50 X 1.20
15'-0" X 4'-0"

First Floor

3.90 X 4.50
13'-0" X 15'-0"

4.30 X 3.20
14'-4" X 10'-8"

4.30 X 3.20
14'-4" X 10'-8"

Second Floor

This dramatic contemporary plan features a comfortable family layout, enhanced by modern interior accents. Just inside, a spacious family room is ideal for casual or formal events. The island snack-bar kitchen is open to the dining area, brightened by a box-bay window. Up a few steps to the right, a den quietly resides behind the garage and laundry room. Upstairs, the master suite features a private bath, while two additional family bedrooms share a full hall bath. This home is designed with a basement foundation.

HPT820068

First Floor: 1,165 square feet
Second Floor: 1,025 square feet
Total: 2,190 square feet
Width: 40'-0" Depth: 44'-0"

© 1986 Donald A. Gardner Architects, Inc.

Bold contemporary lines strike an elegant chord in this two-story plan. The entry foyer leads to a multi-purpose great room with a fireplace and sliding glass doors to a rear deck. The nearby formal dining room connects to the sun room. A U-shaped kitchen features an attached breakfast room and large walk-in pantry. Two bedrooms on this floor share a full bath. The master suite dominates the second floor and features a large walk-in closet, double lavatories, a corner tub and spiral stairs from its private balcony to the sun room below. The upstairs balcony connects it to a study or optional bedroom.

Second Floor

First Floor

HPT820069

First Floor: *1,580 square feet*

Second Floor: *812 square feet*

Total: *2,392 square feet*

Sun Room: *130 square feet*

Width: *47'-4"* **Depth:** *69'-0"*

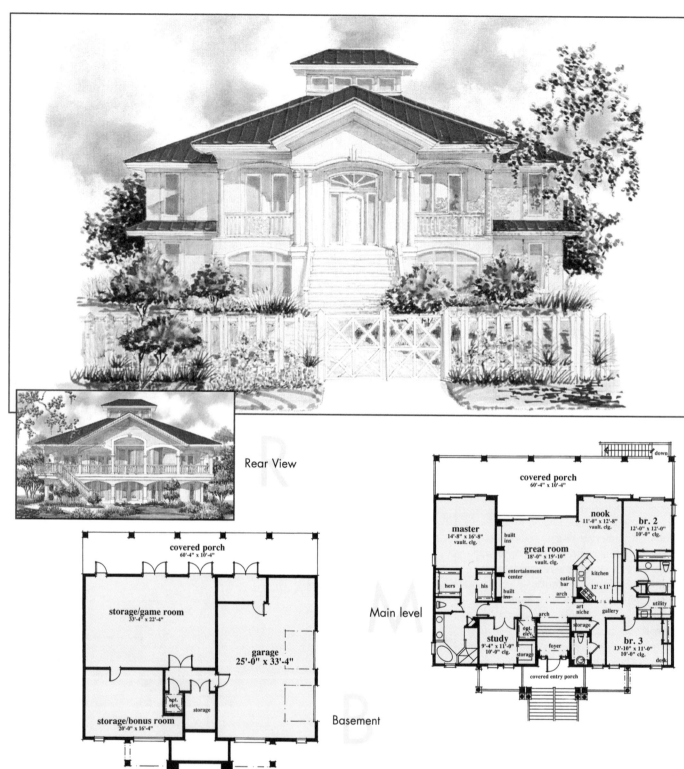

Rear View

covered porch
60'-4" x 10'-4"

covered porch
60'-4" x 10'-4"

Main level

storage/game room
33'-4" x 22'-4"

garage
25'-0" x 33'-4"

storage/bonus room
20'-0" x 16'-4"

Basement

opt. elev.

storage

master
14'-8" x 16'-8"
vault. clg.

built ins

nook
11'-0" x 12'-8"
vault. clg.

br. 2
12'-0" x 12'-0"
10'-0" clg.

great room
18'-0" x 19'-10"
vault. clg.

entertainment center

kitchen
12' x 11'

eating bar

hers

his

built-ins

arch

art niche

storage

gallery

utility

study
9'-4" x 11'-0"
10'-0" clg.

opt. elev.

storage

foyer

br. 3
13'-10" x 11'-0"
10'-0" clg.

desk

arch

down

covered entry porch

HPT820070

Main Level: *2,385 square feet*
Lower Entry: *80 square feet*
Total: *2,465 square feet*
Bonus Space: *1,271 square feet*
Width: *60'-4"* **Depth:** *59'-4"*

A classic pediment and low-pitched roof are topped by a cupola on this gorgeous coastal design, influenced by 19th-Century Caribbean plantation houses. Savory style blended with a contemporary seaside spirit invites entertaining as well as year-round living—plus room to grow. The beauty and warmth of natural light splash the spacious living area with a sense of the outdoors and a touch of *joie de vivre*. The great room features a wall of built-ins designed for even the most technology-savvy entertainment buff. Dazzling views through walls of glass are enlivened by the presence of a breezy porch. The master suite features a luxurious bath, a dressing area and two walk-in closets. Glass doors open to the porch and provide generous views of the seascape, while a nearby study offers an indoor retreat. Please specify pier or block foundation when ordering.

This Mediterranean home offers a dreamy living-by-the-water lifestyle, but it's ready to build in any region. A lovely arch-top entry announces an exquisite foyer with a curved staircase. The family room provides a fireplace and opens to the outdoors on both sides of the plan. An L-shaped kitchen serves a cozy morning area as well as a stunning formal dining room, which offers a bay window. Second-floor sleeping quarters include four bedrooms and two bathrooms. The master suite opens to a balcony and offers a bath with a double-bowl vanity. This home is designed with a basement foundation.

HPT820071

First Floor: 1,065 square feet
Second Floor: 1,032 square feet
Total: 2,097 square feet
Width: 38'-0" Depth: 38'-0"

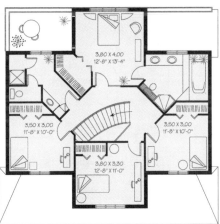

Second Floor

First Floor

Rear View

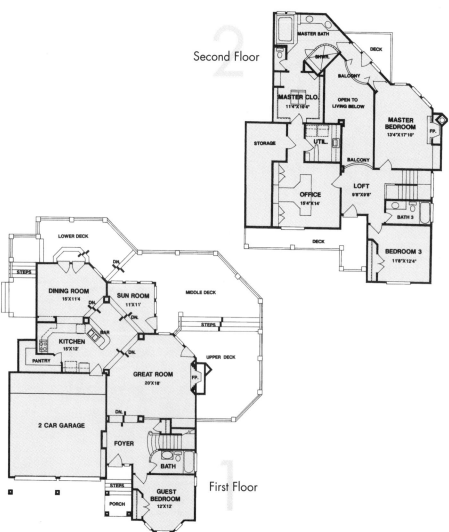

Second Floor

MASTER BATH

DECK

SHWR.

BALCONY

MASTER CLO.
11'4"X10'4"

OPEN TO LIVING BELOW

MASTER BEDROOM
13'4"X17'10"

FP.

STORAGE

UTIL.

BALCONY

OFFICE
15'4"X14'

LOFT
9'8"X9'8"

BATH 3

DECK

BEDROOM 3
11'8"X12'4"

LOWER DECK

STEPS

DN.

DINING ROOM
15'X11'4

SUN ROOM
11'X11'

MIDDLE DECK

DN.

DN.

STEPS

KITCHEN
15'X12'

BAR

DN.

UPPER DECK

PANTRY

GREAT ROOM
20'X18'

FP.

2 CAR GARAGE

DN.

FOYER

BATH

First Floor

STEPS

GUEST BEDROOM
12'X12'

PORCH

Clean, contemporary lines, a unique floor plan and a metal roof with a cupola set this farmhouse apart. Remote-control transoms in the cupola open to create an airy and decidedly unique foyer. The great room, sun room, dining room and kitchen flow from one to another for casual entertaining with flair. The rear of the home is fashioned with plenty of windows overlooking the multi-level deck. A front bedroom and bath would make a comfortable guest suite. The master bedroom and bath upstairs are bridged by a pipe-rail balcony that also gives access to a rear deck. An additional bedroom, home office and bath complete this very special plan.

HPT820072 Ⓛ

First Floor: 1,309 square feet
Second Floor: 1,343 square feet
Total: 2,652 square feet
Width: 44'-4" Depth: 58'-2"

This contemporary home plan offers all the conveniences of modern luxuries. Just inside, a study sits to the immediate left. The living area opens to the formal dining room for easy entertaining and features a warming fireplace. A sun room is located just off the dining room for quiet escapes. The kitchen opens to a breakfast nook. A laundry room, full bath and garage complete the first floor. The master bedroom, two family bedrooms and a full bath are located upstairs. This home is designed with a basement foundation.

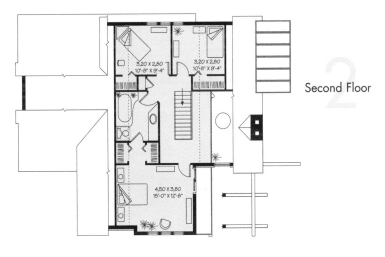

Second Floor

HPT820073

First Floor: 1,062 square feet
Second Floor: 814 square feet
Total: 1,876 square feet
Width: 46'-0" Depth: 40'-0"

First Floor

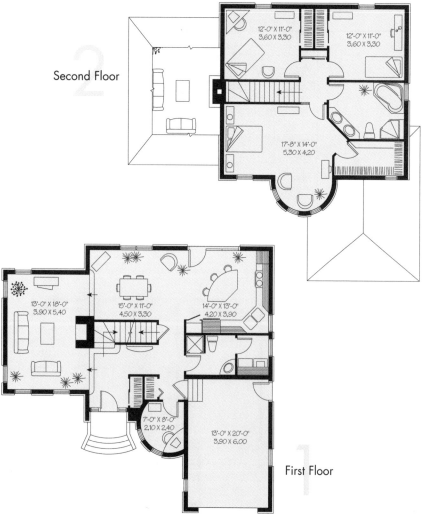

Second Floor

12'-0" X 11'-0"
3.60 X 3.30

12'-0" X 11'-0"
3.60 X 3.30

17'-8" X 14'-0"
5.30 X 4.20

First Floor

13'-0" X 18'-0"
3.90 X 5.40

15'-0" X 11'-0"
4.50 X 3.30

14'-0" X 13'-0"
4.20 X 3.90

7'-0" X 8'-0"
2.10 X 2.40

13'-0" X 20'-0"
3.90 X 6.00

European and contemporary accents dazzle the exterior of this charming design. An arched entry welcomes you inside, while the two-story turret adds an Old World touch. A two-story living room is located to the left and features a warming fireplace. The island snack-bar kitchen is open to the dining area. A laundry/powder room is placed just outside of the garage. Upstairs, the master bedroom provides a bayed sitting area and a huge walk-in closet. Two additional bedrooms share a full hall bath with the master suite. This home is designed with a basement foundation.

HPT820074

First Floor: 1,050 square feet
Second Floor: 917 square feet
Total: 1,967 square feet
Width: 44'-0" Depth: 42'-0"

First Floor

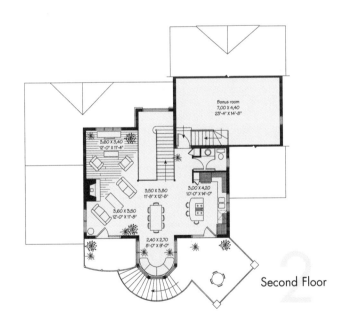

Second Floor

HPT820075

First Floor: 1,209 square feet

Second Floor: 777 square feet

Total: 1,986 square feet

Bonus Room: 342 square feet

Width: 58'-0" **Depth:** 55'-0"

This unusual contemporary design features a stunning facade enhanced by a two-story glass turret and a graceful curving staircase. Stairs lead up to a porch that accesses the main living area. The island snack-bar kitchen is open to the dining area, illuminated by the bayed sitting area. The combined living room and family area is warmed by a fireplace. Below, the first level is reserved for the family bedrooms. All three bedrooms feature double doors to the outdoors. The master suite features a private bath, while the two other bedrooms share a hall bath. A two-car garage with storage space completes the first floor. This home is designed with a basement foundation.

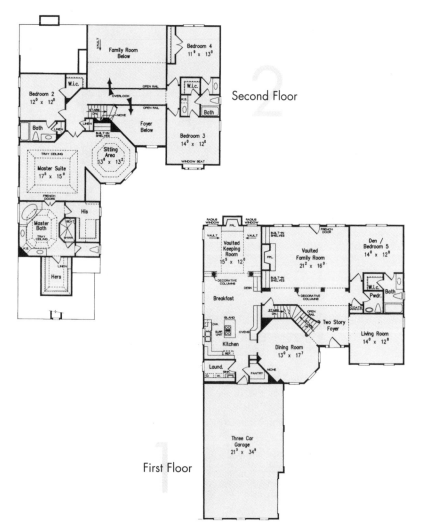

Second Floor

Bedroom 4
11⁹ x 13⁰

Family Room
Below

Bedroom 2
12⁰ x 12⁰

W.i.c.

W.i.c.

Bath

Foyer
Below

Sitting
Area
13⁸ x 13³

Master Suite
17⁵ x 15⁰

Bedroom 3
14⁰ x 12⁰

Master
Bath

His

Hers

First Floor

Vaulted
Keeping Room
15⁵ x 12⁰

Vaulted
Family Room
21² x 16⁰

Den /
Bedroom 5
14⁰ x 12⁰

Breakfast

W.i.c.

Pwdr.

Bath

Kitchen

Two Story
Foyer

Living Room
14⁴ x 12⁸

Dining Room
13⁰ x 17⁷

Laund.

Pantry

Three Car
Garage
21⁵ x 34⁹

Mesmerizing details make this luxurious home a distinct sensation. Stucco and stone, opulent arches and French shutters romanticize the exterior of its blissful perfection. Inside, a radiant staircase cascades into the two-story foyer. The eye-catching stone turret encloses the dining room. The formal living room is illuminated by two enormous arched windows. A wall of windows in the family room offers a breathtaking view of the backyard. The island kitchen adjoins the breakfast area and a walk-in pantry. A three-car garage completes the ground level. Upstairs, the master wing is almost doubled by its private sitting area. Double doors open into the master bath with a corner whirlpool tub. Enormous His and Hers walk-in closets are efficiently designed. Please specify basement or crawlspace foundation when ordering.

HPT820076

First Floor: 2,060 square feet
Second Floor: 1,817 square feet
Total: 3,877 square feet
Width: 54'-0" Depth: 78'-4"

The columned foyer of this home welcomes you into a series of spaces that reach out in all directions. The living room has a spectacular view of the huge covered patio area that's perfect for summer entertaining. The dining room features a tray ceiling and French doors that lead to a covered porch. A secluded master suite affords great views through French doors and also has a tray ceiling. The family wing combines an island kitchen, nook and family gathering space, with the built-in media/ fireplace wall the center of attention. Two secondary bedrooms share a bath. A staircase overlooking the family room takes you up to the sun room complete with a full bath.

HPT820077

First Floor: 2,365 square feet

Second Floor: 364 square feet

Total: 2,729 square feet

Width: 69'-0" Depth: 70'-0"

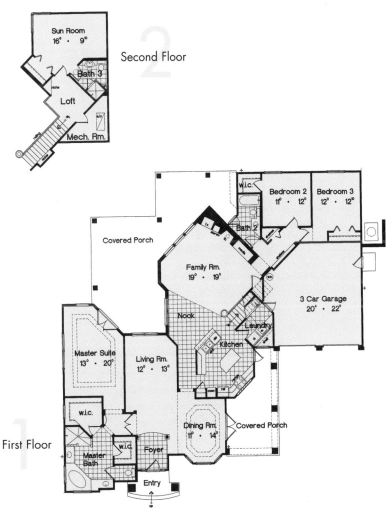

Second Floor

First Floor

First Floor

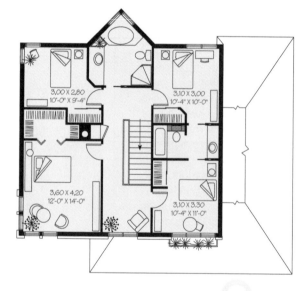

Second Floor

HPT820078

This house design with lovely contemporary accents features a European silhouette with modern interior spaces. Inside, the combined living and dining area is warmed by a fireplace. Radiant two-story windows illuminate this area. The sharp-angled kitchen features a handy snack bar. A casual family room is located at the rear behind the two-car garage. A convenient laundry room completes the first floor. Four family bedrooms and two full baths are located on the second floor. This home is designed with a basement foundation.

First Floor: 926 square feet
Second Floor: 988 square feet
Total: 1,914 square feet
Width: 42'-0" Depth: 34'-0"

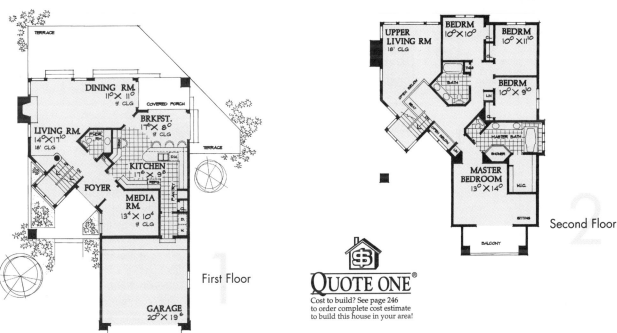

First Floor

Quote One®
Cost to build? See page 246
to order complete cost estimate
to build this house in your area!

Second Floor

HPT820079 L

First Floor: 1,130 square feet
Second Floor: 1,189 square feet
Total: 2,319 square feet
Width: 40'-7" Depth: 57'-8"

This volume home's angled entry opens to a wealth of living potential with a media room to the right and formal living and dining rooms to the left. Open to the dining room, the living room pleases with its marbled hearth and sliding glass doors to the back terrace. A covered porch, accessed from both the dining and breakfast rooms, adds outdoor dining possibilities. The kitchen utilizes a built-in desk, snack bar and breakfast area. A large pantry and closet lead to the laundry near the garage. Upstairs, four bedrooms accommodate a large family well. In the master suite, amenities such as a sitting area and a balcony add definition. The master bath sports a whirlpool tub and a walk-in closet.

Second Floor

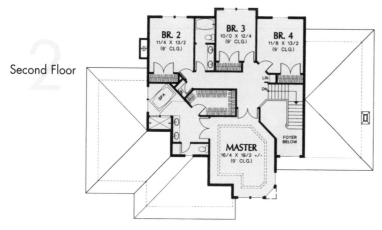

BR. 2
11/4 X 13/2
(9' CLG.)

BR. 3
10/0 X 12/4
(9' CLG.)

BR. 4
11/8 X 13/2
(9' CLG.)

SPA

LIN.
DN.

FOYER
BELOW

MASTER
16/4 X 19/2 +/-
(9' CLG.)

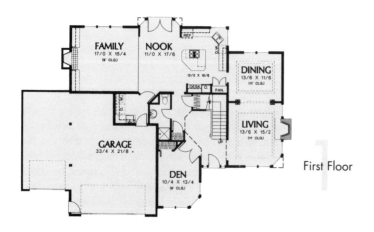

FAMILY
17/0 X 15/4
(9' CLG.)

NOOK
11/0 X 17/6

12/0 X 16/6

REF.
D.W.

DINING
13/6 X 11/6
(11' CLG.)

DESK
D.
PAN.

GARAGE
33/4 X 21/8 +/-

LIVING
13/6 X 15/2
(11' CLG.)

DEN
10/4 X 13/4
(9' CLG.)

First Floor

This two-story home is impressive from the first glance. A two-story bay window graces both the cozy den on the first floor and the deluxe master suite on the second floor. Inside, to the right of the foyer is the formal living room, enhanced by a corner full of windows and by a warming fireplace. This room opens to the rear of the plan into a formal dining room which is just steps away from a large and efficient island kitchen. Casual living is comfortable in the attached nook, with the nearby family room sporting a second fireplace. Upstairs, three family bedrooms offer plenty of storage and share a hall bath. The master suite is impressive with its tray ceiling, large walk-in closet, twin vanities and corner spa. A three-car garage easily holds the family fleet.

HPT820080

First Floor: 1,575 square feet
Second Floor: 1,338 square feet
Total: 2,913 square feet
Width: 66'-0" Depth: 48'-0"

First Floor

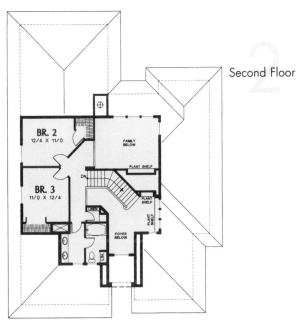

Second Floor

HPT820081

First Floor: 1,896 square feet
Second Floor: 568 square feet
Total: 2,464 square feet
Width: 45'-0" Depth: 64'-0"

Inside the grand entrance of this contemporary home, a large foyer offers a gracious introduction to the formal living and dining rooms. Nearby, the L-shaped island kitchen serves formal and informal areas with equal ease. A two-story family room with a built-in media center and a corner fireplace shares space with a sunny nook. The private master suite features a walk-in closet and a luxurious bath. The second floor contains two bedrooms and a full bath.

Beyond the contemporary facade of this home lies a highly functional floor plan. First-floor living areas include formal living and dining rooms, a private den, and a large family room that connects directly to the breakfast nook and island kitchen. The upper level contains three bedrooms, including a master suite with a nine-foot tray ceiling and a sumptuous master bath which encompasses a huge walk-in closet, whirlpool spa and double vanity. A fine hall bath completes this floor.

Second Floor

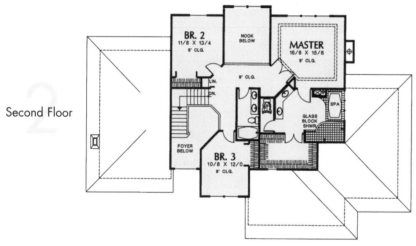

First Floor

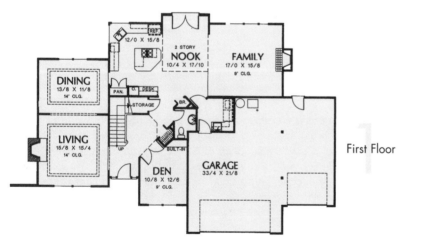

HPT820082 L

First Floor: 1,600 square feet
Second Floor: 1,123 square feet
Total: 2,723 square feet
Width: 68'-0" Depth: 48'-0"

Stucco and Dutch hipped roofs add warmth and charm to this home. The cleverly angled entry spills into the living and dining rooms, both of which share the warmth of the fireplace. The L-shaped kitchen features an island and connects to the well-lit breakfast nook. Upstairs, the master suite includes a double-door entry, a huge walk-in closet and a bath with a picture window. Also on this floor, two family bedrooms share a full bath.

HPT820083

First Floor: 760 square feet

Second Floor: 732 square feet

Total: 1,492 square feet

Width: 35'-0" Depth: 47'-8"

Deck

Brk
9-0x
11-0

Kit
10-9x14-6

Dining
12-0x9-4

Living
15-8x14-0

Up

Porch

Garage
19-4x21-4

First Floor

Second Floor

MBr
11-0x14-8

Br 2
12-0x11-0

Dn

Br 3
12-0x9-9

raised ceiling

Second Floor

BED RM. 11⁸ x 10⁸

CL.

UPPER FAMILY RM.

SLOPED CEILING

MASTER BED RM. 12⁰ x 16⁰

LIN.

BATH

RAILING

CL.

RAILING   DN

W.I.C.

SHLV.

BED RM. 12⁰ x 10⁰

WHIRLPOOL

DRSG.

VANITY

W.I.C.

SHLV.

First Floor

ALCOVE

LIVING RM. 12⁴ x 15⁰

FAMILY RM. 13⁴ x 15⁰ + ALCOVE

DINING RM. 11⁴ x 12⁰

STOR.

CAB. BKCS.

COOK TOP

PDR. RM.

UP   DN

DESK

KITCHEN 14⁰ x 15⁰

FOYER

SER. ENT.

REF'G.

OVEN

CL.

PORCH

CURB

GARAGE 19⁴ x 19⁸

QUOTE ONE®

Cost to build? See page 246
to order complete cost estimate
to build this house in your area!

Interesting detailing marks the exterior
of this home as a beauty. Double doors
on the left open to a large foyer with a
handy coat closet and a powder room
with a curved wall. Living areas of the
home are open and well planned. The
formal living room shares a through-fireplace with the large family room, which
is enhanced by a cabinet-lined alcove.
The adjoining dining room has a pass-
through counter to the efficient L-shaped
kitchen. Each of the three main rooms
on this floor has sliding glass doors to
the rear terrace. Upstairs, the master
bath offers a whirlpool tub, two walk-in
closets and a good-sized dressing area.
Two family bedrooms share a full bath.

HPT820084 LD

First Floor: 1,182 square feet

Second Floor: 927 square feet

Total: 2,109 square feet

Width: 40'-0" Depth: 54'-0"

Here's a bright exterior that blends stately gables with the warmth of stucco. The formal dining room opens off the foyer and is served by a well-organized gourmet kitchen. A flexible floor plan offers the option of a fireplace and an additional window in the great room. French doors open to the first-floor master suite, while double doors to the lavish master bath echo this theme. Upstairs, three additional bedrooms share a full bath and a central hall that leads to a quiet den. Plans for both a two- and three-car garage are included.

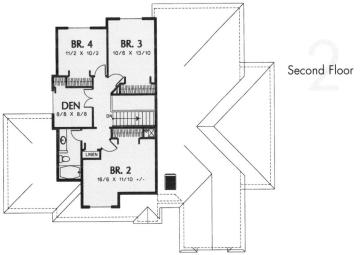

Second Floor

HPT820085

First Floor: 1,655 square feet

Second Floor: 830 square feet

Total: 2,485 square feet

Width: 60'-0" Depth: 54'-0"

First Floor

First Floor

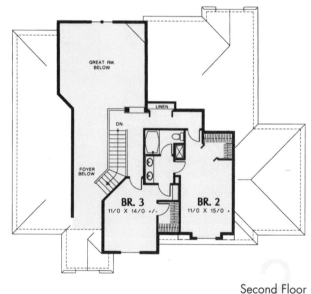

Second Floor

Square columns flank the entry to this contemporary three-bedroom home. The two-story great room provides a fireplace and a wall of windows. A formal dining room, located at the front of the plan, offers a tray ceiling and works well with the kitchen. A bayed den is available for quiet study. The master suite is located on the first floor for privacy and features many amenities such as a spacious master bath and a walk-in closet. Upstairs, two family bedrooms share a full bath.

HPT820086

First Floor: 1,818 square feet
Second Floor: 698 square feet
Total: 2,516 square feet
Width: 60'-0" Depth: 53'-0"

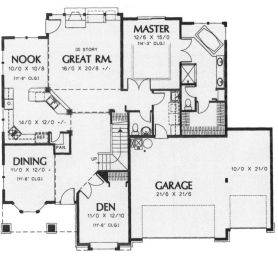

First Floor

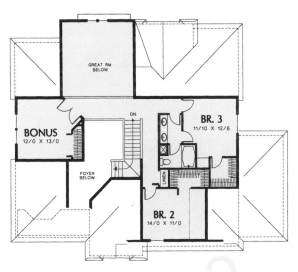

Second Floor

HPT820087

First Floor: 1,786 square feet

Second Floor: 690 square feet

Total: 2,476 square feet

Bonus Room: 204 square feet

Width: 60'-0" Depth: 52'-0"

From the covered porch to the two-story window in the great room, this design is sure to please. The two-story foyer is flanked by a cozy den on the right and a formal dining room with a bay window on the left. A sunny nook is adjacent to the efficient kitchen, which offers a snack bar and a corner sink. The first-floor master suite features a double-door entry, a tray ceiling, a walk-in closet and a bath with a corner tub and separate shower. Upstairs, two family bedrooms—each with a walk-in closet—share a full hall bath. A bonus room completes this level and is available for future development. A three-car garage easily shelters the family fleet.

First Floor

NOOK
10/0 X 12/6
(9' CLG.)

FAMILY RM.
16/6 X 12/6

DINING
13/2 X 11/8

WET BAR

GARAGE
20/0 X 22/0

11/0 X 20/0

1 1/2 STORY
LIVING
13/0 X 13/6

Second Floor

BR. 3
10/8 X 9/11

BR. 2
10/0 X 10/2

MASTER
11/0 X 14/6

BR. 4
11/6 X 10/0

SPA

LIVING RM.
BELOW

Fireplaces in both the living room and family room enhance this home. With an open family room, the kitchen and breakfast nook share the warmth of the fireplace. A few steps down from the foyer, the two-story living room opens to the dining room and a wet bar. Four bedrooms are located on the second floor. The master bedroom features a private bath with a spa and a walk-in closet. The three family bedrooms share a hall bath.

HPT820088

First Floor: 1,255 square feet
Second Floor: 982 square feet
Total: 2,237 square feet
Width: 56'-0" Depth: 45'-0"

Inside and out, this home is packed with delightful details. The entry captivates with its diamond shape, curved stairwell and awesome height. The angled pantry will fit everything you need and living spaces are spiced up with columns set on slants. The family room features a corner entertainment center and the master suite boasts a tub that juts out from the bath. Two second-floor family bedrooms share a hall bath with the bonus room, which is perfect for a home office or playroom.

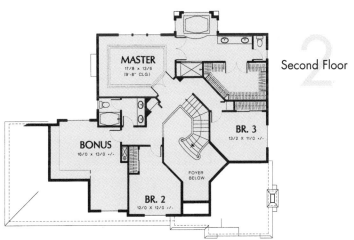

Second Floor

HPT820089

First Floor: 1,547 square feet

Second Floor: 1,160 square feet

Total: 2,707 square feet

Bonus Room: 288 square feet

Width: 60'-0" **Depth:** 50'-0"

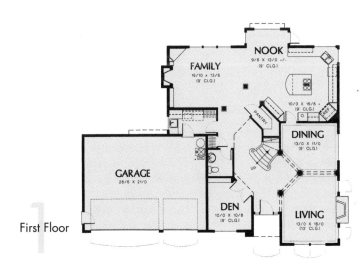

First Floor

First Floor

Second Floor

NOOK
11/0 X 16/0 +/-
(9' CLG.)

VAULTED FAMILY
17/0 X 14/2

13/6 X 17/0 +/-

REF.

PAN.

GARAGE
19/8 X 21/8

10/8 X 19/4

UP

DINING
13/0 X 11/0
(9' CLG.)

W. D.

LIVING
13/0 X 15/4 +/-
(9' CLG.)

MASTER
13/0 X 16/0 +/-
(9'-4" CLG.)

DECK

SPA

FAMILY BELOW

(8' CLG.)

NICHE

BR. 2
11/2 X 12/2

DN.

LIN.

BR. 3
11/6 X 12/8 +/-

LIN.

FOYER BELOW

DEN
9/6 X 11/0

BR. 4
13/0 X 11/0

HPT820090

Here's a contemporary home with a French country spirit! Comfortably elegant formal rooms reside to the front of the plan, with a focal-point fireplace, a bay window and decorative columns to help define the space. A central hall leads to the family area, which includes a gourmet kitchen with an island cooktop counter, a bayed breakfast nook and a vaulted family room with an inglenook. Upstairs, a lavish master suite opens through French doors to a private deck, and a spacious bath boasts a windowed, tile-rimmed spa tub, twin vanities and a generous walk-in closet. Three family bedrooms cluster around a central hall, which opens to a quiet den and enjoys a balcony overlook.

First Floor: 1,466 square feet
Second Floor: 1,369 square feet
Total: 2,835 square feet
Width: 50'-0" Depth: 60'-6"

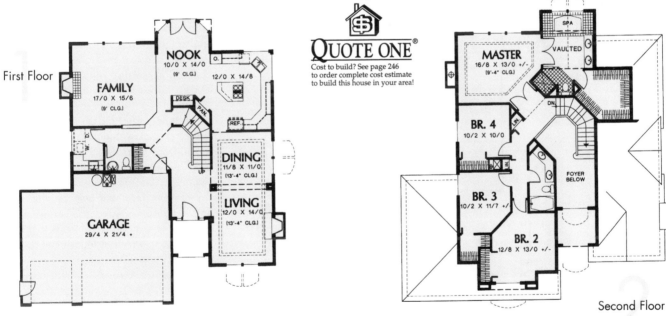

First Floor

NOOK
10/0 X 14/0
(9' CLG.)

FAMILY
17/0 X 15/6
(9' CLG.)

DESK

12/0 X 14/8

W. D.

PAN.

REF.

DINING
11/8 X 11/0
(13'-4" CLG.)

UP

LIVING
12/0 X 14/0
(13'-4" CLG.)

GARAGE
29/4 X 21/4 +

QUOTE ONE®

Cost to build? See page 246
to order complete cost estimate
to build this house in your area!

Second Floor

SPA

MASTER
16/8 X 13/0 +/-
(9'-4" CLG.)

VAULTED

DN.

BR. 4
10/2 X 10/0

FOYER
BELOW

BR. 3
10/2 X 11/7 +/-

BR. 2
12/8 X 13/0 +/-

HPT820091

First Floor: 1,317 square feet

Second Floor: 1,146 square feet

Total: 2,463 square feet

Width: 50'-0" Depth: 54'-0"

This striking stucco home incorporates fine design elements throughout the plan, including a columned formal living and dining area with a boxed ceiling and a fireplace. A gourmet kitchen accommodates the most elaborate—as well as the simplest—meals. The large family room is just off the kitchen for easy casual living. A lovely curved staircase leads to a balcony overlooking the foyer. The master bedroom contains many fine design features, including a luxury bath with a vaulted ceiling and a spa-style bath. Three comfortable family bedrooms share a full hall bath.

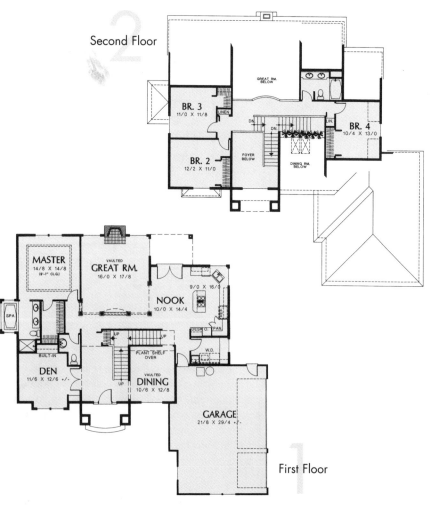

Second Floor

GREAT RM.
BELOW

BR. 3
11/0 X 11/8

LINEN

DN.

DN.

LIN.

BR. 4
10/4 X 13/0

BR. 2
12/2 X 11/0

FOYER
BELOW

DINING RM.
BELOW

MASTER
14/8 X 14/8
(9'-7" CLG.)

VAULTED
GREAT RM.
16/0 X 17/8

9/0 X 16/0

NOOK
10/0 X 14/4

SPA

DESK PAN.

BUILT-IN

W.D.

UP

UP

DEN
11/6 X 12/6 +/-

PLANT SHELF
OVER

VAULTED
DINING
10/6 X 12/8

UP

GARAGE
21/8 X 29/4 +/-

First Floor

This stately contemporary home makes a grand statement inside and out. A volume entry leads to the two-story dining room with a plant shelf and skylights above. The great room with a fireplace flanked by windows is also vaulted. The kitchen provides a desk, a large pantry, an island cooktop and an adjacent breakfast nook with access to a covered porch. Double doors open from the foyer to a den with a built-in cabinet. The master bedroom with a cove ceiling, walk-in closet and amenity-filled bath is conveniently located on the first floor. A two-way staircase leads to the second floor, which includes three family bedrooms and a full bath.

HPT820092 [L]

First Floor: 1,784 square feet
Second Floor: 742 square feet
Total: 2,526 square feet
Width: 64'-0" Depth: 60'-0"

The angular placement of this home's three-car garage creates an expansive and very stylish facade. The foyer is punctuated with a dramatic staircase and opens on the right to formal living areas before continuing back into the inviting family room. A fireplace and plenty of windows in the family room are a nice balance to the country kitchen. Amenities here include a breakfast nook, cooktop island and rear access to the formal dining room. Three family bedrooms and a full hall bath join the luxurious master suite on the second floor.

HPT820093

First Floor: 1,592 square feet

Second Floor: 1,178 square feet

Total: 2,770 square feet

Width: 77'-5" Depth: 64'-7"

Second Floor

First Floor

Second Floor

SPA

MASTER
14/10 X 15/10
(9'-9" CLG)

DINING RM
BELOW

BONUS
11/2 X 13/0 +

FOYER
BELOW

BR. 3
10/8 X 11/8 +

BR. 2
10/0 X 12/0

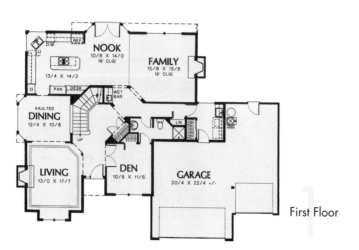

NOOK
10/8 X 14/0
(9' CLG)

FAMILY
15/8 X 15/8
(9' CLG)

13/4 X 14/2

PAN   DESK

WET
BAR

VAULTED
DINING
12/4 X 10/8

LIN

LIVING
13/0 X 17/7

DEN
10/8 X 11/6

GARAGE
30/4 X 22/4 +/-

First Floor

Tall windows dress up a new look in contemporary stucco exteriors and afford wide views inside. The formal living room features a floor-to-ceiling window and opens to the dining room. A gourmet island counter with a cooktop serves planned events as well as casual meals. Choose formal meals in the dining room, or opt for more casual fare in the nook that separates the family room from the L-shaped kitchen. A den is tucked away from the more traffic-laden areas of the home. The spacious master suite defines the second-floor sleeping quarters, which include two additional bedrooms and a full bath with two vanities. A sizable bonus room is available for later development.

HPT820094

First Floor: 1,580 square feet
Second Floor: 943 square feet
Total: 2,523 square feet
Bonus Room: 249 square feet
Width: 63'-0" **Depth:** 50'-0"

This attractive European-styled plan is enhanced by a stucco finish and arched windows complementing the facade. The two-story foyer, with its angled stair, opens to the dramatically vaulted living room on one side and the den with French doors on the other. An efficient L-shaped island kitchen works well with the formal dining room to its left and a sunny nook to the right. A bayed family room with a warming hearth completes this floor. Upstairs, a sumptuous master suite includes a spa tub, shower, twin vanities and a large walk-in closet. Two family bedrooms share a full skylit bath that includes twin vanities. Over the garage is a vaulted bonus room, perfect as a game or hobby room.

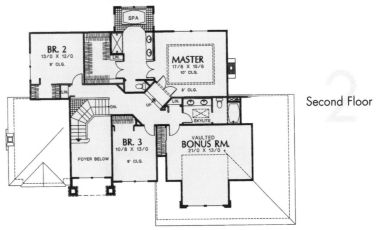

Second Floor

HPT820095 L

First Floor: *1,618 square feet*

Second Floor: *1,212 square feet*

Total: *2,830 square feet*

Bonus Room: *376 square feet*

Width: 68'-0" Depth: 51'-0"

First Floor

Dining
22⁴ · 11⁰

Living Room

Kitchen

Breakfast

opt. media center

Family Room
15⁴ · 14²

pantry

ref

sh

up

Foyer

opt.

Entry

Pdr.

Utility

ac

wh

opt. sink & sh.

ac

Garage

First Floor

Dining Below

opt. trans.

Living Room

Foyer Below

Bath

w.i.c.

down

opt.

Master Bedroom
13⁰ · 11⁶

Second Floor

Study/ Bedroom 4
10⁶ · 10⁰

Bath

Bedroom 3
11⁴ · 11⁰

Bedroom 2
11⁴ · 11⁰

Alternate Elevation

This design accentuates magnificent rear-yard views as all first-floor living areas feature rear-facing windows. The formal living and dining area will serve a variety of situations well. The island kitchen easily accesses the dining room and commands open-floor planning with the breakfast area as well as the family room. The California closet layout in the master bath makes efficient use of space and maximizes storage. Of the other three bedrooms, one could serve as a master sitting room or den, if desired. Blueprints come with options for two different exteriors.

HPT820096

First Floor: 982 square feet
Second Floor: 982 square feet
Total: 1,964 square feet
Width: 40'-0" Depth: 48'-10"

Deck

Sitting

Master Suite
17⁰ • 14⁰

w.i.c.

Gathering Rm.
15⁰ • 25⁰

Covered Patio

Dining Rm.
11⁴ • 13⁸

Master Bath

Kitchen

Foyer

Laun

Pwdr

Nook

Entry

2 Car Garage
21¹ • 23⁴

First Floor

Loft/Bedroom
14⁴ • 11¹⁰

Bath 2

Second Floor

Bedroom 2
11¹ • 11¹

Bath 3

w.i.c.

Bedroom 3
12⁶ • 11⁴

HPT820097

First Floor: 1,698 square feet

Second Floor: 848 square feet

Total: 2,546 square feet

Width: 44'-0" Depth: 64'-8"

The gathering room is the heart of this design, and all other spaces move from its core. The large kitchen with a sunny bayed nook is bathed in light through walls of glass, while the formal dining room has French doors that open onto a private patio. The hub of family activity is the gathering room—it comes complete with a fireplace media wall, which soars two stories with niches and glass transoms. The master suite features a bay-windowed sitting area with a view to the deck area. The bath boasts loads of closet space, and His and Hers vanities flank a soaking tub and separate shower.

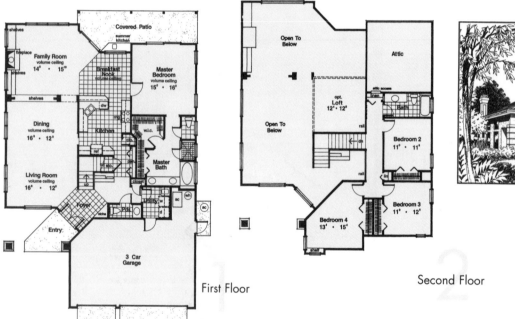

First Floor

Second Floor

Alternate Elevation

No matter where you're building, this design offers two exteriors to heighten the possibilities. The double-door entry opens to the combined formal living and dining areas. Nearby, the kitchen enjoys ample space for gourmet-meal preparations, as well as an attached breakfast nook. In the family room, a volume ceiling and a fireplace are sure to please. The master bedroom, located at the rear of the first floor, accesses the covered patio. It also sports a bath with a double-bowl lavatory, garden tub and large walk-in closet. On the second floor, three bedrooms enjoy peace and quiet and share a hall bath. An optional loft is included in the blueprints.

HPT820098

First Floor: 1,816 square feet
Second Floor: 703 square feet
Total: 2,519 square feet
Width: 45'-0" Depth: 67'-6"

J.N. HANSEN S.DG

Covered Patio

Master Suite
14⁸ · 15⁸

Nook

Family Rm.
16⁸ · 15⁸

w.i.c.

Kitchen

Dining Rm.
16⁴ · 10⁰

Master
Bath

Living Rm.
16⁴ · 13⁸

Laundry

Pwdr.

Foyer

Entry

2 Car Garage
28⁸ · 19⁸

First Floor

Bedroom 2
11⁰ · 13⁸

Loft

Second Floor

Bath 2

w.i.c.

Bedroom 3
10⁴ · 13⁸

Bath

Bedroom 4
13⁴ · 15⁸

HPT820099

First Floor: 1,844 square feet
Second Floor: 1,017 square feet
Total: 2,861 square feet
Width: 45'-0" Depth: 67'-8"

The excitement begins upon entering the foyer of this home where an impressive staircase is its focal point. Spacious living areas include a living/dining room combination and a large family room—complete with a warming fireplace. Just off the nook is a sliding glass door to the covered patio, which includes a wet bar as well as a pool bath. The master suite is generously sized and has a wonderful wall of high transom glass, as well as sliding glass doors to the patio. A spacious loft works well as a game room, study or library—or it can be a fifth bedroom.

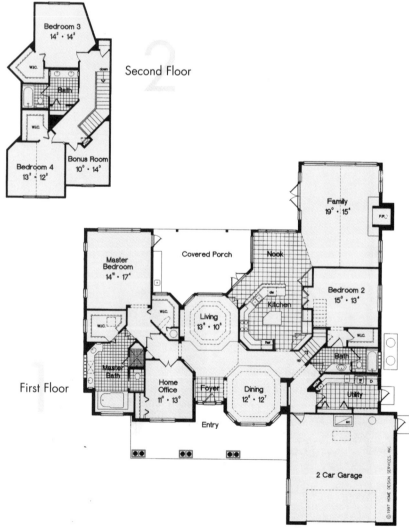

Bedroom 3
14² · 14²

W.I.C.

Second Floor

Bath

down

W.I.C.

Bedroom 4
13² · 12²

Bonus Room
10° · 14³

First Floor

Master
Bedroom
14¹⁰ · 17⁴

Covered Porch

Nook

Family
19° · 15²

F.P.

W.I.C.

W.I.C.

Living
13° · 10³

Kitchen

Bedroom 2
15° · 13²

W.I.C.

Master
Bath

Home
Office
11° · 13°

Foyer

Dining
12³ · 12⁷

Bath

Utility

Entry

2 Car Garage

Warm welcoming porches and brick accents make this elevation an inviting one. The foyer, with a recessed artwork niche, opens up into the formal living and dining room, with playful ceiling elements. Double doors to the master suite are impressive, as is the bedroom and bath layout, with ample closet space and all the expected amenities. The kitchen is the heart of this family home, complete with a work island. The oversized nook provides plenty of space, and the large fireplace is the crowning touch in the large family room. The second floor boasts two large bedrooms with a shared bath and walk-in closets. Another plus is the bonus room, which would be perfect for a computer room or playroom.

HPT820100

First Floor: 2,827 square feet

Second Floor: 696 square feet

Total: 3,523 square feet

Bonus Room: 118 square feet

Width: 72'-8"   Depth: 81'-0"

An incredible combination of curving lines and circles in this ultramodern design makes for an interesting floor plan. The dramatic use of balconies and overlooks highlights a first-floor gathering room, with a fireplace, open to the study and a formal dining room. A kitchen with a circular breakfast room continues the gracious use of curves. A goblet-shaped bedroom on this floor has a balcony and a full bath. Reached by a curved stair, the upper level is dominated by the master suite. A lower-level activities room with a bar and fireplace, and an exercise room with an attached sauna, hot tub and bath overlook the lower terrace. Take special note of the generous use of skylights throughout.

Upper Level

Main Level

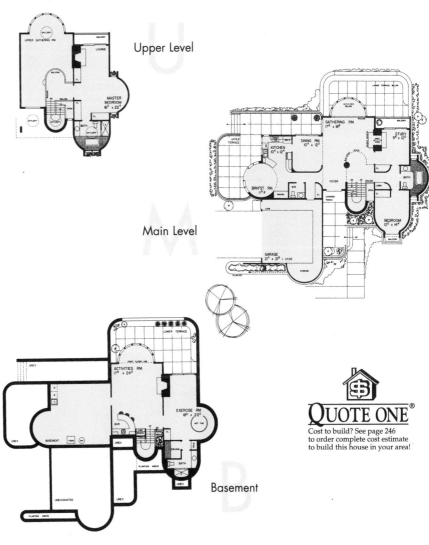

Basement

HPT820101

Main Level: *1,570 square feet*
Upper Level: *598 square feet*
Total: *2,168 square feet*
Finished Basement:
        1,080 square feet
Width: *66'-4"* Depth: *63'-8"*

QUOTE ONE®
Cost to build? See page 246
to order complete cost estimate
to build this house in your area!

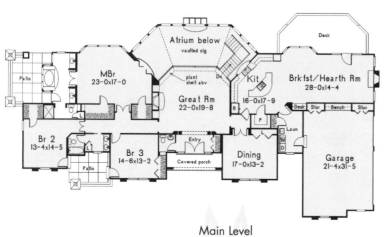

Main Level

Basement

The grand facade on this home is accented by the large window details. Sunbursts, keystones and lintels decorate the arches of the windows. The brightly lit entry connects to the great room with a balcony and a massive bay-shaped atrium. The kitchen features an island snack bar, walk-in pantry, computer area and atrium overlook. The master suite includes a sitting area, two walk-in closets, an atrium overlook and a luxury bath with a private courtyard. The family room/atrium, home theater, game room and guest bedroom comprise the lower level.

HPT820102

Square Footage: 4,826
Finished Basement:
1,776 square feet
Width: 109'-0" Depth: 57'-6"

Contemporary and Mediterranean influences shape the spirit and inner spaces of this fine home. An arched entrance and front covered porch welcome you inside to the formal dining room and great room. The relaxing kitchen/breakfast area is reserved for more intimate and casual occasions. The master suite provides a walk-in closet and private bath while Bedrooms 2 and 3 share a hall bath. Separated from the other sleeping quarters, Bedroom 4 makes the perfect guest suite. A family room, sitting area, wet bar, office and additional bath reside downstairs, furthering the flexibility of this home.

Main Level

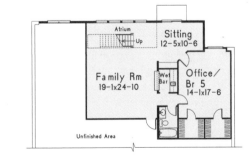

Basement

HPT820103

Square Footage: 2,408

Finished Basement:

1,100 square feet

Width: 75'-8" Depth: 52'-6"

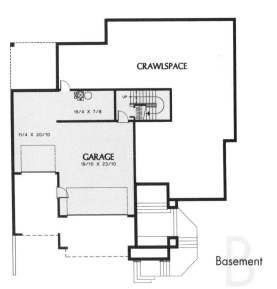

Basement

Main Level

HPT820104

Square Footage: 2,542
Finished Basement:
130 square feet
Width: 60'-0" Depth: 59'-0"

This is a gorgeous design that would easily accommodate a sloping lot. A grand great room sets the tone for this fabulous floor plan, with an elegant tray ceiling and French doors to a private front balcony. With windows and glass panels to take in the view, this design would make an exquisite seaside resort. The formal dining room is off the center of the plan for privacy, and is served by a nearby gourmet kitchen. Three steps up from the foyer, the sleeping level includes a spacious master suite with a sizable private bath. Each of two additional bedrooms privately accesses a shared bath with two vanities.

Homeowners will look forward to coming home to this plan. A spacious gallery hall welcomes you inside. The lower level holds two family bedrooms, a game room and a media room, while the main level includes the kitchen, dining room, great room and master suite. Thoughtful built-ins like a wet bar make this home a prize. Other special amenities such as the corner fireplace in the great room and island workstation in the kitchen are just some of the modern additions found throughout the home. A spacious three-car garage completes the plan.

Main Level

Lower Level

HPT820105

Main Level: 2,157 square feet

Lower Level: 1,754 square feet

Total: 3,911 square feet

Width: 80'-0" Depth: 61'-0"

Basement

First Floor

Second Floor

For an extra-luxurious hillside home, with unfinished space on the lower level, look no further than this grand design. The main and upper levels have spacious living and sleeping areas, a service kitchen for the formal dining room, a den and gourmet kitchen. Two family bedrooms with a shared bath sit on the main level, while the master suite has the entire upper floor to itself. The master bath features twin vanities, an over-sized tub and a separate shower. The lower level holds the three-car garage, game room, shop and a full bath. Please specify basement or crawlspace foundation when ordering.

HPT820106

First Floor: 2,813 square feet
Second Floor: 1,058 square feet
Total: 3,871 square feet
Finished Basement: 806 square feet
Width: 83'-0" Depth: 61'-0"

Keystones, stucco and dramatic rooflines create a stately exterior for this home. The formal living and dining rooms invite elegant occasions, while the clustered family room, breakfast nook and gourmet kitchen take care of casual gatherings. A quiet den with built-in shelves opens off the foyer—perfect for a library or home office. The second-floor master suite, a few steps up from the central hall, features a coffered ceiling and a divided walk-in closet. The master bedroom opens to the spa bath through French doors. Three family bedrooms share a full bath. Unfinished bonus space above the garage can be developed into a hobby room or study.

HPT820107

First Floor: 1,564 square feet

Second Floor: 1,422 square feet

Total: 2,986 square feet

Bonus Room: 430 square feet

Width: 63'-0" **Depth:** 51'-0"

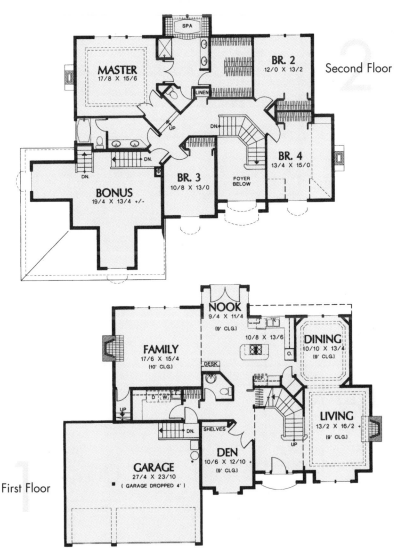

Second Floor

First Floor

UPPER TERRACE

LOWER TERRACE

DINING RM.
11⁴x11⁰

KITCHEN
10⁰x11⁰

NOOK
8⁰x8⁸

FAMILY RM.
15⁰x12⁰

SHELVES

WASH RM.

LAUNDRY

LIVING RM.
21⁴x12⁰

ENTRY

PORCH

GARAGE
22⁸x22⁸

Main Level

ROOF

BALCONY

MASTER BED RM.
15⁰x12⁶

BATH

DRESSING RM.

WALK-IN CLOSET

HALL

DN

BED RM.
11¹x9⁸

BATH

LINEN

ROOF

BED RM.
11⁶x9⁸

BED RM.
11⁶x10⁸

Upper Level

Tri-level living could hardly ask for more than this rustic design has to offer. Not only can you enjoy the three levels but there is also a fourth basement level for bulk storage and a shop area. The interior livability is outstanding. The main level has an L-shaped formal living/dining area with a fireplace in the living room, sliding glass doors in the dining room leading to the upper terrace, a U-shaped kitchen and an informal eating area. Down a few steps to the lower level is the family room with another fireplace and sliding doors to the lower terrace, a washroom and a laundry room. The upper level houses all of the sleeping quarters including three bedrooms, a bath and the master suite.

HPT820108 LD

Main Level: 728 square feet

Upper Level: 874 square feet

Lower Level: 310 square feet

Total: 1,912 square feet

Width: 56'-8" Depth: 36'-5"

This attractive two-story home will fit a sloping lot and fulfill seaside views. The foyer opens to interior vistas through decorative columns, while the two-story great room boasts lovely French doors to a front deck. The gourmet kitchen features an island cooktop counter, a sunny corner sink and a nook with a pass-through to the great room. A formal dining room, a secluded den and a sizable laundry complete the first floor. The second-floor master suite employs a scissor-vault ceiling and a divided-light window for style, and a relaxing bath with a spa tub for comfort. Two family bedrooms, each with a private lavatory, share a full bath on this floor.

HPT820109 L

First Floor: 1,538 square feet

Second Floor: 1,089 square feet

Total: 2,627 square feet

Width: 43'-0" **Depth:** 50'-0"

Basement

QUOTE ONE®
Cost to build? See page 246
to order complete cost estimate
to build this house in your area!

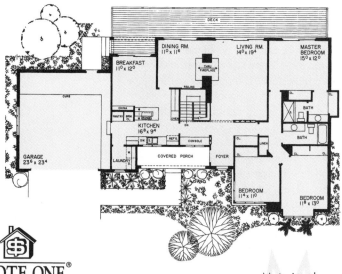

Main Level

HPT820110 L

Think Tudors are only two stories? Think again. This is a magnificent hillside plan, complete with a main-level fireplace, easy-to-reach rear deck (four different rooms lead to it), and plenty of storage space. The lower level is a delight. Note the fireplace, second kitchen with a snack bar, rear terrace, space for an extra bedroom (or two), built-ins galore, and lots of bonus space that could easily be a workroom, exercise room or both.

Square Footage: 1,874
Finished Basement: 1,131 square feet
Width: 78'-10" Depth: 43'-5"

Rear View

Basement

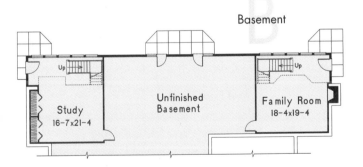

Study
16-7x21-4

Unfinished
Basement

Family Room
18-4x19-4

Up

Up

Main Level

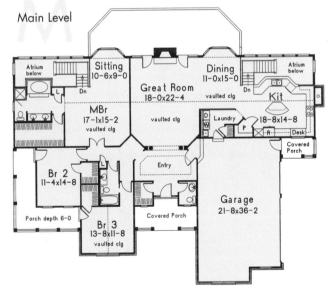

Atrium
below

Sitting
10-6x9-0

Dining
11-0x15-0

Atrium
below

Great Room
18-0x22-4
vaulted clg

Kit
18-8x14-8

MBr
17-1x15-2
vaulted clg

vaulted clg

Laundry

D
W

P

Desk

R

Covered
Porch

Dn

Dn

L

Br 2
11-4x14-8

Entry

L

Garage
21-8x36-2

Porch depth 6-0

Covered Porch

Br 3
13-8x11-8
vaulted clg

HPT820111

Square Footage: 3,199

Finished Basement:

850 square feet

Width: 79'-4" Depth: 59'-6"

Sunbursts over the entryway and front windows add sophistication to this home. The mix of stone and siding adds a versatile feel to this pleasant home. The rear of this home offers plenty of natural lighting as well as porch space. The grand-scale kitchen features bay-shaped cabinetry overlooking an atrium with a two-story window wall. A second atrium dominates the master suite, which boasts a bayed sitting area and a luxurious bath with a whirlpool tub. The lower level contains a study, family room and unfinished space for future expansion.

Rear View

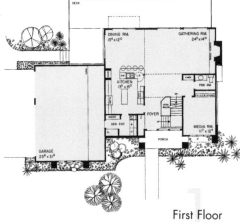

First Floor

Basement

QUOTE ONE®

Cost to build? See page 246
to order complete cost estimate
to build this house in your area!

Second Floor

This attractive multi-level home benefits from the comfort and ease of open planning. The entry foyer leads straight into a large gathering room with a fireplace and is open to the dining room and kitchen. A perfect arrangement for the more informal demands of today! A media room features a built-in area for your TV, VCR and stereo. The sleeping area features two bedrooms on the upper level—one a master suite with His and Hers walk-in closets. The lower level includes an activities room, a wet bar and a third bedroom with a full bath.

HPT820112

Main Level: 1,327 square feet
Upper Level: 887 square feet
Total: 2,214 square feet
Finished Basement: 1,197 square feet
Width: 62'-8" Depth: 44'-0"

This hillside home opens with formal and informal living areas to the left of the central foyer and dining and cooking areas to the right. A large deck to the back adds outdoor enjoyment. The master bedroom, with a full bath, misses nothing in the way of luxury and is joined by two family bedrooms—one with a bay window—and baths. Bonus space to the front makes a perfect office or computer room. Note the lower-level recreation room with a fireplace.

HPT820113

First Floor: 1,315 square feet

Second Floor: 1,312 square feet

Total: 2,627 square feet

Finished Basement:
  404 square feet

Width: 38'-0" **Depth:** 33'-0"

Rear View

Main Level

Basement

QUOTE ONE®
Cost to build? See page 246
to order complete cost estimate
to build this house in your area!

Here's a hillside haven that can easily accommodate the largest of families if necessary. It's perfect for both formal and informal occasions. Straight back from the foyer is a grand gathering room/dining room combination. It is complemented by the breakfast room and a front-facing media room. The sleeping wing contains three bedrooms and two full baths. On the lower level is an activities room with a summer kitchen and a fourth bedroom that makes a perfect guest room. The large upper deck and the lower covered deck allow for formal parties or just quiet relaxation. The lower level can be finished at a later time than the main level—allowing for future expansion.

Square Footage: 3,548
Finished Basement: 1,036 square feet
Width: 74'-0" Depth: 68'-8"

Clean contemporary lines are a prelude to the inside where a foyer leads directly into the sunken great room, which features a fireplace and deck access. The kitchen easily serves both the breakfast room and the formal dining room. Two family bedrooms share a full bath that includes dual lavs. Completing the main level is the master suite, which offers a walk-in closet and a private bath. The lower level is made up of a spacious recreation room with a second fireplace, a fourth bedroom and plenty of storage.

HPT820115 D

Square Footage: 2,184
Finished Basement: 1,130 square feet
Width: 70'-0" Depth: 58'-0"

Main Level

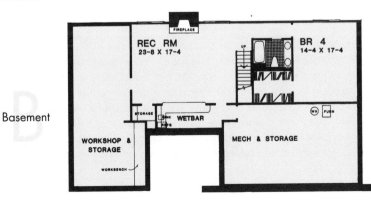

Basement

A. J. YOUNG
FUQUAY VERINA N.C.

Rear View

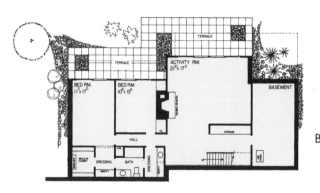

Basement

Main Level

MASTER BED RM.
12' x 16'

STUDY-BED RM.
11' x 13'

GATHERING RM.
22' x 17²

DINING RM.
12² x 10⁴

KITCHEN
12² x 12

LAUNDRY
12² x 7³

WASH. RM.

ENTRY

PORCH

HALL

BATH

DRESSING

VANITY

WALK-IN CLOSET

THRU-FIREPLACE

BALCONY

RAILING

GARAGE
23⁵ x 22⁸

BED RM.
11' x 17¹⁰

BED RM.
10⁸ x 13⁶

ACTIVITY RM.
21⁵ x 17²

TERRACE

TERRACE

BASEMENT

STORAGE

HALL

DRESSING

BATH

DRESSING

VANITY

VANITY

WALK-IN CLOSET

HPT820116

Thoughtful use of space was employed in this design. The result—functional living spaces with options. The main level consists of the gathering room with balcony access and a through-fireplace to the study or optional bedroom. The dining room and kitchen are open areas. Note the convenient island range and amount of counter area for the gourmet. A laundry room (plenty of counter room here, too!) and washroom complete the upper level. The lower level is equally well-planned with a large activity room, two bedrooms with sliding glass doors onto a terrace, and a full bath. One bedroom includes a large walk-in closet with built-in shelves, matching the layout of the master suite.

Square Footage: 1,838
Finished Basement: 1,558 square fee
Width: 61'-8" Depth: 60'-8"

Here is another one-story home that doubles its livability by exposing the lowest level at the rear. Formal living on the main level takes place in the spacious living room and the formal dining area, with any overflow ending out on the rear deck. The island kitchen works well with the sunny nook, which also offers access to the deck. The main-level master suite features its own private balcony. Informal living is accommodated on the lower level by an activity room and study. Two family bedrooms, sharing a full bath, complete this level.

Rear View

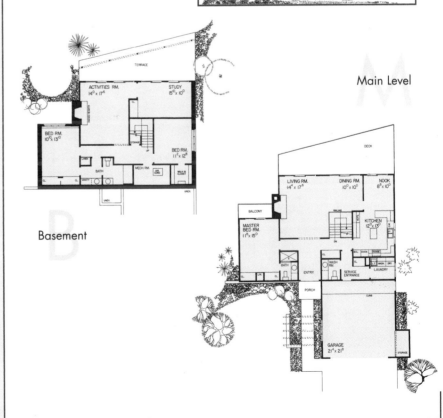

Basement

Main Level

HPT820117 L

Square Footage: 1,242
Finished Basement: 1,242 square feet
Width: 50'-0" Depth: 52'-0"

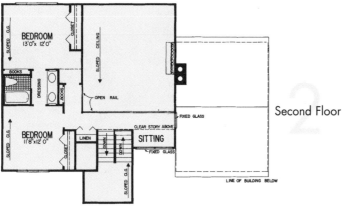

Second Floor

This home is a stunner with its unique angled rooflines, interesting window configurations and mixture of stone and wooden siding facade. Interior spaces are dramatically proportioned because of the long and varied rooflines of this contemporary home. The two-story living area highlights a sloped ceiling, as does the master bedroom and two upper-level bedrooms. Two fireplaces, a huge wooden deck, a small upstairs sitting room and a liberal number of windows make this a most comfortable residence.

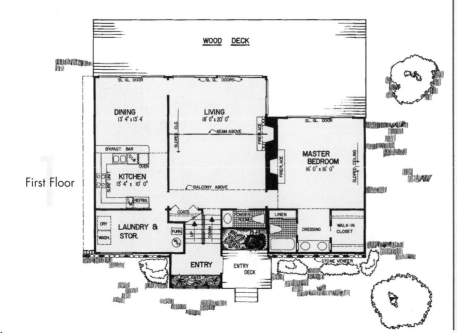

First Floor

HPT820118

First Floor: 1,494 square feet
Second Floor: 597 square feet
Total: 2,091 square feet
Width: 50'-8" **Depth:** 47'-8"

You can't help but feel spoiled by this design. Downstairs from the entry is a large living room with a sloped ceiling and fireplace. Nearby is the U-shaped kitchen with a pass-through to the dining room. Also on this level, the master suite boasts a fireplace and a sliding glass door to the deck. The living and dining rooms also feature deck access. Upstairs are two bedrooms and a shared bath. Finish the lower level when your budget and space needs allow. It includes a play-room with a fireplace, a half-bath, a large bar and sliding glass doors to the patio.

HPT820119 L

Main Level: 1,494 square feet
Upper Level: 597 square feet
Total: 2,091 square feet
Finished Basement: 1,035 square feet
Width: 59'-0" Depth: 69'-8"

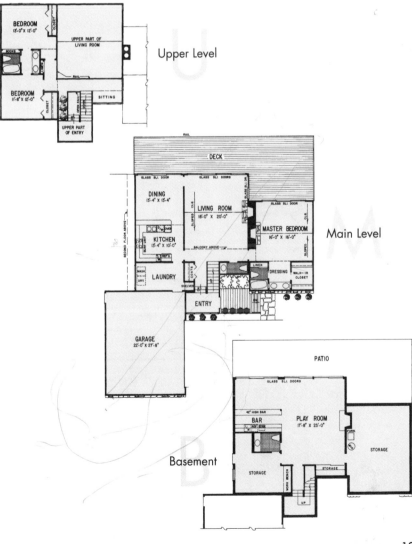

Upper Level

Main Level

Basement

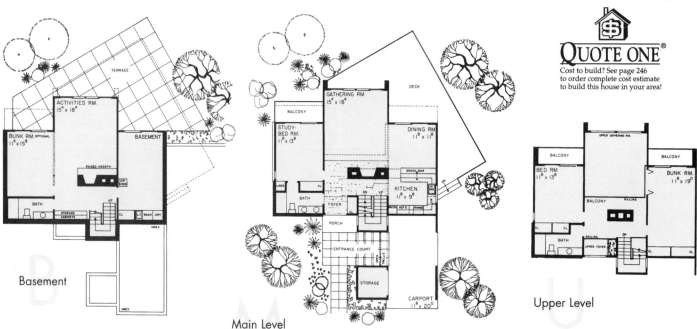

Basement

Main Level

Upper Level

HPT820120 LD

Main Level: 1,043 square feet

Upper Level: 703 square feet

Total: 1,746 square feet

Finished Basement:

794 square feet

Width: 40'-4" Depth: 52'-0"

This outstanding multi-level home comes complete with an outdoor deck and balconies. The main level provides full living space: gathering room with a fireplace, study (or optional bedroom) with a bath, dining room and U-shaped kitchen. A huge deck area wraps around the gathering room and dining room for outdoor enjoyment. A bedroom and bunk room on the upper level are joined by a wide balcony area and full bath. Lower-level space includes a large activities room with a fireplace, an additional bunk room and a full bath. Built-ins and open window areas abound throughout the plan.

Building on a hilly site? If so, this plan may fit right in. It features a terrific master suite. Overlooking the gathering room through shuttered windows, the suite includes a private balcony, a sitting/dressing room and a full bath. Also on this level is a family bedroom with access to a hall bath. Other highlights include a two-story gathering room with a raised-hearth through-fireplace, a sloped ceiling and sliding glass doors to the main balcony. A study shares the fireplace and is located at the front of the plan. The kitchen offers lots of built-ins and a separate dining nook. The lower level contains a large family room, where there's another fireplace; a guest bedroom and full bath; and a rear terrace.

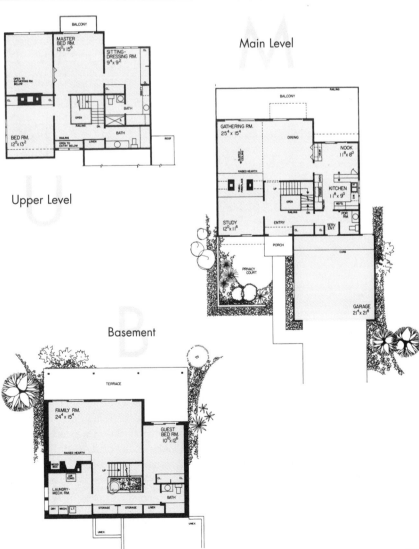

Main Level

Upper Level

Basement

HPT820121 L

Main Level: 1,013 square feet

Upper Level: 885 square feet

Total: 1,898 square feet

Finished Basement: 1,074 square feet

Width: 42'-0" Depth: 52'-0"

Rear View

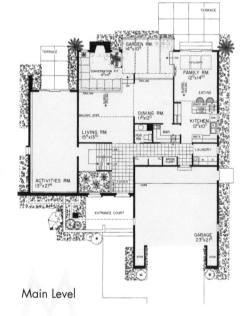

Main Level

Upper Level

This luxurious three-bedroom home offers comfort on many levels. Its modern design incorporates a sunken rear garden room and conversation pit—with a fireplace—off a living room and dining room. Skylights provide natural light in an adjacent family room with a high sloped ceiling. Other features include an entrance court, an activities room with a private terrace, a modern U-shaped kitchen, an upper lounge and a lavish master bedroom suite. Two secondary bedrooms each offer plenty of storage space and share a hall bath.

HPT820122 *L*

Main Level: 1,449 square feet
Upper Level: 1,113 square feet
Total: 2,562 square feet
Width: 54'-0" Depth: 63'-8"

Main Level

Upper Level

Basement

HPT820123

Main Level: 1,809 square feet

Upper Level: 1,293 square feet

Total: 3,102 square feet

Finished Basement: 1,828 square feet

Width: 82'-8" Depth: 40'-0"

A spacious two-story living room is the centerpiece of this plan with its large fireplace and access to the rear deck. Next door are the kitchen and breakfast room and an adjacent formal dining room. Also on this level is an enormous master suite with a fireplace. Upstairs are three bedrooms and a sewing room linked by a balcony overlooking the living room. The lower level consists of a family bedroom with its own bath, a summer kitchen, a family room with a fireplace, a spacious recreation room and a large laundry room.

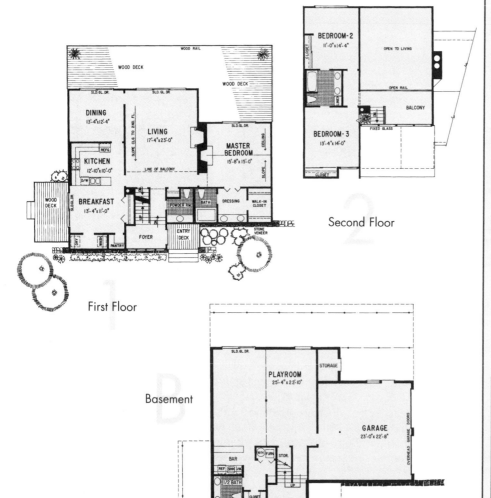

First Floor

Second Floor

Basement

With classic contemporary lines, this three-bedroom home is sure to draw attention in your neighborhood. Entering on the middle level, a spacious living room is just a few steps up and offers a fireplace, sliding glass doors to the rear deck, a sloped ceiling to the second-floor balcony and access to the formal dining room as well as the U-shaped kitchen and breakfast room. The master suite completes this level and contains a fireplace, a walk-in closet, a private bath and access to the rear deck. Two bedrooms and a full bath make up the upper level. The lower level features a huge playroom and access to the garage.

HPT820124 L

First Floor: *1,580 square feet*
Second Floor: *702 square feet*
Total: *2,282 square feet*
Finished Basement: *967 square feet*
Width: *50'-0"* **Depth:** *38'-0"*

This plan opens with the formal living room featuring a raised-hearth fireplace, the dining room with rear-terrace access, and a private media room that keeps noise at bay. The greenhouse off the kitchen adds 147 square feet to the plan and offers access to the clutter room, where gardening or hobby activities may take place. At the opposite end of the house, the master bedroom with a private bath and two family bedrooms and a shared bath make up the sleeping arrangements. A wealth of built-ins throughout the home make it especially inviting.

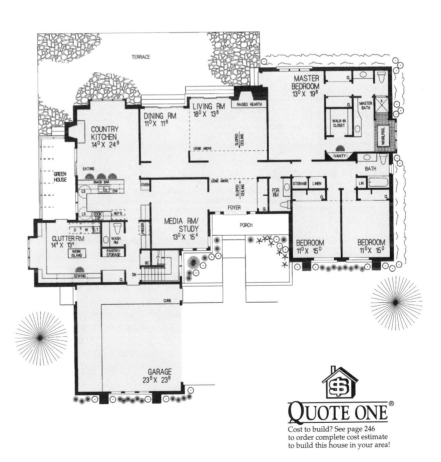

HPT8201 25 L D

Square Footage: 2,913
Greenhouse: 147 square feet
Width: 82'-8" Depth: 74'-0"

QUOTE ONE®
Cost to build? See page 246
to order complete cost estimate
to build this house in your area!

This inviting U-shaped western ranch adaptation offers outstanding living potential behind its double front doors. In only 1,754 square feet there are three bedrooms and 2½ baths. The formal living room is open to the dining area and offers a raised-hearth fireplace and a sloped ceiling. The functional kitchen features an adjacent breakfast nook and easily accesses the informal family room. A rear terrace stretches the width of the home and is accessible from the master bedroom, living room and family room. Stairs lead to a basement which may be developed at a later time.

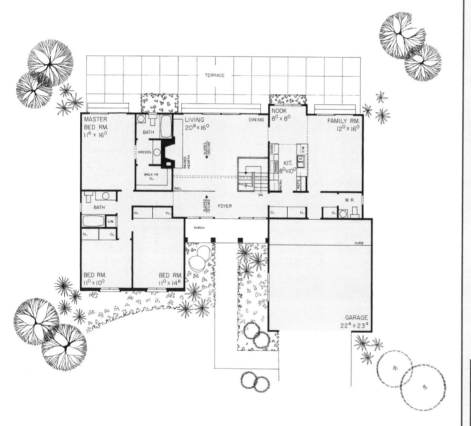

HPT820126 D

Square Footage: 1,754
Width: 64'-0" Depth: 48'-0"

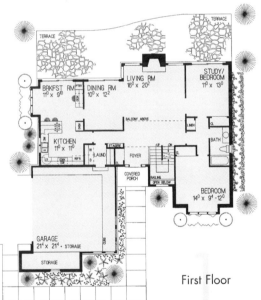

First Floor

Quote One®

Cost to build? See page 246
to order complete cost estimate
to build this house in your area!

Second Floor

HPT820127 [L]

First Floor: 1,467 square feet
Second Floor: 715 square feet
Total: 2,182 square feet
Width: 55'-8" Depth: 55'-0"

Just the right amount of living space is contained in this charming traditional Tudor house and is arranged in a great floor plan. The split-bedroom configuration, with two bedrooms (or optional study) on the first floor and the master suite on the second floor with its own studio, assures complete privacy. The living room has a second-floor balcony overlook and a warming fireplace. The full-width terrace in back is reached through sliding glass doors in each room at the rear of the house.

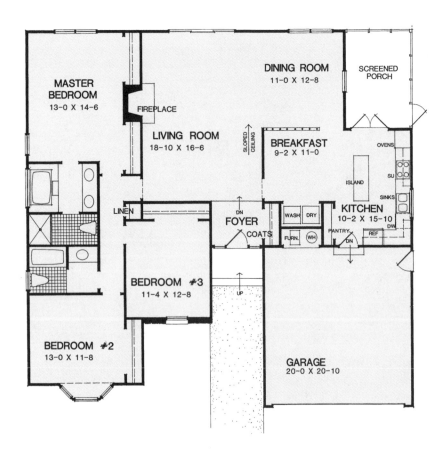

MASTER
BEDROOM
13-0 X 14-6

FIREPLACE

DINING ROOM
11-0 X 12-8

SCREENED
PORCH

LIVING ROOM
18-10 X 16-6

SLOPED
CEILING

BREAKFAST
9-2 X 11-0

OVENS

SU

ISLAND

SINKS

LINEN

DN

FOYER

WASH DRY

KITCHEN
10-2 X 15-10

COATS

FURN. WH

PANTRY

REF

DW

DN

UP

BEDROOM #3
11-4 X 12-8

UP

BEDROOM #2
13-0 X 11-8

GARAGE
20-0 X 20-10

A stone-and-siding exterior and a bayed window—empty-nesters and small families will appreciate the compact design of this sharp little home. A raised foyer leads into the living/dining room, which is warmed by a fireplace. An island kitchen with a breakfast nook and adjacent screened porch offers plenty of storage space. Three bedrooms, one a large master suite with a full bath and twin closets, allow plenty of space for a growing family or visits from grown kids and grandchildren. A two-car garage fulfills all your storage needs.

HPT820128 [L]

Square Footage: 1,811
Width: 53'-0" Depth: 50'-6"

This modest-sized farmhouse has much to offer in the way of livability. It may function as either a two- or three-bedroom home. The huge living room features a fine raised-hearth fireplace and a beamed ceiling. The kitchen revolves around a center island cooktop and a breakfast nook. The handy open stairway to the basement may lead to a future recreation area. In addition to the two full baths, there is an extra washroom. Adjacent is the laundry room and the service entrance from the garage. The blueprints for this design will show details for three delightful elevations: Tudor, Colonial and contemporary.

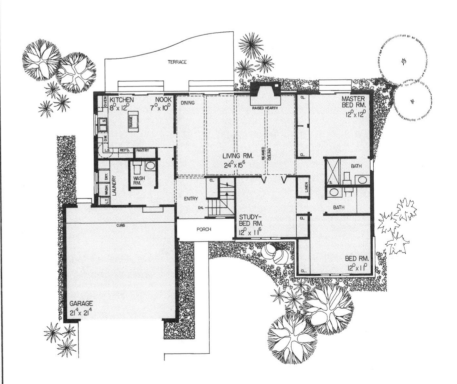

HPT820129 LD

Square Footage: 1,540
Width: 61'-8" Depth: 44'-0"

Quote One®

Cost to build? See page 246
to order complete cost estimate
to build this house in your area!

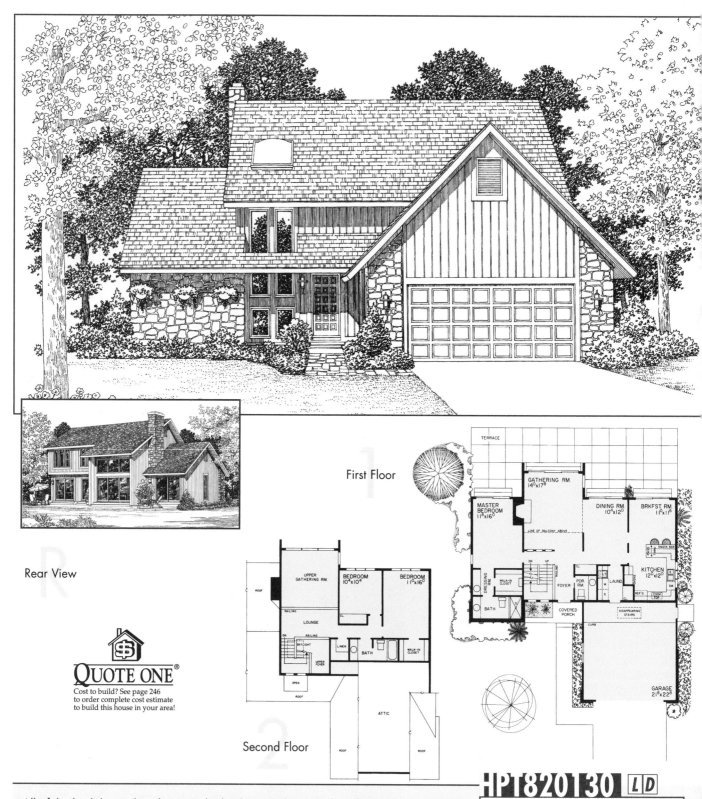

First Floor

Rear View

QUOTE ONE®

Cost to build? See page 246
to order complete cost estimate
to build this house in your area!

Second Floor

HPT820130 L|D

All of the livability in this plan is in the back! With this sort of configuration, this home makes a perfect lakefront or beachfront home. Each first-floor room, except the kitchen, maintains access to the rear terrace via sliding glass doors. However, the kitchen is open to the breakfast room and thus takes advantage of the view. The master bedroom delights with its private bath and walk-in closet. Two secondary bedrooms comprise the second floor. One utilizes a walk-in closet while both make use of a full hall bath. A lounge overlooks the foyer as well as the gathering room below.

First Floor: 1,342 square feet
Second Floor: 619 square feet
Total: 1,961 square feet
Width: 49'-8" Depth: 55'-8"

A high hipped roof allows for a volume look with expansive windows in this two-story plan. The main living areas of the plan are clustered on the first floor with the second floor reserved for two secondary bedrooms and a full hall bath. From the spacious entry, the joined living and dining rooms create a nice place for entertaining. The large family room welcomes casual living with its fireplace. The gourmet kitchen has a great cooktop island that will keep the cook in the loop of family activities. The master suite includes a nearby den, a walk-in closet and a large compartmented bath.

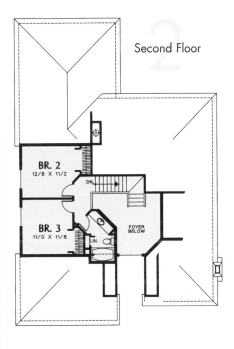

Second Floor

BR. 2
12/8 X 11/2

BR. 3
11/0 X 11/8

FOYER BELOW

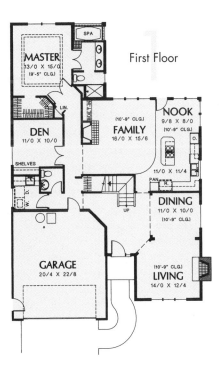

First Floor

MASTER
13/0 X 15/0
(9'-5" CLG.)

SPA

DEN
11/0 X 10/0

FAMILY
16/0 X 15/6
(10'-9" CLG.)

NOOK
9/8 X 8/0
(10'-9" CLG.)

11/0 X 11/4

SHELVES

W. D.

DINING
11/0 X 10/0
(10'-9" CLG.)

UP

GARAGE
20/4 X 22/8

LIVING
14/0 X 12/4
(10'-9" CLG.)

HPT820131 L

First Floor: 1,697 square feet
Second Floor: 433 square feet
Total: 2,130 square feet
Width: 42'-0" **Depth:** 63'-0"

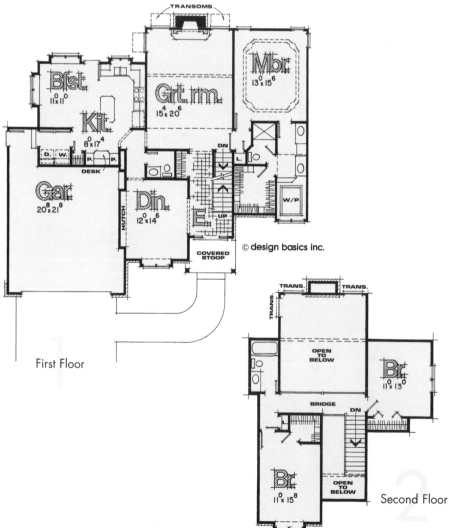

First Floor

TRANSOMS

Bfst.
11'0 x 11'0

Kit.
8'0 x 17'4

Gar.
20'8 x 21'8

Grt. rm.
15'4 x 20'6

Mbr.
13'0 x 15'6

DESK

Dn.
12'0 x 14'6

HUTCH

DN

UP

W/P

COVERED STOOP

© design basics inc.

Second Floor

TRANS.   TRANS.

TRANS.

OPEN TO BELOW

Br.
11'0 x 13'0

BRIDGE

DN

Br.
11'0 x 15'8

OPEN TO BELOW

The varying rooflines, numerous box-bay windows and transoms create a comforting quality on the exterior of this three-bedroom home. A tiled entry opens to the formal dining area with its hutch space and box-bay window. The nearby island kitchen includes a built-in desk and lovely breakfast room with two large box-bay windows. The two-story great room enjoys sun-drenched transoms and a warming fireplace. Filling the right side of the plan, this first-floor master bedroom features a large whirlpool tub, dual vanities and a walk-in closet. The second level holds two family bedrooms and a full bath. Please specify basement, crawlspace or slab foundation when ordering.

HPT820132

First Floor: 1,464 square feet
Second Floor: 541 square feet
Total: 2,005 square feet
Width: 54'-0" **Depth:** 46'-0"

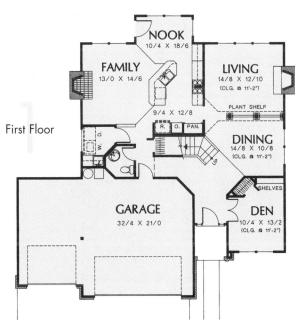

First Floor

NOOK
10/4 X 18/6

FAMILY
13/0 X 14/6

LIVING
14/8 X 12/10
(CLG. @ 11'-2")

9/4 X 12/8

PLANT SHELF

DINING
14/8 X 10/8
(CLG. @ 11'-2")

R. O. PAN.

W. D.

UP

GARAGE
32/4 X 21/0

SHELVES

DEN
10/4 X 13/2
(CLG. @ 11'-2")

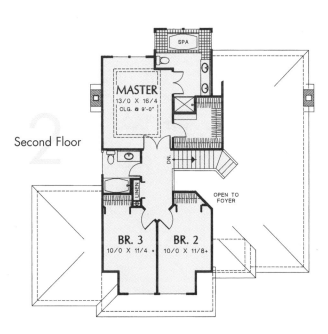

Second Floor

SPA

MASTER
13/0 X 16/4
CLG. @ 9'-0"

DN.

LINEN

OPEN TO
FOYER

BR. 3
10/0 X 11/4 +

BR. 2
10/0 X 11/8+

HPT820133 [L]

First Floor: 1,186 square feet

Second Floor: 895 square feet

Total: 2,081 square feet

Width: 50'-0" Depth: 51'-0"

This plan utilizes fine features in just over 2,000 square feet. Beside the three-car garage, the entry leads to a quiet den on the right, followed by formal dining and living areas. Columns and a plant shelf serve to separate and enhance these areas. The living room features a focal-point fireplace and a wall of windows. The kitchen finds a shared space with the family room and nook. At the top of the open staircase, the master bedroom showcases a walk-in closet and a bath highlighted by a spa tub. Two additional bedrooms even out the second floor.

First Floor

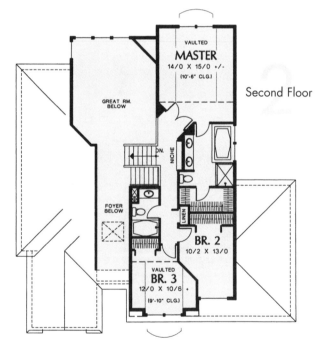

Second Floor

HPT820134

First Floor: 1,476 square feet
Second Floor: 886 square feet
Total: 2,362 square feet
Width: 50'-0" Depth: 55'-0"

Gabled rooflines, arch-topped windows and a three-car garage combine to give this hillside home plenty of curb appeal. The two-story foyer has a cozy den opening directly to the left, with a formal dining room nearby. The angled kitchen offers a corner sink and a snack bar into a sunny nook. A two-story great room features a wall of windows and a corner fireplace. A bedroom, full bath and laundry room inhabit the first floor. Upstairs, two family bedrooms share a full bath, while the master bedroom suite is complete with a walk-in closet, sumptuous bath and vaulted ceiling.

First Floor

Second Floor

HPT820135

First Floor: 1,100 square feet

Second Floor: 970 square feet

Total: 2,070 square feet

Width: 46'-0" Depth: 46'-0"

This new-age contemporary design features two floors full of comfortable modern ameni-ties. An abundance of porch space encourages outdoor activities. A raised front porch welcomes you inside to a foyer accessing the main living area and a computer room illu-minated by an arched window. The kitchen/eating area accesses a petite side porch. The formal dining room overlooks a wraparound back porch. A rustic fireplace warms the liv-ing room, which features yet another first-floor side porch. A few steps down, a garage and laundry room complete the first level. Upstairs, the luxurious master suite features a private balcony, a stunning bath and a walk-in closet. Two additional second-floor bed-rooms share a full hall bath. This home is designed with a basement foundation.

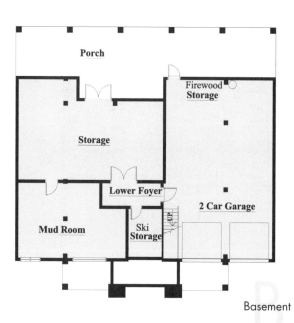

Basement

Main Level

HPT820136

Square Footage: 2,385
Lower Foyer: 109 square feet
Width: 60'-0" Depth: 52'-0"

This trendy cabin is the ideal vacation home for a retreat to the mountain lake. A stone and siding exterior blends well into any country scene. Inside, the foyer steps lead up to the living areas on the main floor. The study is enhanced by a vaulted ceiling and double doors opening to the front balcony. Vaulted ceilings create a spacious feel throughout the home, especially in the central great room, which overlooks the rear deck. The gourmet island kitchen is open to an adjacent breakfast nook. Guest quarters are provided on the right side of the plan. The master suite is placed on the left side of the plan for privacy and offers two walk-in closets and a master bath with a whirlpool tub.

With a rugged stone-and-siding facade, this neighborhood-friendly home sets the pace in ultra-chic places with timeless character. A stately portico presents a warm welcome, while a mid-level foyer eases the transition to the elevated grand salon. Interior vistas extend throughout the living area, made even more inviting by rows of graceful arches and stunningly wide views. A wet bar and pantry serve planned events, and the formal dining room is spacious enough for the most elegant occasions. In the gourmet kitchen, wide counters and a walk-in pantry surround a food-preparation island that sports a vegetable sink. A rambling master suite includes a spacious bath with a whirlpool tub and oversized shower. A private hall leads through a pocket door to a quiet study with built-in cabinetry.

HPT820137

Square Footage: 3,074
Width: 77'-0" Depth: 66'-8"

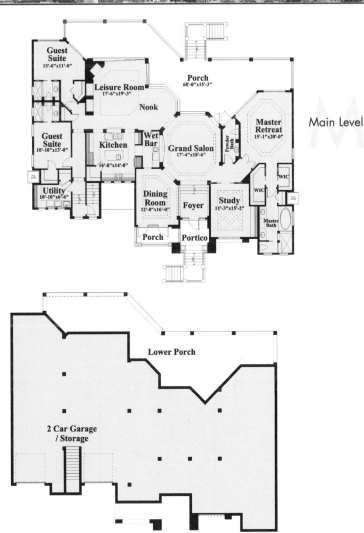

Main Level

Basement

©1991 Donald A. Gardner Architects, Inc.

NATHAN·

Second Floor

BED RM.
11-3 × 11-6

BED RM.
11-3 × 11-6

walk-in closet

balcony

walk-in closet

foyer below

down

bath

skylight

First Floor

DECK

seat   seat

spa

BRKFST.
9-6 × 8-0

DINING
12-8 × 13-4

KIT.
9-6 × 14-0

MASTER BED RM.
13-0 × 15-0

skylight

fireplace

FOYER
9-6 × 10-0

up

sto.

pd. rm.

master bath

GREAT RM.
13-4 × 15-0

cl

UTILITY
9-6 × 7-4

walk-in closet

GARAGE
19-4 × 20-0

©1991 Donald A. Gardner Architects, Inc.

This well-proportioned, compact house provides for a lifestyle that is cozy and inviting. The two-story entrance foyer has windows at the second level, allowing natural light to flood the area. Both the great room and the dining room boast tray ceilings as well as round columns at their entrances. The large master suite is located on the main level and has a gracious private bath with a double-bowl vanity, separate shower and whirlpool tub. Upstairs, two family bedrooms share a full bath.

HPT820138

First Floor: 1,378 square feet
Second Floor: 468 square feet
Total: 1,846 square feet
Width: 49'-8" Depth: 63'-0"

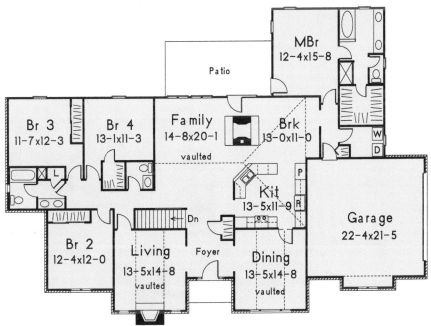

Br 3
11-7x12-3

Br 4
13-1x11-3

Family
14-8x20-1
vaulted

Brk
13-0x11-0

MBr
12-4x15-8

Patio

Kit
13-5x11-9

P
R
W
D

Garage
22-4x21-5

Br 2
12-4x12-0

Living
13-5x14-8
vaulted

Dn

Foyer

Dining
13-5x14-8
vaulted

L

HPT820139

Square Footage: 2,520
Width: 80'-0" Depth: 58'-8"

With an attractive mix of traditional and contemporary accents, this stunning design is sure to be a family favorite. Inside, vaulted living and dining rooms flank the foyer. A fireplace warms the formal living room. Located at the rear of the plan, the casual family room is vaulted and shares a see-through fireplace with the breakfast nook. The gourmet kitchen connects to the formal dining room. The master suite features its own bath with a walk-in closet and private access to the rear patio. Three additional family bedrooms are located on the opposite side of the home. A laundry room connects to the garage.

First Floor

Second Floor

3,90 X 3,30
13'-0" X 11'-0"

3,90 X 3,30
13'-0" X 11'-0"

3,90 X 5,60
13'-0" X 18'-8"

3,90 X 3,30
13'-0" X 11'-0"

3,10 X 3,30
10'-4" X 11'-0"

3,80 X 4,50
12'-8" X 15'-0"

HPT820140

Brick and siding grace the exterior of this contemporary home design. Inside, a combined living and dining area is warmed by a fireplace. The kitchen features a generous snack bar. A casual family room is located at the rear of the plan—a perfect retreat after dinner. An arched window illuminates the stairway. Upstairs, the master suite offers ample closet space and private access to the second-floor bath. Two additional bedrooms are also located on this floor. This home is designed with a basement foundation.

First Floor: 864 square feet
Second Floor: 864 square feet
Total: 1,728 square feet
Width: 28'-0" Depth: 32'-0"

The detailed keystone arch highlights the grand entryway of this home. The vast windows flood the home with natural light throughout. The entry leads into a splendid great room with a sunken solarium. The solarium features U-shaped stairs and a balcony with an arched window. The secluded master suite includes a luxurious bath and a large study with a bay window. A loft, the library and four family bedrooms occupy the second floor.

HPT820141

First Floor: 2,306 square feet
Second Floor: 1,544 square feet
Total: 3,850 square feet
Width: 80'-8" Depth: 51'-8"

Second Floor

Br 5
12-1x14-3

Sunken
Solarium
Below

Br 2
13-11x15-9

Dn

Loft

Br 4
12-1x12-0

Library
15-8x9-8

Br 3
15-5x12-0

open to below

First Floor

Patio

Brk

Hearth Rm
12-1x18-3

Sunken
Solarium

Kit
13-10x8-0

vaulted

Up   Dn

MBr
16-8x13-0

Dining
12-1x16-0

Great Rm
18-0x21-8

Study
16-8x12-3

Garage
30-4x21-4

Entry

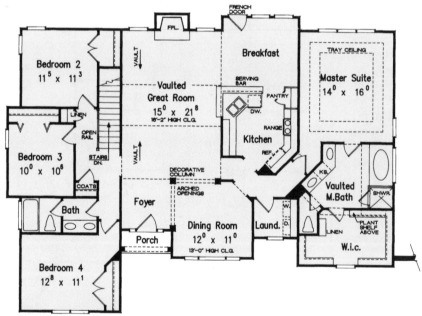

This stunning design is dazzling in stucco and stone accents. A giant front window illuminates the formal dining room accented by arches. The foyer welcomes you into the vaulted great room, warmed by an enormous hearth. The kitchen is set between the dining and breakfast rooms for convenience. The master wing provides a vaulted master bath and huge walk-in closet. On the opposite side of the home, three additional family bedrooms share a hall bath. A handy laundry room completes the floor plan.

HPT820142

Square Footage: 2,032
Width: 58'-6" Depth: 43'-10"

This impressive family design features European and contemporary exterior details. Interior spaces are spacious and flow with ease. The two-story foyer is flanked by formal living and dining rooms. A huge fireplace warms the casual family room. The kitchen overlooks the vaulted, bayed breakfast nook at the rear. The garage features ample storage space. Upstairs, the master suite provides a vaulted sitting area, luxurious bath and huge walk-in closet. Three additional bedrooms share a hall bath. The second-floor laundry room is a convenient touch. Please specify basement or crawlspace foundation when ordering.

HPT820143

First Floor: 1,142 square feet

Second Floor: 1,353 square feet

Total: 2,495 square feet

Width: 57'-4" Depth: 43'-0"

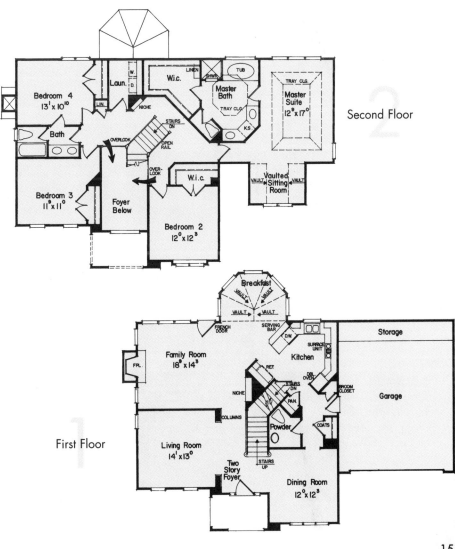

Second Floor

First Floor

151

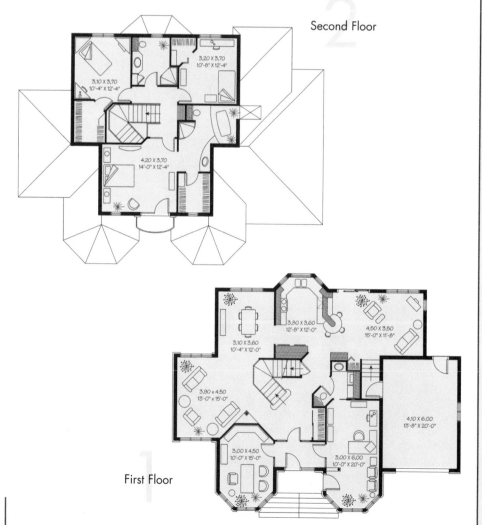

Second Floor

3,20 X 3,70
10'-8" X 12'-4"

3,10 X 3,70
10'-4" X 12'-4"

4,20 X 3,70
14'-0" X 12'-4"

First Floor

3,80 X 3,60
12'-8" X 12'-0"

3,10 X 3,60
10'-4" X 12'-0"

4,50 X 3,50
15'-0" X 11'-8"

3,90 x 4,50
13'-0" X 15'-0"

4,10 X 6.00
13'-8" X 20'-0"

3,00 X 4,50
10'-0" X 15'-0"

3,00 X 6,00
10'-0" X 20'-0"

The stately contemporary proportions and exquisite Mediterranean detailing of this home are sure to please. Like so many European houses, interesting rooflines set the character of this design. Observe the delightful interplay of gable roof, hipped roof and front turrets. A sturdy brick exterior is offset by delicate window detailing, railings and a romantic upstairs balcony above the front entry. Inside is a very livable plan. The kitchen features a circular breakfast counter for casual dining and an adjoining formal dining area. A splendid staircase leads upstairs to the sleeping area, which contains a well-appointed master suite plus two family bedrooms that share a full bath. This home is designed with a basement foundation.

HPT820144

First Floor: 1,468 square feet
Second Floor: 936 square feet
Total: 2,404 square feet
Width: 54'-0" Depth: 44'-0"

First Floor

Second Floor

HPT820145

First Floor: 2,384 square feet

Second Floor: 1,234 square feet

Total: 3,618 square feet

Bonus Room: 314 square feet

Width: 64'-6" Depth: 57'-10"

Stucco and stone, French shutters, a turret-style bay and lovely arches create a magical timeless style. A formal arch romanticizes the front entry, which opens to a two-story foyer. A bayed living room resides to the right, while a formal dining room is set to the left. Straight ahead, the vaulted two-story family room is warmed by an enchanting fireplace. The island kitchen is set between the breakfast and dining rooms. The master suite is enhanced by a tray ceiling and offers a lavish master bath with a whirlpool tub. Upstairs, Bedroom 2 offers another private bath and a walk-in closet. Bedrooms 3 and 4 each provide their own walk-in closets and share a full bath between them. The bonus room is perfect for a future home office or playroom. Please specify basement or crawl-space foundation when ordering.

Rear View

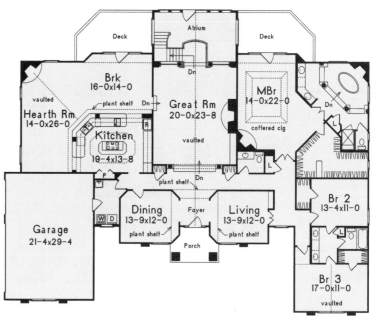

Symmetrically grand, this home features large windows which flood the interior with natural light. The massive sunken great room with a vaulted ceiling includes an exciting balcony overlook of the towering atrium window wall. The open breakfast nook and hearth room adjoin the kitchen. Four fireplaces throughout the house create an overall sense of warmth. A colonnade, a private entrance to the rear deck, and a sunken tub with a fireplace complement the master suite. Two family bedrooms share a dual-vanity bath between them.

Square Footage: 3,566
Width: 88'-0" Depth: 70'-8"

This home is designed to be a home-owner's dream come true. A formal living area opens from the gallery foyer through graceful arches and looks out to the veranda. The veranda hosts an outdoor grill and service counter—perfect for outdoor entertaining. The leisure room offers a private veranda, a cabana bath and a wet bar just off the gourmet kitchen. Walls of windows and a bayed breakfast nook let in natural light and set a bright tone for this area. The master suite opens to the rear property through French doors and boasts a lavish bath with a corner whirlpool tub that overlooks a private garden. An art niche off the gallery hall, a private dressing area and a secluded study complement the master suite. Two family bedrooms occupy the opposite wing of the plan and share a full bath and private hall.

HPT820147

Square Footage: 2,978
Width: 84'-0" Depth: 90'-0"

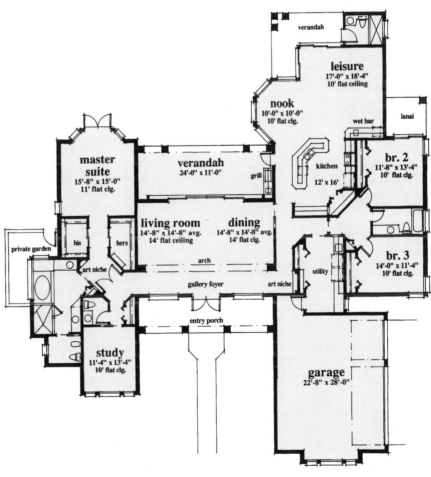

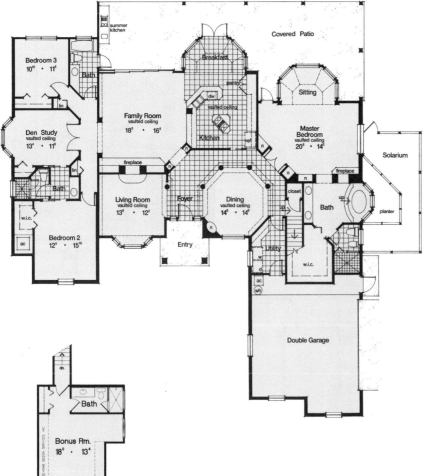

This exquisite design features a contemporary layout for the modern family. Inside, formal rooms flank the entry—the living room is warmed by a fireplace, while columns frame the octagon shape of the dining room. The central island kitchen connects to a bayed nook that opens to the rear covered patio. The master wing features a brilliant bayed sitting area, a private whirlpool bath and a huge walk-in closet. The side solarium is a serene touch. Two additional bedrooms, an optional study and two baths are located on the opposite side of the home.

HPT820148

Square Footage: 2,908
Bonus Room: 379 square feet
Width: 77'-0" Depth: 82'-8"

The facade of this home is a super prelude to an equally impressive interior. The front porch provides entry to a sleeping level, with the master suite on the right and a secondary bedroom on the left. Upstairs, living areas include a family room with a sitting alcove and a living room with special ceiling treatment. The kitchen serves a breakfast room as well as a barrel-vaulted dining room. A third bedroom and two balconies further the custom nature of this home. On the third floor, an observation room with outdoor access is an extra-special touch. Please specify crawlspace or slab foundation when ordering.

Third Floor

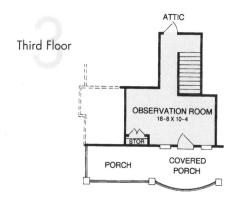

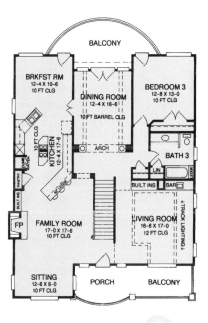

Second Floor

First Floor

HPT820149

First Floor: 1,158 square feet

Second Floor: 1,773 square feet

Total: 2,931 square feet

Observation Room:

    173 square feet

Width: 39'-10" Depth: 58'-11"

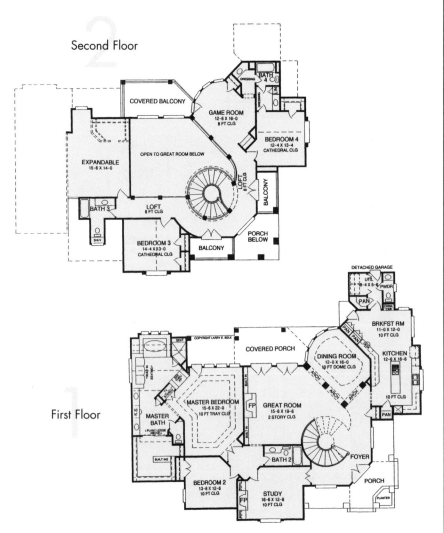

Second Floor

COVERED BALCONY

GAME ROOM
12-6 X 16-0
8 FT CLG

BATH
4

DRESSING

BEDROOM 4
12-4 X 13-4
CATHEDRAL CLG

OPEN TO GREAT ROOM BELOW

LOFT
8 FT CLG

EXPANDABLE
15-6 X 14-0

BALCONY

BATH 3

LOFT
8 FT CLG

SH.V

BEDROOM 3
14-4 X 13-0
CATHEDRAL CLG

BALCONY

PORCH
BELOW

First Floor

COPYRIGHT LARRY E. BELK

COVERED PORCH

DETACHED GARAGE

UTIL
6-4 X 5-6

PWDR

PAN

BRKFST RM
11-0 X 12-0
10 FT CLG

DINING ROOM
12-0 X 16-0
10 FT DOME CLG

KITCHEN
12-6 X 16-6

ARCH

ARCH

ARCH

10 FT CLG

MASTER BEDROOM
15-6 X 22-0
10 FT TRAY CLG

FP

GREAT ROOM
15-6 X 19-6
2 STORY CLG

PAN

MASTER
BATH

+PLANT LEDGE ABOVE+

K.S.

BUILT INS

BEDROOM 2
13-6 X 12-6
10 FT CLG

FP

BATH 2

STUDY
16-6 X 12-8
10 FT CLG

FP

FOYER

PORCH

PLANTER

A truly grand entry—absolutely stunning on a corner lot—sets the eclectic, yet elegant tone of this four-bedroom home. The foyer opens to a dramatic circular stair, then on to the two-story great room that's framed by a second-story balcony. An elegant dining room is set to the side, distinguished by a span of arches. The gourmet kitchen features wrapping counters, a cooktop island and a breakfast room. A front study and a secondary bedroom are nice accompaniments to the expansive master suite. A through-fireplace, a spa-style bath and a huge walk-in closet highlight this area. Upstairs, a loft opens to two balconies overlooking the porch and leads to two family bedrooms and a game room. Please specify crawlspace or slab foundation when ordering.

HPT820150

First Floor: 2,772 square feet
Second Floor: 933 square feet
Total: 3,705 square feet
Width: 74'-8" Depth: 61'-10"

A perfect combination of traditional elements and contemporary design makes this home a stand-out showpiece. A long courtyard and porch lead to the foyer, where traffic is directed either to the living room or down a sunny hall to the dining room and study. The large kitchen features an oversized island and a bayed breakfast nook. Fully accessible balconies frame the second floor, which can be reached by formal and rear staircases. The master suite has a fireplace and luxurious bath. Three family bedrooms each include walk-in closets and private access to a shared bath. Please specify crawlspace or slab foundation when ordering.

HPT820151

First Floor: 1,755 square feet

Second Floor: 2,275 square feet

Total: 4,030 square feet

Width: 74'-0" Depth: 63'-4"

Second Floor

First Floor

A high-arching entrance and dramatic rooflines enhance the facade of this unforgettable family design. Enter inside—formal living and dining rooms flank the entry foyer. The den easily converts to a study. Built-ins and a warming fireplace enhance the spacious family room. The kitchen and nook area overlook the screened porch and deck—great retreats for refreshing relaxation. A roomy three-car garage completes the first floor. Upstairs, the master suite offers a private bath, a walk-in closet and a private sitting area warmed by a fireplace. Three additional family bedrooms are also located on the second floor.

Second Floor

First Floor

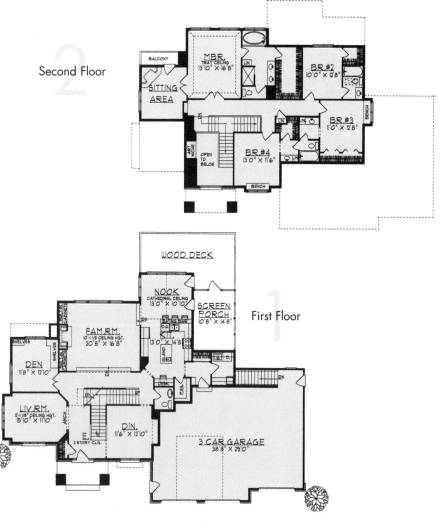

HPT820152

First Floor: 1,776 square feet

Second Floor: 1,537 square feet

Total: 3,313 square feet

Width: 77'-8" Depth: 56'-0"

Varied textures and rooflines, combined with a grand entrance, give this contemporary home plenty of curb appeal. Inside, the foyer opens directly to the family room, which is graced by a corner fireplace, built-in shelves and a wall of sliding glass doors. The efficient kitchen and oversized nook conveniently separate the family room from the game room, providing ease in serving either room. Two family bedrooms share a pool bath and complete this level. Upstairs, privacy is assured with the master suite reigning supreme and enjoying a private covered deck.

HPT820153

First Floor: 2,136 square feet

Second Floor: 1,046 square feet

Total: 3,182 square feet

Width: 74'-0" Depth: 67'-2"

Second Floor

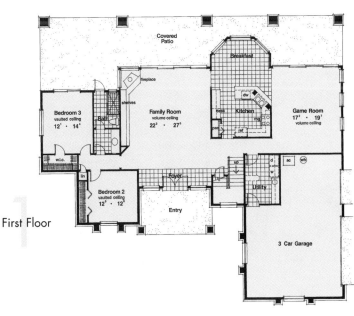

First Floor

Second Floor

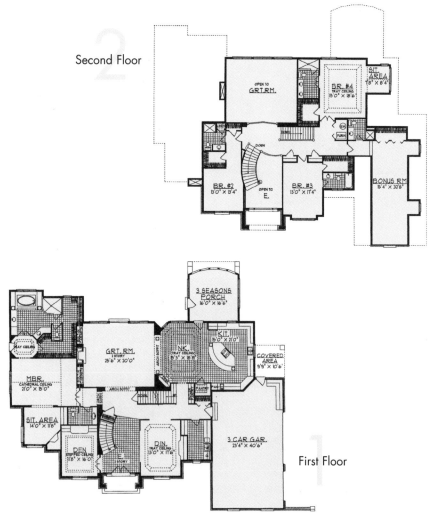

First Floor

Lavish, grand, luxurious—all of these words apply to this beautiful brick mansion with its expansive entrance. Inside, the two-story foyer leads to a formal dining room on the right and a cozy den with built-ins on the left. The huge kitchen is sure to please the gourmet of the family. It includes a large cooktop island with a snack bar, a walk-in pantry, plenty of counter and cabinet space, an adjacent hexagonal nook and access to the three-seasons porch. Lavish is the word for the master suite, which includes among its many amenities a separate sitting area with a fireplace. Upstairs, each bedroom contains a walk-in closet and private bath. The bonus room is available for future expansion and features a full bath and large closet.

HPT820154

First Floor: 3,536 square feet
Second Floor: 1,690 square feet
Total: 5,226 square feet
Bonus Room: 546 square feet
Width: 89'-8" Depth: 76'-0"

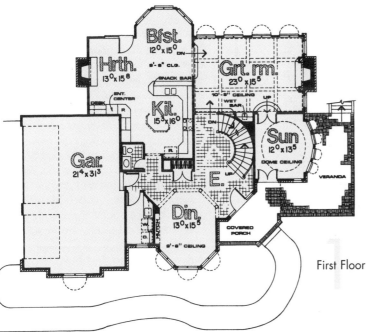

First Floor

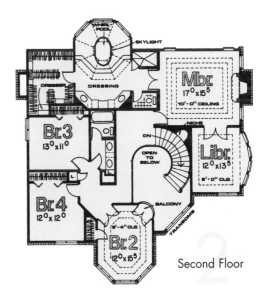

Second Floor

HPT820155

First Floor: 1,719 square feet

Second Floor: 1,688 square feet

Total: 3,407 square feet

Width: 62'-0" Depth: 55'-4"

Two-story bays, luminous windows and brick details embellish this stately traditional castle. Inside, the soaring foyer is angled to provide impressive views of the spectacular curving staircase and columns that define the octagonal dining room. This home's most outstanding feature may be the sun room, which is crowned with a dome ceiling. This room gives access to the multi-windowed great room and an expansive veranda. A cozy hearth room, a breakfast room and an oversized kitchen complete the casual living area. The sumptuous master suite features a fireplace, a library and an opulent master bath with a gazebo ceiling and a skylight above the magnificent whirlpool tub. Three secondary bedrooms and a full hall bath complete the second floor.

Second Floor

First Floor

Semi-circular arches complement the strong linear rooflines and balconies of this exciting contemporary home. The foyer opens to a step-down living room with a dramatic sloped ceiling, a fireplace and four sliding glass doors. A tavern with a built-in wine rack and an adjacent butler's pantry are ideal for entertaining. The family room features a fireplace, sliding glass door and handy snack bar. The kitchen allows for meal preparation, cooking and storage within a step of the central work island. Three second-floor bedrooms, each with a private bath and a balcony, are reached by either of two staircases. The master suite, with His and Hers baths and walk-in closets, a whirlpool tub and a fireplace, adds the finishing touch to this memorable home.

HPT820156 [L]

First Floor: 2,870 square feet
Second Floor: 2,222 square feet
Total: 5,092 square feet
Width: 93'-4" Depth: 82'-8"

Sweeping heights lend a grand stroke to many of the rooms in this estate: the study, the grand foyer, the dining room and the living room. The living and dining room ceilings are coffered. Upstairs, the master suite enjoys a full list of appointments, including an exercise (or bonus) room, a tub tower with a vaulted cove-lit ceiling, and a private deck. Also on this floor is a guest bedroom with an observation deck (or make this a spectacular study to complement the master suite). Other special details include: a pass-through outdoor bar, an outdoor kitchen, a workshop area, two verandas and a glass elevator.

HPT820157

First Floor: *3,667 square feet*

Second Floor: *1,867 square feet*

Total: *5,534 square feet*

Bonus Room: *140 square feet*

Width: *102'-0"* **Depth:** *87'-0"*

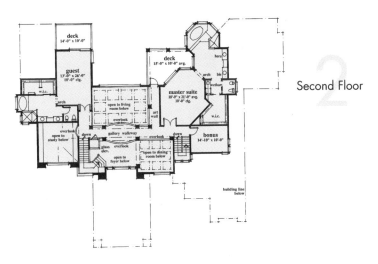

Second Floor

First Floor

Second Floor

First Floor

This fresh and innovative design creates unbeatable ambiance. The breakfast nook and family room both open to a patio—a perfect arrangement for informal entertaining. The dining room is sure to please with elegant pillars separating it from the sunken living room. A media room delights both with its shape and by being convenient to the nearby kitchen—great for snack runs. A private garden surrounds the master bath and its spa tub and enormous walk-in closet. The master bedroom is enchanting with a fireplace and access to the outdoors. Additional family bedrooms come in a variety of different shapes and sizes; Bedroom 4 reigns over the second floor and features its own full bath.

HPT820158

First Floor: 3,770 square feet
Second Floor: 634 square feet
Total: 4,404 square feet
Width: 87'-0" Depth: 97'-6"

Dramatic rooflines and a unique entrance set the mood of this contemporary home. Double doors lead into the foyer, which opens directly to the formal living and dining rooms. A den/study is adjacent to this area and offers a quiet retreat. The spacious kitchen features a large cooktop work island and plenty of counter and cabinet space. The spacious family room expands this area and features a wall of windows and a warming fireplace. Two secondary bedrooms share a full bath. The master suite is designed with pleasure in mind. Included in the suite are a lavish bath and a deluxe walk-in closet, as well as access to the covered patio.

HPT820159

Square Footage: 2,397

Width: 73'-2" Depth: 73'-2"

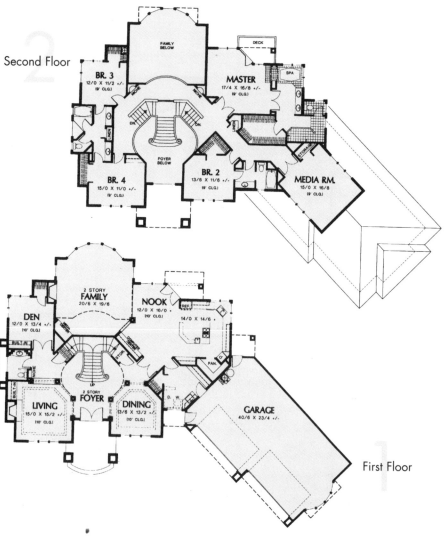

Second Floor

FAMILY BELOW

DECK

SPA

BR. 3
12/0 X 11/2 +/-
(9' CLG.)

MASTER
17/4 X 16/8 +/-
(9' CLG.)

FOYER BELOW

BR. 4
15/0 X 11/0 +/-
(9' CLG.)

BR. 2
13/6 X 11/6 +/-
(9' CLG.)

MEDIA RM.
15/0 X 16/8
(9' CLG.)

2 STORY
FAMILY
20/6 X 19/6

NOOK
12/0 X 16/0 +/-
(10' CLG.)

DEN
12/0 X 13/4 +/-
(10' CLG.)

REF.

14/0 X 14/6 +/-

BUILT-IN

PAN.

LIVING
15/0 X 15/2 +/-
(10' CLG.)

2 STORY
FOYER

DINING
13/6 X 13/2 +/-
(10' CLG.)

D. W

GARAGE
40/6 X 23/4 +/-

First Floor

An impressive entry opens to a two-story foyer with a magnificent staircase. Formal living comes to the forefront with a columned dining room on the right and an inviting living room to the left. The kitchen is a connoisseur's delight, complete with a large pantry and a nook that contains a computer center. The two-story family room is the center of attention with its unique wall of bow windows and a cheerful fireplace. A den and powder room complete the first floor. The second floor holds three secondary bedrooms, two full baths, a media room and an elegant master suite with a private deck and a deluxe master bath.

HPT820160

First Floor: 2,290 square feet
Second Floor: 2,142 square feet
Total: 4,432 square feet
Width: 95'-9" Depth: 73'-0"

J.N.HANSEN S.D.

Covered Patio
17'10" x 37'0"

Master Suite
19'3" x 18'6"

Family Room
25'0" x 21'0"

Nook
8'11" x 10'7"

Master Bath

Kitchen
14'2" x 14'8"

W.I.C.

Dining Room
12'3" x 14'3"

Foyer

Living Room
13'0" x 12'6"

Entry

Utility

2 Car Garage
19'3" x 19'3"

First Floor

Deck

Loft

open to below

Second Floor

W.I.C.

Bedroom 2
14'3" x 10'11"

open to below

Bedroom 3
17'6" x 16'7"

Second Floor

HPT820161

First Floor: 2,051 square feet
Second Floor: 749 square feet
Total: 2,800 square feet
Width: 50'-0" Depth: 74'-0"

At only fifty feet in width, this fabulous design will fit anywhere! From the moment you enter the home from the foyer, this floor plan explodes in every direction with huge living spaces. Flanking the foyer are the living and dining rooms, and the visual impact of the staircase is breathtaking. Two-story ceilings adorn the huge family room with double-stacked glass walls. Sunlight floods the breakfast nook, and the kitchen is a gourmet's dream, complete with cooking island and loads of overhead cabinets. Tray ceilings grace the master suite, which also offers a well-designed private bath. Here, a large soaking tub, doorless shower, private toilet chamber and huge walk-in closet are sure to please. Upstairs, two oversized bedrooms and a loft space—perfect for the home computer—share a full bath.

Second Floor

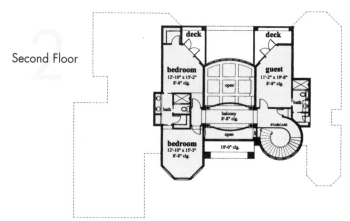

deck

bedroom
12'-10" x 15'-2"
8'-8" clg.

guest
11'-2" x 19'-8"
8'-8" clg.

deck

bath

balcony
8'-8" clg.

bath

STAIRCASE

open

open

bedroom
12'-10" x 15'-5"
8'-8" clg.

10'-0" clg.

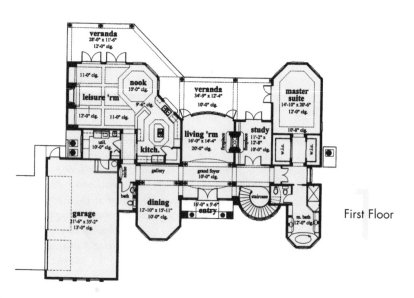

veranda
28'-0" x 11'-6"
12'-0" clg.

11'-0" clg.

nook
10'-0" clg.

veranda
34'-9" x 12'-4"
10'-0" clg.

master suite
14'-10" x 20'-6"
12'-0" clg.

leisure 'rm
12'-0" clg.   11'-0" clg.

9'-6" clg.

living 'rm
16'-0" x 14'-4"
20'-0" clg.

study
11'-2" x
12'-8"
10'-0" clg.

10'-8" clg.

util.
10'-0" clg.

kitch.

w.i.c.   w.i.c.

gallery

grand foyer
10'-0" clg.

bath

staircase

garage
21'-6" x 35'-2"
13'-0" clg.

dining
12'-10" x 15'-11"
10'-0" clg.

19'-0" x 5'-6"
entry

m. bath
12'-0" clg.

First Floor

Assure yourself elegant living with this luxurious plan. A turret, two-story bay windows and plenty of arched glass impart a graceful style to the exterior, while rich amenities inside furnish contentment. A grand foyer decked with columns introduces the living room with a curve of glass windows viewing the rear gardens. A through-fireplace is shared by the study and living room. The master suite enjoys a tray ceiling, two walk-in closets, a separate shower and a garden tub set in a bay window. Informal entertainment will be a breeze with a rich leisure room adjoining the kitchen and breakfast nook and opening to a rear veranda. At the top of a lavish curving staircase are two family bedrooms sharing a full bath and a guest suite with a private deck.

HPT820162

First Floor: 2,841 square feet
Second Floor: 1,052 square feet
Total: 3,893 square feet
Width: 85'-0" Depth: 76'-8"

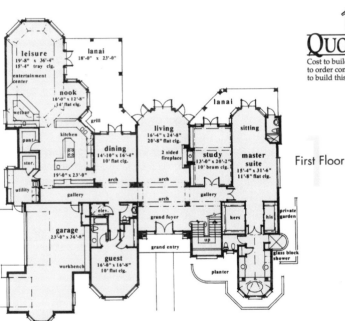

First Floor

QUOTE ONE®

Cost to build? See page 246
to order complete cost estimate
to build this house in your area!

Second Floor

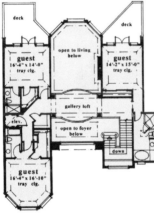

Rear View

HPT820163 ⟨L⟩

First Floor: 4,760 square feet

Second Floor: 1,552 square feet

Total: 6,312 square feet

Width: 98'-0" Depth: 103'-8"

As beautiful from the rear as from the front, this home features a spectacular blend of arch-top windows, French doors and balusters. Dramatic two-story ceilings and tray details add custom spaciousness. An impressive informal leisure room has a sixteen-foot tray ceiling, an entertainment center and a grand ale bar. The large gourmet kitchen is well appointed and easily serves the nook and formal dining room. The master suite has a large bedroom and a bayed sitting area. His and Hers vanities and walk-in closets and a curved, glass-block shower are highlights in the bath. The staircase leads to the deluxe secondary guest suites, two of which have observation decks to the rear, and each includes its own full bath.

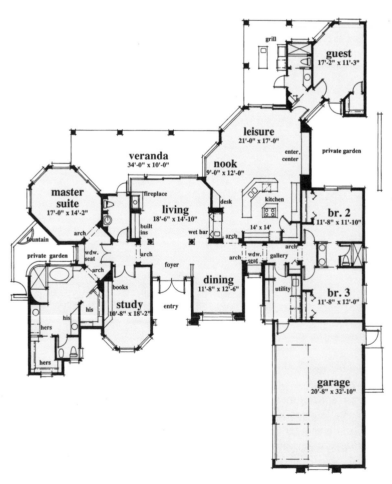

A turret study and a raised entry add elegance to this marvelous stucco home. A guest suite includes a full bath, porch access and a private garden entry, making it perfect for use as an in-law suite. Secondary bedrooms share a full bath. The master suite has a foyer with a window seat overlooking another private garden and fountain area; the private master bath holds dual closets, a garden tub and a curved-glass shower.

HPT820164

Square Footage: 3,265
Width: 80'-0" Depth: 103'-8"

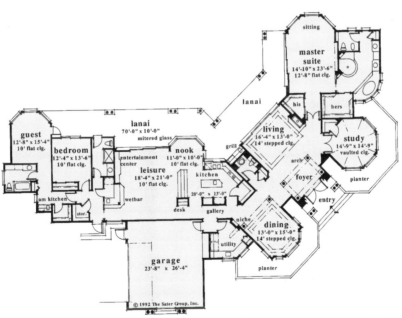

© 1992 The Sater Group, Inc.

HPT820165 LD

Square Footage: 3,866
Width: 120'-0" Depth: 89'-0"

This modern home adds a contemporary twist to the typical ranch-style plan. The turret study and bayed dining room add a sensuous look from the streetscape. The main living areas open up to the lanai and offer broad views to the rear through large expanses of glass and doors. The family kitchen, nook and leisure room focus on the lanai, the entertainment center and an ale bar. The guest suites have separate baths and also access the lanai. The master bath features a curved-glass shower, whirlpool tub, and private toilet and bidet room. Dual walk-in closets and an abundance of light further the appeal of this suite.

First Floor

Second Floor

This award-winning design has been recognized for its innovative use of space, while continuing to keep family living areas combined for maximum enjoyment. The formal spaces separate the master suite and den/study from family space. The master retreat contains a bath with His and Hers vanities, a private toilet room and walk-in closet. The perfect touch in this two-story design is the placement of two bedrooms downstairs with two extra bedrooms on the second floor.

HPT820166

First Floor: 2,624 square feet
Second Floor: 540 square feet
Total: 3,164 square feet
Width: 66'-0" Depth: 83'-0"

If you want to build a home light years ahead of most other designs, non-traditional, yet addresses every need for your family, this showcase home is for you. From the moment you walk into this home, you are confronted with wonderful interior architecture that reflects modern, yet refined taste. The exterior says contemporary; the interior creates special excitement. Note the special rounded corners found throughout the home and the many amenities. The master suite is especially appealing with a fireplace and grand bath. Upstairs are a library/sitting room and a very private den or guest bedroom.

HPT820167

First Floor: *3,236 square feet*
Second Floor: *494 square feet*
Total: *3,730 square feet*
Width: *80'-0"* **Depth:** *89'-10"*

Second Floor

First Floor

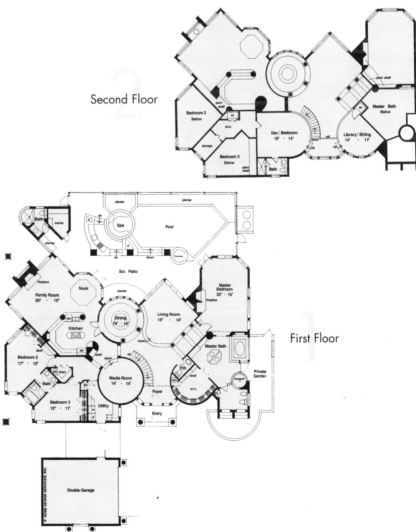

HPT820168

Square Footage: 3,556
Width: 85'-0" Depth: 85'-0"

A beautiful curved portico provides a majestic entrance to this one-story home. To the left of the foyer is a den/bedroom with a private bath, ideal for use as a guest suite. The exquisite master suite features a see-through fireplace and an exercise area with a wet bar. The family wing is geared for casual living with a powder room/patio bath, a huge island kitchen with a walk-in pantry, a glass-walled breakfast nook and a grand family room with a fireplace and media wall. Two family bedrooms share a private bath.

This contemporary masterpiece features many trendsetting details. The exterior lines are clean, but exciting. At the covered entry, a Palladian-style metal grill adds interest. Beyond the foyer, the living room opens up to the lanai through corner glass doors. The doors pocket into the wall, giving the feeling that the outdoors becomes one with the living area. The informal leisure area is perfect for family gatherings. Full guest suites and an exercise or hobby room are located in the guest wing. The master wing features a study with curved glass, a luxurious bath with His and Hers vanities, a large walk-in closet and a large sleeping area and sitting bay.

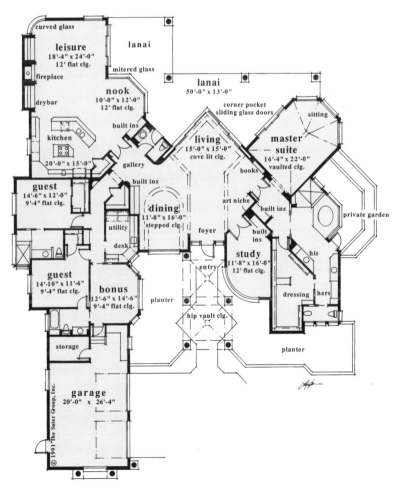

HPT820169 L

Square Footage: 4,187

Width: 84'-8" Depth: 114'-0"

A towering entry welcomes all into the foyer of this soaring contemporary design with a multitude of elegant volume ceilings. The open dining room and living room each have sunny bay windows and built-in features. The spacious family room has a charming corner fireplace, plenty of windows and a breakfast nook easily in reach of the roomy kitchen. Three family bedrooms reside just off the family room. The master suite features a sitting area, twin closets and an oversized bath designed for relaxing.

HPT820170

Square Footage: 2,636
Width: 71'-8" Depth: 71'-4"

A high hipped roof and contemporary fanlight windows set the tone for this elegant plan. The grand foyer opens to the formal dining and living rooms which are set apart with arches, highlighted with art niches and framed with walls of windows. Featuring a gourmet kitchen, breakfast nook and leisure room with a built-in entertainment center, the living area has full view of and access to the lanai. Secondary bedrooms are privately situated through a gallery hall, and both include private baths and walk-in closets. The main wing houses a full study and a master bedroom with a private garden.

HPT820171

Square Footage: 3,244
Width: 90'-0" Depth: 105'-0"

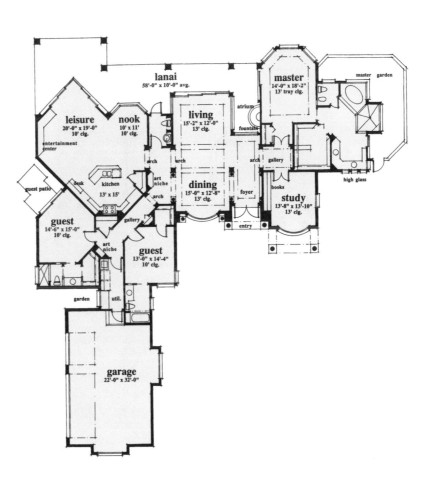

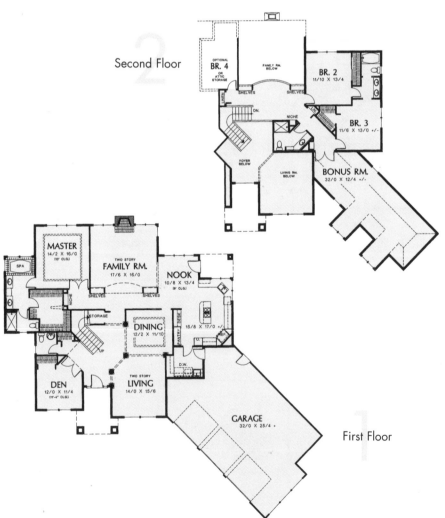

Second Floor

2

OPTIONAL BR. 4 OR ATTIC STORAGE

FAMILY RM. BELOW

BR. 2 11/10 X 13/4

SHELVES   SHELVES

DN.   NICHE

BR. 3 11/6 X 13/0 +/-

FOYER BELOW

LIVING RM. BELOW

BONUS RM. 32/0 X 12/4 +/-

MASTER 14/2 X 16/0 (10' CLG.)

SPA

NICHE

TWO STORY FAMILY RM. 17/6 X 16/0

SHELVES   SHELVES

STORAGE

NOOK 10/8 X 13/4 (9' CLG.)

DINING 12/2 X 11/10

15/8 X 17/0 +/-

PANTRY   REF.

UP

D.W.

DEN 12/0 X 11/4 11'-4" CLG.)

TWO STORY LIVING 14/0 X 15/6

GARAGE 32/0 X 25/4 +

First Floor

1

Dramatic on the highest level, this spectacular plan offers a recessed entry, double rows of multi-pane windows and two dormers over the garage. On the inside, formal living and dining areas reside to the right of the foyer and are separated from it by columns. A private den is also accessed from the foyer through double doors. The family room with a fireplace is to the rear and adjoins the breakfast nook and attached island kitchen. The master suite sits on the first floor to separate it from family bedrooms. Bonus space over the garage can be developed at a later time.

HPT820172 L

First Floor: 2,270 square feet
Second Floor: 788 square feet
Total: 3,058 square feet
Bonus Room: 397 square feet
Width: 84'-9" Depth: 76'-2"

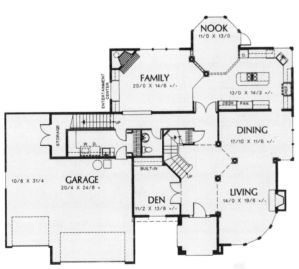

First Floor

Second Floor

HPT820173 L

First Floor: 1,912 square feet

Second Floor: 1,630 square feet

Total: 3,542 square feet

Bonus Room: 300 square feet

Width: 71'-0" Depth: 58'-6"

A sunlit two-story foyer leads to all areas of this exceptional contemporary home. Enter the formal combined living and dining areas highlighted by glass walls and interior columns. The adjacent kitchen blends well with an octagonal nook and a family room with a corner fireplace. A den, a powder room and a utility room complete the first floor. Upstairs, the master suite features a curved-glass wall, a uniquely styled bath and a huge walk-in closet. Three additional bedrooms, two full baths and a bonus room complete the second floor.

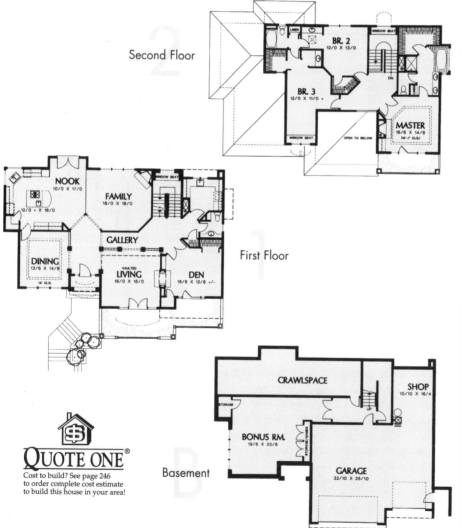

Second Floor

BR. 2
12/0 X 13/0

BR. 3
12/0 X 11/0 +

MASTER
16/6 X 14/8
(10'-1" CLG.)

First Floor

NOOK
10/0 X 17/0

FAMILY
18/0 X 16/0

12/0 + X 16/0

GALLERY

DINING
13/6 X 14/8

VAULTED
LIVING
16/0 X 15/0

DEN
15/6 X 12/8 +/-

10' CLG.

Basement

CRAWLSPACE

SHOP
10/10 X 16/4

STORAGE

BONUS RM.
19/6 X 20/6

GARAGE
32/10 X 25/10

Dramatic balconies and spectacular window treatments enhance this stunning luxury home. Inside, a through-fireplace warms the formal living room and a restful den. Both living spaces open to a balcony that invites quiet reflection on starry nights. The banquet-sized dining room is easily served from the adjacent kitchen. Here, space is shared with an eating nook that provides access to the rear grounds and a family room with a corner fireplace—perfect for casual gatherings. The upper level contains two family bedrooms and a luxurious master suite that enjoys its own private balcony. The lower level accommodates a shop and a bonus room for future development.

HPT820174

First Floor: 1,989 square feet
Second Floor: 1,349 square feet
Total: 3,443 square feet
Bonus Room: 487 square feet
Width: 63'-0" **Depth:** 48'-0"

Main Level

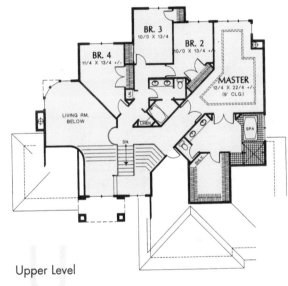

Upper Level

HPT820175

Main Level: 1,894 square feet

Upper Level: 1,544 square feet

Total: 3,438 square feet

Width: 64'-0" Depth: 61'-6"

Sleek, contemporary lines define the exterior of this home. Steps lead up a front-sloping lot to the bright entry. A front-facing den is brightly lit by a curving wall of windows. Built-ins enhance the utility of this room. A two-story living room offers a fireplace and lots of windows. The nearby dining room is capped by an elegant ceiling. The kitchen serves a sunny breakfast nook and an oversized family room. The family will find plenty of sleeping space with four bedrooms on the second level. The master bedroom suite is a real attention getter. Its roomy bath includes a spa tub and a separate shower.

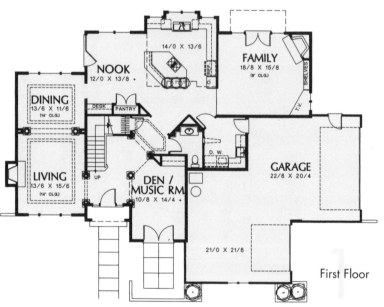

First Floor

NOOK
12/0 X 13/8 +

DINING
13/6 X 11/6
(14' CLG.)

14/0 X 13/6

FAMILY
18/8 X 15/8
(9' CLG.)

DESK · PANTRY

LIVING
13/6 X 15/6
(14' CLG.)

UP

DEN /
MUSIC RM.
10/8 X 14/4 +

D. W.

GARAGE
22/8 X 20/4

21/0 X 21/8

Second Floor

BR. 2
11/8 X 13/4
(9' CLG.)

KITCHEN
BELOW

MASTER
16/8 X 15/8
(10' CLG.)

UP

DN.

(10' CLG.)

SPA

FOYER
BELOW

PLANT SHELF

BR. 3
10/8 X 12/0 +

HPT820176 L

First Floor: 1,762 square feet
Second Floor: 1,233 square feet
Total: 2,995 square feet
Width: 70'-0" Depth: 53'-0"

This stucco contemporary plan is resplendent and quite distinct with wide eaves and inventive window design. The floor plan adds some unique touches as well. The entry foyer leads to a formal living room and dining room on the left and a den or music room on the right. The family room is to the back of the plan and contains a warming corner fireplace. The kitchen is quite different—it boasts a two-story ceiling and is overlooked by the balcony upstairs. Bedrooms include two family bedrooms with a shared bath and a master suite. The master suite includes a private balcony and pampering bath. Cove ceilings can be found in the master suite and also in the dining room and living room.

Clean lines, a hipped roof and a high, recessed entry define this sleek contemporary home. For informal entertaining, gather in the multi-windowed family room with its step-down wet bar and warming fireplace. The open kitchen will delight everyone with its center cooktop island, corner sink and adjacent breakfast nook. Enter the grand master suite through double doors and take special note of the see-through fireplace between the bedroom and bath. An additional see-through fireplace is located between the living room and den. Two family bedrooms both directly access a compartmented bath.

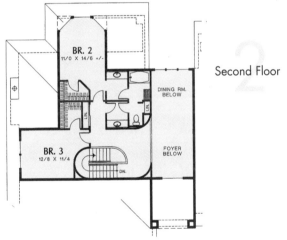

Second Floor

HPT820177 L

First Floor: 2,375 square feet
Second Floor: 762 square feet
Total: 3,137 square feet
Width: 73'-0" **Depth:** 64'-6"

First Floor

185

Second Floor

deck
40'-0" x 10'-0"

open to leisure room below

open to living room below

balcony

master suite
16'-8" x 19'-4"
11' clg.

guest
15'-4" x 12'-8"
9'-4" clg.

overlook

down

open to below

loft

open to below

br. / bonus
12'-0" x 21'-8"
vault. clg.

balcony

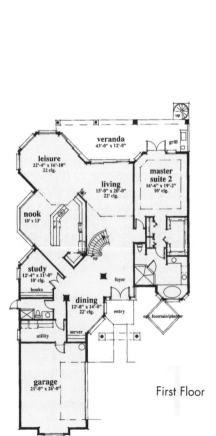

up

leisure
22'-4" x 16'-10"
22 clg.

veranda
43'-0" x 12'-0"

grill

living
15'-0" x 20'-0"
22' clg.

master suite 2
16'-6" x 19'-2"
10' clg.

nook
10' x 13'

up

study
12'-4" x 11'-0"
10' clg.

books

foyer

dining
12'-6" x 14'-0"
22' clg.

entry

out. fountain/planter

server

utility

garage
21'-0" x 26'-0"

First Floor

Double doors open to a grand foyer with a formal dining room to the left. The nearby kitchen and nook combine with a multi-window, two-story leisure room for more casual living, and an adjacent two-story living room for more formal pursuits. The first-floor master suite features a large walk-in closet, a luxurious bath and access to the rear veranda. The second floor contains a guest suite with a private bath and balcony, a bedroom/bonus room with its own balcony and a second master suite. This second master bedroom is highlighted by double doors opening onto a private deck. A walk-in closet and a spacious bath with a bumped-out tub and separate shower provide finishing touches to this private suite.

HPT820178 Ⓛ

First Floor: 2,618 square feet
Second Floor: 1,945 square feet
Total: 4,563 square feet
Width: 54'-8" Depth: 97'-4"

First Floor

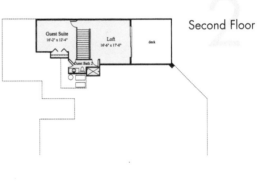

Second Floor

Rear View

HPT820179

First Floor: 3,741 square feet
Second Floor: 657 square feet
Total: 4,398 square feet
Width: 139'-11" Depth: 99'-10"

With contemporary elegance, this stucco home offers a glimpse of ethereal luxury. Double doors open into a spacious vaulted foyer. Straight ahead, an unusually shaped great room is warmed by a focal-point fireplace. This room is open to the elegant dining room. Around the corner, a quiet study is brightened by a bayed window area. Double doors open into a master foyer, flanked on either side by enormous walk-in closets. On the opposite side of the home, the island kitchen features a walk-in pantry and a breakfast nook. The guest suite with a walk-in closet is secluded behind an additional bathroom. A motor court separates the two garages. Above this area, stairs lead to another guest suite with a guest bath—shared by a loft and a second-floor deck.

A towering entry welcomes you to the foyer of this soaring contemporary design. Interior glass walls give openness to the den/study and mirror the arches to the formal dining room. The sunken living room has a bay-window wall, which views the patio. The master-suite wing also holds the den/study, which can access the patio bath. Sliding glass doors from the master suite access the patio. The master bath features dual closets, a sunken vanity/bath area and a doorless shower. The family wing holds the gourmet kitchen, nook and family room with a fireplace.

HPT820180

Square Footage: 2,636
Width: 68'-8" Depth: 76'-0"

An exciting elevation makes the exterior of this home as special as the interior details. A custom grill archway and keystone columns add to the style. The gable roof detail at the entry is carried through to the rear of the house. Columns and archways grace the formal areas of the home. A bow window at the living room overlooks the lanai. A large nook, complete with a buffet server, highlights the family area. The master bedroom has a stepped ceiling and overlooks the lanai. The bath features His and Hers closets, a garden tub and an area for exercise equipment.

HPT820181 L

Square Footage: 3,743

Width: 77'-0" Depth: 94'-4"

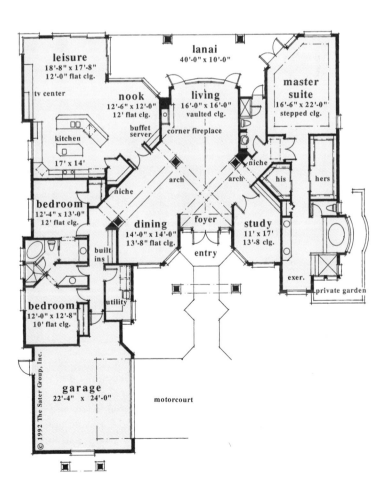

leisure
18'-8" x 17'-8"
12'-0" flat clg.

tv center

lanai
40'-0" x 10'-0"

master
suite
16'-6" x 22'-0"
stepped clg.

nook
12'-6" x 12'-0"
12' flat clg.

living
16'-0" x 16'-0"
vaulted clg.

buffet server

corner fireplace

niche

kitchen
17' x 14'

his

hers

niche

arch

arch

bedroom
12'-4" x 13'-0"
12' flat clg.

dining
14'-0" x 14'-0"
13'-8" flat clg.

foyer

study
11' x 17'
13'-8 clg.

built ins

entry

bedroom
12'-0" x 12'-8"
10' flat clg.

utility

exer.

private garden

© 1992 The Sater Group, Inc.

garage
22'-4" x 24'-0"

motorcourt

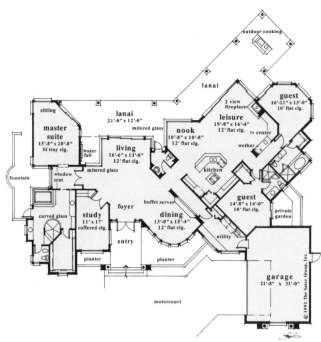

HPT820182 L

Innovative design and attention to detail create true luxury living. This clean, contemporary-style home features a raised, columned entry with an interesting stucco relief archway. The foyer opens to the formal living room, which overlooks the lanai through walls of glass. The formal dining room has a curved wall of windows and a built-in buffet table. Two guest suites each boast a walk-in closet and a private bath. The master suite features a foyer with views of a fountain, and a sunny sitting area that opens to the lanai. The bath beckons with a soaking tub, round shower and large wardrobe area.

Square Footage: 3,944
Width: 98'-0" Depth: 105'-0"

A free-standing entryway is the focal point of this luxurious residence. It has an arch motif that is carried through to the rear using a gabled roof and a vaulted ceiling from the foyer out to the lanai. The kitchen, which features a cooktop island and plenty of counter space, opens to the leisure area with a handy snack bar. Two guest suites with private baths are just off this casual living area. The master wing is truly pampering, stretching the entire length of the home. The suite has a large sitting area, a corner fireplace and a morning kitchen. The bath features an island vanity, a raised tub with a curved glass wall overlooking a private garden, a sauna and separate closets. An exercise room has a curved glass wall and a pocket door to the study, where a wet bar is ready to serve up refreshment.

HPT820183 L

Square Footage: 4,565
Width: 88'-0" Depth: 95'-0"

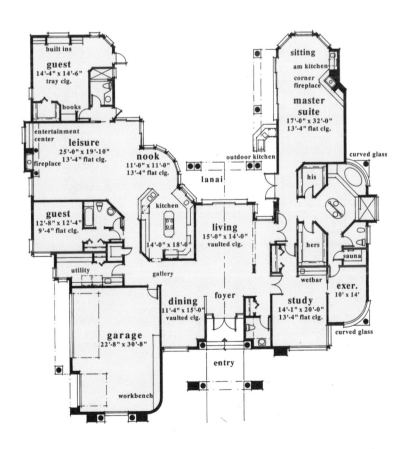

J.N. HANSEN FTL.

Second Floor

Open To Below

Balcony

Loft
volume ceiling
18⁸ · 16⁰

Bedroom 3
volume ceiling
12⁸ · 11⁰

linen

Bath

Bedroom 4
volume ceiling
12⁸ · 11⁰

Bath

Balcony

opt. Bedroom 5
volume ceiling
13⁸ · 11⁰

Optional Layout

Covered Patio

Master
Bedroom
volume ceiling
20⁸ · 14⁸

Courtyard

Bath

Living Room
volume ceiling
15⁸ · 11⁸

w.i.c.

Foyer

Dining
volume ceiling
14⁸ · 11⁸

Entry

Covered Patio

opt.
Pool
Bath

Breakfast

Family Room
volume ceiling
17⁸ · 16⁰

fireplace

summer
kitchen

volume
ceiling

Kitchen

w.i.c. cl

up

Bedroom 2
volume ceiling
11⁸ · 11⁸

Bath

Utility

w   d

wh

Workshop

Double Garage

ac

First Floor

Indoor and outdoor living is enhanced by the beautiful courtyard that decorates the center of this home. A gallery provides views of the courtyard and leads to a kitchen featuring a center work island and adjacent breakfast room. Combined with the family room, this space will be a favorite for informal gatherings. To the left, the gallery leads to the formal living room and master suite. The secluded master bedroom features a tray ceiling and double doors that lead to a covered patio. Retreat to the master bath, where a relaxing tub awaits to pamper and enjoy. The second floor contains a full bath shared by two family bedrooms and a loft that provides flexible space for an additional bedroom.

HPT820184

First Floor: 2,254 square feet
Second Floor: 608 square feet
Total: 2,862 square feet
Width: 66'-0" Depth: 78'-10"

With elegantly formal columns standing at attention around the entryway, this design starts off as impressive and only gets better. Inside, ceiling detail in the foyer and the formal dining room immediately reinforces the graceful qualities of this beautiful home. A large and airy living room awaits to accommodate any entertaining you might have in mind, while the spacious family room encourages more casual encounters with a warming fireplace and access to the covered patio. An angled kitchen is nearby and offers a sunny breakfast room for early morning risers. Three secondary bedrooms accommodate both family and friends, while a lavish master bedroom suite promises pampering for the fortunate homeowner.

HPT820185

Square Footage: 3,091

Width: 62'-0" Depth: 83'-8"

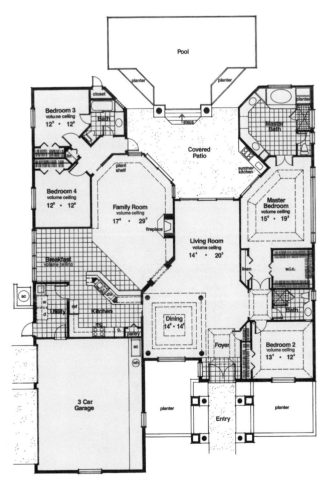

J.N. HANSEN FL.

Second Floor

Deck

Loft
volume ceiling
26⁸ · 22⁴

wet bar

ref

Bath

down

storage

First Floor

Covered Patio

Master
Bedroom
volume ceiling
16⁸ · 21⁴

Covered Patio

Breakfast

fireplace

Family Room
volume ceiling
27⁴ · 23⁴

fireplace

Living Room
volume ceiling
14⁴ · 14⁴

Kitchen

Pdr.

pantry

ref

Bath

w.i.c.

window
seat

Bedroom 3
volume ceiling
12⁴ · 14⁴

Foyer

Dining
volume ceiling
13⁴ · 14⁴

Bath

Den
volume ceiling
11⁴ · 17⁴

w.i.c.

window
seat

Bedroom 2
volume ceiling
13⁴ · 12⁴

Entry

Utility

Courtyard

fountain

3 Car Garage

Old World Mediterranean flavor spills over and combines with classic contemporary lines through the courtyard and at the double-door entry to this three-bedroom home. The formal living room is defined by columns and a glass wall that looks out over the rear patio. The formal dining room offers access to the front courtyard with French doors. A den/library also has French doors to the courtyard and accesses the pool bath for the occasional guest. Double doors bring you into the world of the master suite and sumptuous luxury. A lavish bath features a soaking tub, glass-enclosed shower and His and Hers walk-in closets. Two large family bedrooms, both with bay windows, share a full bath. A spectacular loft awaits upstairs to accommodate a home theater, game room or bedroom.

HPT820186

First Floor: 3,395 square feet
Second Floor: 757 square feet
Total: 4,152 square feet
Width: 71'-0" Depth: 100'-8"

This dynamic exterior invites you in through its columned entry. Inside, the living room and dining room open to a covered rear lanai; built-ins line one wall of the adjacent study, which also opens to the lanai. A resplendent master suite occupies the left wing and provides a private garden, raised whirlpool tub, two walk-in closets and a sitting area. A leisure room to the rear of the plan features a fireplace and a built-in entertainment center. The gourmet kitchen shares an eating bar with the breakfast nook. Other special amenities include art display niches, a wet bar and a computer center.

HPT820187

Square Footage: 4,282
Width: 88'-0" Depth: 119'-0"

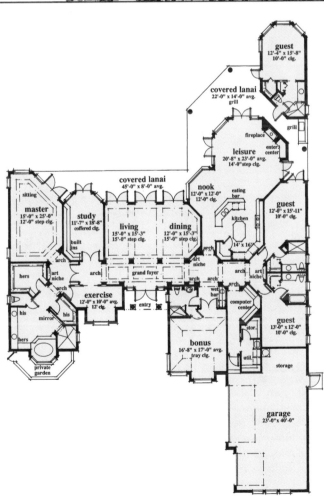

Does your family own a lot of cars? If so, this house is perfect for you. The two garages celebrate the passion for automobiles in a sensible way. The house itself breaks new design ground and addresses many concerns for the large family. A grand foyer leads to the invitingly large living room. Columns flank the formal dining room and help define the large nook across the hall. Family space abounds with the nearby gourmet kitchen, which overlooks the glass-walled family room. The master wing is lavishly designed with a sitting room, private sleeping chamber and ultra-deluxe bath. Two large secondary bedrooms reside on the opposite side of the home and share a full bath that includes dual lavs.

HPT820188

Square Footage: 3,506
Width: 85'-4" Depth: 89'-4"

Contemporary styling coupled with traditional finishes of brick and stucco make this home a standout that caters to the discriminating few. The entry, with a two-story ceiling, steps down into an enormous great room with a see-through fireplace. A formal living room is open from the entry and begins one wing of the home. The bedroom wing provides three bedrooms, each with a large amenity-filled bath, as well as a study area and a recreation room. The opposite wing houses the dining room, kitchen, breakfast room and two more bedrooms. The kitchen offers a curved window overlooking the side yard and a cooktop island with a vegetable sink. A stair leads to a loft overlooking the great room and entry.

HPT820189

First Floor: 5,183 square feet

Second Floor: 238 square feet

Total: 5,421 square feet

Width: 93'-5" Depth: 113'-0"

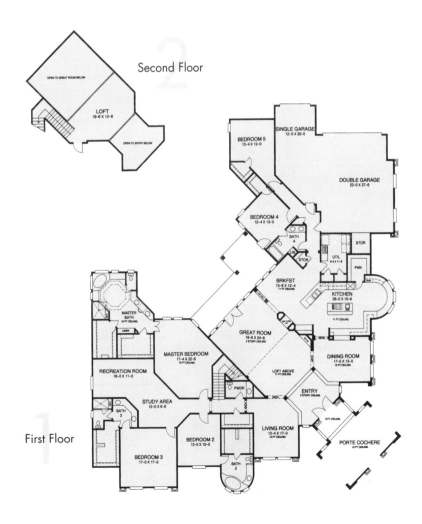

Second Floor

First Floor

Main Level

Lower Level

Rear View

Here's a hillside haven for family living with plenty of room to entertain in style. Enter the main level from a dramatic columned portico that leads to a large entry hall. The gathering room, graced by a fireplace and sliding glass doors to the rear deck, adjoins a formal dining area. A true gourmet kitchen with plenty of room for casual eating and conversation is nearby. The abundantly appointed master suite on this level is complemented by a luxurious bath complete with His and Hers walk-in closets, a whirlpool tub in a bumped-out bay and a separate shower. Note the media room to the front of the house. On the lower level are two more bedrooms—each with access to the rear terrace—a full bath, a large activity area with fireplace and a convenient summer kitchen.

HPT820190 LD

Main Level: 2,662 square feet

Lower Level: 1,548 square feet

Total: 4,210 square feet

Width: 98'-0" Depth: 64'-8"

First Floor

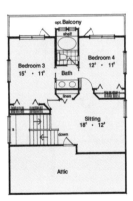

Second Floor

Attic

HPT820191

First Floor: 2,531 square feet

Second Floor: 669 square feet

Total: 3,200 square feet

Width: 82'-4" Depth: 72'-0"

This exquisite brick-and-stucco contemporary home takes its cue from the tradition of Frank Lloyd Wright. The formal living and dining areas combine to provide a spectacular view of the rear grounds. Unique best describes the private master suite, highlighted by a mitered bow window, a raised sitting area complete with a wet bar, oversized His and Hers walk-in closets and a lavish, secluded bath with a relaxing corner tub, a separate shower and twin vanities. The family living area encompasses the left portion of the plan, featuring a spacious family room with a corner fireplace, access to the covered patio from the breakfast area and a step-saving kitchen. Bedroom 2 connects to a private bath. Upstairs, two bedrooms share a balcony, a sitting room and a full bath.

Lower Level

Rear View

Main Level

This spacious, modern contemporary home offers plenty of livability on many levels. The main level includes a breakfast room in addition to a dining room. Adjacent is a living room with a raised hearth. The upper level features an isolated master bedroom suite with an adjoining study or sitting room and a balcony. The family level includes a long, rectangular family room with an adjoining terrace on one end and a bar with a washroom at the other end. A spacious basement is included. Two other bedrooms are positioned in the lower level with their own view of the terrace. The rear deck provides lots of space for outdoor entertaining and relaxation.

HPT820192

Main Level: 1,179 square feet
Lower Level: 2,004 square feet
Total: 3,183 square feet
Width: 65'-0" Depth: 57'-0"

The impressive stonework facade of this contemporary home is as dramatic as it is practical, and it contains a grand floor plan. Three rooms—the living room, media room and family room—are all located a few steps down from the elegant foyer. Notice the nearby wet bar and the raised-hearth fireplace in the family room. The large L-shaped kitchen is highlighted by an island work center and a pass-through snack bar. It provides easy access to the formal dining room, via a butler's pantry, as well as to the breakfast room and the sunny atrium. A double curved staircase leads to the second floor, where four bedrooms and three full baths are found. The master suite is luxurious, with a cozy fireplace, private deck and separate dressing area.

HPT820193 L

First Floor: 2,861 square feet

Second Floor: 1,859 square feet

Total: 4,720 square feet

Width: 103'-0" Depth: 47'-8"

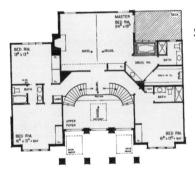

Second Floor

QUOTE ONE®
Cost to build? See page 246
to order complete cost estimate
to build this house in your area!

First Floor

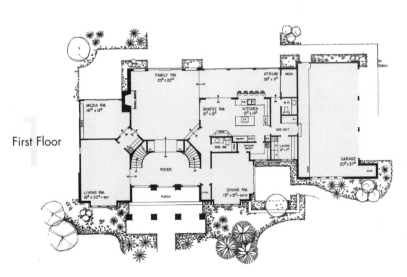

Main Level

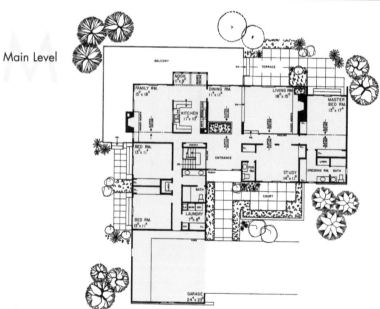

This sleek contemporary home has two faces. From the street, this design gives all the appearances of being a one-story L-shaped home. When viewed from the rear, a whole new countenance is shown off by the sloping terrain. Inside, formal and informal living are both accommodated, from the sunken living room to the cozy family room—both with fireplaces. A U-shaped kitchen easily serves both the formal dining room and the nearby nook. A study offers outdoor access, perfect for an in-home office. Sleeping arrangements, which include two family bedrooms separated from a deluxe master suite, all offer private patios. The finished basement features a spacious activities room with yet another fireplace, a card room and a convenient summer kitchen.

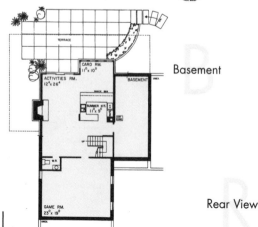

Basement

Rear View

HPT820194 L

Square Footage: 2,606
Finished Basement:
 1,243 square feet
Width: 71'-8" Depth: 74'-8"

Basement

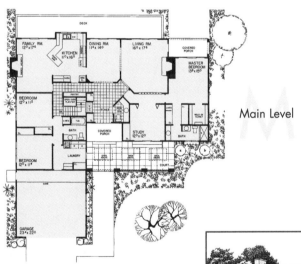

Main Level

Rear View

HPT820195

Square Footage: 2,341
Finished Basement:
    1,380 square feet
Width: 66'-0" Depth: 66'-0"

The street view of this contemporary Spanish-style home shows a beautifully designed one-story home, but now take a look at the rear elevation. This home has been de-signed to be built into a hill, so the lower level is open to the sun. With an abundance of casual living space on the lower level, including a game room, full bath, a lounge with a fireplace, and even a summer kitchen with a full-sized snack bar, the formal liv-ing space can be reserved for the main floor. From the foyer, the formal living room and dining room take center stage. The large kitchen has an angled snack bar that is open to the family room. The master suite includes a covered porch and split-vanity bath. Two family bedrooms share a full hall bath.

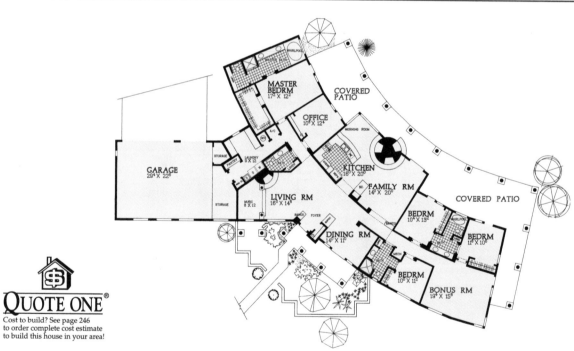

Cost to build? See page 246
to order complete cost estimate
to build this house in your area!

QUOTE ONE®

HPT820196 L

An in-line floor plan follows the tradition of the original Santa Fe-style homes. The slight curve to the overall configuration lends an interesting touch. From the front courtyard, the plan opens to a formal living room and dining room, complemented by a family room and a kitchen with an adjoining morning room. The master suite is found to one side of the plan while family bedrooms share space at the opposite end. There's also a huge office and a bonus/study area for private times.

Square Footage: 3,428
Width: 120'-0" Depth: 86'-0"

This one-story home matches traditional Southwestern design elements such as stucco, tile and exposed rafters (called vigas) with an up-to-date floor plan. The forty-three-foot gathering room provides a dramatic multi-purpose living area. Interesting angles highlight the kitchen, which offers plenty of counter and cabinet space, a planning desk, a snack-bar pass-through into the gathering room, and a morning room with a bumped-out bay. A media room could serve as a third bedroom. The luxurious master bedroom contains a walk-in closet and an amenity-filled bath with a whirlpool tub. A three-car garage easily serves the family fleet.

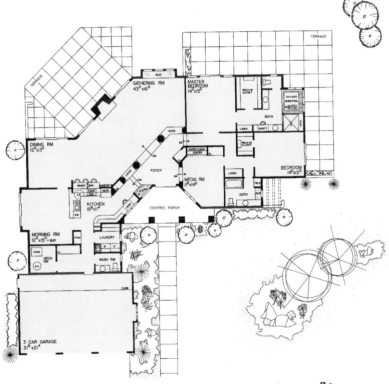

HPT820197

Square Footage: 2,922
Width: 82'-0" Depth: 77'-0"

QUOTE ONE®
Cost to build? See page 246
to order complete cost estimate
to build this house in your area!

Second Floor

Glass-block walls and a foyer with a barrel-vaulted ceiling create an interesting exterior. Covered porches to the front and rear provide for excellent indoor/outdoor living relationships. Inside, a large planter and through-fireplace enhance the living room and family room. A desk, eating area and snack bar are special features in the kitchen. The master suite is highlighted by a large walk-in closet, a bath with a separate shower and tub, and a private deck.

Quote One®
Cost to build? See page 246 to order complete cost estimate to build this house in your area!

HPT820198 [L]

First Floor: 1,481 square feet
Second Floor: 1,287 square feet
Total: 2,768 square feet
Width: 64'-0" **Depth:** 56'-2"

First Floor

This Southwestern contemporary home offers a distinctive look for any neighborhood—both inside and out. The formal living areas are concentrated in the center of the plan, perfect for entertaining. To the right, the kitchen and family room function well together as a working and living area. The first-floor sleeping wing includes a guest suite and a master suite. Upstairs, two family bedrooms are reached by a balcony overlooking the living room. Each bedroom has a walk-in closet and a dressing area with a vanity, while sharing a compartmented bath that includes a linen closet.

Rear View

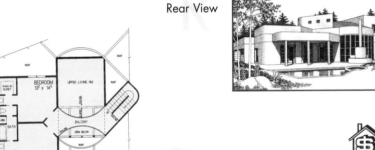

Second Floor

HPT820199 L

First Floor: 2,422 square feet

Second Floor: 714 square feet

Total: 3,136 square feet

Width: 77'-8" Depth: 62'-0"

First Floor

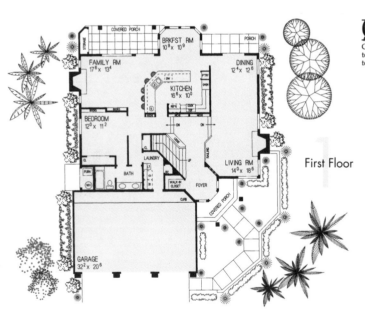

First Floor

QUOTE ONE®

Cost to build? See page 246
to order complete cost estimate
to build this house in your area!

Second Floor

HPT820200

Here's a two-story Spanish design with an appealing angled exterior. Inside, an interesting floor plan contains rooms with a variety of shapes. Formal areas are to the right of the entry tower: a sunken living room with a fireplace and a large dining room with access to the rear porch. The kitchen contains loads of counter space and is complemented by a bumped-out breakfast room. Note the second fireplace in the family room and the first-floor bedroom, which could also be a guest suite. Three second-floor bedrooms, including the deluxe master suite, radiate around the upper foyer. Among the master suite's many amenities are a private balcony, walk-in closet and sumptuous bath.

First Floor: 1,776 square feet
Second Floor: 1,035 square feet
Total: 2,811 square feet
Width: 52'-0" Depth: 64'-4"

Heavily influenced by the Spanish Eclectic style, the tower and second-floor balcony on this two-story home will clearly draw attention. The dramatic two-story foyer is breathtaking with the grand staircase, tiled floor and decorative columns that lead to the great room. The kitchen is situated neatly between the sunlit dining room and the breakfast nook. Beyond the island snack bar, find the great room with a fireplace and access to the rear porch. Upstairs, the master suite boasts an efficient private bath while two additional bedrooms share a full bath.

HPT820201

First Floor: 1,000 square feet

Second Floor: 780 square feet

Total: 1,780 square feet

Width: 40'-0" Depth: 66'-6"

First Floor

Second Floor

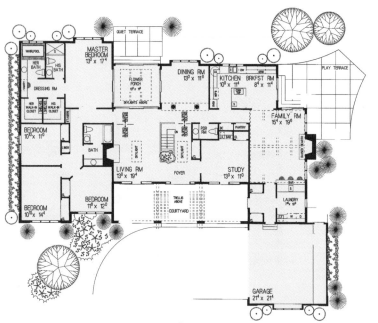

Quote One®

Cost to build? See page 246
to order complete cost estimate
to build this house in your area!

HPT820202 L

Natural light pours in through skylights and plenty of large windows to illuminate a floor plan well designed for formal entertaining, for family togetherness and for quiet solitude. The living room stretches from the front covered courtyard to a sunny flower porch at the back of the plan. Perfectly placed for both formal and informal meals, the bay-windowed dining room also adjoins the flower porch. With access from either the front courtyard or the foyer, the study is well insulated from the bustle of the rest of the house. Amenities in the living areas include two fireplaces, a built-in desk in the breakfast room and wet bars in the study and the family room. The four-bedroom sleeping area includes a sumptuous master suite with His and Hers bathrooms and walk-in closets, a whirlpool tub and a large dressing room.

Square Footage: 3,054
Width: 85'-8" Depth: 70'-2"

Here is a perfect example of what 1,800 square feet can deliver in comfort and convenience. The setting reminds one of the sun country of Arizona. However, this design would surely be an attractive and refreshing addition to any region. The covered front porch, with its adjacent open trellis area, shelters the center entry. From here, traffic flows efficiently to the sleeping, living and kitchen zones. There is much to recommend each: the sleeping area with its fine bath and closet facilities; the living area with its spaciousness, fireplace and adjacent dining room; the kitchen with its handy nook, excellent storage, nearby laundry and extra washroom.

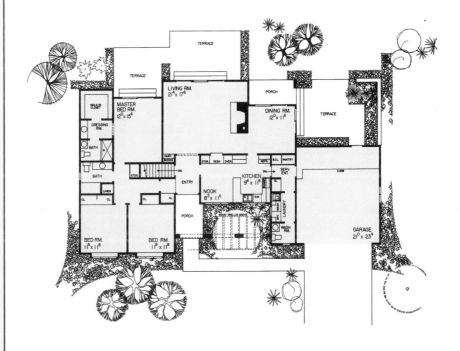

HPT820203 D

Square Footage: 1,842
Width: 76'-0" Depth: 42'-0"

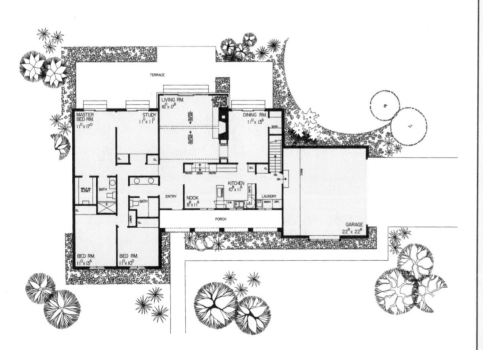

This eye-catching design with a flavor of the Spanish Southwest will be as interesting to live in as it is to look at. The character of the exterior is set by the wide overhanging roof with its exposed beams, the massive arched pillars, the arching of the brick over the windows, and the vertical siding that contrasts with the brick. The master bedroom/ study suite is a focal point of the interior. However, if necessary, the study could become the fourth bedroom. The large living and dining rooms are separated by a massive raised-hearth fireplace. Don't miss the planter, the book niches and the china storage. The breakfast nook and the laundry flank the U-shaped kitchen. Notice the twin pantries, the built-in planning desk and the pass-through. A big lazy Susan is located to the right of the kitchen sink.

HPT820204

Square Footage: 1,955
Width: 80'-8" Depth: 45'-8"

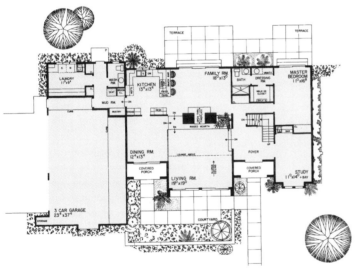

First Floor

Second Floor

HPT820205 LD

First Floor: 2,121 square feet
Second Floor: 913 square feet
Total: 3,034 square feet
Width: 84'-0" Depth: 48'-0"

This striking contemporary design with Spanish good looks offers outstanding livability for today's active lifestyles. A three-car garage leads to a mudroom, laundry and wash-room. An efficient, spacious kitchen opens to a large dining room, with a pass-through also leading to the family room. This room and the adjoining master bedroom suite overlook a backyard terrace. Just off the master bedroom is a sizable study that opens to a foyer. Stairs just off the foyer make upstairs access quick and easy. The hub of this terrific plan is a living room that faces the front courtyard, and a lounge above the living room. Upstairs, three family bedrooms share a bath and the spacious lounge.

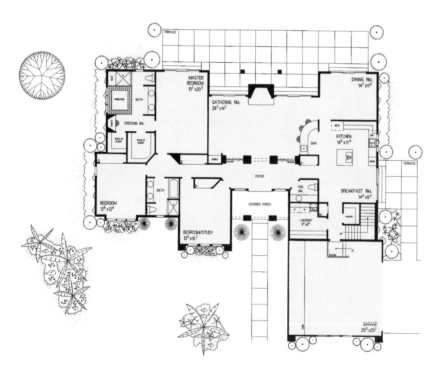

A natural desert dweller, this stucco tile-roofed beauty is equally comfortable in any climate. Inside, there's a well-planned design. Common living areas—the gathering room, formal dining room and breakfast room—are offset by a quiet study that could be used as a bedroom or guest room. A master suite features two walk-in closets, a double vanity and whirlpool spa. The two-car garage provides a service entrance; close by is a laundry area and a pantry. A lovely hearth warms the gathering room and complements the snack bar.

HPT820206

Square Footage: 2,559
Width: 74'-0" Depth: 66'-10"

HPT820207

Square Footage: 2,715
Width: 72'-0" Depth: 64'-8"

This exquisite Sun Country villa features stunning Mediterranean accents that combine Old World style with modern convenience. Three arches welcome you to a covered front porch, which opens to a spacious tiled foyer. Enchanting arches frame the great room and formal dining room. The island snack-bar kitchen opens to a casual gathering room warmed by a fireplace. At the rear, a covered courtyard is a relaxing retreat, featuring a serene built-in fountain. The luxurious master wing is full of amenities, such as a private covered terrace with a spa, a kitchenette, a whirlpool bath and two huge walk-in closets—one with built-in dressers. A laundry room is placed just outside of the three-car garage. Please specify basement, crawlspace or slab foundation when ordering.

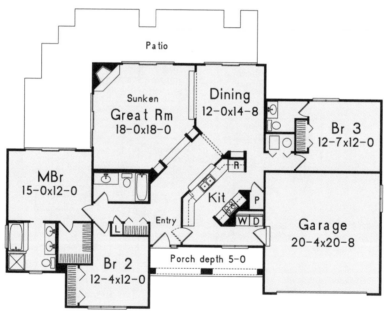

Patio

Sunken
Great Rm
18-0x18-0

Dining
12-0x14-8

Br 3
12-7x12-0

MBr
15-0x12-0

R

Kit

P

Entry

W D

Garage
20-4x20-8

L

Br 2
12-4x12-0

Porch depth 5-0

A stylish stucco exterior enhances this home's curb appeal. A sunken great room offers a corner fireplace flanked by wide patio doors. A well-designed kitchen features an ideal view of the great room and fireplace through the breakfast-bar opening. The rear patio offers plenty of outdoor entertaining and relaxing space. The master suite features a private bath and walk-in closet. The master bath contains dual vanities, while the two family bedrooms each access a bath. A spacious two-car garage completes this plan.

HPT820208

Square Footage: 1,712
Width: 67'-0" Depth: 42'-4"

This classic stucco home is designed to make the most of family entertainment. The first floor includes a game room, a front-facing bedroom that would be perfect for out-of-town guests, and a large family room with a fireplace and access to a rear covered patio. The spacious angled kitchen features a snack bar and a corner pantry and is located conveniently close to both the bayed breakfast room and the combination dining/living room. The elegant staircase provides a perfect focal point for family portraits or your favorite artist's work. The master bedroom features a private deck, two closets and a corner whirlpool tub. Two additional bedrooms share a galley-style bath.

HPT820209 L

First Floor: 1,861 square feet
Second Floor: 1,039 square feet
Total: 2,900 square feet
Width: 64'-0" **Depth:** 52'-0"

Second Floor

QUOTE ONE®
Cost to build? See page 246
to order complete cost estimate
to build this house in your area!

First Floor

Screened Deck
16⁰ x 13⁷

CATHEDRAL CEILING

Nook
12⁰ x 11⁰

10'-0" CEILING

Br. #3
12⁰ x 12⁰

Great Room
16⁰ x 22⁷

SNACK BAR

Mbr.
17⁰ x 14⁰

10'-0" CEILING

Kit.
14³ x 14¹⁰

11'-0" CEILING

Br. #2
12⁰ x 12⁸

LIN

WHIRLPOOL

BOOKS

Den
12⁰ x 12³

10'-0" CEILING

OPT. GUEST SUITE

FOYER

Din.
12⁰ x 16⁰

10'-0" CEILING

D.

W.

F.

COVERED STOOP

3-Car Garage
22⁰ x 31⁰

© dbi

A convenient one-story floor plan is provided for this attractive Sun Country home. A covered front porch welcomes you inside to a foyer flanked on either side by a den and a formal dining room. A fireplace in the great room warms family and friends. The kitchen opens to a breakfast nook. The rear screened porch is enhanced by a cathedral ceiling. The master suite features a luxurious bath and a huge walk-in closet. Bedrooms 2 and 3 share a full bath. A laundry room is placed just outside the entrance to the three-car garage. Please specify basement, crawlspace or slab foundation when ordering.

HPT820210

Square Footage: 2,647
Width: 66'-8" Depth: 79'-8"

Rear View

First Floor

Second Floor

Quote One®
Cost to build? See page 246
to order complete cost estimate
to build this house in your area!

HPT820211 L

First Floor: 2,495 square feet
Second Floor: 1,080 square feet
Total: 3,575 square feet
Width: 67'-0" Depth: 72'-6"

Spacious rooms are the rule in this home. A sunken living room stretches for a full twenty-five feet. The family room with a fireplace is impressive in size, and even the kitchen abounds in space with a separate eating area (with a coffered ceiling), snack bar, island cooktop and walk-in pantry. The first-floor master bedroom contains His and Hers walk-in closets, a three-way fireplace, whirlpool tub and double-bowl vanity. Three bedrooms upstairs share a compartmented bath. Back on the first floor, a fifth bedroom with a private bath is perfect for guest quarters.

Second Floor

Open To Family Room Below

Bedroom 2
14² · 13⁸

Bath

ac

Bedroom 3
11⁰ · 10⁰

Bedroom 4
13⁴ · 10⁰

down

First Floor

Master Bedroom
vaulted ceiling
18⁰ · 13⁰

Covered Patio

Breakfast

Family Room
volume ceiling
17⁸ · 16⁰
fireplace

Living Room
vaulted ceiling
13⁰ · 11⁰

Kitchen

w.i.c.

Bath

Foyer

Dining
vaulted ceiling
15⁰ · 10⁸

Utility

Pdr.

Entry

up

Double Garage

The vaulted two-story ceilings of this plan belie the fact that it is, in fact, a two-story home. The excitement and openness were made possible by placing the majority of the second floor bedrooms over the kitchen and garage areas. The privacy and quietness of the master wing is assured, as well. A decorative niche is the focal point of the master suite, which is complete with a windowed bed wall and sliding glass doors to the patio. The eyes gaze upward as you enter the two-story family room with a majestic media/fireplace wall and twelve-foot sliders to the rear yard. As you ascend the staircase, you can view the formal dining room below and then enjoy a beautiful view of the family room from a balcony. Three generously sized bedrooms share a hall bath.

HPT820212

First Floor: 1,735 square feet

Second Floor: 674 square feet

Total: 2,409 square feet

Width: 59'-8" Depth: 45'-0"

© 1994 Donald A. Gardner Architects, Inc.

Arched windows and a dramatic arched entry enhance this exciting contemporary home. The expansive great room, highlighted by a cathedral ceiling and a fireplace, offers direct access to the rear patio and the formal dining room—a winning combination for both formal and informal get-togethers. An efficient U-shaped kitchen provides plenty of counter space and easily serves both the dining room and the great room. Sunlight fills the master bedroom through a wall of windows, which affords views of the rear grounds. The master bath invites relaxation with its soothing corner tub and separate shower. Two secondary bedrooms (one serves as an optional study) share an adjacent bath.

HPT820213

Square Footage: 1,838
Width: 60'-0" Depth: 60'-4"

© 1994 Donald A. Gardner Architects, Inc.

First Floor

Second Floor

Quote One®

Cost to build? See page 246
to order complete cost estimate
to build this house in your area!

HPT820214 LD

Practical to build, this wonderful transitional plan combines the best of contemporary and traditional styling. Its stucco exterior is enhanced by arched windows and a recessed, arched entry plus a lovely balcony off the second-floor master bedroom. A walled entry court extends the living room to the outside. The double front doors open to a foyer with a hall closet and powder room. The service entrance is just to the right and accesses the two-car garage. The large living room adjoins directly to the dining room. The family room is set off behind the garage and features a sloped ceiling and fireplace. Sleeping quarters consist of two secondary bedrooms with a shared bath and a generous master suite.

First Floor: 1,023 square feet
Second Floor: 866 square feet
Total: 1,889 square feet
Width: 52'-4" Depth: 34'-8"

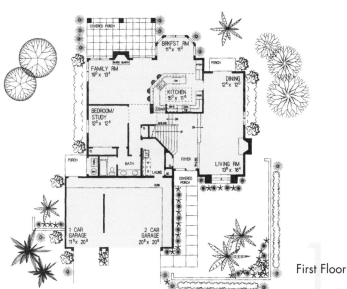

First Floor

Second Floor

Quote One®
Cost to build? See page 246
to order complete cost estimate
to build this house in your area!

HPT820215 L

First Floor: 1,739 square feet
Second Floor: 1,376 square feet
Total: 3,115 square feet
Width: 57'-4" Depth: 63'-6"

From the dramatic, open entry to the covered back porch, this home delivers a full measure of livability in a Spanish design. Formal living areas (the living and dining rooms) have a counterpoint in the family room and the glassed-in breakfast room. The kitchen is the hub for both areas. Notice that the first-floor study includes an adjacent bath, making it a fine guest room when needed. On the second floor, the activities room serves two family bedrooms and the grand master suite.

223

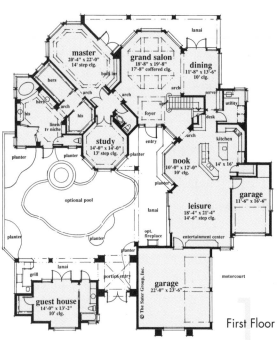

First Floor

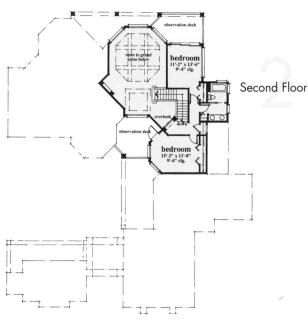

Second Floor

HPT820216 [L]

First Floor: 2,853 square feet
Second Floor: 627 square feet
Total: 3,480 square feet
Width: 80'-0" Depth: 96'-0"

A unique courtyard provides a happy marriage of indoor/outdoor relationships for this design. Inside, the foyer opens to a grand salon with a wall of glass, providing unobstructed views of the backyard. Informal areas include a leisure room with an entertainment center and glass doors that open to a covered poolside lanai. An outdoor fireplace enhances casual gatherings. The master suite is filled with amenities that include a bayed sitting area, access to the rear lanai, His and Hers closets and a soaking tub. Upstairs, two family bedrooms—both with private decks—share a full bath. A detached guest house has a cabana bath and an outdoor grill area.

Luxurious living begins as soon as you step into the entryway of this home. Double doors open to the foyer, which features columns and a barrel-vaulted ceiling; combined living and dining rooms are straight ahead. The octagonal kitchen serves this area with a pass-through counter. Two master suites characterize this plan as the perfect vacation retreat. Two guest rooms enjoy quiet locales and direct access to the master baths. Outdoor living areas include a master lanai and another lanai that stretches around the back of the house. A pool bath is easily accessible from the lanai. A two-car garage and a utility room finish off the plan.

HPT820217 L

Square Footage: 2,473

Width: 60'-0" Depth: 83'-0"

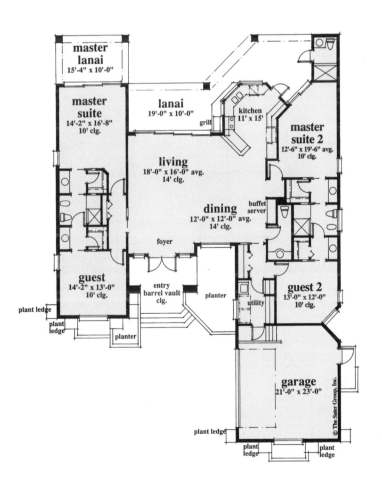

Main Level

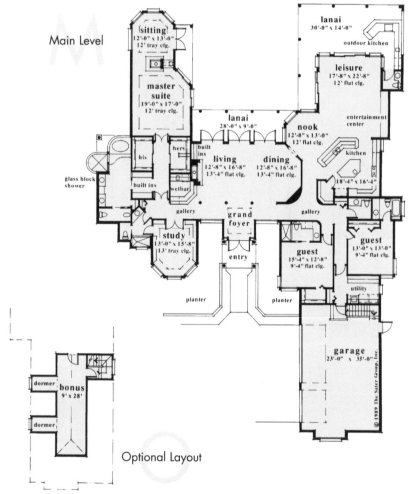

sitting
12'-0" x 13'-0"
12' tray clg.

master
suite
19'-0" x 17'-0"
12' tray clg.

lanai
30'-0" x 14'-0"

outdoor kitchen

leisure
17'-8" x 22'-8"
12' flat clg.

his   hers

built
ins

built
ins

glass block
shower

lanai
28'-0" x 9'-0"

living
12'-8" x 16'-8"
13'-4" flat clg.

dining
12'-8" x 16'-8"
13'-4" flat clg.

nook
12'-0" x 13'-0"
12' flat clg.

entertainment
center

kitchen

18'-4" x 16'-4"

wetbar

gallery

grand
foyer

gallery

study
13'-0" x 15'-8"
13' tray clg.

entry

guest
15'-4" x 12'-8"
9'-4" flat clg.

guest
13'-0" x 13'-0"
9'-4" flat clg.

planter   planter

utility

garage
23'-0" x 35'-0"

© 1989 The Sater Group, Inc.

dormer

bonus
9' x 28'

dormer

Optional Layout

This elegant exterior blends a classical look with a contemporary feel. Corner quoins and round columns highlight the front elevation. The formal living room, complete with a fireplace and a wet bar, and the formal dining room access the lanai through three pairs of French doors. The well-appointed kitchen features an island prep sink, a walk-in pantry and a desk. The secondary bedrooms are full guest suites, located away from the master suite. This suite enjoys enormous His and Hers closets, built-ins, a wet bar and a three-sided fireplace that separates the sitting room and the bedroom. The luxurious bath features a stunning rounded glass-block shower and a whirlpool tub.

HPT820218 [L]

Square Footage: 3,896
Bonus Room: 356 square feet
Width: 90'-0" Depth: 120'-8"

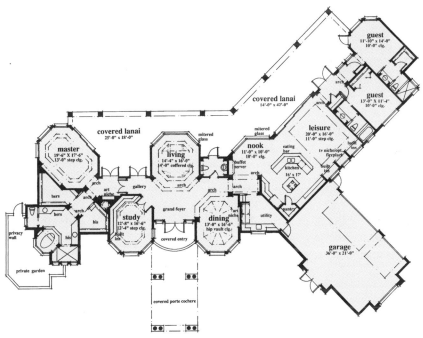

Floor plan labels:

- guest — 11'-10" x 14'-0" — 10'-0" clg.
- guest — 13'-0" X 11'-4" — 10'-0" clg.
- covered lanai — 14'-0" x 42'-0"
- covered lanai — 25'-0" x 18'-0"
- master — 19'-6" X 17'-6" — 13'-0" step clg.
- living — 14'-4" x 16'-0" — 14'-0" coffered clg.
- mitered glass
- leisure — 20'-0" x 16'-0" — 11'-0" step clg.
- nook — 11'-0" x 10'-0" — 10'-0" clg.
- mitered glass
- eating bar
- tv niche/opt. fireplace
- buffet server
- built ins
- kitchen — 16' x 17'
- art niche
- gallery
- hers
- hers
- his
- his
- study — 12'-8" x 16'-6" — 12'-4" step clg.
- built ins
- grand foyer
- art niche
- dining — 13'-0" x 16'-6" — hip vault clg.
- utility
- pantry
- privacy wall
- private garden
- covered entry
- garage — 36'-0" x 21'-0"
- covered porte cochere

HPT820219

Square Footage: 3,398
Width: 121'-5" Depth: 96'-2"

Bringing the outdoors in through a multitude of bay windows is what this design is all about. The grand foyer opens to the living room with a magnificent view to the covered lanai. The study and dining room flank the foyer. The master suite is found on the left with an opulent private bath and views of the private garden. To the right, the kitchen adjoins the nook that boasts a mitered-glass bay window overlooking the lanai. Beyond the leisure room are two guest rooms, each with a private bath.

Second Floor

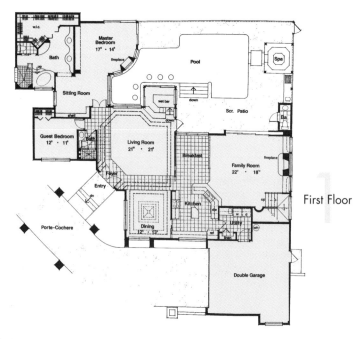
First Floor

Rooflines, arches and corner quoins adorn the facade of this magnificent home. A porte cochere creates a stunning prelude to the double-door entry. A wet bar serves the sunken living room and overlooks the pool area. The dining room has a tray ceiling and is located near the gourmet kitchen with a food-preparation island and angled counter. A guest room opens off the living room. The generous family room, warmed by a fireplace, opens to the screened patio. The master suite provides a sitting room and a fireplace that's set into an angled wall. Its luxurious bath includes a step-up tub. Upstairs, two bedrooms share the oversized balcony and nearby observation room.

HPT820220

First Floor: 2,669 square feet
Second Floor: 621 square feet
Total: 3,290 square feet
Width: 78'-0" Depth: 84'-6"

This stunning contemporary cottage has a heart of gold, with plenty of windows to bring in a wealth of natural light. Open planning allows the first-floor living and dining room to share the wide views of the outdoors. Glass doors frame the fireplace and open to the deck. A second-floor mezzanine enjoys an overlook to the living area and leads to a generous master suite with a walk-in closet, private bath and a sitting area. This home is designed with a basement foundation.

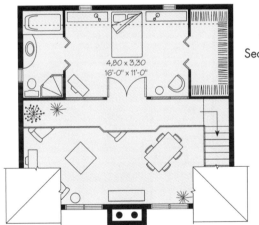

Second Floor

HPT820221

First Floor: *728 square feet*

Second Floor: *420 square feet*

Total: *1,148 square feet*

Width: *28'-0"* **Depth:** *26'-0"*

First Floor

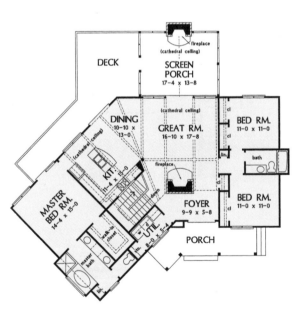

DECK

SCREEN PORCH
17-4 x 13-8

fireplace
(cathedral ceiling)

(cathedral ceiling)

DINING
10-10 x 13-0

GREAT RM.
16-10 x 17-8

BED RM.
11-0 x 11-0

KIT.
11-4 x 15-0

MASTER BED RM.
14-4 x 15-0

fireplace

bath

FOYER
9-9 x 5-8

BED RM.
11-0 x 11-0

walk-in closet

UTIL

master bath

PORCH

GARAGE
22-0 x 22-0

Rear View

This rustic retreat is updated with contemporary angles and packs a lot of living into a small space. Start off with the covered front porch, which leads to a welcoming foyer. The beamed-ceiling great room opens directly ahead and features a fireplace, a wall of windows and access to the screened porch (with its own fireplace!) and is adjacent to the angled dining area. A highly efficient island kitchen is sure to please with a cathedral ceiling, access to the rear deck and tons of counter and cabinet space. Two family bedrooms, sharing a full bath, are located on one end of the plan while the master suite is secluded for complete privacy at the other end. The master suite includes a walk-in closet and a pampering bath. ©1997 Donald A. Gardner Architects, Inc.

HPT820222

Square Footage: 3,333
Width: 62'-8" Depth: 59'-10"

2,60 X 3,40
8'-8" X 11'-4"

2,80 X 3,40
9'-4" X 11'-4"

7,00 X 4,00
23'-4" X 13'-4"

First Floor

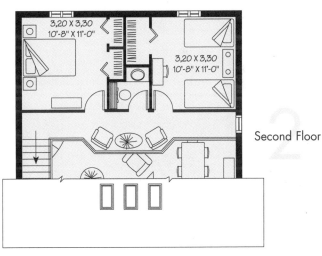

3,20 X 3,30
10'-8" X 11'-0"

3,20 X 3,30
10'-8" X 11'-0"

Second Floor

HPT820223

First Floor: 728 square feet
Second Floor: 442 square feet
Total: 1,170 square feet
Width: 28'-0" Depth: 26'-0"

This petite vacation design features contemporary accents and comfortable accommodations for any lakefront setting. A wall of windows and brilliant skylights fill the front of the home with sensational light. Double doors open inside to a combined living and dining room, overlooked by a second-floor sitting area. A compact U-shaped kitchen, a full bath and laundry facilities are located at the rear on the first level. Upstairs, the second floor hosts two bedrooms with ample closet space, a powder bath and a sitting area.

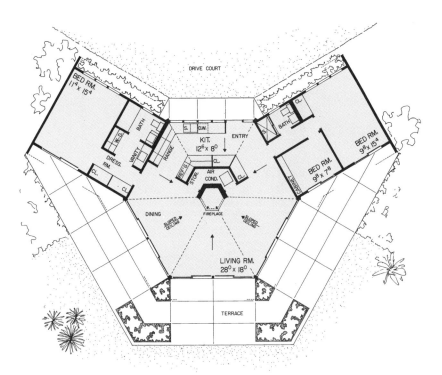

BED RM.
11⁴ x 15⁴

DRIVE COURT

BATH

W.C.L

DRESS.
RM.

VANITY

RANGE

CL.

S. D.W.

KIT.
12⁶ x 8⁰

ENTRY

CL.

BATH

S.

CL.

BED RM.
9⁸ x 15⁴

CL.

REF'G.

STOR.

AIR
COND.

CL.

CABINET

BED RM.
9⁸ x 7⁸

DINING

SLOPED CEILING

FIREPLACE

SLOPED CEILING

LIVING RM.
28⁰ x 18⁰

TERRACE

Here is an exciting design—unusual in character, yet fun to live in. This design, with its frame exterior and large glass areas, has as its dramatic focal point a hexagonal living area that gives way to interesting angles. The spacious living area features sliding glass doors through which traffic may pass to the terrace stretching across the entire length of the house. The wide overhanging roofs project over the terraces, thus providing partial protection from the weather. The sloping ceilings converge above the unique open fireplace. The sleeping areas are located in each wing, away from the hexagonal center.

HPT820224

Square Footage: 1,336
Width: 69'-2" Depth: 40'-0"

If you have the urge to make your vacation home one that has a distinctive flair of individuality, definite consideration should be given to this design. Not only does this plan present a unique exterior, it also offers an exceptional living pattern. The basic living area is a hexagon. To this space, conscious geometric shape is incorporated with the sleeping wings and baths. The center of the living area enjoys a warming fireplace as its focal point.

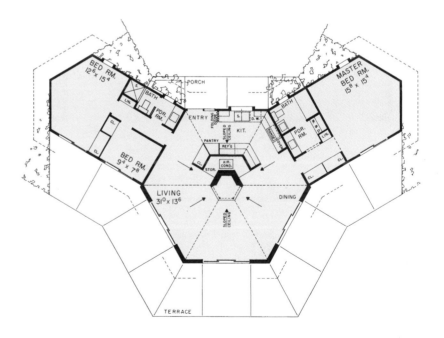

HPT820225

Square Footage: 1,400
Width: 66'-6" Depth: 38'-0"

Lower Level

Main Level

HPT820226

Main Level: 787 square feet
Lower Level: 787 square feet
Total: 1,574 square feet
Width: 32'-4" Depth: 24'-4"

This chalet-style design offers wonderful views for vacations and plenty of comfort for year-round living. The main level includes complete living quarters with one bedroom, a full bath and an open living/dining area accessing the front. Sliding glass doors lead from the eat-in kitchen to the wraparound deck, and a V-shaped fireplace warms the entire area. The lower level provides two more bedrooms, a full bath with laundry facilities, and a family room with outdoor access. This home is designed with a basement foundation.

A true vacationer's delight, this two-bedroom home offers the finest contemporary livability. Two sets of sliding glass doors open off the kitchen and living room where a sloped ceiling lends added dimension. In the kitchen, full counter space and cabinetry assure ease in meal preparation. A pantry stores all of your canned and boxed goods. In the living room, a fireplace serves as a relaxing as well as a practical feature. The rear of the plan is comprised of two bedrooms of identical size. A nearby full bath holds a washer/dryer unit. Two additional closets, as well as two linen closets, add to storage capabilities.

HPT820227

Square Footage: 864
Width: 24'-0" Depth: 36'-0"

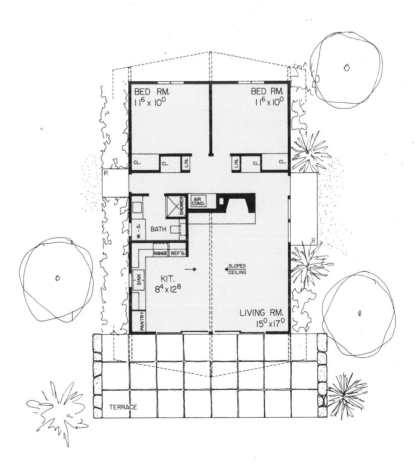

© 1989 Donald A. Gardner Architects, Inc.

BED RM.
11-2 × 11-4

BED RM.
11-2 × 11-4

cl cl

lin.

bath

KITCHEN
11-0×12-8

wash
dry

FOYER
12-1 × 8-7

up

DINING

cl

balcony above

GREAT RM.
27-4 × 15-0

fireplace

DECK

First Floor

© 1989 Donald A. Gardner Architects, Inc.

storage

MASTER
BED RM.
14-0 × 17-0

storage

tub

master
bath

walk-in
closet

storage

LOFT
14-0 × 12-4

stairs

down

foyer
below

railing

paddle fan

great room below

Second Floor

HPT820228

This rustic three-bedroom vacation home allows for casual living both inside and out. The two-story great room offers dramatic space for entertaining with windows stretching clear to the roof, maximizing the outdoor view. A stone fireplace is the focal point of this room. Two family bedrooms on the first floor share a full hall bath. The second floor holds the master bedroom with a spacious master bath and a walk-in closet. A large loft area overlooks the great room and entrance foyer.

First Floor: 1,374 square feet
Second Floor: 608 square feet
Total: 1,982 square feet
Width: 40'-0" Depth: 60'-8"

MASTER BED RM.
13-4 × 13-4

walk-in closet

master bath

cl

KITCHEN
13-10 × 12-0

w
d

sto.

up

cl

FOYER
9-6×5-0

balcony above

DINING/GREAT RM.
24-8 × 16-8

fireplace

First Floor

DECK

storage

BED RM.
11-0×11-4

storage

cl

down

BED RM.
11-0 × 12-0

bath

foyer below

cl

LOFT

Second Floor

railing

dining/great room below

HPT820229

First Floor: 1,150 square feet

Second Floor: 470 square feet

Total: 1,620 square feet

Width: 41'-10" Depth: 61'-6"

This rustic three-bedroom vacation home allows for casual living both inside and out. The two-level great room offers a dramatic space with sloping windows along with an impressive rock fireplace. The generous kitchen boasts a cooking island with a serving counter and direct access to the deck. The master bedroom suite is located on the first floor for both convenience and privacy. Two additional bedrooms are on the second floor with plenty of storage and a loft area. ©1993 Donald A. Gardner Architects, Inc.

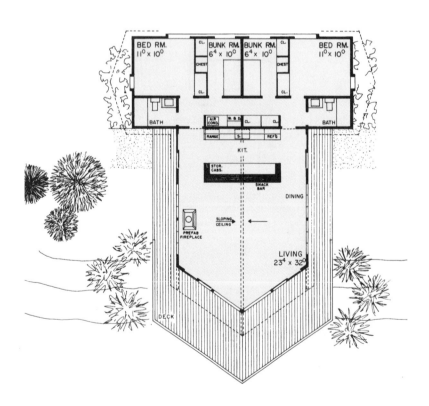

Here is a wonderfully organized plan with an exterior that will command the attention of each and every passerby. The rooflines and the pointed glass gable-end wall will be noticed immediately—the delightful deck will be quickly noticed, too. Inside visitors will be thrilled by the spaciousness of the huge living room. The ceilings slope upward to the exposed ridge beam. A free-standing fireplace will make its contribution to a cheerful atmosphere. The sleeping zone has two bedrooms, two bunk rooms, two full baths, two built-in chests and fine closet space.

HPT820230

Square Footage: 1,312
Width: 40'-0" Depth: 48'-0"

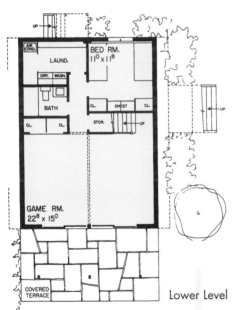

Lower Level

Main Level

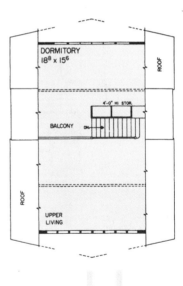

Upper Level

HPT820231

Main Level: 896 square feet

Upper Level: 298 square feet

Lower Level: 896 square feet

Total: 2,090 square feet

Width: 28'-0" Depth: 48'-0"

A steeply pitched roof and an impressive window wall are just a couple of the distinguishing features of this unique plan. Three levels accommodate family needs with a delightful informality. A dormitory balcony overlooks the main-level living room, which offers deck access. A well-equipped kitchen will easily accommodate meals. The plan offers sleeping quarters on each of the three levels—two bedrooms and a dormitory—plus extra space for games and recreation. Two full baths, a laundry room and extra storage space in the lower level complete the plan.

First Floor

ROOF

P.

STORAGE

BATH

BED RM.
10⁴x9⁰

REF'G.

RANGE

SINK

KITCHEN

CL.

CL.

UP

DINING

LIVING
19⁸x15⁶

ROOF

ROOF

DECK

DN

A. J. YOUNG
FUQUAY VARINA NC

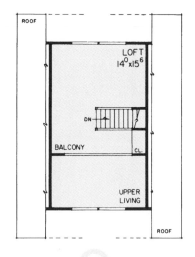

Second Floor

ROOF

LOFT
14⁰x15⁶

DN

BALCONY

CL.

UPPER
LIVING

ROOF

HPT820232

Wherever situated—in the northern woods or on the southern coast—this enchanting A-frame will be the perfect retreat. Whether called upon to serve as a ski lodge or a summer haven, you will find great livability in its simple design. The first floor has a living and dining area and a corner kitchen. A private bedroom and a full bath round out this floor. The second level is devoted to a spacious loft that looks out not only over the living room, but the picture windows and beautiful views beyond.

First Floor: 576 square feet
Second Floor: 234 square feet
Total: 810 square feet
Width: 24'-0" Depth: 36'-0"

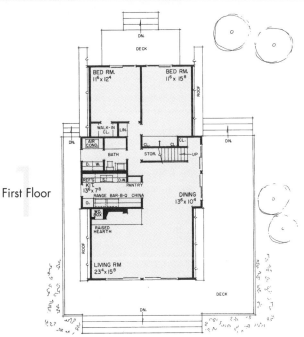

First Floor

Second Floor

HPT820233

First Floor: 1,224 square feet

Second Floor: 464 square feet

Total: 1,688 square feet

Width: 44'-0" Depth: 48'-4"

This dramatic A-frame will surely command its share of attention wherever located. Its soaring roof and large glass areas put this design in a class all on its own. Raised wood decks on all sides provide delightful outdoor living areas. In addition, there is a balcony outside the second-floor master bedroom. The living room is the focal point of the interior. The attractive raised-hearth fireplace is a favorite feature. Another favored highlight is the lounge area of the second floor overlooking the living room. The kitchen work center has all the conveniences of home. Note the barbecue unit, pantry and china cabinet—sure to make living easy. Two secondary bedrooms complete this plan.

*A new Web site, **www.eplans.com**, provides a way for you to*

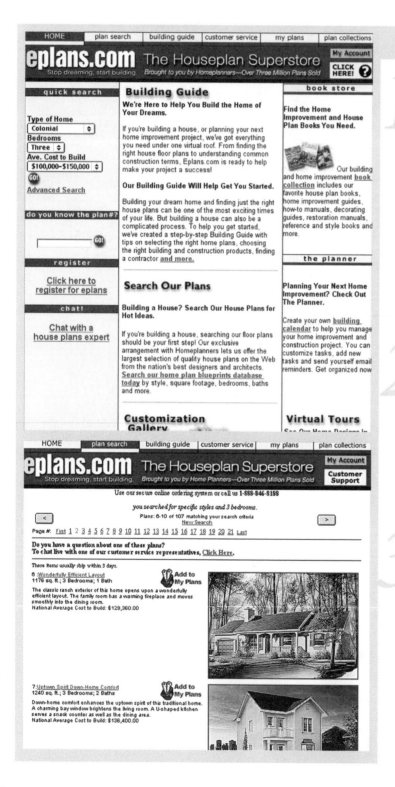

THE EPLANS SITE

SEARCH FOR PLANS

The heart of the site is the Plan Search feature that offers an extensive database of plans for your consideration. Do a simplified search by style, number of bedrooms and approximate cost to build in order to find appropriate homes in your range. Or, choose a more advanced search that includes choices for square footage, number of floors, number of bedrooms and baths, width and depth, style, amenities, garage size and, if you prefer, a specified designer.

Either way, you gain access to a selection of homes that meets your specifications, allowing you to easily make comparisons. The site shows front perspectives as well as detailed floor plans for each of your choices. You can even look at enlarged versions of the drawings to make more serious analyses.

SAVE FAVORITE PLANS

As you're doing your searches, you can save favorite plans to a personal portfolio called My Plans so that you can easily recall them for future reference and review. This feature stores summary information for each of the plans you select and allows you to review details of the plan quickly without having to re-search or re-browse. You can even compare plans, deleting those that don't measure up and keeping those that appeal, so you can narrow down your search more quickly.

PURCHASE PLANS

Once you've made your final choice, you can proceed to purchase your plan, either by checking out through our secure online ordering process or by calling the toll-free number offered in the site. If you choose to check out online, you'll receive information about foundation options for your chosen plan, plus other helpful products such as a building cost estimator to help you gauge costs to build the plan in your zip code area, a materials list specific to your plan, color and line renderings of the plan, and mirror and full reverses. Information relating to all of these products can also be reviewed with a customer service representative if you choose to order by phone.

search for home plans that is as simple as pointing and clicking.

also on the EPLANS site...

VIRTUAL TOURS

In order to help you more completely visualize the homes as built, eplans offers virtual tours of a select group of homes. Showing both interior and exterior features of the homes, the virtual tour gives you a complete vision of how the floor plans for the home will look when completed. All you have to do is choose a home in the Virtual Tour gallery, then click on an exterior or interior view. The view pops up and immediately begins a slow 360° rotation to give you the complete picture. Special buttons allow you to stop the rotation anywhere you like, reverse the action, or move it up or down, and zoom in on a particular element. There's even a large-screen version to allow you to review the home in greater detail.

CUSTOMIZATION GALLERY

For a special group of plans, a customization option allows you to try out building product selections to see which look the best and to compare styles, colors and textures. You'll start with an eplans design rendering and then be given options for such elements as roofing, columns, siding and trim, among others. A diverse grouping of materials and color options is available in each product category. As you choose each option, it will appear on the rendering, allowing you to mix and match options and try out various design ideas. When you're satisfied with your choices, you can enlarge the view, print it out or save it in your personalized Home Project Folder for future reference.

The eplans site is convenient and contains not only the best home plans in the business, but also a host of other features and services. Like Home Planners handy books and magazines, it speaks your language in user-friendly fashion.

In fact, if you want or need more help, there is a Live Person, real-time chat opportunity available with one of our customer service representatives right on the site to answer questions and help you make plans selections.

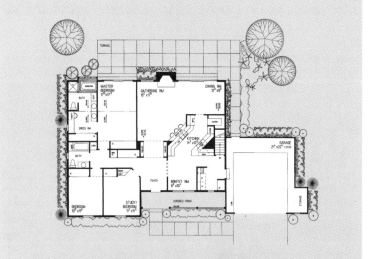

also on the EPLANS site...

BUILDING GUIDE AND TASK PLANNER

Because building a home is a complicated process, eplans gets you started with a step-by-step Building Guide. Covering everything from choosing a lot to settling into your new home, the Building Guide gives tips and valuable information to help you understand the entire process of constructing your new home. Learn about the steps in framing your home, different foundation types and which might work best for your building situation, financing your project, home products such as appliances, and much, much more. A handy glossary is available in each section that helps define terms that relate to the information in that section.

Within the Building Guide is a unique Task Planner outlining each of the various tasks involved in residential construction over the entire 16-week (average) life of the project. Simply tell Task Planner when you plan to start construction or when you plan to move into the finished home, and it will create a calendar that shows each of the many steps involved in building your home. You can customize tasks, add new tasks, and send yourself email reminders that help you manage the building project. In addition, each task in the calendar is linked to a tip or information piece in the Building Guide to help make the process easier to follow and understand. Choose the Calendar View, which shows a month-by-month progression of construction, or the Task View, which lists each task by category and shows its due date.

Customize your plan----without spending a penny or hammering a nail! The Customization Gallery lets you "try on" various material colors and styles before you make decisions.

The *eplans.com* Advantage

While there are hundreds of home plans sites on the Web, only eplans.com offers the variety, quality and ease of use you want when doing a search for the perfect home. From expert advice to online ordering of plans, eplans gives you a full complement of services, information, home plans and planning tools to make your building experience easy and enjoyable. Log on to www.eplans.com to begin your search for the home you've always wanted.

LET US SHOW YOU OUR HOME BLUEPRINT PACKAGE.

BUILDING A HOME? PLANNING A HOME?

OUR BLUEPRINT PACKAGE HAS NEARLY EVERYTHING YOU NEED TO GET THE JOB DONE RIGHT,

whether you're working on your own or with help from an architect, designer, builder or subcontractors. Each Blueprint Package is the result of many hours of work by licensed architects or professional designers.

QUALITY

Hundreds of hours of painstaking effort have gone into the development of your blueprint plan. Each home has been quality-checked by professionals to insure accuracy and buildability.

VALUE

Because we sell in volume, you can buy professional quality blueprints at a fraction of their development cost. With our plans, your dream home design costs substantially less than the fees charged by architects.

SERVICE

Once you've chosen your favorite home plan, you'll receive fast, efficient service whether you choose to mail or fax your order to us or call us toll free at 1-800-521-6797. After you have received your order, call for customer service toll free 1-888-690-1116.

SATISFACTION

Over 50 years of service to satisfied home plan buyers provide us unparalleled experience and knowledge in producing quality blueprints.

ORDER TOLL FREE 1-800-521-6797

After you've looked over our Blueprint Package and Important Extras, call toll free on our Blueprint Hotline: 1-800-521-6797, for current pricing and availability prior to mailing the order form on page 253. We're ready and eager to serve you. After you have received your order, call for customer service toll free 1-888-690-1116.

Each set of blueprints is an interrelated collection of detail sheets which includes components such as floor plans, interior and exterior elevations, dimensions, cross-sections, diagrams and notations. These sheets show exactly how your house is to be built.

SETS MAY INCLUDE:

FRONTAL SHEET
This artist's sketch of the exterior of the house gives you an idea of how the house will look when built and landscaped. Large floor plans show all levels of the house and provide an overview of your new home's livability, as well as a handy reference for deciding on furniture placement.

FOUNDATION PLANS
This sheet shows the foundation layout including support walls, excavated and unexcavated areas, if any, and foundation notes. If slab construction rather than basement, the plan shows footings and details for a monolithic slab. This page, or another in the set, may include a sample plot plan for locating your house on a building site.

DETAILED FLOOR PLANS
These plans show the layout of each floor of the house. Rooms and interior spaces are carefully dimensioned and keys are given for cross-section details provided later in the plans. The positions of electrical outlets and switches are shown.

HOUSE CROSS-SECTIONS
Large-scale views show sections or cut-aways of the foundation, interior walls, exterior walls, floors, stairways and roof details. Additional cross-sections may show important changes in floor, ceiling or roof heights or the relationship of one level to another. Extremely valuable for construction, these sections show exactly how the various parts of the house fit together.

INTERIOR ELEVATIONS
Many of our drawings show the design and placement of kitchen and bathroom cabinets, laundry areas, fireplaces, bookcases and other built-ins. Little "extras," such as mantelpiece and wainscoting drawings, plus molding sections, provide details that give your home that custom touch.

EXTERIOR ELEVATIONS
These drawings show the front, rear and sides of your house and give necessary notes on exterior materials and finishes. Particular attention is given to cornice detail, brick and stone accents or other finish items that make your home unique.

INTRODUCING IMPORTANT PLANNING AND CONSTRUCTION AIDS DEVELOPED BY OUR PROFESSIONALS TO HELP YOU SUCCEED IN YOUR HOME-BUILDING PROJECT

MATERIALS LIST

(Note: Because of the diversity of local building codes, our Materials List does not include mechanical materials.)

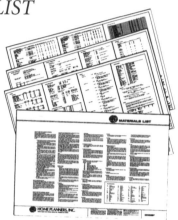

For many of the designs in our portfolio, we offer a customized materials take-off that is invaluable in planning and estimating the cost of your new home. This Materials List outlines the quantity, type and size of materials needed to build your house (with the exception of mechanical system items). Included are framing lumber, windows and doors, kitchen and bath cabinetry, rough and finish hardware, and much more. This handy list helps you or your builder cost out materials and serves as a reference sheet when you're compiling bids. Some Materials Lists may be ordered before blueprints are ordered, call for information.

SPECIFICATION OUTLINE

This valuable 16-page document is critical to building your house correctly. Designed to be filled in by you or your builder, this book lists 166 stages or items crucial to the building process. It provides a comprehensive review of the construction process and helps in choosing materials. When combined with the blueprints, a signed contract, and a schedule, it becomes a legal document and record for the building of your home.

QUOTE ONE®

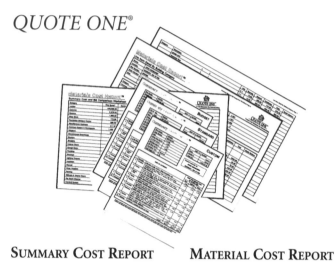

SUMMARY COST REPORT   **MATERIAL COST REPORT**

A product for estimating the cost of building select designs, the Quote One® system is available in two separate stages: The Summary Cost Report and the Material Cost Report.

The **Summary Cost Report** is the first stage in the package and shows the total cost per square foot for your chosen home in your zip-code area and then breaks that cost down into various categories showing the costs for building materials, labor and installation. The report includes three grades: Budget, Standard and Custom. These reports allow you to evaluate your building budget and compare the costs of building a variety of homes in your area.

Make even more informed decisions about your home-building project with the second phase of our package, our **Material Cost Report.** This tool is invaluable in planning and estimating the cost of your new home. The material and installation (labor and equipment) cost is shown for each of over 1,000 line items provided in the Materials List (Standard grade), which is included when you purchase this estimating tool. It allows you to determine building costs for your specific zip-code area and for your chosen home design. Space is allowed for additional estimates from contractors and subcontractors, such as for mechanical materials, which are not included in our packages. This invaluable tool includes a Materials List. A Material Cost Report cannot be ordered before blueprints are ordered. Call for details. In addition, ask about our Home Planners Estimating Package.

If you are interested in a plan that is not indicated as Quote One®, please call and ask our sales reps. They will be happy to verify the status for you. To order these invaluable reports, use the order form.

CONSTRUCTION INFORMATION

IF YOU WANT TO KNOW MORE ABOUT TECHNIQUES— and deal more confidently with subcontractors — we offer these useful sheets. Each set is an excellent tool that will add to your understanding of these technical subjects. These helpful details provide general construction information and are not specific to any single plan.

PLUMBING

The Blueprint Package includes locations for all the plumbing fixtures, including sinks, lavatories, tubs, showers, toilets, laundry trays and water heaters. However, if you want to know more about the complete plumbing system, these Plumbing Details will prove very useful. Prepared to meet requirements of the National Plumbing Code, these fact-filled sheets give general information on pipe schedules, fittings, sump-pump details, water-softener hookups, septic system details and much more. Sheets also include a glossary of terms.

ELECTRICAL

The locations for every electrical switch, plug and outlet are shown in your Blueprint Package. However, these Electrical Details go further to take the mystery out of household electrical systems. Prepared to meet requirements of the National Electrical Code, these comprehensive drawings come packed with helpful information, including wire sizing, switch-installation schematics, cable-routing details, appliance wattage, doorbell hook-ups, typical service panel circuitry and much more. A glossary of terms is also included.

CONSTRUCTION

The Blueprint Package contains information an experienced builder needs to construct a particular house. However, it doesn't show all the ways that houses can be built, nor does it explain alternate construction methods. To help you understand how your house will be built—and offer additional techniques—this set of Construction Details depicts the materials and methods used to build foundations, fireplaces, walls, floors and roofs. Where appropriate, the drawings show acceptable alternatives.

MECHANICAL

These Mechanical Details contain fundamental principles and useful data that will help you make informed decisions and communicate with subcontractors about heating and cooling systems. Drawings contain instructions and samples that allow you to make simple load calculations, and preliminary sizing and costing analysis. Covered are the most commonly used systems from heat pumps to solar fuel systems. The package is filled with illustrations and diagrams to help you visualize components and how they relate to one another.

THE HANDS-ON HOME FURNITURE PLANNER

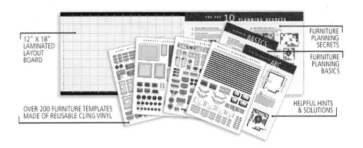

Effectively plan the space in your home using The **Hands-On Home Furniture Planner**. It's fun and easy—no more moving heavy pieces of furniture to see how the room will go together. And you can try different layouts, moving furniture at a whim.

The kit includes reusable peel and stick furniture templates that fit onto a 12" x 18" laminated layout board—space enough to layout every room in your home.

Also included in the package are a number of helpful planning tools. You'll receive:

- ✓ Helpful hints and solutions for difficult situations.
- ✓ Furniture planning basics to get you started.
- ✓ Furniture planning secrets that let you in on some of the tricks of professional designers.

The **Hands-On Home Furniture Planner** is the one tool that no new homeowner or home remodeler should be without. It's also a perfect housewarming gift!

To Order, Call Toll Free
1-800-521-6797

After you've looked over our Blueprint Package and Important Extras on these pages, call for current pricing and availability prior to mailing the order form. We're ready and eager to serve you. After you have received your order, call for customer service toll free 1-888-690-1116.

THE DECK BLUEPRINT PACKAGE

Many of the homes in this book can be enhanced with a professionally designed Home Planners Deck Plan. Those homes marked with a **D** have a complementary Deck Plan, sold separately, which includes a Deck Plan Frontal Sheet, Deck Framing and Floor Plans, Deck Elevations and a Deck Materials List. A Standard Deck Details Package, also available, provides all the how-to information necessary for building *any* deck. Our Complete Deck Building Package contains one set of Custom Deck Plans of your choice, plus one set of Standard Deck Building Details, all for one low price. Our plans and details are carefully prepared in an easy-to-understand format that will guide you through every stage of your deck-building project. This page shows a sample Deck layout to match your favorite house. See Blueprint Price Schedule for ordering information.

THE LANDSCAPE BLUEPRINT PACKAGE

For the homes marked with an **L** in this book, Home Planners has created a front-yard Landscape Plan that is complementary in design to the house plan. These comprehensive blueprint packages include a Frontal Sheet, Plan View, Regionalized Plant & Materials List, a sheet on Planting and Maintaining Your Landscape, Zone Maps and Plant Size and Description Guide. These plans will help you achieve professional results, adding value and enjoyment to your property for years to come. Each set of blueprints is a full 18" x 24" in size with clear, complete instructions and easy-to-read type. A sample Landscape Plan is shown below. See Blueprint Price Schedule for ordering information.

CONTEMPORARY LEISURE DECK
Deck ODA021

CAPE COD COTTAGE
Landscape OLA003

REGIONAL ORDER MAP

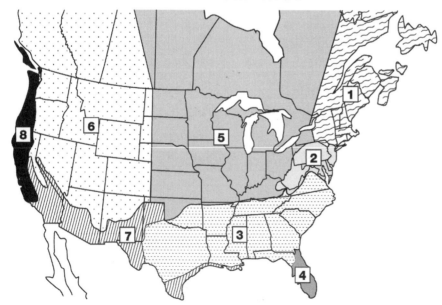

Most Landscape Plans are available with a Plant & Materials List adapted by horticultural experts to 8 different regions of the country. Please specify the Geographic Region when ordering your plan. See Blueprint Price Schedule for ordering information and regional availability.

Region	1	Northeast
Region	2	Mid-Atlantic
Region	3	Deep South
Region	4	Florida & Gulf Coast
Region	5	Midwest
Region	6	Rocky Mountains
Region	7	Southern California & Desert Southwest
Region	8	Northern California & Pacific Northwest

BLUEPRINT PRICE SCHEDULE

Prices guaranteed through December 31, 2002

TIERS	1-SET STUDY PACKAGE	4-SET BUILDING PACKAGE	8-SET BUILDING PACKAGE	1-SET REPRODUCIBLE*
P1	$20	$50	$90	$140
P2	$40	$70	$110	$160
P3	$70	$100	$140	$190
P4	$100	$130	$170	$220
P5	$140	$170	$210	$270
P6	$180	$210	$250	$310
A1	$440	$480	$520	$660
A2	$480	$520	$560	$720
A3	$520	$560	$600	$780
A4	$565	$605	$645	$850
C1	$610	$655	$700	$915
C2	$655	$700	$745	$980
C3	$700	$745	$790	$1050
C4	$750	$795	$840	$1125
L1	$825	$875	$925	$1240
L2	$900	$950	$1000	$1340
L3	$1000	$1050	$1100	$1500
L4	$1100	$1150	$1200	$1650

* Requires a fax number

OPTIONS FOR PLANS IN TIERS A1–L4

Additional Identical Blueprints
in same order for "A1–L4" price plans ....**$50 per set**
Reverse Blueprints (mirror image)
with 4- or 8-set order for "A1–L4" plans...............................**$50 fee per order**
Specification Outlines..**$10 each**
Materials Lists for "A1–C3" plans ....**$60 each**
Materials Lists for "C4–L4" plans..**$70 each**

OPTIONS FOR PLANS IN TIERS P1–P6

Additional Identical Blueprints
in same order for "P1–P6" price plans..**$10 per set**
Reverse Blueprints (mirror image) for "P1–P6" price plans ....**$10 fee per order**
1 Set of Deck Construction Details ....**$14.95 each**
Deck Construction Package ....**add $10 to Building Package price**
*(includes 1 set of "P1–P6" plans, plus
1 set Standard Deck Construction Details)*

IMPORTANT NOTES

• The 1-set study package is marked "not for construction."
• Prices for 4- or 8-set Building Packages honored only at time of original order.
• Some foundations carry a $225 surcharge.
• Right-reading reverse blueprints, if available, will incur a $165 surcharge.
• Additional identical blueprints may be purchased within 60 days of original order.

TO USE THE INDEX,

refer to the design number listed in numerical order (a helpful page reference is also given). Note the price tier and refer to the House Blueprint Price Schedule above for the cost of one, four or eight sets of blueprints or the cost of a reproducible drawing. Additional prices are shown for identical and reverse blueprint sets, as well as a very useful Materials List for some of the plans. Also note in the Plan Index those plans that have Deck Plans or Landscape Plans. Refer to the schedules above for prices of these plans. The letter "Y" identifies plans that are part of our Quote One® estimating service and those that offer Materials Lists.

TO ORDER,

Call toll free 1-800-521-6797 for current pricing and availability prior to mailing the order form. FAX: 1-800-224-6699 or 520-544-3086.

PLAN INDEX

DESIGN	PRICE	PAGE	MATERIALS LIST	QUOTE ONE®	DECK	DECK PRICE	LANDSCAPE	LANDSCAPE PRICE	REGIONS
HPT820001	C4	5							
HPT820002	L1	8							
HPT820003	L3	13							
HPT820004	A1	12		Y					
HPT820005	C4	10					OLA004	P3	123568
HPT820006	C3	14	Y				OLA001	P3	123568
HPT820007	L1	15							
HPT820008	C3	16	Y						
HPT820009	C2	17					OLA004	P3	123568
HPT820010	A4	18							
HPT820011	C2	19							

PLAN INDEX

DESIGN	PRICE	PAGE	MATERIALS LIST	QUOTE ONE®	DECK	DECK PRICE	LANDSCAPE	LANDSCAPE PRICE	REGIONS
HPT820012	A4	20							
HPT820013	C1	21							
HPT820014	C1	22							
HPT820015	C2	23							
HPT820016	A4	24							
HPT820017	C1	25							
HPT820018	A3	26							
HPT820019	C2	27	Y	Y	ODA012	P3	OLA018	P3	12345678
HPT820020	A4	28							
HPT820021	A4	29							
HPT820022	A4	30							
HPT820023	C1	31	Y	Y			OLA035	P3	12345678
HPT820024	A4	32							
HPT820025	A3	33	Y				OLA001	P3	123568
HPT820026	A2	34	Y						
HPT820027	A4	35	Y						
HPT820028	C2	36	Y	Y			OLA039	P3	3478
HPT820029	C3	37	Y	Y			OLA036	P4	123568
HPT820030	A3	38	Y						
HPT820031	C2	39	Y	Y			OLA028	P4	12345678
HPT820032	A3	40	Y	Y	ODA002	P2	OLA035	P3	12345678
HPT820033	A4	41	Y	Y	ODA015	P2	OLA035	P3	12345678
HPT820034	C3	42	Y						
HPT820035	C2	43	Y						
HPT820036	C2	44	Y		ODA002	P2	OLA035	P3	12345678
HPT820037	A4	45	Y		ODA014	P2			
HPT820038	A4	46	Y		ODA018	P3			
HPT820039	A4	47	Y						
HPT820040	A4	48	Y						
HPT820041	C1	49	Y		ODA018	P3	OLA029	P3	12345678
HPT820042	A4	50	Y				OLA032	P4	12345678
HPT820043	A3	51			ODA021	P2			
HPT820044	A2	52	Y	Y	ODA014	P2	OLA027	P3	12345678
HPT820045	C2	53	Y	Y					
HPT820046	A3	54	Y						
HPT820047	A3	55	Y						
HPT820048	A4	56	Y	Y	ODA013	P2	OLA030	P3	12345678
HPT820049	C1	57	Y				OLA035	P3	12345678
HPT820050	C1	58							
HPT820051	A3	59	Y						
HPT820052	A3	60	Y						
HPT820053	A3	61	Y						
HPT820054	A4	62							
HPT820055	A4	63							
HPT820056	A4	64	Y	Y	ODA006	P2	OLA030	P3	12345678
HPT820057	A4	65	Y						
HPT820058	A3	66	Y	Y			OLA030	P3	12345678
HPT820059	A3	67	Y						
HPT820060	A3	68	Y		ODA016	P2	OLA003	P3	123568
HPT820061	C1	69	Y		ODA002	P2			
HPT820062	A3	70							
HPT820063	C1	71	Y	Y	ODA006	P2	OLA023	P3	123568
HPT820064	A3	72	Y						
HPT820065	C1	73	Y						
HPT820066	A4	74	Y						
HPT820067	A2	75	Y						
HPT820068	A4	76	Y						
HPT820069	A4	77	Y						
HPT820070	C1	78							
HPT820071	C2	79	Y						
HPT820072	C1	80					OLA001	P3	123568
HPT820073	A3	81	Y						
HPT820074	A3	82	Y						
HPT820075	A3	83	Y						
HPT820076	C3	84							
HPT820077	C1	85							
HPT820078	A3	86	Y						
HPT820079	A4	87	Y	Y			OLA039	P3	3478
HPT820080	C1	88	Y						
HPT820081	A4	89	Y						
HPT820082	C1	90	Y				OLA005	P3	123568
HPT820083	A3	91	Y						
HPT820084	A4	92	Y	Y	ODA011	P2	OLA039	P3	3478
HPT820085	A4	93							
HPT820086	C1	94							
HPT820087	A4	95							
HPT820088	A4	96							
HPT820089	C1	97							
HPT820090	C1	98	Y						
HPT820091	A4	99	Y	Y					
HPT820092	C1	100	Y				OLA008	P4	1234568
HPT820093	C1	101	Y						
HPT820094	C1	102	Y						
HPT820095	C1	103	Y				OLA005	P3	123568
HPT820096	A4	104							
HPT820097	C1	105							
HPT820098	A4	106							
HPT820099	C1	107							
HPT820100	C3	108							
HPT820101	C3	109	Y	Y					
HPT820102	C4	110	Y						
HPT820103	C1	111	Y						
HPT820104	C1	112							
HPT820105	C3	113							
HPT820106	C3	114							
HPT820107	C2	115	Y						
HPT820108	A4	116	Y	Y	ODA013	P2	OLA029	P3	12345678
HPT820109	C1	117	Y				OLA001	P3	123568
HPT820110	C2	118	Y	Y			OLA021	P3	123568
HPT820111	C2	119	Y						
HPT820112	C2	120	Y	Y					
HPT820113	C3	121							
HPT820114	L2	122	Y	Y			OLA031	P4	12345678
HPT820115	C2	123	Y		ODA013	P2			
HPT820116	C3	124	Y						
HPT820117	C1	125	Y				OLA030	P3	12345678
HPT820118	A4	126							
HPT820119	C2	127	Y				OLA032	P4	12345678
HPT820120	C1	128	Y	Y	ODA009	P2	OLA030	P3	12345678
HPT820121	C1	129	Y				OLA030	P3	12345678
HPT820122	C1	130	Y				OLA030	P3	12345678
HPT820123	C4	131	Y						

BEFORE FILLING OUT THE ORDER FORM, PLEASE CALL US ON OUR TOLL-FREE BLUEPRINT HOTLINE 1-800-521-6797. YOU MAY WANT TO LEARN MORE ABOUT OUR SERVICES AND PRODUCTS. HERE'S SOME INFORMATION YOU WILL FIND HELPFUL.

OUR EXCHANGE POLICY

With the exception of reproducible plan orders, we will exchange your entire first order for an equal or greater number of blueprints within our plan collection within 90 days of the original order. The entire content of your original order must be returned before an exchange will be processed. Please call our customer service department for your return authorization number and shipping instructions. If the returned blueprints look used, redlined or copied, we will not honor your exchange. Fees for exchanging your blueprints are as follows: 20% of the amount of the original order...plus the difference in cost if exchanging for a design in a higher price bracket or less the difference in cost if exchanging for a design in a lower price bracket. **(Reproducible blueprints are not exchangeable or refundable.)** Please call for current postage and handling prices. Shipping and handling charges are not refundable.

ABOUT REPRODUCIBLES

When purchasing a reproducible you may be required to furnish a fax number. The designer will fax documents that you must sign and return to them before shipping will take place.

ABOUT REVERSE BLUEPRINTS

Although lettering and dimensions will appear backward, reverses will be a useful aid if you decide to flop the plan. See Price Schedule and Plans Index for pricing.

REVISING, MODIFYING AND CUSTOMIZING PLANS

Like many homeowners who buy these plans, you and your builder, architect or engineer may want to make changes to them. We recommend purchase of a reproducible plan for any changes made by your builder, licensed architect or engineer. As set forth below, we cannot assume any responsibility for blueprints which have been changed, whether by you, your builder or by professionals selected by you or referred to you by us, because such individuals are outside our supervision and control.

ARCHITECTURAL AND ENGINEERING SEALS

Some cities and states are now requiring that a licensed architect or engineer review and "seal" a blueprint, or officially approve it, prior to construction due to concerns over energy costs, safety and other factors. Prior to application for a building permit or the start of actual construction, we strongly advise that you consult your local building official who can tell you if such a review is required.

ABOUT THE DESIGNS

The architects and designers whose work appears in this publication are among America's leading residential designers. Each plan was designed to meet the requirements of a nationally recognized model building code in effect at the time and place the plan was drawn. Because national building codes change from time to time, plans may not comply with any such code at the time they are sold to a customer. In addition, building officials may not accept these plans as final construction documents of record as the plans may need to be modified and additional drawings and details added to suit local conditions and requirements. We strongly advise that purchasers consult a licensed architect or engineer, and their local building official, before starting any construction related to these plans.

LOCAL BUILDING CODES AND ZONING REQUIREMENTS

At the time of creation, our plans are drawn to specifications published by the Building Officials and Code Administrators (BOCA) International, Inc.; the Southern Building Code Congress (SBCCI) International, Inc.; the International Conference of Building Officials (ICBO); or the Council of American Building Officials (CABO). Our plans are designed to meet or exceed national building standards. Because of the great differences in geography and climate throughout the United States and Canada, each state, county and municipality has its own building codes, zone requirements, ordinances and building regulations. Your plan may need to be modified to comply with local requirements regarding snow loads, energy codes, soil and seismic conditions and a wide range of other matters. In addition, you may need to obtain permits or inspections from local governments before and in the course of construction. Prior to using blueprints ordered from us, we strongly advise that you consult a licensed architect or engineer—and speak with your local building official—before applying for any permit or beginning construction. We authorize the use of our blueprints on the express condition that you strictly comply with all local building codes, zoning requirements and other applicable laws, regulations, ordinances and requirements. Notice: Plans for homes to be built in Nevada must be re-drawn by a Nevada-registered professional. Consult your building official for more information on this subject.

 TOLL FREE 1-800-521-6797

REGULAR OFFICE HOURS:
8:00 a.m.-9:00 p.m. EST
Monday-Friday.

If we receive your order by 3:00 p.m. EST, Monday-Friday, we'll process it and ship within **two business days**. When ordering by phone, please have your credit card or check information ready. We'll also ask you for the Order Form Key Number at the bottom of the order form.

By FAX: Copy the Order Form on the next page and send it on our FAX line: 1-800-224-6699 or 520-544-3086.

**Canadian Customers
Order Toll Free 1-877-223-6389**

DISCLAIMER

The designers we work with have put substantial care and effort into the creation of their blueprints. However, because they cannot provide on-site consultation, supervision and control over actual construction, and because of the great variance in local building requirements, building practices and soil, seismic, weather and other conditions, WE CANNOT MAKE ANY WARRANTY, EXPRESS OR IMPLIED, WITH RESPECT TO THE CONTENT OR USE OF THE BLUEPRINTS, INCLUDING BUT NOT LIMITED TO ANY WARRANTY OF MERCHANTABILITY OR OF FITNESS FOR A PARTICULAR PURPOSE. ITEMS, PRICES, TERMS AND CONDITIONS ARE SUBJECT TO CHANGE WITHOUT NOTICE. REPRODUCIBLE PLAN ORDERS MAY REQUIRE A CUSTOMER'S SIGNED RELEASE BEFORE SHIPPING.

TERMS AND CONDITIONS

These designs are protected under the terms of United States Copyright Law and may not be copied or reproduced in any way, by any means, unless you have purchased Reproducibles which clearly indicate your right to copy or reproduce. We authorize the use of your chosen design as an aid in the construction of one single family home only. You may not use this design to build a second or multiple dwellings without purchasing another blueprint or blueprints or paying additional design fees.

HOW MANY BLUEPRINTS DO YOU NEED?

Although a standard building package may satisfy many states, cities and counties, some plans may require certain changes. For your convenience, we have developed a Reproducible plan which allows a local professional to modify and make up to 10 copies of your revised plan. As our plans are all copyright protected, with your purchase of the Reproducible, we will supply you with a Copyright release letter. The number of copies you may need: 1 for owner; 3 for builder; 2 for local building department and 1-3 sets for your mortgage lender.

 **ORDER TOLL FREE!**

For information about any of our services or to order call 1-800-521-6797

Browse our website: www.eplans.com

BLUEPRINTS ARE NOT REFUNDABLE EXCHANGES ONLY

For Customer Service, call toll free 1-888-690-1116.

 HOME PLANNERS, LLC wholly owned by Hanley-Wood, LLC
3275 WEST INA ROAD, SUITE 110 • TUCSON, ARIZONA • 85741

THE BASIC BLUEPRINT PACKAGE
Rush me the following (please refer to the Plans Index and Price Schedule in this section):
___ Set(s) of reproducibles*, plan number(s) _____ $_____
    indicate foundation type _____ surcharge (if applicable): $_____
___ Set(s) of blueprints, plan number(s) _____ $_____
    indicate foundation type _____ surcharge (if applicable): $_____
___ Additional identical blueprints (standard or reverse) in same order @ $50 per set $_____
___ Reverse blueprints @ $50 fee per order. Right-reading reverse @ $165 surcharge $_____

IMPORTANT EXTRAS
Rush me the following:
___ Materials List: $60 (Must be purchased with Blueprint set.) Add $10 for Schedule C4–L4 plans $_____
___ **Quote One®** Summary Cost Report @ $29.95 for one, $14.95 for each additional,
    for plans _____ $_____
    Building location: City _____ Zip Code _____
___ **Quote One®** Material Cost Report @ $120 Schedules P1–C3; $130 Schedules C4–L4,
    for plan_____ (Must be purchased with Blueprints set.) $_____
    Building location: City _____ Zip Code _____
___ Specification Outlines @ $10 each $_____
___ Detail Sets @ $14.95 each; any two $22.95; any three $29.95; all four for $39.95 (save $19.85) $_____
    ❏ Plumbing ❏ Electrical ❏ Construction ❏ Mechanical
___ Home Furniture Planner @ $15.95 each $_____

DECK BLUEPRINTS
(Please refer to the Plans Index and Price Schedule in this section)
___ Set(s) of Deck Plan _____. $_____
___ Additional identical blueprints in same order @ $10 per set. $_____
___ Reverse blueprints @ $10 fee per order. $_____
___ Set of Standard Deck Details @ $14.95 per set. $_____
___ Set of Complete Deck Construction Package (Best Buy!) Add $10 to Building Package.
    Includes Custom Deck Plan _____ Plus Standard Deck Details

LANDSCAPE BLUEPRINTS
(Please refer to the Plans Index and Price Schedule in this section.)
___ Set(s) of Landscape Plan _____ $_____
___ Additional identical blueprints in same order @ $10 per set $_____
___ Reverse blueprints @ $10 fee per order $_____
Please indicate appropriate region of the country for Plant & Material List. Region _____

POSTAGE AND HANDLING *SIGNATURE IS REQUIRED FOR ALL DELIVERIES.*	1–3 sets	4+ sets
DELIVERY No CODs (Requires street address—No P.O. Boxes)		
•Regular Service (Allow 7–10 business days delivery)	❏ $20.00	❏ $25.00
•Priority (Allow 4–5 business days delivery)	❏ $25.00	❏ $35.00
•Express (Allow 3 business days delivery)	❏ $35.00	❏ $45.00
OVERSEAS DELIVERY	fax, phone or mail for quote	

Note: All delivery times are from date Blueprint Package is shipped.

POSTAGE (From box above) $_____
SUBTOTAL $_____
SALES TAX (AZ & MI residents, please add appropriate state and local sales tax.) $_____
TOTAL (Subtotal and tax) $_____

YOUR ADDRESS (please print legibly)
Name _____
Street _____
City _____ State _____ Zip _____
Daytime telephone number (required) (_____) _____
* Fax number (required for reproducible orders) _____
TeleCheck® Checks By Phone℠ available
FOR CREDIT CARD ORDERS ONLY
Credit card number _____ Exp. Date: (M/Y) _____
Check one ❏ Visa ❏ MasterCard ❏ Discover Card ❏ American Express

Order Form Key

HPT82

Signature (required) _____
Please check appropriate box: ❏ Licensed Builder-Contractor ❏ Homeowner

 **ORDER TOLL FREE!**
1-800-521-6797

BY FAX: Copy the order form above and send it on our FAXLINE: 1-800-224-6699 OR 520-544-3086

1 BIGGEST & BEST

1001 of our best-selling plans in one volume. 1,074 to 7,275 square feet. 704 pgs $12.95 1K1

2 ONE-STORY

450 designs for all lifestyles. 800 to 4,900 square feet. 384 pgs $9.95 OS

3 MORE ONE-STORY

475 superb one-level plans from 800 to 5,000 square feet. 448 pgs $9.95 MO2

4 TWO-STORY

443 designs for one-and-a-half and two stories. 1,500 to 6,000 square feet. 448 pgs $9.95 TS

5 VACATION

430 designs for recreation, retirement and leisure. 448 pgs $9.95 VS3

6 HILLSIDE

208 designs for split-levels, bi-levels, multi-levels and walkouts. 224 pgs $9.95 HH

7 FARMHOUSE

300 Fresh Designs from Classic to Modern. 320 pgs. $10.95 FCP

8 COUNTRY HOUSES

208 unique home plans that combine traditional style and modern livability. 224 pgs $9.95 CN

9 BUDGET-SMART

200 efficient plans from 7 top designers, that you can really afford to build! 224 pgs $8.95 BS

10 BARRIER-FREE

Over 1,700 products and 51 plans for accessible living. 128 pgs $15.95 UH

11 ENCYCLOPEDIA

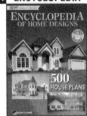

500 exceptional plans for all styles and budgets—the best book of its kind! 528 pgs $9.95 ENC

12 ENCYCLOPEDIA II

500 completely new plans. Spacious and stylish designs for every budget and taste. 352 pgs $9.95 E2

13 AFFORDABLE

300 Modest plans for savvy homebuyers.256 pgs. $9.95 AH2

14 VICTORIAN

210 striking Victorian and Farmhouse designs from today's top designers. 224 pgs $15.95 VDH2

15 ESTATE

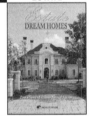

Dream big! Eighteen designers showcase their biggest and best plans. 224 pgs $16.95 EDH3

16 LUXURY

170 lavish designs, over 50% brand-new plans added to a most elegant collection. 192 pgs $12.95 LD3

17 EUROPEAN STYLES

200 homes with a unique flair of the Old World. 224 pgs $15.95 EURO

18 COUNTRY CLASSICS

Donald Gardner's 101 best Country and Traditional home plans. 192 pgs $17.95 DAG

19 COUNTRY

85 Charming Designs from American Home Gallery. 160 pgs. $17.95 CTY

20 TRADITIONAL

85 timeless designs from the Design Traditions Library. 160 pgs $17.95 TRA

21 COTTAGES

245 Delightful retreats from 825 to 3,500 square feet. 256 pgs. $10.95 COOL

22 CABINS TO VILLAS

Enchanting Homes for Mountain Sea or Sun, from the Sater collection. 144 pgs $19.95 CCV

23 CONTEMPORARY

The most complete and imaginative collection of contemporary designs available anywhere. 256 pgs. $10.95 CM2

24 FRENCH COUNTRY

Live every day in the French countryside using these plans, landscapes and interiors. 192 pgs. $14.95 PN

25 SOUTHERN

207 homes rich in Southern styling and comfort. 240 pgs $8.95 SH

26 SOUTHWESTERN

138 designs that capture the spirit of the Southwest. 144 pgs $10.95 SW

27 SHINGLE-STYLE

155 Home plans from Classic Colonials to Breezy Bungalows. 192 pgs. $12.95 SNG

28 NEIGHBORHOOD

170 designs with the feel of main street America. 192 pgs $12.95 TND

29 CRAFTSMAN

170 Home plans in the Craftsman and Bungalow style. 192 pgs $12.95 CC

30 GRAND VISTAS

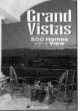

200 Homes with a View. 224 pgs $10.95 GV

31 DUPLEX & TOWNHOMES

115 Duplex, Multiplex & Townhome Designs. 128 pgs. $17.95 MFH

32 WATERFRONT

200 designs perfect for your waterside wonderland. 208 pgs $10.95 WF

33 NATURAL LIGHT

223 Sunny home plans for all regions. 240 pgs. $8.95 NA

34 NOSTALGIA

100 Time-Honored designs updated with today's features. 224 pgs. $14.95 NOS

35 STREET OF DREAMS

Over 300 photos showcase 54 prestigious homes. 256 pgs $19.95 SOD

36 NARROW-LOT

250 Designs for houses 17' to 50' wide. 256 pgs. $9.95 NL2

37 SMALL HOUSES

Innovative plans for sensible lifestyles. 224 pgs. $8.95 SM2

38 GARDENS & MORE

225 gardens, landscapes, decks and more to enhance every home. 320 pgs. $19.95 GLP

39 EASY-CARE

41 special landscapes designed for beauty and low maintenance. 160 pgs $14.95 ECL

40 BACKYARDS

40 designs focused solely on creating your own specially themed backyard oasis. 160 pgs $14.95 BYL

41 BEDS & BORDERS
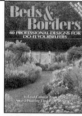
40 Professional designs for do-it-yourselfers 160 pgs. $14.95 BB

42 BUYER'S GUIDE

A comprehensive look at 2700 products for all aspects of landscaping & gardening. 128 pgs $19.95 LPBG

LANDSCAPE DESIGNS

43 OUTDOOR

74 easy-to-build designs, lets you create and build your own backyard oasis. 128 pgs $9.95 YG2

44 GARAGES
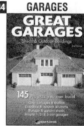
145 exciting projects from 64 to 1,900 square feet. 160 pgs. $9.95 GG2

45 DECKS

A brand new collection of 120 beautiful and practical decks. 144 pgs. $9.95 DP2

46 HOME BUILDING

Everything you need to know to work with contractors and subcontractors. 212 pgs $14.95 HBP

47 RURAL BUILDING

Everything you need to know to build your home in the country. 232 pgs. $14.95 BYC

48 VACATION HOMES

Your complete guide to building your vacation home. 224 pgs. $14.95 BYV

PROJECT GUIDES

Book Order Form

To order your books, just check the box of the book numbered below and complete the coupon. We will process your order and ship it from our office within two business days. Send coupon and check (in U.S. funds).

YES! Please send me the books I've indicated:

❑ 1:1K1 ....$12.95	❑ 17:EURO...$15.95	❑ 33:NA..........$8.95
❑ 2:OS............$9.95	❑ 18:DAG $17.95	❑ 34:NOS $14.95
❑ 3:MO2.........$9.95	❑ 19:CTY.....$17.95	❑ 35:SOD $19.95
❑ 4:TS $9.95	❑ 20:TRA.....$17.95	❑ 36:NL2......$9.95
❑ 5:VS3..........$9.95	❑ 21:COOL...$10.95	❑ 37:SM2......$8.95
❑ 6:HH............$9.95	❑ 22:CCV....$19.95	❑ 38:GLP.....$19.95
❑ 7:FCP........$10.95	❑ 23:CM2.....$10.95	❑ 39:ECL.....$14.95
❑ 8:CN............$9.95	❑ 24:PN......$14.95	❑ 40:BYL.....$14.95
❑ 9:BS............$8.95	❑ 25:SH........$8.95	❑ 41:BB........$14.95
❑ 10:UH $15.95	❑ 26:SW.....$10.95	❑ 42:LPBG ...$19.95
❑ 11:ENC.......$9.95	❑ 27:SNG.....$12.95	❑ 43:YG2......$9.95
❑ 12:E2 ....$9.95	❑ 28:TND.....$12.95	❑ 44:GG2 .....$9.95
❑ 13:AH2........$9.95	❑ 29:CC......$12.95	❑ 45:DP2......$9.95
❑ 14:VDH2 ...$15.95	❑ 30:GV......$10.95	❑ 46:HBP $14.95
❑ 15:EDH3 ...$16.95	❑ 31:MFH....$17.95	❑ 47:BYC.....$14.95
❑ 16:LD3......$12.95	❑ 32:WF.......$10.95	❑ 48:BYV....$14.95

Books Subtotal $_____
ADD Postage and Handling (allow 4–6 weeks for delivery) $ 4.00
Sales Tax: (AZ & MI residents, add state and local sales tax.) $_____
YOUR TOTAL (Subtotal, Postage/Handling, Tax) $_____

YOUR ADDRESS (PLEASE PRINT)
Name _____
Street _____
City _____ State _____ Zip _____
Phone (_____) _____ — _____

YOUR PAYMENT
TeleCheck® Checks By Phone℠ available
Check one: ❑ Check ❑ Visa ❑ MasterCard ❑ Discover ❑ American Express
Required credit card information:
Credit Card Number _____
Expiration Date (Month/Year)_____/_____
Signature Required _____

Canadian Customers Order Toll Free 1-877-223-6389

Home Planners, LLC
3275 W. Ina Road, Suite 110, Dept. BK, Tucson, AZ 85741

HPT82

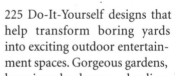